# Contemporary Political Theory

# Contemporary Political Theory

## A Reader

Edited by
Colin Farrelly

SAGE Publications
Los Angeles • London • New Delhi • Singapore
www.sagepublications.com

Editorial material © Colin Farrelly 2004

First Published 2004. Reprinted 2007

Apart from any fair dealing for the purposes of research or private study, or criticism or review, as permitted under the Copyright, Designs and Patents Act, 1988, this publication may be reproduced, stored or transmitted in any form, or by any means, only with the prior permission in writing of the publishers, or in the case of reprographic reproduction, in accordance with the terms of licences issued by the Copyright Licensing Agency. Enquiries concerning reproduction outside those terms should be sent to the publishers.

SAGE Publications Ltd
1 Oliver's Yard
55 City Road
London EC1Y 1SP

SAGE Publications Inc
2455 Teller Road
Thousand Oaks
California 91320

SAGE Publications India Pvt. Ltd
B 1/I 1 Mohan Cooperative Industrial Area
Mathura Road, New Delhi 110 044
India

SAGE Publications Asia-Pacific Pte Ltd
33 Pekin Street #02-01
Far East Square
Singapore 048763

**British Library Cataloguing in Publication Data**

A catalogue record for this book is available
from the British Library

ISBN-13 978-0-7619-4184-2 (pbk)
ISBN-13 978-0-7619-4183-5 (hbk)

**Library of Congress Control Number 2003106177**

Typeset by C&M Digitals (P) Ltd, Chennai, India
Printed in Great Britain by Cpod, Trowbridge, Wiltshire

To my parents

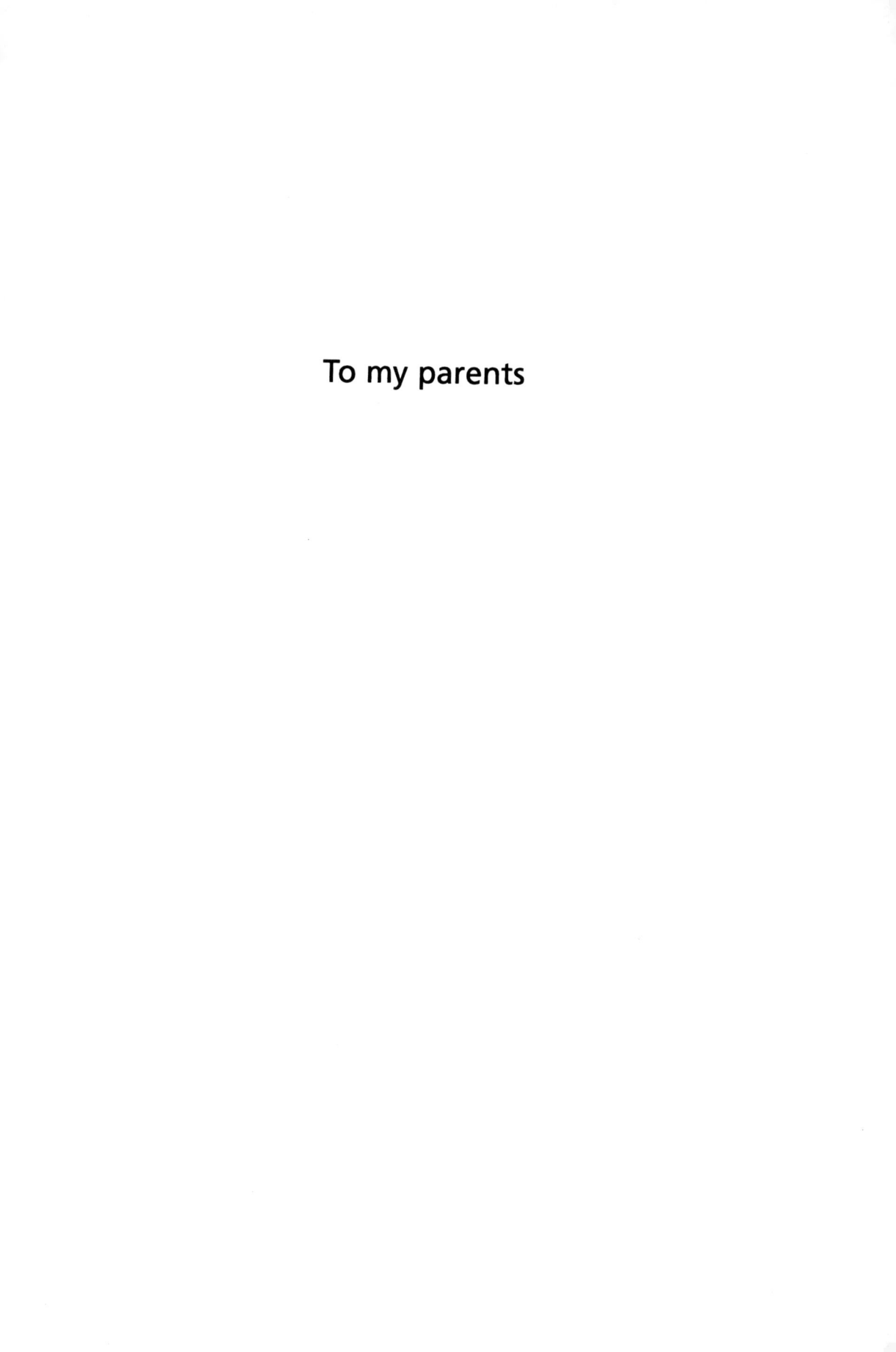

# Contents

| | |
|---|---|
| Preface | ix |
| Acknowledgements | x |
| **Part One  Egalitarian-Liberalism** | 1 |
| Introduction | 3 |
| 1  John Rawls, *Justice as Fairness* | 13 |
| 2  John C. Harsanyi, *The Maximin Principle* | 22 |
| 3  Richard J. Arneson, *Primary Goods Reconsidered* | 31 |
| 4  Alex Callinicos, *Equality of What?* | 36 |
| 5  John Kekes, *A Question for Egalitarians* | 45 |
| **Part Two  Libertarianism** | 51 |
| Introduction | 53 |
| 6  Robert Nozick, *The Entitlement Theory of Justice* | 61 |
| 7  Eric Mack, *How Liberty Upsets Patterns* | 69 |
| 8  Robert E. Litan, *On Rectification in Nozick's Minimal State* | 81 |
| 9  David Gauthier, *Justice as Mutual Advantage* | 89 |
| 10  Allen Buchanan, *A Critique of Justice as Reciprocity* | 99 |
| **Part Three  Communitarianism** | 107 |
| Introduction | 109 |
| 11  Michael J. Sandel, *The Procedural Republic and the Unencumbered Self* | 113 |
| 12  Will Kymlicka, *Liberal Individualism and Liberal Neutrality* | 126 |
| 13  Michael Walzer, *Complex Equality* | 134 |
| **Part Four  Republicanism** | 145 |
| Introduction | 147 |
| 14  Philip Pettit, *Freedom as Antipower* | 151 |
| 15  Alan Patten, *The Republican Critique of Liberalism* | 159 |
| 16  James Bohman, *Cosmopolitan Republicanism* | 169 |

| | |
|---|---:|
| Part Five  Feminism | 179 |
| Introduction | 181 |
| 17  Susan Moller Okin, *The Public/Private Dichotomy* | 185 |
| 18  Iris Marion Young, *The Ideal of Community and the Politics of Difference* | 195 |
| 19  Nancy Fraser, *Recognition or Redistribution?* | 205 |
| Part Six  Deliberative Democracy | 221 |
| Introduction | 223 |
| 20  Iris Marion Young, *The Deliberative Model* | 227 |
| 21  Amy Gutmann and Dennis Thompson, *Deliberative Democracy Beyond Process* | 232 |
| 22  John S. Dryzek, *Legitimacy and Economy in Deliberative Democracy* | 242 |
| Part Seven  Multiculturalism | 261 |
| Introduction | 263 |
| 23  Charles Taylor, *The Politics of Recognition* | 269 |
| 24  Bhikhu Parekh, *Equality of Difference* | 282 |
| 25  Chandran Kukathas, *Liberalism and Multiculturalism* | 288 |
| Index | 295 |

# Preface

Political theorists are primarily concerned with how we *ought*, collectively, to live together. A diverse range of political arrangements can, and have been, defended by reference to values such as justice, freedom, equality and democracy. The job of the political theorist is to bring some precision to these vague and contested concepts so that one can provide convincing arguments for the particular social arrangements they believe we should be aspiring towards. This Reader brings together a diverse array of contributions from theorists of different theoretical perspectives. I believe the positions covered in this volume – egalitarian-liberalism, libertarianism, communitarianism, republicanism, feminism, deliberative democracy and multiculturalism – not only cover the most significant theoretical debates in contemporary political theory, but the readings chosen will help motivate students to think critically about the different arguments political theorists have advanced. In each chapter I have included a brief introduction to help provide some background to the readings and the issues and topics covered by these different theoretical positions.

# Acknowledgements

Arneson, Richard. 'Primary Goods Reconsidered', *Nous*, 24, 1990: 429–54 [excerpts from pp. 429, 441–45].
Bohman, James. 'Cosmopolitan Republicanism: Citizenship, Freedom and Global Political Authority', *The Monist*, 84(1), 2001: 3–21 [excerpts from pp. 3–5, 9–10, 12–19].
Buchanan, Allen. 'Justice as Reciprocity versus Subject-Centered Justice', *Philosophy and Public Affairs*, 19(3), 1990: 227–52 [excerpts from pp. 227–33, 236–38].
Callinicos, Alex. *Equality*. (Cambridge: Polity Press, 2000) [excerpts from pp. 52–64].
Dryzek, John. 'Legitimacy and Economy in Deliberative Democracy', *Political Theory*, 29(5), 2001: 651–69.
Fraser, Nancy. 'Recognition or Redistribution? A Critical Reading of Iris Young's *Justice and the Politics of Difference*', *The Journal of Political Philosophy*, 3(2), 1995: 166–80.
Gauthier, David. *Morals by Agreement*. (New York: Oxford University Press, 1986) [excerpts from pp. 1–5, 13–19].
Gutmann, Amy and Thompson, Dennis. 'Deliberative Democracy Beyond Process', *The Journal of Political Philosophy*, 10(2), 2002: 153–74 [excerpts from pp. 153–55, 158–65, 174].
Harsanyi, John. 'Can the Maximin Principle Serve as a Basis for Morality? A Critique of John Rawls's Theory', *American Political Science Review*, 69, 1975: 594–606 [excerpts from pp. 594–98].
Kekes, John. 'A Question for Egalitarians', *Ethics*, 107, 1997: 658–69 [excerpts from pp. 658–64].
Kukathas, Chandran. 'Liberalism and Multiculturalism: The Politics of Indifference', *Political Theory*, 26(5), 1998: 686–99 [excerpts from pp. 686–87, 690–96, 698].
Kymlicka, Will. 'Liberal Individualism and Liberal Neutrality', *Ethics*, 99(4), 1989: 883–905 [excerpts from 883–86, 899–902].
Litan, Robert. 'On Rectification in Nozick's Minimal State', *Political Theory*, 5(2), 1977: 233–46 [excerpts from pp. 233–39, 244–46].
Mack, Eric. 'Self-Ownership, Marxism and Egalitarianism: Part 1: Challenges to Historical Entitlement', *Politics, Philosophy and Economics*, 1(1), 2002: 75–108 [excerpts from pp. 81–91].
Nozick, Robert. *Anarchy, State, and Utopia*. (New York: Basic Books, 1974) [excerpts from pp. 32–33, 152–53, 160–62, 168–70, 174–77].
Okin, Susan. *Justice, Gender and the Family*. (New York: Basic Books, 1989) [excerpts from pp. 124–33].

Parekh, Bhikhu. *Rethinking Multiculturalism: Cultural Diversity and Political Theory*. (Basingstoke: Palgrave, 2000) [excerpts from pp. 243–49].

Patten, Alan. 'The Republican Critique of Liberalism', *British Journal of Political Science*, 26, 1996: 25–44 [excerpts from pp. 28–36].

Pettit, Phillip. 'Freedom as Antipower', *Ethics*, 106(3), 1996: 576–604 [excerpts from pp. 595–603].

Rawls, John. *Justice as Fairness: A Restatement*. (Cambridge, Mass: Harvard University Press, 2001) [excerpts from pp. 5–11, 14–18, 41–43].

Sandel, Michael. 'The Procedural Republic and the Unencumbered Self', *Political Theory*, 12(1), 1984: 81–96.

Taylor, Charles. 'The Politics of Recognition'. In A. Gutmann (ed.), *Multiculturalism* (Princeton: Princeton University Press, 1994) [excerpts from pp. 25–44].

Walzer, Michael. *Spheres of Justice*. (New York: Basic Books, 1983) [excerpts from pp. 3–12, 17–18].

Young, Iris Marion. 'The Ideal of Community and the Politics of Difference', *Social Theory and Practice*, 12(1), 1986: 1–26 [excerpts from pp. 1–2, 14–23].

———. *Inclusion and Democracy*. (Oxford: Oxford University Press, 2000) [excerpts from pp. 21–26].

# Part One: Egalitarian-Liberalism

# Introduction

Over the course of the last thirty years there has emerged a distinctive brand of liberal political theory called 'egalitarian-liberalism'. Egalitarian-liberals are primarily concerned with the issue of *distributive justice*; that is, how the benefits and burdens of social cooperation are to be distributed. As is evident by its name, egalitarian-liberals believe that liberty and equality are compatible political values and that the demands of these two values should be taken seriously when considering what the just division of burdens and benefits are. There is of course no consensus among egalitarian-liberals concerning what distributive outcome constitutes the best complement of liberty and equality. As shall become evident in Chapter 4, liberals have adopted a negative conception of liberty that equates freedom with the absence of interference.[1] Liberals endorse the negative conception of liberty as it captures many of the central concerns they believe a just public philosophy should emphasise. For example, the idea of limited government, the importance of toleration and respect for individual autonomy. These concerns are core concerns of liberals.

But egalitarian-liberals believe that the demands of justice go well beyond the demands of respecting the liberty of all. The value of equality is also a central concern, indeed some egalitarian-liberals argue that equality is the fundamental value of liberalism.[2] It is the 'egalitarian' component of 'egalitarian-liberalism' that has received the most attention (both positive and negative) from political philosophers in the past few decades. This first part begins with the most influential egalitarian-liberal – John Rawls. In *A Theory of Justice* Rawls revitalised the social contract tradition of John Locke, Jean-Jacques Rousseau and Immanuel Kant. Rawls defends the theory he calls 'justice as fairness'. Justice as fairness is primarily concerned with 'the way in which major social institutions distribute fundamental rights and duties and determine the division of advantages from social cooperation' (Rawls, 1999: 6).[3] As such, justice as fairness is a theory designed to apply to what Rawls calls the 'basic structure' – the political, social and economic institutions of society. It provides a normative ideal by which we are to judge the political constitution of society and the principal economic and social arrangements. The just society, according to justice as fairness, is one governed by the two principles of justice. These principles are:

(a) Each person has the same indefensible claim to a fully adequate scheme of equal basic liberties, which scheme is compatible with the same scheme of liberties for all (*equal basic liberties principle*).
(b) Social and economic inequalities are to satisfy two conditions. First, they are to be attached to offices and positions open to all under conditions of fair equality of opportunity (*fair equality of opportunity principle*); and second, they are to be to the greatest benefit of the least-advantaged members of society (*difference principle*).

The principles are presented in 'lexical order'. This means that they are listed in order of priority. The equal basic liberties principle must be satisfied before the second principle is invoked and the fair equality of opportunity principle must be satisfied before the difference principle can be invoked.

Rawls argues that the two principles of justice would be the principles parties in an impartial choice situation would choose as the principles to govern their society. This impartial choice situation is called the 'original position'. The parties in this original position are placed behind a 'veil of ignorance' so that knowledge of things like one's social position and natural talents cannot influence their choice of the principles of justice. In such a scenario Rawls believes the parties would choose the two principles of justice over the principle of utility. In *Contemporary Ethics: Taking Account of Utilitarianism* William Shaw claims that two fundamental ideas underlie utilitarianism: 'first, that the results of our actions are the key to their moral evaluation, and second, that one should assess and compare those results in terms of the happiness they cause (or more broadly, in terms of their impact on people's well-being)' (Shaw, 1999: 2). When stated like this it is easy to see why utilitarianism has enjoyed an eminent list of devotees that includes David Hume, Adam Smith, Jeremy Bentham and J.S. Mill. It captures some of our most basic moral intuitions concerning the importance of, for example, impartiality and human welfare. Utilitarians have put forth diverse accounts of what constitutes 'happiness', or 'utility', but they share the belief that the best outcome is the one that *maximises* overall happiness or utility.

In *A Theory of Justice* Rawls invokes two main concepts of ethics – the right and the good – in order to illustrate how his contractarian theory differs from utilitarianism. 'The structure of an ethical theory', claims Rawls, is 'largely determined by how it defines and connects these two basic notions' (Rawls, 1999: 21). Rawls distinguishes between the following two ways of relating the right and the good. The first way is to define the good independently from the right, and then the right as that which maximises the good. Suppose, for example, one defines the good as material prosperity. If we accept this definition of the good then we can determine which laws and policies are the right ones by simply choosing the institutional arrangement that will bring about the greatest level of material prosperity. Institutions and acts are right if, of the available alternatives, they produce the most good. Rawls calls this type of theory a 'teleological theory'. It is contrasted with a 'deontological theory'. Deontological theories can be defined as theories 'that either do not specify the good independently from the right, or do not interpret the right as maximising the good' (Rawls, 1999: 26). Rawls wants to defend a theory that is deontological in this second sense, that is, it gives a priority of the right over the good.

The appeal of the deontological position can be brought out by considering the example noted above. A teleological theory instructs us to maximise the good. If we define the good as material prosperity, for example, the institutions of our society should be designed to maximise overall material prosperity. But such a goal may be pursued by measures we think are unjust. Maximising overall material prosperity might justify restricting the number of children people can have or forcing people to do jobs they are best suited to do but do not want to do. By asserting a priority of the right over the good Rawls seeks to avoid the injustices which may be made in the name of maximising utility. As Rawls puts it, 'each person possesses an inviolability founded on justice that even the welfare of society as a whole cannot override' (Rawls, 1999: 3)

The main target of Rawls's critique is the classical utilitarian doctrine espoused by Jeremy Bentham and Henry Sidgwick. This version maintains that 'society is rightly ordered, and therefore just, when its major institutions are arranged so as to achieve the greatest net balance of satisfaction summed over all the individuals belonging to it' (Rawls, 1999: 20). Such an approach extends what is a commonsensical approach to the principle of choice for one person to the principle of choice for an association of people. Rawls explains how, as a principle of choice for one person, the utilitarian ethic seems like a rational ethic:

> Each man in realising his own interests is certainly free to balance his own losses against his own gains. We may impose a sacrifice on ourselves now for the sake of a greater advantage later. A person quite properly acts, at least when others are not affected, to achieve his own greatest good, to advance his rational ends as far as possible. (Rawls, 1999: 21)

But the reasoning that is appropriate for the choice of one person should not, argues Rawls, be extended to the choice for an association of people. But this is what utilitarianism does. In doing so it does not take seriously the distinction between persons. There are some things we should not do to people, even if doing it achieves the greatest net balance of satisfaction for all. In particular, Rawls argues that 'in a just society the basic liberties are taken for granted and the rights secured by justice are not subject to political bargaining or to the calculus of social interests' (Rawls, 1999: 25). Utilitarianism treats questions of distributive justice as questions of efficient administration. 'The nature of the decision made by the ideal legislator is not, therefore, materially different from that of an entrepreneur deciding how to maximise his profit by producing this or that commodity, or that of a consumer deciding how to maximise his satisfaction by the purchase of this or that collection of goods' (Rawls, 1999: 24). But justice, claims Rawls, must trump the virtue of efficiency. The right is prior to the good. Justice denies that the loss of freedom for some is made right by a greater good shared by others.

The first excerpt in this part is from Rawls's recent re-statement of the theory of justice as fairness. Rawls revised various parts of his theory over the course of a quarter of a century and the excerpt covers some of the central aspects of his account including his discussion of society as a fair system of cooperation and the original position. The second excerpt considers the utilitarian reply to Rawls's argument. John Harsyani focuses on Rawls's discussion of the maximin strategy. This strategy instructs the parties in the original position to evaluate possible institutional arrangements in terms of how well the least advantaged fare and opt for the scheme that maximises the prospects of the members of this group. The two principles of justice ensure that the interests of the least advantaged are better secured than they would be in a society governed by the principle of utility and thus Rawls believes it is rational to choose the two principles of justice. But Harsanyi questions whether it is rational to abide by the dictates of the principle of maximin.

Richard Arneson focuses on Rawls's difference principle in the excerpt from 'Primary Goods Reconsidered'. Arneson, an egalitarian, is concerned with the scope

Rawls leaves for the issue of personal responsibility when he defines the least advantaged with respect to the primary goods[4] individuals possess. According to Rawls's difference principle, membership in the category of the 'least advantaged' appears to be settled in terms of primary goods that individuals enjoy over the course of their lives and this, argues Arneson, has counterintuitive consequences. He illustrates this with the example of the life choices of four individuals – Smith, Black, Jones, and Johnson. Smith and Black both graduate from an elite law school with high grades and can choose among several career options. Black chooses to be a Wall Street lawyer, the work is stressful but the income is high. Smith opts for the life of a bohemian artist, the income is meagre but the work is like play. Jones and Johnson did not go to college and both graduated from formal schooling with very little in terms of marketable skills. Jones chooses to be a bohemian artist and Johnson an unskilled labourer.

According to Rawls's definition of the least advantaged, Smith is one of the least advantaged. That is, his income falls below both the median income and that which the unskilled worker would get. The difference principle requires us to maximise the prospects of the least advantaged and both Smith and Johnson are members of this group. But our moral intuitions tell us that these two individuals should not be treated the same. Smith had lots of opportunities. With his law degree he could have chosen a variety of jobs that would have secured him a high income. But he *chose* to be a bohemian artist and the low level of subsistence that comes with it. This contrasts with Johnson. Due to his low level of marketable skills he never had a choice between high income and low income jobs. In addition to this, he chose to work for a living doing hard labour rather than live the life of a bohemian artist. Johnson is one of the *deserving* poor, argues Arneson, while Smith is not. Smith is poor by choice and thus should not receive the same benefits that Johnson receives. Justice does not require us to compensate individuals for inequalities they have voluntarily chosen.

Rawls's attempt to combine considerations of liberty with those of equality has inspired political theorists to take more seriously the idea that something should be *equally* distributed among us and thus many authors have sought to give some precision to exactly what this egalitarian metric is. This has come to be known as the 'Equality of What?' debate, named after an influential article by Amartya Sen (1980). This debate has largely evolved out of concerns stemming from Rawls's account of justice. Two central concerns have arisen with respect to the way Rawls defines the least advantaged members of society in *A Theory of Justice*. First, Rawls stipulates that he constructs a theory of justice for the simpler case of a society of 'normal, fully cooperating members'. But this tactic makes Rawls's theory less attractive to those who believe that inequalities in the natural lottery of life should be a central concern of a theory of justice. By excluding the severely handicapped from the category of the least advantaged Rawls's theory does not take seriously the egalitarian intuition that inequalities in our natural endowments should be compensated. Second, critics like Arneson have argued that Rawls includes many of the undeserving poor in the category of the 'least advantaged' and the idea of maximising the prospects of those who choose to be non-productive does not cohere with our moral sensibilities. There is a difference between someone who is less advantaged as a result of circumstances beyond their control (for example, being born with a severe handicap) and someone who is less advantaged as a result of their own choice (for example, choosing to live off welfare payments instead of working). A concern for these two issues has given rise to the position Elizabeth Anderson (1999) calls 'luck egalitarianism'.[5] Luck egalitarians construct their theories around what is called the choice/chance (or choice/circumstances) distinction. 'People's fates are determined by their choices and their circumstances' (Dworkin, 2000: 322) and this must remain, argue luck egalitarians, a fundamental insight when considering what constitutes a just distribution.

Luck egalitarians disagree on exactly what should be equalised (for example, resources, opportunity for welfare, etc.) but they believe that inequalities in the advantages that people enjoy are just if they derive from the choices people have voluntarily made, and conversely that inequalities deriving from unchosen features of people's circumstances are unjust. In the excerpt from Alex Callinicos's *Equality* he surveys the main egalitarian positions that have been defended and the concerns that have been raised against these distinct positions. One of the most influential accounts of luck egalitarianism is Ronald Dworkin's argument for 'equality of resources'. Dworkin begins *Sovereign Virtue* by declaring:

> No government is legitimate that does not show equal concern for the fate of all those citizens over whom it claims dominion and from whom it claims allegiance. Equal concern is the sovereign virtue of political community – without it government is only tyranny – and when a nation's wealth is very unequally distributed, as the wealth of even very prosperous nations now is, then its equal concern is suspect. For the distribution of wealth is the product of a legal order: a citizen's wealth massively depends on which laws his community has enacted – not only its laws governing ownership, theft, contract, and tort, but its welfare law, tax law, labor law, civil rights law, environmental regulation law, and laws of practically everything else. (Dworkin, 2000: 1)

Like Rawls, Dworkin believes that the basic structure of society should be publicly justified to all citizens. But unlike Rawls, Dworkin does not believe that this can be accomplished by emphasising a version of 'political liberalism'[6] that does not invoke ethical assumptions and controversies about the good life. On the contrary, Dworkin appeals to a diverse array of general ethical values. His version of 'comprehensive liberalism' rests on two fundamental principles of ethical individualism – the principle of equal importance and the principle of special responsibility. These principles maintain the following:

> Principle of Equal Importance: It is important, from an objective point of view, that human lives be successful rather than wasted, and this is equally important, from an objective point of view, for each human life.

> Principle of Special Responsibility: though we must all recognise the equal objective importance of the success of a human life, one person has a special and final responsibility for that success – the person whose life it is. (Dworkin, 2000: 5)

These two principles make different demands on government. The principle of equal importance requires 'government to adopt laws and policies that insure that its citizens' fates are, so far as government can achieve this, insensitive to who they otherwise are – their economic background, gender, race, or particular set of skills and handicaps' (Dworkin, 2000: 6). The principle of special responsibility 'demands that the government work, again as far as it can achieve this, to make their fates sensitive to the choices they have made' (Dworkin, 2000: 6). Over the course of *Sovereign Virtue* Dworkin elaborates on what the content of these twin demands are by considering a number of theoretical issues and political controversies.

When someone declares themselves to be an 'egalitarian' we commonly assume that they hold particular beliefs concerning what might be called *distributional equality*. They might, for example, believe that everyone should have equal incomes or be equally happy. Distributional equality concerns the index of goods an egalitarian believes should be equally distributed. Dworkin's main concern is with distributional equality and he considers two general theories – equality of welfare and equality of resources.

> Equality of Welfare: A distributional scheme treats people as equals when it distributes or transfers resources among them until no further transfer would leave them more equal in welfare.
>
> Equality of Resources: A distributional scheme treats people as equals when it distributes or transfers so that no further transfer would leave their shares of the total resources more equal. (Dworkin, 2000: 12)

Utilitarianism is the main tradition that adopts a welfarist metric when assessing the merits of actions and policies/laws. The right action or policy, argue utilitarians, is that which promotes the greatest happiness of the greatest number. One could define 'welfare' in many distinct ways (for example, sensation of pleasure, preference satisfaction, etc.). Whatever one's account of welfare is, the ideal of equality of welfare seems appealing as it coheres with the first of the two principles of ethical individualism Dworkin emphasises – the principle of equal importance. Equality of welfare would require, for example, that those whose welfare is impeded by handicaps receive extra resources so that they can enjoy the same level of welfare as those who do not face such burdens.

But equality of welfare fails to accommodate the second principle which Dworkin takes to be fundamental, the principle of special responsibility. If equality of welfare is the goal then it cannot provide sufficient room for the idea that we have special and final responsibility for the success of our lives. I may have less welfare than another due, not to factors beyond my control (for example, a handicap I was born with), but to factors I can be personally responsible for (for example, expensive tastes). Perhaps I have cultivated expensive tastes and thus need extra resources in order for me to achieve the same level of welfare that others (with less expensive tastes) have. According to equality of welfare my demand for extra resources, like those of the person with a handicap, is legitimate. Equality of welfare fails as a distributive ideal because it does not permit sufficient room for considerations of personal responsibility. Like Rawls's difference principle, equality of welfare fails to distinguish between the deserving and undeserving poor. Dworkin puts forth his account of equality of resources as an alternative distributive ideal that incorporates both the principle of equal importance and the principle of special responsibility.

Dworkin's argument for equality of resources is a rich and sophisticated one and we can only briefly consider some of the main components of it. Dworkin's attempt to merge the two fundamental principles of ethical individualism are most stark in his hypothetical tale of shipwrecked survivors who are washed up on a desert island that has abundant resources. These immigrants agree to divide the resources of the island equally among them. Each immigrant is given 100 clam shells to bid on the various resources. These people will obviously have different preferences and this will be reflected in what they spend their clam shells on. If the majority of immigrants have a preference for sun-tanning on the beach then those parts of the beach will be very costly. If the majority have a preference for living as farmers then those parts of the island conducive to agriculture will be very costly, etc. The distribution that would result from such an auction would be 'ambition-sensitive'. That is, the bundle of goods people end up with would reflect only the choices they made. No one could complain that someone else received preferential treatment as all started with 100 clam shells and were free to bid on whatever resources they wanted. Of course some resources will be more expensive than others but this is not grounds for a complaint as this stems from your own personal preferences and those of the other immigrants. You could change your preferences so that you could appropriate more of the less expensive resources. Such an auction will treat all as equals if it satisfies what Dworkin calls the 'envy test'. The envy test maintains that 'no division of resources is an equal division if, once the distribution is complete, any immigrant would prefer someone else's bundle of resources to his own bundle' (Dworkin, 2000: 67).

The first part of Dworkin's hypothetical story captures the concern for the principle of special responsibility. The initial bundle of goods the immigrants have are the result of their own ambitions, tastes, etc. But what happens once the auction is completed and the immigrants begin to produce things? Given the fact that some immigrants will be more skilful, others will fall sick etc., it will not be long before the conditions of the envy test will fail to be met. These events thus threaten to undermine the first fundamental principle of ethical individualism – the principle of equal importance. This principle maintains that it is important that human lives be successful rather than wasted. But a 'starting-gate' theory that holds that justice requires equal initial resources and *laissez-faire* thereafter will undermine the requirements of this principle. Dworkin argues that we must not allow the distribution of resources to be *endowment-sensitive*, that is, 'to be affected by differences in ability of the sort that produce income differences in a *laissez-faire* economy among people with the same ambitions' (Dworkin, 2000: 89).

Dworkin introduces the hypothetical insurance scheme to alleviate the concerns about abandoning the ideal of an endowment-insensitive distribution. He modifies the auction story by declaring that, prior to the auction, the immigrants are denied information about their natural endowments and are given the opportunity to purchase insurance against handicaps and unequal skills. Under these conditions of uncertainty people would be willing to part with some of their 100 clam shells to guard against having disabilities or lacking skills. Those who fare poorly in these respects will receive compensation in the form of extra resources paid out by these insurance schemes. Such schemes will be funded by those who are fortunate not to have to make an insurance claim but who will have to pay an insurance premium.

The hypothetical auction Dworkin invokes is likely to cause some confusion in terms of understanding how it relates to the real world, where we don't begin with equal resources nor do we have insurance schemes in place for things like skill. Dworkin attempts to make the link between the theory and real world by tackling a number of applied topics in part II of *Sovereign Virtue*, including health care, welfare programmes, electoral reform and affirmative action. In the real world, for example, there is a need for taxation and redistribution. Income tax is a device society can use to neutralise the effects of handicaps and differential talents. But a tax system can only roughly approximate the results of the insurance scheme and will not achieve a truly 'ambition-sensitive/endowment-insensitive' distribution. Nor is there one simple solution which will do justice to the demands of the two fundamental principles of ethical individualism. Dworkin endorses, for example, a decent minimum of medical care for all citizens and the option to buy private health insurance. But his endorsement of universal coverage is not founded on the rescue principle, which instructs us to spend all we can on health care 'until the next dollar would buy no gain in health and life expectancy at all' (Dworkin, 2000: 309). Equal concern for all does not necessarily entail that we spend exorbitant amounts of public funds trying to save the lives of those who have little chance of surviving for long. Society must make tough decisions regarding which medical tests and procedures should be deemed 'necessary and appropriate' for coverage under the publicly funded health care system and also allow individuals to choose for themselves how much more they wish to spend to insure themselves against other possible misfortunes. Such an arrangement is a just compromise between the demands of the principle of equal importance and the principle of special responsibility.

The idea that we should attempt to implement some egalitarian metric is rejected by John Kekes in his article 'A Question for Egalitarians'. An excerpt from that article is included in Chapter 5. Kekes argues that the egalitarian belief that the just society should aim to eliminate or reduce unjustified inequalities has some absurd consequences. Kekes illustrates this point by considering the inequalities in life expectancy between men and women. Life expectancy, argues Kekes, has at least as strong a claim to being a primary good as any other candidate. Thus if we include it in our list of inequalities that should be compensated then we should support some absurd policies, such as giving men shorter working days and longer vacations than women. Kekes's point is that not all serious inequalities are unjust, preventable or due to institutional arrangements.

## Notes

1 See Isaiah Berlin (1997).
2 See Dworkin (1985), chapter nine.
3 All references to *A Theory of Justice* are to the second edition.
4 These goods are rights and liberties, powers and opportunities, income and wealth and self-respect.
5 Those who endorse this position include, among others, Ronald Dworkin (2000), Richard Arneson (1989), G.A. Cohen (1989) and Philippe Van Parijs (1995).
6 See Rawls (1993).

## References

Anderson, Elizabeth. 'What is the Point of Equality?', *Ethics,* 109(2), 1999: 287-337.
Arneson, Richard. 'Equality and Equal Opportunity for Welfare', *Philosophical Studies,* 56, 1989: 77-93.
Berlin, Isaiah. 'Two Concepts of Liberty.' In P. Pettit and R. Goodin (eds.) *Contemporary Political Philosophy* (Oxford: Blackwell Publishers, 1997).
Cohen, G.A. 'On the Currency of Egalitarian Justice', *Ethics,* 99(4), 1989: 906-44.
Dworkin, Ronald. *A Matter of Principle.* (Cambridge, Mass: Harvard University Press, 1985).
─── *Sovereign Virtue* (Cambridge, Mass.: Harvard University Press, 2000).
Rawls, John. *A Theory of Justice* (second edition) (Oxford: Oxford University Press, 1999).
─── *Political Liberalism.* (New York: Columbia University Press, 1993).
Sen, Amartya. 'Equality of What?'. In S.M. McMurrin (ed.), *The Tanner Lectures on Human Values,* vol. 1 (Salt Lake City: University of Utah Press, 1980).
Shaw, William. *Contemporary Ethics: Taking Account of Utilitarianism.* (Oxford: Blackwell Publishers, 1999).
Van Parijs, Philippe. *Real Freedom for All* (Oxford: Oxford University Press, 1995).

# 1 Justice as Fairness

## John Rawls

One practicable aim of justice as fairness is to provide an acceptable philosophical and moral basis for democratic institutions and thus to address the question of how the claims of liberty and equality are to be understood. To this end we look to the public political culture of a democratic society, and to the traditions of interpretation of its constitution and basic laws, for certain familiar ideas that can be worked up into a conception of political justice. It is assumed that citizens in a democratic society have at least an implicit understanding of these ideas as shown in everyday political discussion, in debates about the meaning and ground of constitutional rights and liberties, and the like.[1]

Some of these familiar ideas are more basic than others. Those we use to organize and to give structure to justice as fairness as a whole I count as fundamental ideas. The most fundamental idea in this conception of justice is the idea of society as a fair system of social cooperation over time from one generation to the next (*Theory*, §1: 4). We use this idea as the central organizing idea in trying to develop a political conception of justice for a democratic regime.

This central idea is worked out in conjunction with two companion fundamental ideas. These are: the idea of citizens (those engaged in cooperation) as free and equal persons (§7); and the idea of a well-ordered society, that is, a society effectively regulated by a public conception of justice (§3).

As indicated above, these fundamental intuitive ideas are viewed as being familiar from the public political culture of a democratic society. Even though such ideas are not often expressly formulated, nor their meanings clearly marked out, they may play a fundamental role in society's political thought and in how its institutions are interpreted, for example, by courts and in historical or other texts regarded as being of enduring significance. That a democratic society is often viewed as a system of social cooperation is suggested by the fact that from a political point of view, and in the context of the public discussion of basic questions of political right, its citizens do not regard their social order as a fixed natural order, or as an institutional structure justified by religious doctrines or hierarchical principles expressing aristocratic values. Nor do they think a political party may properly, as a matter of its declared program, work to deny any recognized class or group its basic rights and liberties.

The central organizing idea of social cooperation has at least three essential features:

(a) Social cooperation is distinct from merely socially coordinated activity—for example, activity coordinated by orders issued by an absolute central authority. Rather, social cooperation is guided by publicly recognized rules and procedures which those cooperating accept as appropriate to regulate their conduct.
(b) The idea of cooperation includes the idea of fair terms of cooperation: these are terms each participant may reasonably accept, and sometimes should accept, provided that everyone else likewise accepts them. Fair terms of cooperation specify an idea of reciprocity, or mutuality: all who do their part as the recognized rules require are to benefit as specified by a public and agreed-upon standard.
(c) The idea of cooperation also includes the idea of each participant's rational advantage, or good. The idea of rational advantage specifies what it is that those engaged in cooperation are seeking to advance from the standpoint of their own good.

Throughout I shall make a distinction between the reasonable and the rational, as I shall refer to them. These are basic and complementary ideas entering into the fundamental idea of society as a fair system of social cooperation. As applied to the simplest case, namely to persons engaged in cooperation and situated as equals in relevant respects (or symmetrically, for short), reasonable persons are ready to propose, or to acknowledge when proposed by others, the principles needed to specify what can be seen by all as fair terms of cooperation. Reasonable persons also understand that they are to honor these principles, even at the expense of their own interests as circumstances may require, provided others likewise may be expected to honor them. It is unreasonable not to be ready to propose such principles, or not to honor fair terms of cooperation that others may reasonably be expected to accept; it is worse than unreasonable if one merely seems, or pretends, to propose or honor them but is ready to violate them to one's advantage as the occasion permits.

Yet while it is unreasonable, it is not, in general, not rational. For it may be that some have a superior political power or are placed in more fortunate circumstances; and though these conditions are irrelevant, let us assume, in distinguishing between the persons in question as equals, it may be rational for those so placed to take advantage of their situation. In everyday life we imply this distinction, as when we say of certain people that, given their superior bargaining position, their proposal is perfectly rational, but unreasonable all the same. Common sense views the reasonable but not, in general, the rational as a moral idea involving moral sensibility.[2]

## Two Principles of Justice

To try to answer our question, let us turn to a revised statement of the two principles of justice discussed in *Theory*, §§11–14. They should now read:

(a) Each person has the same indefeasible claim to a fully adequate scheme of equal basic liberties, which scheme is compatible with the same scheme of liberties for all; and

(b) Social and economic inequalities are to satisfy two conditions: first, they are to be attached to offices and positions open to all under conditions of fair equality of opportunity; and second, they are to be to the greatest benefit of the least-advantaged members of society (the difference principle).[3]

As I explain below, the first principle is prior to the second; also, in the second principle fair equality of opportunity is prior to the difference principle. This priority means that in applying a principle (or checking it against test cases) we assume that the prior principles are fully satisfied. We seek a principle of distribution (in the narrower sense) that holds within the setting of background institutions that secure the basic equal liberties (including the fair value of the political liberties) as well as fair equality of opportunity. How far that principle holds outside that setting is a separate question we shall not consider.[4]

The role of the principles of justice (as part of a political conception of justice) is to specify the fair terms of social cooperation (*Theory*, §1). These principles specify the basic rights and duties to be assigned by the main political and social institutions, and they regulate the division of benefits arising from social cooperation and allot the burdens necessary to sustain it. Since in a democratic society citizens are regarded from the point of view of the political conception as free and equal persons, the principles of a democratic conception of justice may be viewed as specifying the fair terms of cooperation between citizens so conceived.

By way of these specifications, the principles of justice provide a response to the fundamental question of political philosophy for a constitutional democratic regime. That question is: what is the most acceptable political conception of justice for specifying the fair terms of cooperation between citizens regarded as free and equal and as both reasonable and rational, and (we add) as normal and fully cooperating members of society over a complete life, from one generation to the next? This question is fundamental because it has been the focus of the liberal critique of monarchy and aristocracy and of the socialist critique of liberal constitutional democracy. It is also the focus of the present conflict between liberalism and conservative views over the claims of private property and the legitimacy (as opposed to the effectiveness) of social policies associated with the so-called welfare state.[5]

In using the conception of citizens as free and equal persons we abstract from various features of the social world and idealize in certain ways. This brings out one role of abstract conceptions: they are used to gain a clear and uncluttered view of a question seen as fundamental by focusing on the more significant elements that we think are most relevant in determining its most appropriate answer. Unless explicitly stated otherwise, we do not try to answer any question except the fundamental question stated above.

## The Idea of a Well-Ordered Society

As stated, the fundamental idea of a well-ordered society—a society effectively regulated by a public conception of justice—is a companion idea used to specify the central organizing idea of society as a fair system of cooperation. Now to say that a political society is well ordered conveys three things:

First, and implied by the idea of a public conception of justice, it is a society in which everyone accepts, and knows that everyone else accepts, the very same political conception of justice (and so the same principles of political justice). Moreover, this knowledge is mutually recognized: that is, people know everything they would know if their acceptance of those principles were a matter of public agreement.

Second, and implied by the idea of effective regulation by a public conception of justice, society's basic structure—that is, its main political and social institutions and the way they hang together as one system of cooperation—is publicly known, or with good reason believed, to satisfy those principles of justice.

Third, and also implied by the idea of effective regulation, citizens have a normally effective sense of justice, that is, one that enables them to understand and apply the publicly recognized principles of justice, and for the most part to act accordingly as their position in society, with its duties and obligations, requires.

In a well-ordered society, then, the public conception of justice provides a mutually recognized point of view from which citizens can adjudicate their claims of political right on their political institutions or against one another.

## The Idea of the Basic Structure

Another fundamental idea is the idea of the basic structure (of a well-ordered society). This idea is introduced so as to formulate and present justice as fairness as having an appropriate unity. Along with the idea of the original position (§6), it is needed to complete other ideas and to order them into a perspicuous whole. The idea of the basic structure may be seen in that light.

As indicated above, the basic structure of society is the way in which the main political and social institutions of society fit together into one system of social cooperation, and the way they assign basic rights and duties and regulate the division of advantages that arises from social cooperation over time (*Theory*, §2: 6). The political constitution with an independent judiciary, the legally recognized forms of property, and the structure of the economy (for example, as a system of competitive markets with private property in the means of production), as well as the family in some form, all belong to the basic structure. The basic structure is the background social framework within which the activities of associations and individuals take place. A just basic structure secures what we may call background justice.

One main feature of justice as fairness is that it takes the basic structure as the primary subject of political justice (*Theory*, §2). It does so in part because the effects of the basic structure on citizens' aims, aspirations, and character, as well as on their opportunities and their ability to take advantage of them, are pervasive and present from the beginning of life (§§15–16). Our focus is almost entirely on the basic structure as the subject of political and social justice.

Since justice as fairness starts with the special case of the basic structure, its principles regulate this structure and do not apply directly to or regulate internally institutions and associations within society.[6] Firms and labor unions, churches, universities, and the family are bound by constraints arising from the principles of justice, but these constraints arise indirectly from just background institutions within which associations and groups exist, and by which the conduct of their members is restricted.

For example, while churches can excommunicate heretics, they cannot burn them; this constraint is to secure liberty of conscience. Universities cannot discriminate in certain ways: this constraint is to help to establish fair equality of opportunity. Parents (women equally with men) are equal citizens and have equal basic rights including the right of property; they must respect the rights of their children (which the latter have as prospective citizens) and cannot, for instance, deprive them of essential medical care. Moreover, to establish equality between men and women in sharing the work of society, in preserving its culture and in reproducing itself over time, special provisions are needed in family law (and no doubt elsewhere) so that the burden of bearing, raising, and educating children does not fall more heavily on women, thereby undermining their fair equality of opportunity.

## The Idea of the Original Position

Let us begin with how we might be led to the original position and the reasons for using it. The following line of thought might lead us to it: we start with the organizing idea of society as a fair system of cooperation between free and equal persons. Immediately the question arises as to how the fair terms of cooperation are specified. For example: Are they specified by an authority distinct from the persons cooperating, say, by God's law? Or are these terms recognized by everyone as fair by reference to a moral order of values,[7] say, by rational intuition, or by reference to what some have viewed as "natural law"? Or are they settled by an agreement reached by free and equal citizens engaged in cooperation, and made in view of what they regard as their reciprocal advantage, or good?

Justice as fairness adopts a form of the last answer: the fair terms of social cooperation are to be given by an agreement entered into by those engaged in it. One reason it does this is that, given the assumption of reasonable pluralism, citizens cannot agree on any moral authority, say a sacred text or a religious institution or tradition. Nor can they agree about a moral order of values or the dictates of what some view as natural law. So what better alternative is there than an agreement between citizens themselves reached under conditions that are fair for all?

Now this agreement, like any other, must be entered into under certain conditions if it is to be a valid agreement from the point of view of political justice. In particular, these conditions must situate free and equal persons fairly and must not permit some to have unfair bargaining advantages over others. Further, threats of force and coercion, deception and fraud, and so on must be ruled out. So far, so good. These considerations are familiar from everyday life. But agreements in everyday life are made in determinate situations within the background institutions of the basic structure; and the particular features of these situations affect the terms of the agreements reached. Clearly, unless those situations satisfy the conditions for valid and fair agreements, the terms agreed to will not be regarded as fair.

Justice as fairness hopes to extend the idea of a fair agreement to the basic structure itself. Here we face a serious difficulty for any political conception of justice that uses the idea of contract, whether or not the contract is social. The difficulty is this: we must specify a point of view from which a fair agreement between free and equal persons can be reached; but this point of view must be removed from and not distorted by the particular features and circumstances of the existing basic structure. The original position, with the feature I have called the "veil of ignorance" (*Theory*, §24), specifies this point of view. In the original position, the parties are not allowed to know the social positions or the particular comprehensive doctrines of the persons they represent. They also do not know persons' race and ethnic group, sex, or various native endowments such as strength and intelligence, all within the normal range. We express these limits on information figuratively by saying the parties are behind a veil of ignorance.[8]

One reason why the original position must abstract from the contingencies—the particular features and circumstances of persons—within the basic structure is that the conditions for a fair agreement between free and equal persons on the first principles of justice for that structure must eliminate the bargaining advantages that inevitably arise over time within any society as a result of cumulative social and historical tendencies. "To persons according to their threat advantage" (or their de facto political power, or wealth, or native endowments) is not the basis of political justice. Contingent historical advantages and accidental influences from the past should not affect an agreement on principles that are to regulate the basic structure from the present into the future.[9]

The idea of the original position is proposed, then, as the answer to the question of how to extend the idea of a fair agreement to an agreement on principles of political justice for the basic structure. That position is set up as a situation that is fair to the parties as free and equal, and as properly informed and rational. Thus any agreement made by the parties as citizens' representatives is fair. Since the content of the agreement concerns the principles of justice for the basic structure, the agreement in the original position specifies the fair terms of social cooperation between citizens regarded as such persons. Hence the name: justice as fairness.

Observe that, as stated in *Theory*, the original position generalizes the familiar idea of the social contract (*Theory*, §3). It does so by making the object of agreement the first principles of justice for the basic structure, rather than a particular form of government, as in Locke. The original position is also more abstract: the agreement must be regarded as both hypothetical and nonhistorical.

(i) It is hypothetical, since we ask what the parties (as described) could, or would, agree to, not what they have agreed to.
(ii) It is nonhistorical, since we do not suppose the agreement has ever, or indeed ever could actually be entered into. And even if it could, that would make no difference.

The second point (ii) means that what principles the parties would agree to is to be decided by analysis. We characterize the original position by various stipulations—each with its own reasoned backing—so that the agreement that would be reached can be worked out deductively by reasoning from how the parties are situated and described, the alternatives open to them, and from what the parties count as reasons and the information available to them. We return to this in Part III.

Here there may seem to be a serious objection: since hypothetical agreements are not binding at all, the agreement of the parties in the original position would appear to be of no significance.[10] In reply, the significance of the original position lies in the fact that it is a device of representation or, alternatively, a thought-experiment for the purpose of public- and self-clarification. We are to think of it as modeling two things:

First, it models what we regard—here and now—as fair conditions under which the representatives of citizens, viewed solely as free and equal persons, are to agree to the fair terms of cooperation whereby the basic structure is to be regulated.

Second, it models what we regard—here and now—as acceptable restrictions on the reasons on the basis of which the parties, situated in fair conditions, may properly put forward certain principles of political justice and reject others.

Thus if the original position suitably models our convictions about these two things (namely, fair conditions of agreement between citizens as free and equal, and appropriate restrictions on reasons), we conjecture that the principles of justice the parties would agree to (could we properly work them out) would specify the terms of cooperation that we regard—here and now—as fair and supported by the best reasons. This is because, in that case, the original position would have succeeded in modeling in a suitable manner what we think on due reflection are the reasonable considerations to ground the principles of a political conception of justice.

... [o]ur question is: viewing society as a fair system of cooperation between citizens regarded as free and equal, what principles of justice are most appropriate to specify basic rights and liberties, and to regulate social and economic inequalities in citizens' prospects over a complete life? These inequalities are our primary concern.

To find a principle to regulate these inequalities, we look to our firmest considered convictions about equal basic rights and liberties, the fair value of the political liberties as well as fair equality of opportunity. We look outside the sphere of distributive justice more narrowly construed to see whether an appropriate distributive principle is singled out by those firmest convictions once their essential elements are represented in the original position as a devise of representation (§6). This device is to assist us in working out which principle, or principles, the representatives of free and equal citizens would select to regulate social and economic inequalities in these prospects over a complete life when they assume that the equal basic liberties and fair opportunities are already secured.

The idea here is to use our firmest considered convictions about the nature of a democratic society as a fair system of cooperation between free and equal citizens—as modeled in the original position—to see whether the combined assertion of those convictions so expressed will help us to identify an appropriate distributive principle for the basic structure with its economic and social inequalities in citizens' life-prospects. Our convictions about principles regulating those inequalities are much less firm and assured; so we look to our firmest convictions for guidance where assurance is lacking and guidance is needed (*Theory*, §§4, 20).

## Notes

1. The exposition of justice as fairness starts with these familiar ideas. In this way we connect it with the common sense of everyday life. But because the exposition begins with these ideas does not mean that the argument for justice as fairness simply assumes them as a basis. Everything depends on how the exposition works out as a whole and whether the ideas and principles of this conception of justice, as well as its conclusions, prove acceptable on due reflection. See §10.
2. This kind of distinction between the reasonable and the rational was made by W. M. Sibley in "The Rational versus the Reasonable," *Philosophical Review* 62 (October 1953): 554–560. The text connects the distinction closely with the idea of cooperation among equals and specifies it accordingly for this more definite idea. From time to time we come back to the distinction between the reasonable and the rational. See §23.2 and §23.3. It is of central importance in understanding the structure of justice as fairness, as well as T. M. Scanlon's general contractualist moral theory. See his "Contractualism and Utilitarianism," in *Utilitarianism and Beyond*, ed. Amartya Sen and Bernard Williams (Cambridge: Cambridge University Press, 1982).
3. This section summarizes some points from "The Basic Liberties and Their Priority," *Tanner Lectures on Human Values*, vol. 3, ed. Sterling McMurrin (Salt Lake City: University of Utah Press, 1982), §I, reprinted in *Political Liberalism*. In that

essay I try to reply to what I believe are two of the more serious objections to my account of liberty in *Theory* raised by H.L.A. Hart in his splendid critical review essay, "Rawls on Liberty and Its Priority," *University of Chicago Law Review* 40 (Spring 1973): 551–555, reprinted in his *Essays in Jurisprudence and Philosophy* (Oxford: Oxford University Press, 1983). No changes made in justice as fairness in this restatement are more significant than those forced by Hart's review.

4 Some have found this kind of restriction objectionable; they think a political conception should be framed to cover all logically possible cases, or all conceivable cases, and not restricted to cases that can arise only within a specified institutional context. See for example Brian Barry, *The Liberal Theory of Justice* (Oxford: Oxford University Press, 1973), p. 112. In contrast, we seek a principle to govern social and economic inequalities in democratic regimes as we know them, and so we are concerned with inequalities in citizens' life-prospects that may actually arise, given our understanding of how certain institutions work.

5 I say "so-called welfare state" because Part IV distinguishes between a property-owning democracy and a capitalist welfare state and maintains that the latter conflicts with justice as fairness.

6 This seems obvious in most cases. Clearly the two principles of justice (§13) with their political liberties are not supposed to regulate the internal organization of churches and universities. Nor is the difference principle to govern how parents are to treat their children or to allocate the family's wealth among them. See Part IV, §50, on the family.

7 This order I assume to be viewed as objective as in some form of moral realism.

8 [See Rawls, *Political Liberalism* (New York: Columbia University Press, 1993), pp. 24–25.]

9 This is an essential feature of justice as fairness as a form of the contract doctrine. It differs from Locke's view in this respect, and also from the contract views of Robert Nozick in *Anarchy, State, and Utopia* (New York: Basic Books, 1974), of James Buchanan in *The Limits of Liberty* (Chicago: University of Chicago Press, 1975), and of David Gauthier in *Morals by Agreement* (Oxford: Oxford University Press, 1986). In these three works citizens' basic rights, liberties, and opportunities, as secured by the basic structure, depend on contingencies of history, and social circumstance and native endowment, in ways excluded by justice as fairness. We come back to this in §16.1.

10 This question is discussed by Ronald Dworkin in §1 of his critical review entitled "Justice and Rights," *University of Chicago Law Review* (1973), reprinted in *Taking Rights Seriously* (Cambridge, Mass.: Harvard University Press, 1977), as chap. 6. I have discussed his interpretation briefly in "Justice as Fairness: Political Not Metaphysical," *Philosophy and Public Affairs* 14 (Summer 1985): 236f., n. 19; reprinted in Rawls, *Collected Papers*, ed. Samuel Freeman (Cambridge, Mass.: Harvard University Press, 1999), 400f., n. 19.

# 2 The Maximin Principle

## John C. Harsanyi

John Rawls's *A Theory of Justice*[1] is an important book. It is an attempt to develop a viable alternative to *utilitarianism*, which up to now in its various forms was virtually the only ethical theory proposing a reasonably clear, systematic, and purportedly rational concept of morality. I shall argue that Rawls's attempt to suggest a viable alternative to utilitarianism does not succeed. Nevertheless, beyond any doubt, his book is a significant contribution to the ongoing debate on the nature of rational morality.

Rawls distinguishes two major traditions of systematic theory in post medieval moral philosophy. One is the *utilitarian* tradition, represented by Hume, Adam Smith, Bentham, John Stuart Mill, Sidgwick, Edgeworth, and many others, including a number of contemporary philosophers and social scientists. The other is the *contractarian* (social-contract) tradition of Locke, Rousseau, and Kant. The latter has never been developed as systematically as the utilitarian tradition, and, clearly, one of Rawls's objectives is to remedy this situation. He regards his own theory as a generalization of the classical contractarian position, and as its restatement at a higher level of abstraction (p. 11).

Rawls argues that the "first virtue" of social institutions (i.e., the most fundamental moral requirement they ought to satisfy) is *justice* (or *fairness*). Suppose that all members of a society—or, more precisely, all "heads of families" (p. 128; *pace* Women's Lib!)—have to agree on the general principles that are to govern the institutions of their society. All of them are supposed to be rational individuals caring only about their own personal interests (and those of their own descendants). But, in order to ensure that they would reach a fair-minded agreement (p. 12), Rawls assumes that they would have to negotiate with each other under what he calls the *veil of ignorance*, i.e., without knowing their own social and economic positions, their own special interests in the society, or even their own personal talents and abilities (or their lack of them). This hypothetical situation in which all participants would have to agree on the most basic institutional arrangements of their society while under this veil of ignorance, is called by Rawls the *original position*. In his theory, this purely hypothetical—and rather abstractly defined—original position replaces the historical or semi-historical "social contract" of earlier contractarian philosophers. He considers the institutions of a given society to be *just* if they are organized according to the principles that presumably would have been agreed upon by rational individuals in the original position (p. 17).

What decision rule would rational individuals use in the original position in deciding whether a given set of institutions was or was not acceptable to them? In the terminology of modern decision theory, the initial position would be a situation of *uncertainty* because, by assumption, the participants would be uncertain about what their personal circumstances would be under any particular institutional framework to be agreed upon.

There are two schools of thought about the decision rule to be used by a rational person under uncertainty. One proposes the *maximin principle*, or some generalization or modification of this principle, as the appropriate decision rule.[2] From the mid-'forties (when the problem first attracted wider attention) to the mid-'fifties this was the prevailing opinion. But then came a growing realization that the maximin principle and all its relatives lead to serious paradoxes because they often suggest wholly unacceptable practical decisions.[3] The other—Bayesian—school of thought, which is now dominant, proposes *expected-utility maximization* as decision rule under uncertainty.[4]

In my opinion, the concept of the original position is a potentially very powerful analytical tool for clarifying the concept of justice and other aspects of morality. In actual fact, this concept played an essential role in my own analysis of moral value judgements,[5] prior to its first use by Rawls in 1957[6] (though I did not use the term "original position"). But the usefulness of this concept crucially depends on its being combined with a satisfactory decision rule. Unfortunately, Rawls chooses the maximin principle as decision rule for the participants in the original position. By the very nature of the maximin principle, this choice cannot fail to have highly paradoxical implications.

## The Maximin Principle and its Paradoxes

Suppose you live in New York City and are offered two jobs at the same time. One is a tedious and badly paid job in New York City itself, while the other is a very interesting and well paid job in Chicago. But the catch is that, if you wanted the Chicago job, you would have to take a plane from New York to Chicago (e.g., because this job would have to be taken up the very next day). Therefore there would be a very small but positive probability that you might be killed in a plane accident. Thus, the situation can be represented by the double-entry table [Table 2.1, see over]:

The maximin principle says that you must evaluate every policy available to you in terms of the *worst possibility* that can occur to you if you follow that particular policy. Therefore, you have to analyze the situation as follows. If you choose the New York job then the worst (and, indeed, the only) possible outcome will be that you will have a poor job but you will

**TABLE 2.1**

|  | If the N.Y.–Chicago plane has an accident | If the N.Y.–Chicago plane has no accident |
|---|---|---|
| If you choose the N.Y. job | You will have a poor job, but will stay alive | You will have a poor job, but will stay alive |
| If you choose the Chicago job | You will die | You will have an excellent job and will stay alive |

stay alive. (I am assuming that your chances of dying in the near future for reasons other than a plane accident can be taken to be zero.) In contrast, if you choose the Chicago job then the worst possible outcome will be that you may die in a plane accident. Thus, the worst possible outcome in the first case would be much better than the worst possible outcome in the second case. Consequently, if you want to follow the maximin principle then you must choose the New York job. Indeed, you must not choose the Chicago job *under any condition*—however unlikely you might think a plane accident would be, and however strong your preference might be for the excellent Chicago job.

Clearly, this is a highly irrational conclusion. Surely, if you assign a low enough probability to a plane accident, and if you have a strong enough preference for the Chicago job, then by all means you should take your chances and choose the Chicago job. This is exactly what Bayesian theory would suggest you should do.

If you took the maximin principle seriously then you could not ever cross a street (after all, you might be hit by a car); you could never drive over a bridge (after all, it might collapse); you could never get married (after all, it might end in a disaster), etc. If anybody really acted this way he would soon end up in a mental institution.

Conceptually, the basic trouble with the maximin principle is that it violates an important continuity requirement: It is extremely irrational to make your behavior wholly dependent on some highly unlikely unfavorable contingencies *regardless of how little probability you are willing to assign to them.*

Of course, Rawls is right when he argues that in *some* situations the maximin principle will lead to reasonable decisions (pp. 154–156). But closer inspection will show that this will happen only in those situations where the maximin principle is essentially *equivalent* to the expected-utility maximization principle (in the sense that the policies suggested by the former will yield expected-utility levels as high, or almost as high, as the policies suggested by the latter would yield). Yet, the point is that in cases where the two principles suggest policies very dissimilar in their consequences so that they are far from being equivalent, it is always the expected-utility maximization principle that is found on closer inspection to suggest reasonable policies, and it as always the maximin principle that is found to suggest unreasonable ones.

## The Maximin Principle in the Original Position

In the last section I have argued that the maximin principle would often lead to highly irrational decisions in everyday life. This is already a sufficient reason for rejecting it as a decision rule appropriate for the original position. This is so because the whole point about the concept of the original position is to imagine a number of individuals ignorant of their personal circumstances and then to assume that under these conditions of ignorance they would act in a *rational manner*, i.e., in accordance with some decision rule which consistently leads to reasonable decisions under ignorance and uncertainty. But, as we have seen, the maximin principle is most definitely *not* a decision rule of this kind.

Yet, after considering the performance of the maximin principle in everyday life, I now propose to consider explicitly the more specific question of how well this principle would perform in the original position itself. In particular, do we obtain a satisfactory concept of justice if we imagine that the criteria of justice are chosen by people in the original position in accordance with the maximin principle?

As Rawls points out, use of the maximin principle in the original position would lead to a concept of justice based on what he calls the *difference principle*, which evaluates every possible institutional arrangement in terms of the interests of the *least advantaged* (i.e., the poorest, or otherwise worst-off) individual (pp. 75–78). This is so because in the original position nobody is assumed to know what his own personal situation would be under any specific institutional arrangement. Therefore, he must consider the possibility that he might end up as the worst-off individual in the society. Indeed, according to the maximin principle, he has to evaluate any particular institutional framework *as if* he were *sure* that this was exactly what would happen to him. Thus, he must evaluate any possible institutional framework by identifying with the interests of the worst-off individual in the society.[7]

Now, I propose to show that the difference principle often has wholly unacceptable moral implications. As a first example, consider a society consisting of one doctor and two patients, both of them critically ill with pneumonia. Their only chance to recover is to be treated by an antibiotic, but the amount available suffices only to treat one of the two patients. Of these two patients, individual A is a basically healthy person, apart from his present attack of pneumonia. On the other hand, individual B is a terminal cancer victim but, even so, the antibiotic could prolong his life by several months. Which patient should be given the antibiotic? According to the difference principle, it should be given to the cancer victim, who is obviously the less fortunate of the two patients.

In contrast, utilitarian ethics—as well as ordinary common sense—would make the opposite suggestion. The antibiotic should be given to A because it would do "much more good" by bringing him back to normal health than it would do by slightly prolonging the life of a hopelessly sick individual.

As a second example, consider a society consisting of two individuals. Both of them have their material needs properly taken care of, but society still has a surplus of resources left over. This surplus can be used either to provide education in higher mathematics for individual A, who has a truly exceptional mathematical ability, and has an all-consuming interest in receiving instruction in higher mathematics. *Or*, it could be used to provide remedial training for individual B, who is a severely retarded person. Such training could achieve only trivial improvements in B's condition (e.g., he could perhaps learn how to tie his shoelaces); but presumably it would give him some minor satisfaction. Finally, suppose it is not possible to divide up the surplus resources between the two individuals.

Again, the difference principle would require that these resources should be spent on B's remedial training, since he is the less fortunate of the two individuals. In contrast, both utilitarian theory and common sense would suggest that they should be spent on A's education, where they would accomplish "much more good," and would create a much deeper and much more intensive human satisfaction.[8]

Even more disturbing is the fact that the difference principle would require us to give *absolute* priority to the interests of the worst-off individual, *no matter what*, even under the most extreme conditions. Even if his interest were affected only in a very minor way, and all other individuals in society had opposite interests of the greatest importance, his interests would always override anybody else's. For example, let us assume that society would consist of a large number of individuals, of whom one would be seriously retarded. Suppose that some extremely expensive treatment were to become available, which could very slightly improve the retarded individual's condition, but at such high costs that this treatment could be financed only if some of the most brilliant individuals were deprived of all higher education. The difference principle would require that the retarded individual should all the same receive this very expensive treatment at any event—*no matter how many* people would have to be denied a higher education, and *no matter how strongly* they would desire to obtain one (and no matter how great the satisfaction they would derive from it).

Rawls is fully aware that the difference principle has implications of this type. But he feels these are morally desirable implications because in his view they follow from Kant's principle that people should "treat one another not as means only but as ends in themselves" (p. 179). If society were to give priority to A's interests over B's on the utilitarian grounds that by satisfying A's interests "more good" or "more utility" or "more human satisfaction" would be produced (e.g., because A could derive a greater benefit from medical treatment, or from education, or from whatever else), this would amount to "treating B as means only, and not as end in himself."

To my own mind, this is a very artificial and very forced interpretation of the Kantian principle under discussion. The natural meaning of the phrase "treating B as a means only, and not as end in himself" is that it refers to using B's *person*, i.e., his mental or physical faculties or his body itself, as *means* in the service of other individuals' interests, without proper concern for B's own interests. One would have to stretch the meaning of this phrase quite a bit even in order to include an unauthorized use of B's material *property* (as distinguished from his person) in the service of other individuals.

This, however, is still not the case we are talking about. We are talking about B's merely being *denied* the use of certain resources over which he has no prior property rights, and this is done on the ground that other individuals have "greater need" for these resources, i.e., can derive greater utility from them (and let us assume, as may very well be the case, that almost all impartial observers would agree that this was so). But there is no question at all of using B's person or property for the benefit of other individuals. Therefore, it is very hard to understand how the situation could be described as "treating B as a means only, and not as end in himself."

In any case, even if we did accept such an unduly broad interpretation of the Kantian principle, the argument would certainly cut both ways—and indeed, it would go much more against the difference principle than in favor of it. For suppose we accept the argument that it would be a violation of the Kantian principle if we gave priority to a very important need of A over a relatively unimportant need of B, because it would amount to treating B as a mere means. Then, surely, the opposite policy of giving absolute priority to B's *unimportant* need will be an even stronger violation of the Kantian principle and will amount *a fortiori* to treating A now as a mere means rather than as an end.

## Do Counterexamples Matter?

Most of my criticism of Rawls's theory up to now has been based on counterexamples. How much weight do arguments based on counterexamples have? Rawls himself seems to have considerable reservations about such arguments. He writes (p. 52): "Objections by way of counterexamples are to be made with care, since these may tell us only what we know already, namely that our theory is wrong somewhere. The important thing is to find out how often and how far it is wrong. All theories are presumably mistaken in places. The real question at any given time is which of the views already proposed is the best approximation overall."

To be sure, counterexamples to some minor details of an ethical theory may not prove very much. They may prove no more than that the theory needs correction in some minor points, and this fact may have no important implications for the basic principles of the theory. But it is a very different matter when the counterexamples are directed precisely against the most fundamental principles of the theory, as are the maximin principle and the difference principle for Rawls's theory. In this case, if the counterexamples are valid, it can only mean that the theory is *fundamentally* wrong.

Admittedly, all my counterexamples refer to rather special situations. It is quite possible that, in *most* everyday situations posing no special problems,

Rawls's theory would yield quite reasonable practical conclusions. Indeed, it is my impression that in most situations the practical implications of Rawls's theory would not be very different from those of utilitarian theories. But of course, if we want to *compare* Rawls's theory with utilitarian theories in order to see which of the two yields more reasonable practical conclusions, we have to concentrate on those cases where they yield significantly different conclusions.

Clearly, as far as Rawls's theory often has implications similar to those of utilitarian theories, I must agree with his point that counterexamples do not prove that his theory does not have at least *approximate* validity in most cases. But my understanding is that Rawls claims more than approximate validity *in this sense* for his theory. Though he does not claim that his theory is absolutely correct in every detail, he does explicitly claim that at the very least the basic principles of his theory yield more satisfactory results than the basic principles of utilitarian theories do. Yet, in my opinion, my counterexamples rather conclusively show that the very opposite is the case.

## An Alternative Model of Moral Value Judgments

All difficulties outlined in Section 3 [p. 25] can be avoided if we assume that the decision rule used in the original position would not be the maximin principle but would rather be the expected-utility maximization principle of Bayesian theory.

In the two papers already quoted,[9] I have proposed the following model. If an individual expresses his preference between two alternative institutional arrangements, he will often base his preference largely or wholly on his personal interests (and perhaps on the interests of his family, his friends, his occupational group, his social class, etc.). For instance, he may say: "I know that under capitalism I am a wealthy capitalist, whereas under socialism I would be at best a minor government official. Therefore, I prefer capitalism." This no doubt would be a very natural judgment of personal preference from his own point of view. But it certainly would not be what we would call a *moral* value judgment by him about the relative merits of capitalism and socialism.

In contrast, most of us will admit that he would be making a moral value judgment if he chose between the two social systems *without knowing* what his personal position would be under either system. More specifically, let us assume that society consists of $n$ individuals, and that the individual under consideration would choose between the two alternative social systems on the assumption that under either system he would have the same probability, $1/n$, of taking the place of the best-off individual, or the second-best-off individual, or the third-best-off individual, etc., up to the worst-off individual. This I shall call the *equi-probability assumption*. Moreover, let us assume that in choosing between the two social systems he would use the principle of expected-utility maximization as his decision rule. (This is my own version of the concept of the "original position.")

It is easy to verify that under these assumptions our individual would always choose that social system which, in his opinion, would yield the higher *average utility level* to the individual members of the society. More generally, he would evaluate every possible social arrangement (every possible social system, institutional framework, social practice, etc.) in terms of the average utility level likely to result from it. This criterion of evaluation will be called the *principle of average utility*.

Of course, in real life, when people express a preference for one social arrangement over another, they will often have a fairly clear idea of what their own personal position would be under both. Nevertheless, we can say that they are expressing a *moral value judgment*, or that they are expressing a *moral preference* for one of these social arrangements, if they make a serious effort to *disregard* this piece of information, and make their choice *as if* they thought they would have the same probability of taking the place of any particular individual in the society.

Thus, under this model, each individual will have two different sets of preferences: he will have a set of *personal preferences*, which may give a particularly high weight to his personal interests (and to those of his close associates); and he will have a set of *moral preferences*, based on a serious attempt to give the same weight to the interests of every member of the society, in accordance with the principle of average utility.

While Rawls's approach yields a moral theory in the contractarian tradition, my own model yields a moral theory based on the principle of average utility and, therefore, clearly belonging to the utilitarian tradition.

## Notes

1 Cambridge, Mass.: Harvard University Press, 1971.
2 See Abraham Wald, *Statistical Decision Functions* (New York: John Wiley & Sons, 1950); Leonid Hurwicz, "Optimality Criteria for Decision Making Under Ignorance," *Cowles Commission Discussion Paper*, Statistics #370 (1951, mimeographed); and Leonard J. Savage, "The Theory of Statistical Decision." *Journal of the American Statistical Association*, 46 (March, 1951), 55–67.
3 See Roy Radner and Jacob Marschak, "Note on Some Proposed Decision Criteria," in R. M. Thrall, C. H. Coombs, and R. L. Davis, eds., *Decision Processes* (New York: John Wiley & Sons, 1954), pp. 61–68.
4 See, e.g., Leonard J. Savage, *The Foundations of Statistics* (New York: John Wiley & Sons, 1954).
5 See John C. Harsanyi, "Cardinal Utility in Welfare Economics and in the Theory of Risk-Taking," *Journal of Political Economy*, 61 (October, 1953), 434–435; and "Cardinal Welfare, Individualistic Ethics, and Interpersonal Comparisons of Utility," *Journal of Political Economy*, 63 (August, 1955), 309–321.
6 John Rawls, "Justice as Fairness," *Journal of Philosophy*, 54 (October, 1957), 653–662; and "Justice as Fairness," *Philosophical Review*, 67 (April, 1958), 164–194. The 1957 paper is a shorter version of the 1958 paper with the same title.
7 In cases where a more specific principle is necessary, Rawls favors the *lexicographical* difference principle: In comparing two possible societies, first compare

them from the point of view of the *worst-off* individual. If they turn out to be equally good from his point of view, then compare them from the point of view of the *second-worst-off* individual. If this still does not break the tie, then compare them from the point of view of the *third-worst-off* individual, etc.
8   This argument of course presupposes the possibility of interpersonal utility comparisons, at least in a rough and ready sense.
9   Harsanyi, "Cardinal Utility ...," and Harsanyi, "Cardinal Welfare...."

# 3  Primary Goods Reconsidered

## Richard J. Arneson

Among the more noteworthy initial lines of criticism provoked by John Rawls's theory of justice is a challenge to his claim that the advantages and disadvantages of social cooperation should be reckoned in terms of shares of primary goods. The challengers assert that using primary goods shares to compare individual situations is unfair to those individuals for whom primary goods will not be particularly useful for the successful pursuit of their life plans. In *A Theory of Justice* Rawls stipulates that primary goods are those that any rational person prefers more rather than less of, whatever her final aims. Rawls's challengers assert that it is nonetheless the case that primary goods can be expected to be differentially useful to people depending on their final aims, and in particular that a primary goods standard of distributive justice will be biassed in favor of people with individualistic goals and against those whose fundamental goals are communal in nature.

I call this line of criticism the Nagel-Schwartz objection, after Thomas Nagel and Adina Schwartz, who in separate articles first vigorously stated it (Nagel, p. 228; Schwartz, pp. 298-304). The present article reconsiders the objection, examines to what extent Rawls's more recent writings successfully respond to it, and concludes that a principle of distributive justice in a liberal theory ought to use individual opportunities for preference satisfaction rather than primary goods as the basis of interpersonal comparisons. The root issue at stake here is in what sense, if any, a theory of distributive justice could be and ought to be neutral with respect to the conceptions of the good upheld and pursued by its citizens.

## Voluntary Avoidability Versus the Difference Principle

An important Rawlsian counter-reply to the Nagel-Schwartz objection has so far not been mentioned. To repeat, the objection is that primary goods will be differentially useful to individuals, depending on their fundamental values. Primary goods, even though necessary to any rational life plan, may nonetheless not enable individuals with idiosyncratic as opposed to widely shared, expensive rather than cheap, or communal rather than individualistic personal values to have a reasonably good expectation of fulfilling them. Rawls stoutly denies that this claim, the truth of which he does not contest, gives rise to any valid objection against the idea of using primary goods to measure distributive shares. Rawls asserts that the life goals or basic preferences of individuals are not afflictions, but lie within their voluntary control (FG, p. 553; KC, p. 544; SU, p. 169). Given a fair allotment of primary goods, individuals must take responsibility for their own final aims and for the quality of their lives as structured by these final aims.

As just stated, this reply is vulnerable to the objection that the voluntary choice of preferences is a much less significant phenomenon than Rawls supposes (cf. Scanlon, pp. 192-201). Genetic predisposition and early social conditioning interact to instill in citizens preferences that they could alter or expunge only at considerable cost or by dint of hard effort (if they are lucky enough to have inherited the motivation to put forth such effort). Rawls gives us no reason to think that distributing social benefits according to his principles of justice would render it any easier to rid oneself of preferences by voluntary choice, so he has no reason to deny that compensating individuals for nonvoluntary expensive or burdensome preferences may be fair policy.

This objection perhaps reduces the scope of Rawls's reply but not its argumentative force, in my judgment. Rawls's point could be restated so: To whatever extent it is reasonable to hold individuals personally responsible for their preferences, to that extent adjusting individuals' distributive shares according to how expensive their preferences are to satisfy is unfair. I accept this formulation of Rawls's point. In this essay I shall attempt no further exploration of the issue of what determines a reasonable attribution of individual responsibility.

What calls for attention is rather that the background moral requirement to which Rawls seems committed by this reply is clearly violated by his own favored difference principle regulating justified inequalities in social and economic benefits (i.e. in primary goods other than basic liberties) (TJ, p. 302). This background requirement, to which Rawls's reply appeals, holds that a just society should not assume responsibility for correcting any distributive outcome that could have been avoided by reasonable voluntary choice on the part of the individual who is disadvantaged by that outcome, so long as the individual was capable of making such a voluntary choice and standing fast by it. Call this the "voluntary avoidability" restriction on principles of distributive justice.

Rawls's own difference principle straightforwardly violates this restriction. This much-discussed principle holds that inequalities in social and economic benefits among citizens should be instituted just to the point at which they are to the greatest advantage of the worst off class. According to Rawls, the worst off class in society comprises those individuals who both (1) are born into that class whose members have the smallest share of primary goods and (2) remain in that class throughout their lives. The trouble is that membership in the worst off class according to Rawls's definition of it is partly fixed by individual voluntary choices. For this reason, to run a political economy according to the difference principle is to commit the state to continuing redistribution of resources of a sort that violates the "voluntary avoidability" restriction.

Interestingly, Rawls occasionally suggests that the theory of justice should be conceived to have as its subject matter inequalities in the initial range of opportunities open to citizens. According to Rawls, a theory of justice issues in principles concerned to regulate "the basic structure of society, or more exactly, the way in which major social institutions distribute fundamental rights and duties and determine the division of advantages from social cooperation." Rawls continues:

> The basic structure is the primary subject of justice because its effects are so profound and present from the start. The intuitive notion here is that this structure contains various social positions and that men born into different social positions have different expectations of life determined, in part, by the social system as well as by economic and social circumstances. In this way the institutions of society favor certain starting places over others. These are especially deep inequalities. Not only are they pervasive, but they affect men's initial choices in life; yet they cannot possibly be justified by an appeal to the notions of merit or desert. It is these inequalities ... to which the principles of justice in the first instance apply (TJ, p. 7).

Consider in the light of these comments the life choices of Smith, Black, Jones, and Johnson. Having graduated from an elite law school with high grades, Smith and Black each can choose among several career options: Wall Street lawyer (large income, stressful work), small-town lawyer (small income, relaxed work), unskilled laborer (smaller income, hard work), bohemian artist (hand-to-mouth subsistence, work as play), and unemployment (the dole, no work). Black chooses to be a Wall Street lawyer and Smith opts for the life of a bohemian artist. Lacking the option of college and having graduated from formal schooling with very little by way of marketable skills, Jones and Johnson must choose among bohemian life, unskilled labor, and unemployment. Jones chooses to be a bohemian artist, Johnson an unskilled laborer. If inequalities that are not voluntarily chosen are the primary subject of justice, than principles of justice scanning society for inequalities ought to register as problematic the inequalities in the opportunity sets faced by Black and Smith on the one hand and by Johnson and Jones on the other. If there emerges an inequality in the lifetime primary goods share enjoyed by Smith as compared to what Black gets, or by Jones as compared to Johnson, these are not the sorts of inequalities with which the theory of justice is primarily concerned. Nor should the redistributive institutions of a just society treat the two bohemian artists, Smith and Jones, on a par—for example, with respect to income tax policy. Redistributive policies, insofar as they aim to promote equality, should strive for equality in the initial opportunity sets that persons enjoy.

According to Rawls's general conception of justice, there is a presumption in favor of equality in people's shares of primary social goods. (The presumption gives way when inequalities work to maximize the share of the least advantaged, according to the difference principle.) Rawls does not fully acknowledge the implications for his favored interpretation of distributive equality of his notion of the basic structure as the subject of justice. In saying that principles of justice apply in the first instance to the basic structure of society, he means that they are not meant to regulate individual transactions but rather the long-term prospects, as measured by shares of primary goods, of the least advantaged class in society. But membership in the least advantaged class appears to be settled purely in terms of the amounts of primary goods that individuals enjoy over the course of their lives, rather than the amounts they have the opportunity to enjoy. This would appear to identify Smith in the example above as a member of the least advantaged class—implausibly, in my view. Referring to the view that ideally people should be compensated for their expensive preferences, Rawls observes that insofar as people's unfortunate plight is due to their voluntary choice of preferences, society does not owe them compensation for their predicament (FG, p. 553; SU, p. 169). But by parity of reasoning, insofar as people's subpar holdings of primary goods are due to their voluntary choices, society does not owe them compensation to increase those holdings (see Cohen, pp. 915-916). To the extent that we agree that from the standpoint of distributive justice it is best to measure people's resource holdings by a primary goods standard, our distributive principles should be sensitive to people's opportunities for primary goods, not their actual lifelong primary goods shares, despite Rawls's commitment to the latter.

In recent writings Rawls occasionally touches on the problem I am discussing. Rawls seems to think the problem concerns the proper specification of the primary goods. He observes, for example, that if need be a Rawlsian society could count leisure among the primary goods, in order to avoid the embarrassment of being required by one's principles to count the permanently and willfully unemployed among the worst off class (PR, p. 257, fn. 7). But the problem goes deeper. Notice that the Smith-Jones-Johnson-Black case developed above still stands as a counter-example even if leisure is added to the list of primary goods. The force of the counter-example is to insist that distributive justice should be concerned with the inequalities in the opportunity sets that individuals face, rather than what use presumably rational individuals make of their opportunities.

The upshot of this discussion is as follows. Against the objection that a primary goods standard is unfair to those with expensive, hard-to-satisfy preferences, Rawls urges that our preferences are at least to some extent the result of our voluntary choices, so the expected frustration of our preferences is not a basis for government redistributive intervention in a liberal society. But this objection can be turned successfully against the difference principle. An individual's lifelong share of primary goods is not to be considered manna from heaven. The size of any individual's expected share is to some large extent determined by the voluntary choices made by the individual. So the objection that rules out equal proportionate satisfaction of preferences as a principle of distributive justice also rules out the difference principle. What this shows is that Rawls's expressed concern for voluntariness does not in fact bear on the choice between a primary goods standard and a preference satisfaction standard. Rawls's voluntary avoidability restriction on principles of distributive justice is met by any principle that rates individuals' situations for purposes of distributive justice in terms of the opportunities they enjoy, not the actual outcomes they reach.

## References

Cohen, G. A. 1989 "On the Currency of Egalitarian Justice," *Ethics* 99, 906-944.
Nagel, Thomas 1973 "Rawls on Justice," *The Philosophical Review* 82, 220-234.
Rawls, John 1971 *A Theory of Justice* (Cambridge, MA: Harvard University Press) (cited as TJ).
Rawls, John 1975 "Fairness to Goodness," *The Philosophical Review* 84, 536-554 (cited as FG).
Rawls, John 1980 "Kantian Constructivism in Moral Theory: The Dewey Lectures 1980," *The Journal of Philosophy* 77, 515-572 (cited as KC).
Rawls, John 1982 "Social Unity and Primary Goods," in Amartya Sen and Bernard Williams, eds., *Utilitarianism and Beyond* (Cambridge: Cambridge University Press), pp. 159-185 (cited as SU).
Rawls, John 1988 "The Priority of Right and Ideas of the Good," *Philosophy and Public Affairs* 17, 251-276 (cited as PR).
Scanlon, T. M. 1988 "The Significance of Choice," in Sterling M. McMurrin, ed., *The Tanner Lectures on Human Values*, vol. 8 (Salt Lake City: University of Utah Press), pp. 149-216.
Schwartz, Adina 1973 "Moral Neutrality and Primary Goods," *Ethics* 83, 294-307.

# 4 Equality of What?

## Alex Callinicos

Debates about equality, Amartya Sen has suggested, raise two central questions: '(1) Why equality? (2) Equality of what?' He argues that it is the second question that is mainly at issue in contemporary controversy over equality. There are various respects in which people may be treated equally or unequally: 'Equality is judged by comparing some particular aspect of a person (such as income, or wealth, or happiness, or opportunities, or rights, or need-fulfilments) with the same aspect of another person.' The inherent diversity of human beings means that treating them equally with respect to one such 'focal variable' may lead to considerable inequalities in other dimensions. It is a rare theorist who does not favour equalizing some variable: 'Ethical plausibility is hard to achieve unless everyone is given equal consideration in *some* space that is important to the particular theory.' Nozick, for example, defends equalizing individual freedom (in effect equated with self-ownership) at the price of deep inequalities of wealth and income. Thus: 'The engaging question turns out to be "equality of what?"'[1]

It is certainly true that human diversity is sometimes bewilderingly reflected in the different focal variables that various egalitarian liberals have argued should be used in the inter-personal comparisons on which redistribution should be based. Apart from Rawls's primary social goods, the main candidates for equalization are welfare, resources, access to advantage (or opportunity for welfare) and capabilities. Considering these in turn may help to clarify not simply the nature of the redistributions proposed, but also the deep ethical reasons for seeking to achieve equality in the first place.[2]

To take *equality of welfare* first, one might consider this a modified version of utilitarianism. Both are instances of welfarism, as Sen puts it, 'the view that the goodness of a state of affairs is to be judged entirely by the goodness of the utilities in that state'.[3] Once again utility or welfare is understood here as either pleasurable mental states or the satisfaction of a person's preferences. Two objections to equality of welfare are what Cohen calls 'the *offensive tastes* and *expensive tastes* criticisms'.[4]

The first is stated by Rawls: for welfarism, 'if men take a certain pleasure in discriminating against one another, in subjecting others to a lesser liberty as a means of enhancing their self-respect, then the satisfaction of these desires must be weighed in our deliberations according to their intensity, or whatever, along with other desires'.[5] There is something profoundly wrong with a conception of justice that treats my preference for torturing you as, in principle, equally worthy of satisfaction as a homeless person's preference for shelter.

Not only do all preferences seem not to be of equal value, but satisfying some may cost more than satisfying others. Such is the nub of the second criticism, put most systematically by Dworkin: 'Equality of welfare seems to recommend that those with champagne tastes, who need more income simply to achieve the same level of welfare as those with less expensive tastes, should have more income on that account.' In particular, what of those who deliberately cultivate expensive tastes? If it seems unreasonable to regard satisfying their desires as just as urgent as satisfying those of people who have remained content with more modest tastes, then we need to select a different focal variable to equalize.[6]

Once we start to consider the process through which individuals' preferences are formed, a third objection to equality of welfare emerges – to my mind the most important one. Preferences often adapt to circumstances. As Sen puts it, '[a] thoroughly deprived person, leading a very reduced life, might not appear too badly off in terms of the mental metric of desire and its fulfilment, if the hardship is accepted with non-grumbling resignation.'[7] This is the problem of sour grapes, or (to put it in more highfalutin terms) of adaptive preferences: one gives up wanting what one believes one cannot get. It may be particularly dangerous in situations of acute inequality and poverty to go by the preferences of the worst off, since they may have given up hope of any improvement in their condition.[8]

In place of equality of welfare, Dworkin proposes *equality of resources*. He imagines an auction in which all material productive resources are sold to individuals each with an equal amount of money with which to bid. Sub-auctions allow them also to insure themselves against being handicapped or lacking various skills. Underlying this proposal is a particular view of the rationale for equality. On this view, as Cohen puts it, 'a large part of the fundamental egalitarian aim is to extinguish the influence of brute luck on distribution'.[9] Dworkin distinguishes between two kinds of luck – 'option luck', 'which is a matter of how deliberate and calculated gambles turn out', and 'brute luck', which is 'a matter of how risks fall out that are not in that sense deliberate gambles'.[10] A victim of brute luck cannot be held responsible for the resulting disadvantage. Being born poor is one relevant example of brute luck. One of Rawls's most important contributions to egalitarian thought has been to argue that the distributions of natural talents among individuals represents, in effect, another case of brute luck, from which those advantaged are only entitled to benefit if allowing them to do so will improve the condition of the worst off.

Dworkin argues that the case for equality of resources 'produces a certain view of the distinction between a person and his circumstances, and assigns his tastes and ambitions to his person, and his physical and mental powers to his circumstances'.[11] A person can thus be held responsible for her tastes and ambitions, but not for her physical and mental powers. The latter are, like the socio-economic position into which she is born, matters of brute luck. An initial equal distribution of resources would, when undergirded by a hypothetical insurance market to compensate for inequalities in natural assets, place individuals in the same circumstances. Their responses to these circumstances would differ according to their tastes and ambitions, producing unequal outcomes. A driven and abstemious individual will end up with more resources than someone more laid-back who has expensive tastes. But *this* inequality will be a consequence of individual choices rather than the brute luck of being born with more wealth or talent than others.

Cohen comments: 'Dworkin has, in effect, performed for egalitarianism the considerable service of incorporating within it the most powerful idea in the arsenal of the anti-egalitarian right: the idea of choice and responsibility.'[12] But the relationship between choice, preferences and circumstances is complex. There is, in the first place, the problem we have already encountered of adaptive preferences. Dworkin contends that individuals are responsible for their preferences as long as they identify with them. However, John Roemer objects that it is wrong to hold people 'accountable for their choices, even if they follow from preferences which were in part or entirely formed under influences beyond their control ... Preferences are often adjusted to what the person falsely deems to be necessity, and society does her no favour by accepting the consequences that follow from exercising them.'[13]

Secondly, individuals may, for reasons outside their control, benefit differently form the same share of resources. Sen imagines two people, A and B: 'person A as a cripple gets half the utility that the pleasure-wizard B does from a given level of income'. Neither Rawls's difference principle nor Dworkin's equality of resources takes this 'utility disadvantage', for which it would be absurd to hold A responsible, into account. Such cases illustrate the general fact that 'the conversion of goods to capabilities varies substantially from person to person and the equality of the former may still be far from the equality of the latter'.[14] These considerations also count against equality of income, advocated, for example, by Shaw, who wrote: 'The really effective incentive to work is our needs, which are equal.'[15] The case of A and B shows that our needs are *not* equal: to give A the same income as B would be to treat her unfairly.

This second objection led Cohen to propose, in answer to Sen's question, *equality of access to advantage*, where 'advantage' refers to 'a heterogeneous collection of desirable states of the person reducible neither to his resources bundle nor to his welfare level'.[16] He offers the following rationale for this proposal:

> For Dworkin it is not choice but preference which excuses what would otherwise be an unjustly unequal distribution. He proposes compensation for power deficiencies, but not for expensive tastes, whereas I believe that we should compensate for disadvantage beyond a person's control, as such, and that we should not, accordingly, draw a line between unfortunate

resource endowment and unfortunate utility functions. A person with *wantonly* expensive tastes has no claim on us, but neither does a person whose powers are feeble because he has recklessly failed to develop them. There is no moral difference, from an egalitarian point of view, between a person who irresponsibly acquires (or blamelessly chooses to develop) an expensive taste and a person who irresponsibly loses (or blamelessly chooses to consume) a valuable resource. The right cut is between responsibility and bad luck, not between preferences and resources.[17]

Cohen's approach dovetails with various attempts to develop the idea of 'deep' equality of opportunity. For Roemer, for example, this idea means that 'society should do what it can to "level the playing field" among individuals who compete for positions, or, more generally, that it level the playing field among individuals during their periods of formation, so that all those with relevant potential will eventually be admissible to pools of candidates competing for positions'. The 'mounds and troughs in the playing field' correspond to 'the differential circumstances for which they [i.e. individuals] should not be held accountable and which affect their ability to achieve or have access to the kind of advantage that is being sought'.[18]

Sen, however, offers a different solution to the inadequacies of welfare and resources as focal variables: *equality of capabilities*. This idea depends on distinguishing between achievement, the means of achievement, and freedom to achieve. Welfarism concentrates on achievement – the actual satisfactions that individuals derive from various states of affairs. This is an inadequate measure of equality for the reasons we have seen above. Both Rawls's primary goods and Dworkin's resources represent a shift towards the *means* of achievement. This is a step in the right direction, but it does not go far enough. The diversity of human beings means that, as we have already seen, someone who is mentally or physically disabled or prone to some serious illness, for example, will not extract the same benefit from a given bundle of resources as someone who does not suffer from these disadvantages. The extent of their freedom to achieve, as well as their actual achievements, will therefore differ. Thus: 'Primary goods suffers from a fetishist handicap' in that it 'is concerned with good things rather than with what these good things *do* to human beings'.[19]

To remedy these defects, Sen proposes that we think of a person's well-being as depending on the quality of 'a set of interrelated "functionings", consisting of beings and doings'. These 'can vary from such elementary things as being adequately nourished, being in good health, avoiding escapable morbidity and premature mortality, etc., to more complex achievements such as being happy, having self-respect, taking part in the life of the community, and so on'. The *'capability* to function … represents the various combinations of functionings (beings and doings) that the person can achieve'. It thus reflects 'the person's freedom to lead one type of life rather than another'. It is equality in these capabilities that Sen proposes that we should seek to achieve: 'individual claims are not to be assessed in terms of the resources or primary goods the persons respectively hold, but by the freedoms they actually enjoy to choose the lives they have reason to value'.[20]

Most unusually for a normative political theory, Sen's capability approach has had a considerable impact on more empirical social-science literature: it has, for example, helped to inspire the efforts of the United Nations Development Programme to construct various indicators that measure development in Third World countries better than the crude indices offered by national-income statistics such as growth in gross national product.[21] From a philosophical point of view, it has the considerable interest that it seeks to relate freedom and equality. Equality of capabilities is concerned with individuals' freedom to achieve the functionings they value. 'This freedom, reflecting a person's opportunities of well-being, must be valued at least for *instrumental* reasons, e.g. in judging how good a "deal" a person has in the society. But, in addition, freedom may be seen as intrinsically important for a good social structure.' If choosing is seen as a constituent part of the good life, then 'at least some types of capabilities contribute *directly* to well-being, making one's life richer with the opportunity of reflective choice'.[22]

Sen's attempt to relate liberty and equality is important for at least two reasons. First, as we have seen, neo-liberals such as Nozick attack egalitarianism on the grounds that its achievement would drastically reduce individual freedom. But Sen argues that counterposing liberty and equality in this way 'reflects a "category mistake". They are not alternatives. Liberty is among the possible *fields of application* of equality, and equality is among the possible *patterns* of distribution of liberty.'[23] Secondly, the capability approach offers a positive rationale for equality. Rawls, Dworkin and Cohen offer effectively a negative reason for seeking to achieve equality in the preferred dimension: people should not suffer the consequences of disadvantages for which they are not responsible, whether these disadvantages derive from the distribution of productive resources or the incidence of natural talents. But one might also value equality for the more positive reason that, by equalizing individuals' freedom to achieve well-being, it contributes towards what Tawney called 'the growth towards perfection of individual human beings'.[24]

Tawney here offers a very clear statement of the ethical doctrine that Rawls calls 'perfectionism', which understands the good as the achievement of personal well-being. Rawls argues that this doctrine cannot be part of a theory of justice: the parties to the original position do not know their conception of the good, reflecting the fact that in liberal societies conceptions of the good are inherently diverse.[25] Sen approaches this subject with caution. He gives the capability approach a genealogy that includes both Aristotle, who offered a theory of the good conceived as an objectively knowable condition of well-being (*eudaimonia*), and Marx, who tacitly relied on such a theory when he argued that individuals fulfil themselves through free activity. But Sen also rejects Martha Nussbaum's proposal that he extend his own theory by 'introducing an objective normative account of human functioning', maintaining that 'quite different specific theories of value may be consistent with the capability approach'.[26]

One advantage of developing the capability approach in the direction suggested by Nussbaum is that it would offer a way of integrating two of the core values common to both traditional socialism and the Third Way, namely autonomy and equality. One might, for example, understand equality as equal access to well-being, and well-being itself as critically involving (though not reducible to) individuals' ability successfully to pursue goals that they have chosen for themselves, but which are conceived as having value independently of being chosen and pursued.[27] At the very least, Sen suggests that we should value equality not so much as a passive condition, but rather as enabling us actively to engage with the world, and through doing so to live the kind of life we desire.

It is, however, this very running together of equality and autonomy that gives Cohen pause. Sen is right, he argues, to reject the welfarist idea that 'the whole relevant effect on a person of his bundle of primary goods is on, or in virtue of, his mental reactions to what they can do for him'. Sen has identified what Cohen calls 'midfare', 'the non-utility effect of goods', which consists of 'states of the person produced by goods, states in virtue of which utility levels take the values they do'. But midfare cannot be reduced to the capabilities with which goods endow individuals, or the exercise of these capabilities, since 'goods cause further desirable states directly, without any exercise of capability on the part of their beneficiary'.[28]

It is not clear how damaging this criticism is. Sen understands functionings to embrace both 'beings' and 'doings': that is, states as well as activities. Cohen proposes equalizing access to advantage, which, he acknowledges, 'is, like Sen's "functioning" …, a heterogeneous collection of desirable state'[29] Sen himself notes that 'if advantage is seen specifically in terms of well-being (ignoring the agency aspect), then Cohen's "equality of access to advantage" would be very like equality of well-being freedom'.[30] The difference between the two perspectives seems to lie less in what they seek to equalize than in their underlying rationales for equality: Cohen's concern is to eliminate the consequences of brute luck, while Sen is drawn towards a perfectionist theory, where equalizing capabilities enables people to realize themselves. Either equality implies a very considerable redistribution of wealth and income. For the purposes of my argument in the following chapter, I shall treat them as equivalent.

Writing from a position very similar to Cohen's, Richard Arneson criticizes Sen for failing to come up with an index that would allow us to rank individual capabilities. In the absence of such an index, it is very hard, given the diversity of human beings that Sen himself stresses, to compare and therefore to seek to equalize the capabilities of different persons. Arneson effectively confronts Sen with a dilemma. We can take individual preferences into account, in which case we are back to welfarism. But any objective ranking of functionings and capabilities independent of preferences presupposes 'the adequacy of an as yet unspecified perfectionist doctrine the like of which has certainly not yet been defended and is in my opinion indefensible'.[31]

Arneson's own preferred egalitarian currency, equality of opportunity for welfare, also goes beyond individuals' actual preferences. He argues that we should take 'hypothetical preferences' as 'the measure of an individual's welfare'. These are the preferences 'I would have if I were to engage in thoroughgoing deliberation about my preferences with full pertinent information, in a calm mood, while thinking clearly and making no reasonable errors'. Idealizing preferences in this way is essential if Arneson's position is not to collapse into straight equality of welfare, with all the difficulties that this involves. But, he concedes, the effect is to require 'a normative account of preference formation that is not preference-based. A perfectionist component may thus be needed in a broadly welfarist egalitarianism.'[32] Arneson is thus caught in the same dilemma between welfarism and perfectionism with which he confronts Sen.

The difficulty that faces Arneson's critique of Sen is significant for two reasons. First, it supports Roemer's conclusion: 'Some objective measure of a person's condition should, it seems, surely count in the measure of advantage salient for distributive justice, for a subjective measure does not appear to permit a solution to the tamed housewife problem' – that is, to the adaptation of preferences to confined circumstances.[33] Despite Rawls's strenuous resistance to perfectionism, the theory of egalitarian justice is incomplete without an objective account of human well-being. Secondly, this means that egalitarian liberalism must confront the same kind of objection that is often made to Marx's critique of capitalism, namely that it counterposes people's real needs and interests to the actual preferences they have. The latter, according to the Marxist theory of ideology, tend to reflect the effect of capitalist social relations, which leads to individual desires being distorted or adjusted downwards.[34]

Egalitarian liberals may resist being drawn on to this hotly contested terrain. It is hard to see how they can avoid it, however, for their more radical redistributive proposals are likely to be met by appeals to common sense. Thus the Labour Party's Commission on Social Justice, in its extraordinarily conservative discussion of equality, invokes popular intuitions to dismiss Rawls's opposition to basing justice on the notion of desert. For example: 'Few people believe' that 'no rewards ... are ... a matter of desert'. Or again: 'people ... rightly think that redistribution of income is not an aim in itself'. Insofar as the authors of these assertions are not simply dressing up their own views as what they claim 'people' think, they are making the prevailing beliefs in society the benchmark of social justice. Indeed, they declare that 'it is certain that the British public would not recognize in such a theory [i.e. Rawls's], or in any other theory with such ambitions, all its conflicting ideas and feelings about social justice'.[35]

The question of how to validate any theory of justice is undoubtedly a difficult one, but it is hard to see what the point of political philosophy is if it merely serves up the 'conflicting ideas and feelings' that happen at any given time to predominate on the subject. In particular, making these the benchmark of what we mean by social justice may give theoretical sanction to attitudes that reflect the belief of those who hold them that they cannot hope for anything better. Egalitarian liberalism cannot simply take actual preferences and the beliefs that justify them at face value. Thus, rather surprisingly, it joins hands with Marxist ideology-critique.

## Notes

1. A. Sen, *Inequality Reexamined* (Oxford, 1992), pp. 12, 1, 3, 4. Sen first presented the issue in these terms in a celebrated 1980 lecture, 'Equality of What?', reprinted in id., *Choice, Welfare and Measurement* (Oxford, 1982). As so often, Aristotle made the point first: 'Justice is held by all to be a certain equality ... But equality in what sort of things and inequality in what sort of things – that should not be overlooked': *The Politics* (Chicago, 1985), 3.12, p. 103. I am grateful to Gordon Finlayson for this reference. It is, incidentally, a striking indication of the gap that continues to separate Anglophone from Continental intellectual culture, that Bobbio (and his translator) should apparently believe Sen to be a woman: see *Left and Right* (Cambridge, 1996), p. 112 n. 3.
2. J. Roemer, *Theories of Distributive Justice* (Cambridge, MA, 1996), chs 5–8, offers a lucid introduction to recent debates, albeit one accompanied by much axiomatic economic theorizing. I have also benefited from reading a helpful survey, M. Clayton and A. Williams, 'Egalitarian Justice and Interpersonal Comparison', *Morell Studies in Toleration*, Discussion Paper Series No. 146, University of York, April 1999.
3. Sen, 'Equality of What?', p. 359.
4. G.A. Cohen, 'The Currency of Egalitarian Justice', *Ethics*, 99 (1989), p. 912.
5. Rawls, *Theory*, pp. 30–1.
6. R. Dworkin, 'What is Equality? Part 1: Equality of Welfare', *Philosophy and Public Affairs*, 10 (1981), pp. 228–40 (quotation from p. 228).
7. Sen, *Inequality Reexamined*, p. 55.
8. See J. Elster, *Sour Grapes* (Cambridge, 1983). Roemer is the egalitarian theorist who has had the merit of most strongly stressing this problem, though he tends towards an excessively determinist view of the relationship between circumstances and preferences, arguing that 'every individual in society can be represented as a vector of circumstances': *Theories of Distributive Justice*, p. 242.
9. Cohen, 'Currency of Egalitarian Justice', p. 931.
10. Dworkin, 'Equality of Resources', p. 292.
11. Ibid., p. 302.
12. Cohen, 'Currency of Egalitarian Justice', p. 933.
13. Roemer, '*Equality of Opportunity*, pp. 19, 20. See also *Theories of Distributive Justice*, ch. 7.
14. Sen, 'Equality of What?', pp. 357, 365, 368.
15. G.B. Shaw, *The Intelligent Woman's Guide to Socialism and Capitalism* (London, 1928), p. xiv. In fact, Shaw acknowledges individual differences to the extent of proposing that those doing less attractive work should be compensated with more leisure: ibid., pp. 77–9.
16. G.A. Cohen, 'Equality of What? On Welfare, Goods, and Capabilities', in M. Nussbaum and A. Sen, eds, *The Quality of Life* (Oxford, 1993), p. 28.
17. Id., 'Currency of Egalitarian Justice', p. 922.
18. Roemer, *Equality of Opportunity*, pp. 1, 5.
19. Sen, 'Equality of What?', p. 368. See also, for example, id., *Inequality Reexamined*, pp. 27ff and 73–87.
20. Id., *Inequality Reexamined*, pp. 39–40, 81.

21  See, for example, United Nations Development Programme, *Human Development Report 1999* (New York, 1999), pp. 127–246.
22  Sen, *Inequality Reexamined*, p. 41.
23  Ibid., pp. 22–3.
24  R.H. Tawney, *Equality* (4th edn; London, 1952), p. 84.
25  Rawls, *Theory of Justice*, pp. 325–32.
26  A. Sen, 'Capability and Well-Being', in Sen and Nussbaum, eds, *The Quality of Life*, pp. 47–8. See also M. Nussbaum, 'Non-Relative Virtues: An Aristotelian Approach', in the same volume, and R.W. Miller, 'Marx and Aristotle: A Kind of Consequentialism', in A. Callinicos, ed., *Marxist Theory* (Oxford, 1989).
27  For an account of well-being in these terms, albeit one critical of egalitarianism, see J. Raz, *The Morality of Freedom* (Oxford, 1986).
28  Cohen, 'Equality of What?', p. 18. See also id., 'Amartya Sen's Unequal World', *New Left Review*, 203 (1994).
29  Cohen, 'Equality of What?', p. 28. See also id., 'Currency of Egalitarian Justice', pp. 920-1.
30  Sen, 'Capability and Well-Being', p. 46.
31  R. Arneson, 'Equality and Equal Opportunity for Welfare', *Philosophical Studies*, 56 (1989), pp. 90–2 (quotation from p. 92).
32  Ibid., pp. 82, 83, 93 n. 19. See Roemer, *Theories of Distributive Justice*, p. 268. In a more recent comment on Elizabeth Anderson's attack on 'luck egalitarianism' (see the next section), Arneson goes so far as to make the fundamental yardstick of distributive justice well-being, understood as 'achievement of what is objectively worthwhile or choiceworthy in human life' (p. 2): http://www.brown.edu/Departments/Philosophy/bears/9904arne.html. See also R. Arneson, 'Equality of Opportunity for Welfare Defended and Recanted', *Journal of Political Philosophy*, 7 (1999).
33  Roemer, *Theories of Distributive Justice*, p. 309.
34  For further discussion of these issues, see A. Callinicos, *Making History* (Cambridge, 1987), ch. 3.
35  Commission on Social Justice, *The Justice Gap* (London, 1993), pp. 13, 6. David Miller has recently sought to offer a more careful defence of such a conception of political philosophy, arguing that 'a normative theory of justice ... is to be tested, in part, by its correspondence with our evidence concerning everyday beliefs about justice. Seen in this way, a theory of justice brings out the deep structure of a set of everyday beliefs that, on the surface, are to some degree ambiguous, confused, and contradictory': *Principles of Social Justice* (Cambridge, MA, 1999), p. 51. But, as he himself notes, his approach is vulnerable to the objection that 'to see justice in this way is to abandon its most basic critical function; our theory cannot judge an entire society, *including it beliefs*, to be radically unjust' (p. 279 n. 16). Exactly. In fact the theory of justice Miller outlines in this book goes a long way beyond the commonsense beliefs it supposedly articulates. To that extent, he cannot simply appeal to these beliefs to corroborate his theory. Miller, in other words, is in the same boat as Rawls and other egalitarian liberals whom he criticizes for seeking to revise our intuitions about justice.

# 5 A Question for Egalitarians

## John Kekes

It is a basic egalitarian belief that serious unjustified inequalities are morally objectionable and that the measure of a just society is the extent to which it eliminates or at least reduces them. Inequalities are serious if they affect primary goods, which are goods necessary for living a good life, such as adequate income, health care, education, physical security, housing, and so forth. There are several egalitarian views about what serious inequalities are unjustified, but only one of them will be considered here. According to it, all serious inequalities are unjustified unless they benefit everyone in one's society, especially those who are worst off. The best-known defenders of this view are probably John Rawls and Thomas Nagel. In order to avoid pedantry and verbosity, this view will be referred to simply as "egalitarian," although egalitarianism has other versions as well.

One obvious implication of egalitarianism is that overcoming serious unjustified inequalities requires the redistribution of primary goods, which involves taking them from those who are better off and giving them to those who are worse off. The effect of such redistribution is to make the worst off better off and thus gradually reduce the unjustified inequalities. This is one aim and justification of many policies intimately connected with the welfare state, namely, graduated taxation, affirmative action and equal opportunity programs, the preferential treatment of various minorities and women, and a whole panoply of antipoverty policies inaugurated by the Great Society legislations.

Consider now Table 5.1 which is extracted from table 114 in the *Statistical Abstract of the United States*.[1] The figures there make it obvious that American men born between 1970 and 2010 have an actual or projected life expectancy significantly lower than American women born in the same years. Since the difference in the life expectancy of men and women is between seven and eight years, and since life expectancy ranges from sixty-seven to eighty-one years, it may be said that the life expectancy of American men born in the relevant years is about one-tenth lower than the life expectancy of women born in the same years.

**TABLE 5.1** EXPECTATIONS OF LIFE AT BIRTH, 1970–92, AND PROJECTIONS, 1995–2010

| Year | Men | Women |
|---|---|---|
| 1970 | 67.1 | 74.7 |
| 1975 | 68.8 | 76.6 |
| 1980 | 70.0 | 77.4 |
| 1981 | 70.4 | 77.8 |
| 1982 | 70.8 | 78.1 |
| 1983 | 71.0 | 78.1 |
| 1984 | 71.1 | 78.2 |
| 1985 | 71.1 | 78.2 |
| 1986 | 71.2 | 78.2 |
| 1987 | 71.4 | 78.3 |
| 1988 | 71.4 | 78.3 |
| 1989 | 71.7 | 78.5 |
| 1990 | 71.8 | 78.8 |
| 1991 | 72.0 | 78.9 |
| 1992 | 72.3 | 79.0 |
| Projections: | | |
| 1995 | 72.8 | 79.7 |
| 2000 | 73.2 | 80.2 |
| 2005 | 73.8 | 80.7 |
| 2010 | 74.5 | 81.3 |

There is thus an inequality in respect to the life expectancy of men and women. (The qualification that it holds for Americans born between 1970 and 2010 will from now on be omitted, but it should be understood to hold.) This inequality is serious because life expectancy has at least as strong a claim to being a primary good as any other candidate. Normally, it is better to live longer. Normally, however, men tend to have lives about one-tenth shorter than women. In respect to the primary good of life expectancy, men form a group whose members tend to be worse off than women. Since there are only two groups, men in this respect are not only worse off, but also the worst off.

But is this inequality unjustified? It may be justified, but only if it could be shown that it is in everybody's interest, and especially in the interest of men, who in this case are the worst off. It is obvious, however, that this is not so. In the first place, it is not in the interest of men to live shorter lives. In the second place, it is not in the interest of women either, since the lives of men and women are intertwined in countless relationships, such as love, friendship, parenthood, and so on, and men provide knowledge, skill, and services that women rely on. Women, of course, do the same for men, but that is beside the point in the present context. The shorter life expectancy of men thus constitutes a loss not just for men, but for women as well, to the extent to which women wish for the continuation of these valued relationships and rely on men.

If egalitarians mean it when they say that "the gap between the life prospects of the best-off and the worst-off individuals, in terms of wealth, income, education, access to medical care, employment or leisure-time options, and any other index of well-being one might care to name, is enormous.... Confronting these disparities, the egalitarian holds that it would be a better state of affairs if everyone enjoyed the same level of social and economic benefits";[2] or that "how could it not be an evil that some people's prospects at birth are radically inferior to others?"[3] or that "undeserved inequalities call for redress; and since inequalities of birth and natural endowments are undeserved, these inequalities are to be somehow compensated for.... The idea is to redress the bias of contingencies in the direction of equality,"[4] then they must find the serious and unjustified inequality between the life expectancy of men and women morally objectionable.

If this inequality is morally objectionable, then the question arises as to what ought to be done about it. Egalitarians give a clear answer: "What makes a system egalitarian is the priority it gives to the claims of those ... at the bottom.... Each individual with a more urgent claim has priority ... over each individual with a less urgent claim."[5] Such a priority system follows the "lexical difference principle," which is: "first maximize the welfare of the worst off ... second ... the welfare of the second worst off and so on until the last case."[6] All this is guided by the belief that "those who have been favored by nature ... may gain from their good fortune only in terms that improve the situation of those who have lost out."[7]

These egalitarian policies cannot be applied directly to unequal life expectancy, for life expectancy is not a good, like money, that can be taken from one and given to another. But it is easy to see how the policies could be applied indirectly. Available resources that tend to lengthen life expectancy ought to be redistributed from women to men and "undeserved inequalities ... are to be somehow compensated for."[8] Redistribution and compensation will not eliminate this unjustified inequality, but they will reduce the morally objectionable gap between the well off and the worst off.

What policies would bring about the appropriate redistribution? The most obvious one affects health care. Men ought to have more and better health care than women. How much more and how much better are difficult questions of fine-tuning. The general answer, however, is that redistribution ought to aim to equalize the life expectancy of men and women by making men have longer and women shorter lives. But life expectancy is also affected by stressful, demeaning, soul-destroying, and hazardous jobs. So obviously what ought to be done is to employ fewer men and more women in these undesirable jobs. Another factor affecting life expectancy is leisure. Men therefore ought to have shorter working days and longer vacations than women. This will not lead to diminished productivity if loss in man-hours is counter-balanced by gain in woman-hours.

Yet a further policy follows from the realization that since men have shorter lives than women, they are less likely to benefit after retirement from social security payments and medicare treatments. As things are, in their present inegalitarian state, men and women are required to contribute an equal percentage of their earnings to the social security and medicare funds. This is clearly unjust from the egalitarian point of view: why should men be required to subsidize the health and wealth of women in their declining years? The policy this suggests is to decrease the levy on men, or to increase it on women, or possibly to do both at once. There is thus much that egalitarians could do by way of redistribution to reduce the unjustified inequality in respect to the life expectancy of men and women.

However much that is, it will affect only future generations. There remains the question of how to compensate men born between 1970 and 2010 for the unjustified inequality of having lives one-tenth shorter than women. No compensation can undo the damage, but it may make it easier to bear. The obvious policy is to set up preferential treatment programs designed to provide for men at least some of the goods that they would have enjoyed had their life expectancy been equal to women's. There is a lot of pleasure that could be had in those seven to eight years that men are not going to have. And since those years would have come at the end of their lives, when they are more likely to know their minds, their loss affects not only the quantity but also the quality of their not-to-be-had pleasures. One efficient way of compensating them for their loss is to set up government-sponsored pleasure centers in which men may spend the hours and days gained from having shorter working days and longer vacations.

Having dwelt on the absurd policies that follow from egalitarianism, the time has come to ask the question promised in the title: what is wrong with these policies? Let it be said immediately that this question will not be answered here. Indeed, the very point of the argument is to raise the question and then leave it to egalitarians to try to answer it. They should try because the absurd policies follow from basic egalitarian beliefs, and their absurdity casts doubt on the beliefs from which they follow. That of course means that the justification that is customarily given for the policies which are more usually associated with egalitarianism, namely, antipoverty programs, various welfare legislations, the preferential treatment of minorities and women, and so forth, is called into question as well.

There is also another reason why they should try to answer it. The very absurdity of the policies discussed above will create the suspicion in some minds not completely set in the ideological mold of egalitarianism that the policies more usually associated with egalitarianism suffer from analogous absurdity. Such uncommitted people may suspect that the reason why the familiar egalitarian policies do not appear absurd has more to do with familiarity produced by repetition than with the justification available for them. Egalitarians should try to answer the question to dispel that suspicion.

It is a safe bet, however, that if egalitarians do not ignore the question altogether, then they will claim that it has an obvious answer. It is impossible to tell what all of these yet-to-be-given answers may be, but there are three predictable ones, and it needs to be discussed why they fail.

The first is to claim that there is a significant disanalogy between men being worst off in respect to life expectancy and the poor, minorities, and women being worst off in respect to some other primary goods. The disanalogy, egalitarians may say, is that members of these other groups are worst off because preventable injustice has been done to them, such as exploitation, discrimination, prejudice, and so forth, while this is not true of men.

A moment of thought shows, however, that this answer is untenable. In the first place, the group of men includes minorities and the poor who, according to egalitarians, have suffered from injustice. And the groups of minorities and women include high achievers, middle- and upper-class people, people with considerable wealth, as well as recent immigrants who came to this country voluntarily and who could not have suffered from injustice here. It is but the crudest prejudice to think of men as Archie Bunkers, of women as great talents sentenced to housewifery, and of blacks and Hispanics as ghetto dwellers doomed by injustice to a life of poverty, crime, and addiction. Many men have been victims of injustice, and many women and minorities have not suffered from it.

It will be said against this that there still is a disanalogy because the poor, minorities, and women are more likely to have been victims of injustice than men. Suppose that this is so. What justice requires then, according to egalitarians, is the redistribution of the relevant primary goods and compensation for their loss. But these policies will be just only if they benefit victims of injustice, and the victims cannot be identified simply as poor, minorities, or women because they, as individuals, may not have suffered any injustice. Moreover, those members of these groups who do lack primary goods may do so, not because of injustice, but because of bad luck, personal defects, or having taken risks and lost. Overcoming injustice requires, therefore, a much more precise identification of the victims than merely membership in such amorphous groups as those of women, minorities, or the poor. This more precise identification requires asking and answering the question of why people who lack primary goods lack them.

Answering it, however, must include consideration of the possibility that people may cause or contribute to their own misfortune and that it is their lack of merit, effort, or responsibility, not injustice, that explains why they lack primary goods. The consideration of this possibility, however, is regarded as misguided by egalitarians. According to them, the mere fact of being worst off is sufficient to warrant redistribution and compensation.

It need not be considered here whether or not egalitarians are right about this, for, right or wrong, they face a dilemma. If the policies of redistribution and compensation do take into account the degree to which people are responsible for being among the worst off, then the justification of these policies must go beyond what egalitarians have been willing to provide. For the justification must then involve consideration of merit, desert, effort, and so forth. To the extent to which this is done, the justification ceases to be egalitarian.

If, on the other hand, the policies of redistribution and compensation do not take into account the degree of responsibility people have for being among the worst off, then there is no disanalogy between men, who are worst off in respect to life expectancy, and women, minorities, or the poor, who are worst off in other respects. Consistent egalitarian policies would then have to aim to overcome all inequalities, and that is just what produces the absurd policies noted above.

## Notes

1. U.S. Bureau of Census, *Statistical Abstract of the United States*, 114th ed. (Washington, D.C., 1994), p. 87.
2. Richard J. Arneson, "Equality," in *A Companion to Contemporary Political Philosophy*, ed. Robert E. Goodin and Philip Pettit (Oxford: Blackwell, 1993), pp. 489–507, p. 489.
3. Thomas Nagel, *Equality and Partiality* (New York: Oxford University Press, 1991), p. 28.
4. John Rawls, *A Theory of Justice* (Cambridge, Mass.: Harvard University Press, 1971), pp. 100–101.
5. Thomas Nagel, "Equality," in *Mortal Questions* (Cambridge: Cambridge University Press, 1979), pp. 106–27, pp. 117–18.
6. Rawls, p. 83.
7. Ibid., p. 101.
8. Ibid., p. 100.

# Part Two: Libertarianism

# Introduction

The just society, according to Rawls, is one that protects citizens' basic liberties and arranges socio-economic inequalities so that they are to the greatest benefit of the least advantaged and attached to offices and positions open to all under conditions of fair equality of opportunity. This contrasts with the conception of justice defended by the libertarian Robert Nozick. Justice, for Nozick, actually rules out the kind of redistribution that Rawls envisions. In *Anarchy, State, and Utopia* Nozick defends the minimal state. The state should be 'limited to the narrow functions of protection against force, theft, fraud, enforcement of contracts and so on' (Nozick, 1974: ix). Any state that extends its functions beyond this narrow range of functions is unjust. So, for example, the requirements of Rawls's fair equality of opportunity principle and the difference principle would be ruled out. Such an extensive state, argues Nozick, violates people's rights.

There are certain affinities between egalitarian-liberals and libertarians, namely the emphasis they place on the value of liberty. But libertarians hold that a minimal state is the only justified state and thus reject the considerations of equality that egalitarian-liberals like Rawls invoke. Liberty and equality are, argues Nozick, incompatible. If one is truly committed to the value of freedom then any attempt to enforce, through the coercive apparatus of the state, a particular distributive arrangement, be it egalitarian or otherwise, will violate the freedom of individuals and thus be unjust. Nozick's appeal to the primacy of the value of freedom is a sophisticated appeal and the first excerpt from *Anarchy, State, and Utopia* covers the main components of his argument.

Central to Nozick's argument is an appeal to moral side constraints. 'Side constraints upon action reflect the underlying Kantian principle that individuals are ends and not merely means, they may not be sacrificed or used for the achieving of other ends without their consent' (Nozick, 1974: 30–1). Individuals are, argues Nozick, inviolable. Recall that this line of argument was also central to Rawls's rejection of utilitarianism. By defining the right as that which maximises the good utilitarianism fails to take seriously the distinction between persons. Maximising utility might justify violating individual rights. But justice, argues Rawls, denies that the loss of freedom for some is made right by a greater good shared by others. It would thus appear that Rawls and Nozick share the same starting point. But this is not so. The scope of individual freedom that Nozick appeals to is more expansive than that of Rawls. The central issue that divides Rawls and Nozick is the stance they take on *property rights*. While Rawls does include among the basic liberties of the person the right to hold and have the exclusive use of personal property, he does not include the wider conception of the right which extends this right to include certain rights of acquisition and bequest, as well as the right to own means of production and natural resources (Rawls, 1993: 298). Nozick's libertarian argument is premised on *absolute* property rights: rights of ownership over oneself and over things in the world (Wolff, 1991: 4).

It is thus obvious why, for Nozick, freedom and equality are incompatible. If freedom includes absolute property rights then such freedom will be limited by the egalitarian measures of, for example, Rawls's difference principle. The important question is – should we accept this wide conception of property rights? Nozick believes that such a conception of property rights follows from a commitment to the thesis that underlies our commitment to side constraints – the thesis of self-ownership. This thesis states 'that each person is the morally rightful owner of his own person and powers, and, consequently, that each is free (morally speaking) to use those powers as he wishes, provided that he does not deploy them aggressively against others' (Cohen, 1995: 67).

The so-called 'eye lottery' example is usually invoked to illustrate the intuitive appeal of the thesis of self-ownership and how it captures our concern for side constraints.

> Suppose that transplant technology reaches such a pitch of perfection that it becomes possible to transplant eyeballs with a one hundred per cent chance of success. Anyone's eyes may be transplanted into anyone else, without complications. As some people are born with defective eyes, or with no eyes at all, should we redistribute eyes? That is, should we take one eye from some people with two healthy eyes, and give eyes to the blind? Of course, some people may volunteer their eyes for transplant. But what if there were not enough volunteers? Should we have a national lottery, and force the losers to donate an eye? (Wolff, 1991: 7–8)

The eye lottery example represents a clear case where our commitment to self-ownership trumps considerations of equality. If one is truly convinced by the egalitarian aspiration of Rawls's claim that morally arbitrary factors should be mitigated, argues Nozick, then one should support the policy of an eye lottery. Nozick claims that 'an application of the principle of maximising the position of those worst off might involve forceable redistribution of bodily parts' (Nozick, 1974: 206). Those born with two healthy eyes do not deserve their eyes. If we can mitigate the misfortune of the natural lottery by adopting an eye lottery wouldn't such a policy be just? The fact that we feel that such a policy is unjust is evidence of our commitment to the thesis of self-ownership. And if we are to take this thesis seriously, argues Nozick, we should also object to the redistributive policies of Rawlsian justice. Such policies, like the eye lottery, violate the thesis of self-ownership. The only institutional arrangement that respects persons as self-owners is the minimal state. Nozick believes that 'taxation of earnings from labor is on a moral par with forced labor' (Nozick, 1974: 169).

Nozick defends an entitlement theory of justice which states: *whatever arises from a just situation by just steps is itself just* (Nozick, 1974: 151). He illustrates the intuitive appeal of the entitlement theory of justice with his Wilt Chamberlain example. The example runs like this. Let us suppose that we begin with a just distribution, call it D1. Nozick allows us to characterise D1 in whatever way we want. Let's assume, being an egalitarian, one claims that D1 is the equal society. In this just equal society an individual, Wilt Chamberlain, is in great demand by basketball teams. He is a great gate attraction and utilises this bargaining advantage to work out the following lucrative deal with the owners of the team. In each home game, twenty-five cents from the price of each ticket of admission goes to him. The season starts, and the cheerful fans attend his team's games, each time dropping a separate twenty-five cents of their admission price into a special box with Chamberlain's name on it. By the end of the season one million fans have attended his home games and thus he winds up with $250 000, which makes him much richer than everyone else. We now have a new distribution – D2. D2 is not the egalitarian distribution we started with. We now have an unequal society. Is this new distribution just?

Nozick argues that D2 is just. The entitlement theory of justice tells us that whatever arises from a just distribution by just steps is itself just. D2 satisfies the requirements of the entitlement theory. The initial distribution was just. Recall that Nozick allows us complete freedom in describing what the initial distribution is so the egalitarian cannot complain that D1 itself was unjust. The steps away from D1 are also just. The contract between Chamberlain and the owners was a fully voluntary contract. The fans who paid the separate twenty-five cents also voluntarily agreed to this arrangement. They could have spent their money on other things such as going to the movies. Thus, having fulfilled the requirements of the entitlement theory of justice, it appears that D2 must be just.

The Wilt Chamberlain example illustrates a important point in Nozick's libertarian argument: liberty upsets patterns. If you allow people to be free they will inevitably engage in activities which will upset the pattern the 'pie-cutting' theorist says is just. The only way to maintain a pattern is to violate the rights of individuals – namely, to violate their right to choose what to do with their entitlements. The egalitarian will argue that the state should step in in D2 and tax Chamberlain's new wealth in order to bring things back to an equal distribution. Maintaining a distributional pattern, argues Nozick, is individualism with a vengeance (Nozick, 1974: 167). The only way a distributive pattern can be maintained is by constantly interfering with the fully voluntary transactions of individuals. By doing so we fail to respect the requirements of the thesis of self-ownership.

In the excerpt from 'Self-Ownership, Marxism and Egalitarianism' Eric Mack considers some of the criticisms raised against Nozick's 'How Liberty Upsets Patterns' argument. Instead of presenting Nozick's argument as one pointing to a conflict between respecting liberty and maintaining a distributive paradigm, Mack reconstructs Nozick's argument. According to Mack, Nozick's argument 'points to a tension between advocating a justice-*initiating* application of a favored end-state or pattern and being committed to the *repeated* application of that end-state or pattern in a way that negates the outcome of individuals employing as they see fit the holdings established by the justice-initiating application of that end-state or pattern' (Mack, 2002: 81).

Most examinations of Nozick's entitlement theory tend to focus on only two of the three principles the theory is premised on – the principle of just transfer and the principle of just initial acquisition. These two principles help us to determine when one is entitled to a good or holding. Namely, if they have been acquired in accordance with the principles of both justice in acquisition and justice in transfer. But in reality people do not always abide by the requirements of these two principles. Human history is not one of just initial acquisition nor just transfers. It is a history of slavery, conquest, theft and fraud. To remedy such injustices the entitlement theory must invoke a third principle – the principle of rectification. This principle is 'an essential part [of Nozick's entitlement theory]; for, without it, owing to the inductive nature of the definition of entitlement, if there has been a single injustice in the history of the state, no matter how far back, the state will not be able to achieve a just distribution of goods in the present' (Davis, 1982: 348). Nozick recognises that the principle of rectification raises many complex questions for his entitlement theory of justice.

> If past injustice has shaped present holdings in various ways, some identifiable and some not, what now, if anything, ought to be done to rectify these injustices? What obligations do the performers of injustice have toward those whose position is worse than it would have been had the injustice not been done? Or, than it would have been had compensation been paid promptly? How, if at all, do things change if the beneficiaries and those made worse off are not the direct parties in an act of injustice, but, for example, their descendants? How far back must one go in wiping clean the historical slate of injustices? What may victims of injustice permissibly do in order to rectify the injustices being done to them, including the many injustices done by persons acting through their government? (Nozick, 1974: 152)

Given the actual history of human acquisition and transfers it is surprising that Nozick's historical theory does not make the principle of rectification more central to *Anarchy, State, and Utopia*. The topic 'rectification' appears only five times in the index and totals a meagre seven pages in a book that exceeds 350 pages. Thus we are not given a great deal of information as to how the rectification principle could be applied to remedy past injustices. Robert Litan considers these issues in 'On Rectification in Nozick's Minimal State'. Once this aspect of Nozick's argument is considered one sees that Nozick's theory gives rise to some surprising conclusions.

The second main theory covered in this part is the contractarian argument of David Gauthier. Like Nozick, Gauthier rejects the suggestion that justice requires the kind of egalitarian redistribution that is entailed by Rawls's difference principle. But Gauthier's argument is in fact radically different from both Rawls's egalitarian-liberalism and Nozick's entitlement theory of justice. Rawls and Nozick share some methodological assumptions concerning how to construct and defend a theory of justice. Both theorists appeal to the moral sensibilities we have concerning what is just. By characterising his original position as the 'appropriate initial status quo' Rawls appeals to our moral sensibilities of fairness, equality and impartiality. Nozick's entitlement theory of justice appeals to the weight we place on the thesis of self-ownership and the importance of moral side constraints. This approach to political theory is rejected by those who opt for what Arthur Ripstein calls 'foundationalism'.

> Foundationalist political theories attempt to justify political institutions without presupposing any political considerations. In a foundationalist theory, some set of considerations is held to support a particular form of political order, without itself depending on any substantive assumptions about the legitimacy of particular forms of human interaction. Hence the metaphor of a foundation, which holds up an edifice without itself being supported by anything else. (Ripstein, 1987: 115)

The main proponent of foundationalism is Thomas Hobbes (1588–1679). In *Leviathan* Hobbes attempts to justify an absolute sovereign by showing that it would be rational for people to agree to accept this arrangement. The last two decades has witnessed renewed interest in Hobbes.[1] While rejecting, for obvious reasons, Hobbes's conclusion (i.e. that an absolute sovereign is justified), contemporary authors have been inspired by the foundationalism of the Hobbesian project. This is

# Introduction

most evident in the contractarian theory of David Gauthier whose theory is the focus of the last two excerpts in this chapter. Like Rawls, Gauthier appeals to the idea of a social contract as is evident in the title of his influential book *Morals by Agreement*. But unlike Rawls, Gauthier rejects the idea that a theory of justice can be justified by appealing to our moral intuitions. On the contrary, justice must be based on *non-moral* premises. To base justice on moral premises is simply to assume what one is trying to justify in the first place. The non-moral premises that Gauthier founds his moral theory on are the premises of rational choice. Gauthier argues that 'the rational principles for making choices, or decisions among possible actions, include some that constrain the actor pursuing his own interest in an impartial way. These we identify as moral principles' (Gauthier, 1986: 3). Gauthier's argument is a complex one and the excerpt is a brief overview of the main components of his theory, including minimax relative concession, constrained maximisation and the Lockean proviso.

Gauthier's claim that moral duties are rationally grounded has sparked much debate among moral and political philosophers. One of the main concerns raised against Gauthier concerns the scope of other-regarding demands. Justice, according to Gauthier, only arises among parties who are roughly equal in physical and mental capacities.

> Only beings whose physical and mental capacities are either roughly equal or mutually complementary can expect to find co-operation beneficial to all. Humans benefit from their interaction with horses, but they do not co-operate with horses and may not benefit them. Among unequals, one party may benefit most by coercing the other, and on our theory would have no reason to refrain. We may condemn all coercive relationships, but only within the context of mutual benefit can our condemnation appeal to a rationally grounded morality. (Gauthier, 1986: 17)

If justice only applies to those who are roughly equal in physical and mental powers, then what about people who do not satisfy this condition (for example, the young, old, infirm and unborn)? Critics of Gauthier's contractarianism point to these cases as the most effective way of illustrating the shortcomings of justice as mutual advantage. In the final excerpt in this part Allen Buchanan argues that Gauthier's type of project, which Buchanan calls 'justice as self-interested reciprocity', gives rise to the *reciprocity thesis*. The reciprocity thesis states that only those who do (or at least can) make a contribution to the cooperative surplus have rights to social resources (Buchanan, 1990: 230). One might find that the reciprocity thesis does cohere with some of our intuitions about what is fair. For example, that free-riders who *choose* not to contribute should not expect to receive something back from society. But the reciprocity thesis rules out entitlements for *all* free-riders, those that have chosen to free-ride and those who, for reasons beyond their control, must free-ride if they are to survive or live meaningful lives. This second category of free-riders would include people who are born with handicaps so severe that they would never be able to contribute. These individuals would not, according to justice as mutual advantage, be entitled to provisions such as publicly funded health care services for such a policy would violate the reciprocity thesis by permitting these individuals to free-ride off those who contribute and pay the taxes for such programmes. As Buchanan points out, the implications of Gauthier's theory might be even more radical than denying noncontributors rights of distributive justice:

> If justice as reciprocity is extended to all rights, not just rights of distributive justice, it is even more radical and, one is tempted to say, even more inhumane. If, as Gauthier believes, all moral rights, including the so-called negative rights to refrain from injuring and killing, are rationally ascribable only to potential contributors to social wealth, then we violate no rights if we choose to use noncontributors in experiments on the nature of pain or for military research on the performance of various designs of bullets when they strike human tissue, slaughter them for food, or bronze them to make lifelike statues. (Buchanan, 1990: 232)

Buchanan argues that justice as mutual advantage fails to recognise 'that questions of justice arise not only with respect to relations among contributors but also at the deeper level of what sort of cooperative institutions we ought to have, insofar as the character of these institutions will determine in part who can contribute' (Buchanan, 1990: 238). Buchanan's point can be illustrated by reflecting on how our own society has evolved over time and with it who counts as a contributor. Many people who have physical or mental handicaps can contribute in our present society due to changes in, for example, technology. Consider the case of Stephen Hawking, the eminent physicist. No one would dispute the fact that he has made a very important contribution to our society. But 200 years ago someone with Lou Gehrig's disease would not have had the opportunity to make such a contribution. Changes in technology have brought changes in who counts as a contributor. Even something as basic as making the workplace accessible to people in wheelchairs widens the range of people who can qualify as contributors.

The basic skills necessary for qualifying as a contributor have also changed over the course of the last century. One's level of physical strength was more of an asset in an agrarian society, but in the complex information age of the modern world an ever increasing number of occupations require skills such as reading, writing and computer literacy. Given the fact that the capacity to be a contributor is socially determined, Buchanan argues that Gauthier's version of contractarianism is incomplete and thus defective because it does not consider the question of whether the scheme of cooperation unjustly excludes some persons from participating.

Proponents of justice as mutual advantage will not be moved by many of the objections we have just raised. Claims about the rights of the infirm are premised on moral intuitions and thus cannot be backed up by non-moral premises. The mutual advantage theorist rejects the methodological assumptions of striving for a 'reflective equilibrium'.[2] It is counterproductive, they argue, to construct a theory which coheres to our moral sensibilities as it is an open question as to whether or not these sensibilities are themselves justified. In order to be justified they must, argues Gauthier, reflect what rational individuals would agree to in a mutually advantageous bargain. The debate between those contractarians partial to Rawls's approach and those partial to Gauthier's is thus a difficult one to assess as the proponents disagree on the criteria by which a theory should be assessed. Those who defend the appeal to our moral sensibilities claim that Gauthier's theory is so counterintuitive that it should not even be called a theory of justice. Those who are attracted to Gauthier's project will claim that such an objection is merely question begging. It presupposes that one already knows what is moral or just.

## Notes

1   See, for example, David Gauthier (1986), Jean Hampton (1986), Gregory Kavka (1986) and Quentin Skinner (1996).
2   This is the process whereby we seek to find a 'fit' between the conclusions of a theory of justice and our initial moral convictions.

## References

Buchanan, Allen. 'Justice as Reciprocity versus Subject-Centered Justice', *Philosophy and Public Affairs*, 19(3), 1990: 227–252.
Cohen, G.A. *Self-Ownership, Freedom and Equality*. (Cambridge: Cambridge University Press, 1995).
Davis, Lawrence. 'Nozick's Entitlement Theory'. In J. Paul (ed.) *Reading Nozick: Essays on Anarchy, State, and Utopia*. (Oxford: Blackwell Publishers, 1982).
Gauthier, David. *Morals by Agreement*. (New York: Oxford University Press, 1986).
Hampton, Jean. *Hobbes and the Social Contract Tradition*. (Cambridge: Cambridge University Press, 1986).
Kavka, Gregory. *Hobbesian Moral and Political Theory*. (Princeton: Princeton Unviersity Press, 1986).
Mack, Eric. 'Self-Ownership, Marxism and Egalitarianism: Part 1: Challenges to Historical Entitlement', *Politics, Philosophy and Economics*, 1(1), 2002: 75–108.
Nozick, Robert. *Anarchy, State, and Utopia*. (New York: Basic Books, 1974).
Rawls, John. *Political Liberalism*. (New York: Columbia University Press, 1993).
Ripstein, Arthur. 'Foundationalism in Political Thoery', *Philosophy and Public Affairs*, 16(2), 1987: 115–137.
Skinner, Quentin. *The Foundations of Modern Political thought*, 2 volumes. (Cambridge: Cambridge University Press, 1996).
Wolff, Jonathan. *Robert Nozick: Property, Justice and the Minimal State*. (Cambridge: Polity Press, 1991).

# 6 The Entitlement Theory of Justice

## Robert Nozick

Political philosophy is concerned only with *certain* ways that persons may not use others; primarily, physically aggressing against them. A specific side constraint upon action toward others expresses the fact that others may not be used in the specific ways the side constraint excludes. Side constraints express the inviolability of others, in the ways they specify. These modes of inviolability are expressed by the following injunction: "Don't use people in specified ways." An end-state view, on the other hand, would express the view that people are ends and not merely means (if it chooses to express this view at all), by a different injunction: "Minimize the use in specified ways of persons as means." Following this precept itself may involve using someone as a means in one of the ways specified. Had Kant held this view, he would have given the second formula of the categorical imperative as, "So act as to minimize the use of humanity simply as a means," rather than the one he actually used: "Act in such a way that you always treat humanity, whether in your own person or in the person of any other, never simply as a means, but always at the same time as an end."[1]

Side constraints express the inviolability of other persons. But why may not one violate persons for the greater social good? Individually, we each sometimes choose to undergo some pain or sacrifice for a greater benefit or to avoid a greater harm: we go to the dentist to avoid worse suffering later; we do some unpleasant work for its results; some persons diet to improve their health or looks; some save money to support themselves when they are older. In each case, some cost is borne for the sake of the greater overall good. Why not, *similarly*, hold that some persons have to bear some costs that benefit other persons more, for the sake of the overall social good? But there is no *social entity* with a good that undergoes some sacrifice for its own good. There are only individual people, different individual people, with their own individual lives. Using one of these people for the benefit of others, uses him and benefits the others. Nothing more. What happens is that something is done to him for the sake of others. Talk of an overall social good covers this up. (Intentionally?) To use a person in this way does not sufficiently respect and take account of the fact that he is a separate person,[2] that his is the only life he has. *He* does not get some overbalancing good from his sacrifice, and no one is entitled to force this upon him—least of all a state or government that claims his allegiance (as other individuals do not) and that therefore scrupulously must be *neutral* between its citizens.

Not all actual situations are generated in accordance with the two principles of justice in holdings: the principle of justice in acquisition and the principle of justice in transfer. Some people steal from others, or defraud them, or enslave them, seizing their product and preventing them from living as they choose, or forcibly exclude others from competing in exchanges. None of these are permissible modes of transition from one situation to another. And some persons acquire holdings by means not sanctioned by the principle of justice in acquisition. The existence of past injustice (previous violations of the first two principles of justice in holdings) raises the third major topic under justice in holdings: the rectification of injustice in holdings. If past injustice has shaped present holdings in various ways, some identifiable and some not, what now, if anything, ought to be done to rectify these injustices? What obligations do the performers of injustice have toward those whose position is worse than it would have been had the injustice not been done? Or, than it would have been had compensation been paid promptly? How, if at all, do things change if the beneficiaries and those made worse off are not the direct parties in the act of injustice, but, for example, their descendants? Is an injustice done to someone whose holding was itself based upon an unrectified injustice? How far back must one go in wiping clean the historical slate of injustices? What may victims of injustice permissibly do in order to rectify the injustices being done to them, including the many injustices done by persons acting through their government? I do not know of a thorough or theoretically sophisticated treatment of such issues. Idealizing greatly, let us suppose theoretical investigation will produce a principle of rectification. This principle uses historical information about previous situations and injustices done in them (as defined by the first two principles of justice and rights against interference), and information about the actual course of events that flowed from these injustices, until the present, and it yields a description (or descriptions) of holdings in the society. The principle of rectification presumably will make use of its best estimate of subjunctive information about what would have occurred (or a probability distribution over what might have occurred, using the expected value) if the injustice had not taken place. If the actual description of holdings turns out not to be one of the descriptions yielded by the principle, then one of the descriptions yielded must be realized.[3]

The general outlines of the theory of justice in holdings are that the holdings of a person are just if he is entitled to them by the principles of justice in acquisition and transfer, or by the principle of rectification of injustice (as specified by the first two principles). If each person's holdings are just, then the total set (distribution) of holdings is just. To turn these general outlines into a specific theory we would have to specify the details of each of the three principles of justice in holdings: the principle of acquisition of holdings, the principle of transfer of holdings, and the principle of rectification of violations of the first two principles. I shall not attempt that task here. (Locke's principle of justice in acquisition is discussed below.)

## How Liberty Upsets Patterns

It is not clear how those holding alternative conceptions of distributive justice can reject the entitlement conception of justice in holdings. For suppose a distribution favored by one of these non-entitlement conceptions is realized. Let us suppose it is your favorite one and let us call this distribution $D_1$; perhaps everyone has an equal share, perhaps shares vary in accordance with some dimension you treasure. Now suppose that Wilt Chamberlain is greatly in demand by basketball teams, being a great gate attraction. (Also suppose contracts run only for a year, with players being free agents.) He signs the following sort of contract with a team: In each home game, twenty-five cents from the price of each ticket of admission goes to him. (We ignore the question of whether he is "gouging" the owners, letting them look out for themselves.) The season starts, and people cheerfully attend his team's games; they buy their tickets, each time dropping a separate twenty-five cents of their admission price into a special box with Chamberlain's name on it. They are excited about seeing him play; it is worth the total admission price to them. Let us suppose that in one season one million persons attend his home games, and Wilt Chamberlain winds up with $250,000, a much larger sum than the average income and larger even than anyone else has. Is he entitled to this income? Is this new distribution $D_2$, unjust? If so, why? There is *no* question about whether each of the people was entitled to the control over the resources they held in $D_1$; because that was the distribution (your favorite) that (for the purposes of argument) we assumed was acceptable. Each of these persons *chose* to give twenty-five cents of their money to Chamberlain. They could have spent it on going to the movies, or on candy bars, or on copies of *Dissent* magazine, or of *Montly Review*. But they all, at least one million of them, converged on giving it to Wilt Chamberlain in exchange for watching him play basketball. If $D_1$ was a just distribution, and people voluntarily moved from it to $D_2$, transferring parts of their shares they were given under $D_1$ (what was it for if not to do something with?), isn't $D_2$ also just? If the people were entitled to dispose of the resources to which they were entitled (under $D_1$), didn't this include their being entitled to give it to, or exchange it with, Wilt Chamberlain? Can anyone else complain on grounds of justice? Each other person already has his legitimate share under $D_1$. Under $D_1$, there is nothing that anyone has that anyone else has a claim of justice against. After someone transfers something to Wilt Chamberlain, third parties *still* have their legitimate shares; *their* shares are not changed. By what process could such a transfer among two persons give rise to a legitimate claim of distributive justice on a portion of what was transferred, by a third party who had no claim of justice on any holding of the others *before* the transfer?[4]

Patterned principles of distributive justice necessitate *re*distributive activities. The likelihood is small that any actual freely-arrived-at set of holdings fits a given pattern; and the likelihood is nil that it will continue to fit the pattern as people exchange and give. From the point of view of an entitlement theory, redistribution is a serious matter indeed, involving, as it does, the violation of people's rights. (An exception is those takings that fall under the principle of the rectification of injustices.) From other points of view, also, it is serious.

Taxation of earnings from labor is on a par with forced labor.[5] Some persons find this claim obviously true: taking the earnings of *n* hours labor is like taking *n* hours from the person; it is like forcing the person to work *n* hours for another's purpose. Others find the claim absurd. But even these, *if* they object to forced labor, would oppose forcing unemployed hippies to work for the benefit of the needy.[6] And they would also object to forcing each person to work five extra hours each week for the benefit of the needy. But a system that takes five hours' wages in taxes does not seem to them like one that forces someone to work five hours, since it offers the person forced a wider range of choice in activities than does taxation in kind with the particular labor specified. (But we can imagine a gradation of systems of forced labor, from one that specifies a particular activity, to one that gives a choice among two activities, to … ; and so on up.) Furthermore, people envisage a system with something like a proportional tax on everything above the amount necessary for basic needs. Some think this does not force someone to work extra hours, since there is no fixed number of extra hours he is forced to work, and since he can avoid the tax entirely by earning only enough to cover his basic needs. This is a very uncharacteristic view of forcing for those who *also* think people are forced to do something *whenever* the alternatives they face are considerably worse. However, *neither* view is correct. The fact that others intentionally intervene, in violation of a side constraint against aggression, to threaten force to limit the alternatives, in this case to paying taxes or (presumably the worse alternative) bare subsistence, makes the taxation system one of forced labor and distinguishes it from other cases of limited choices which are not forcings.

The man who chooses to work longer to gain an income more than sufficient for his basic needs prefers some extra goods or services to the leisure and activities he could perform during the possible nonworking hours; whereas the man who chooses not to work the extra time prefers the leisure activities to the extra goods or services he could acquire by working more. Given this, if it would be illegitimate for a tax system to seize some of a man's leisure (forced labor) for the purpose of serving the needy, how can it be legitimate for a tax system to seize some of a man's goods for that purpose? Why should we treat the man whose happiness requires certain material goods or services differently from the man whose preferences and desires make such goods unnecessary for his happiness? Why should the man who prefers seeing a movie (and who has to earn money for a ticket) be open to the required call to aid the needy, while the person who prefers looking at a sunset (and hence need earn no extra money) is not? Indeed, isn't it surprising that redistributionists choose to ignore the man whose pleasures are so easily attainable without extra labor, while adding yet another burden to the poor unfortunate who must work for his pleasures? If anything, one would have expected the reverse. Why is the person with the nonmaterial or nonconsumption desire allowed to proceed unimpeded to his most favored feasible alternative, whereas the man whose pleasures or desires involve material things and who must work for extra money (thereby serving whomever considers his activities valuable enough to pay him) is constrained in what he can realize?

## Locke's Theory of Acquisition

Before we turn to consider other theories of justice in detail, we must introduce an additional bit of complexity into the structure of the entitlement theory. This is best approached by considering Locke's attempt to specify a principle of justice in acquisition. Locke views property rights in an unowned object as originating through someone's mixing his labor with it. This gives rise to many questions. What are the boundaries of what labor is mixed with? If a private astronaut clears a place on Mars, has he mixed his labor with (so that he comes to own) the whole planet, the whole uninhabited universe, or just a particular plot? Which plot does an act bring under ownership? The minimal (possibly disconnected) area such that an act decreases entropy in that area, and not elsewhere? Can virgin land (for the purposes of ecological investigation by high-flying airplane) come under ownership by a Lockean process? Building a fence around a territory presumably would make one the owner of only the fence (and the land immediately underneath it).

Why does mixing one's labor with something make one the owner of it? Perhaps because one owns one's labor, and so one comes to own a previously unowned thing that becomes permeated with what one owns. Ownership seeps over into the rest. But why isn't mixing what I own with what I don't own a way of losing what I own rather than a way of gaining what I don't? If I own a can of tomato juice and spill it in the sea so that its molecules (made radioactive, so I can check this) mingle evenly throughout the sea, do I thereby come to own the sea, or have I foolishly dissipated my tomato juice? Perhaps the idea, instead, is that laboring on something improves it and makes it more valuable; and anyone is entitled to own a thing whose value he has created. (Reinforcing this, perhaps, is the view that laboring is unpleasant. If some people made things effortlessly, as the cartoon characters in *The Yellow Submarine* trail flowers in their wake, would they have lesser claim to their own products whose making didn't *cost* them anything?) Ignore the fact that laboring on something may make it less valuable (spraying pink enamel paint on a piece of driftwood that you have found). Why should one's entitlement extend to the whole object rather than just to the *added value* one's labor has produced? (Such reference to value might also serve to delimit the extent of ownership; for example, substitute "increases the value of" for "decreases entropy in" in the above entropy criterion.) No workable or coherent value-added property scheme has yet been devised, and any such scheme presumably would fall to objections (similar to those) that fell the theory of Henry George.

It will be implausible to view improving an object as giving full ownership to it, if the stock of unowned objects that might be improved is limited. For an object's coming under one person's ownership changes the situation of all others. Whereas previously they were at liberty (in Hohfeld's sense) to use the object, they now no longer are. This change in the siuation of others (by removing their liberty to act on a previously unowned object) need not worsen their situation. If I appropriate a grain of sand from Coney Island, no one else may now do as they will with *that* grain of sand. But there are plenty of other grains of sand left for them to do the same with. Or if not grains of sand, then other things. Alternatively, the things I do with the grain of sand I appropriate might improve the position of others, counterbalancing their loss of the liberty to use that grain. The crucial point is whether appropriation of an unowned object worsens the situation of others.

Locke's proviso that there be "enough and as good left in common for others" (sect. 27) is meant to ensure that the situation of others is not worsened. (If this proviso is met is there any motivation for his further condition of nonwaster?) It is often said that this proviso once held but now no longer does. But there appears to be an argument for the conclusion that if the proviso no longer holds, then it cannot ever have held so as to yield permanent and inheritable property rights. Consider the first person $Z$ for whom there is not enough and as good left to appropriate. The last person $Y$ to appropriate left $Z$ without his previous liberty to act on an object, and so worsened $Z$'s situation. So $Y$'s appropriation is not allowed under Locke's proviso. Therefore the next to last person $X$ to appropriate left $Y$ in a worse position, for $X$'s act ended permissible appropriation. Therefore $X$'s appropriation wasn't permissible. But then the appropriator two from last, $W$, ended permissible appropriation and so, since it worsened $X$'s position, $W$'s appropriation wasn't permissible. And so on back to the first person $A$ to appropriate a permanent property right.

This argument, however, proceeds too quickly. Someone may be made worse off by another's appropriation in two ways: first, by losing the opportunity to improve his situation by a particular appropriation or any one; and second, by no longer being able to use freely (without appropriation) what he previously could. A *stringent* requirement that another not be made worse off by an appropriation would exclude the first way if nothing else counterbalances the diminution in opportunity, as well as the second. A *weaker* requirement would exclude the second way, though not the first. With the weaker requirement, we cannot zip back so quickly from $Z$ to $A$, as in the above argument; for though person $Z$ can no longer *appropriate*, there may remain some for him to *use* as before. In this case $Y$'s appropriation would not violate the weaker Lockean condition. (With less remaining that people are at liberty to use, users might face more inconvenience, crowding, and so on; in that way the situation of others might be worsened, unless appropriation stopped far short of such a point.) It is arguable that no one legitimately can complain if the weaker provision is satisfied. However, since this is less clear than in the case of the more stringent proviso, Locke may have intended this stringent proviso by "enough and as good" remaining, and perhaps he meant the non-waste condition to delay the end point from which the argument zips back.

Is the situation of persons who are unable to appropriate (there being no more accessible and useful unowned objects) worsened by a system allowing appropriation and permanent property? Here enter the various familiar social considerations favoring private property: it increases the social product by putting means of production in the hands of those who can use them most efficiently (profitably); experimentation is encouraged, because with separate persons controlling resources, there is no one person or small group whom someone with a new idea must convince to try it out; private property enables people to decide on the pattern and types of risks they wish to bear, leading to specialized types of risk bearing; private property protects future persons by leading some to hold back resources from current consumption for future markets; it provides alternate sources of employment for unpopular persons who don't have to convince any one person or small group to hire them, and so on.

## Notes

1  *Groundwork of the Metaphysic of Morals*. Translated by H. J. Paton, *The Moral Law* (London: Hutchinson, 1956), p. 96.
2  See John Rawls, *A Theory of Justice*, sects. 5, 6, 30.
3  If the principle of rectification of violations of the first two principles yields more than one description of holdings, then some choice must be made as to which of these is to be realized. Perhaps the sort of considerations about distributive justice and equality that I argue against play a legitimate role in *this* subsidiary choice. Similarly, there may be room for such considerations in deciding which otherwise arbitrary features a statute will embody, when such features are unavoidable because other considerations do not specify a precise line; yet a line must be drawn.
4  Might not a transfer have instrumental effects on a third party, changing his feasible options? (But what if the two parties to the transfer independently had used their holdings in this fashion?) I discuss this question below, but note here that this question concedes the point for distributions of ultimate intrinsic noninstrumental goods (pure utility experiences, so to speak) that are transferable. It also might be objected that the transfer might make a third party more envious because it worsens his position relative to someone else. I find it incomprehensible how this can be thought to involve a claim of justice. On envy, see Chapter 8.

   Here and elsewhere in this chapter, a theory which incorporates elements of pure procedural justice might find what I say acceptable, *if* kept in its proper place; that is, if background institutions exist to ensure the satisfaction of certain conditions on distributive shares. But if these institutions are not themselves the sum or invisible-hand result of people's voluntary (nonaggressive) actions, the constraints they impose require justification. At no point does *our* argument assume any background institutions more extensive than those of the minimal night-watchman state, a state limited to protecting persons against murder, assault, theft, fraud, and so forth.

5 I am unsure as to whether the arguments I present below show that such taxation merely *is* forced labor; so that "is on a par with" means "is one kind of." Or alternatively, whether the arguments emphasize the great similarities between such taxation and forced labor, to show it is plausible and illuminating to view such taxation in the light of forced labor. This latter approach would remind one of how John Wisdom conceives of the claims of metaphysicians.

6 Nothing hangs on the fact that here and elsewhere I speak loosely of *needs*, since I go on, each time, to reject the criterion of justice which includes it. If, however, something did depend upon the notion, one would want to examine it more carefully. For a skeptical view, see Kenneth Minogue, *The Liberal Mind*, (New York: Random House, 1963), pp. 103–112.

# 7 How Liberty Upsets Patterns

## Eric Mack

Nozick's best-known argument against all end-state and pattern theories is contained in a section of *Anarchy, State, and Utopia* that is entitled 'How Liberty Upsets Patterns' (N: 160–164[1]). Nozick and most commentators represent this argument as pointing to a conflict between respecting the liberty of individuals and maintaining allegiance to some favorite end-state or pattern as the measure of justice: 'no end-state principle or distributional patterned principle of justice can be continuously realized without continuous interference with people's lives' (N: 163). In contrast with this representation, the argument that I ascribe to Nozick perhaps with an excess of generosity, is an argument that points to a tension between advocating a justice-*initiating* application of a favored end-state or pattern and being committed to the *repeated* application of that end-state or pattern in a way that negates the outcome of individuals employing as they see fit the holdings established by the justice-initiating application of that end-state or pattern.

Nozick asks his reader to envision a world in which distribution of holdings $D_1$ obtains, where $D_1$ is the distribution that, among all possible distributions in that world, best realizes the reader's own favorite pattern. From the perspective of the pattern-friendly reader, the institutionalization of $D_1$ is the institutionalization of justice. Nozick then asks the reader to envision a set of voluntary exchanges among some of the (relatively well-endowed) inhabitants of that world that alters the distribution of holdings. These exchanges are envisioned as enhancing to some unspecified degree the holdings of each of the parties to the exchanges while not affecting the holdings of the non-participants. In fact, Nozick might, instead, have asked his pattern-friendly reader to envision the simpler yet case of relatively well-endowed individuals increasing their respective holdings under $D_1$ through purely unilateral action — through these individuals separately engaging in enhancing transformations of their assigned resources (or the resources that they have purchased with their assigned income under $D_1$). Indeed, he could also have asked the friend of structure to envision relatively ill-endowed individuals *decreasing* their respective holdings under $D_1$ through purely unilateral action — through these individuals separately engaging in diminishing transformations of their assigned resources (or the resources that they have purchased with their assigned income under $D_1$).[2]

Nozick then points out that the distribution of holdings $D_2$ that results from the envisioned voluntary exchanges (or, he might have said, that results from those unilaterally enhancing or diminishing actions) will almost certainly count as unjust in terms of the very pattern that certified the starting distribution $D_1$ as just. For it will almost certainly be the case that $D_2$ will not be the distribution that, of all the distributions possible *after* the exchanges (or transformations) that brought it into existence, most fully realizes the pattern that anointed $D_1$. Since, the pattern befriended by the pattern theorist will typically embody some preference for equality in holdings, I have described exchanges or transformations that increase inequality in holdings and so, in terms of this preference for equality, tend to make the conversion from $D_1$ into $D_2$ a transition from a just to an unjust distribution. However, friends of non-egalitarian patterns could be presented with different voluntary exchanges or unilateral transformations by different individuals that would, in terms of their favored structure, tend to move the world from justice to injustice. For example, friends of distribution in accordance with virtue could be presented with a transition from $D_1$ to $D_2$ brought about by the virtuous virtuously donating their holdings to the wicked. Whatever the character of the favored pattern, the resulting distribution $D_2$ will be unjust in terms of that certifying pattern if it is possible to convert $D_2$ (presumably through finely tuned tax and subsidy measures) into another distribution $D_3$ that better realizes the reigning pattern than does $D_2$ or $D_1$.

According to Nozick, the pattern theorist must say both that $D_1$ is just when it is created and that the $D_2$ that is envisioned to discomfort him is unjust when it arises. In one way, the pattern theorist has no trouble at all explaining the injustice of $D_2$ when it arises. $D_2$, he says, is unjust simply because it realizes the certifying pattern less fully than some other distribution $D_3$ into which $D_2$ can be converted. But, Nozick contends that the pattern theorist is obligated to provide a different sort of explanation for the (purported) injustice of $D_2$. He must explain *how* $D_2$ has become *infected* with injustice even though $D_2$'s existence and structure is entirely a function of just allocation $D_1$ and individuals deploying their just holdings as they respectively see fit without in any way impinging upon anyone else's just holding. How could the sort of activities that are envisioned as transforming $D_1$ into $D_2$ *introduce* injustice into the world? These questions are not answered by pointing again to the fact that $D_2$ can be converted into $D_3$, which better realizes the favored pattern. For these questions precisely challenge the proposition that a distribution is unjust if it can be converted into another that more fully realizes some esteemed structure. The questions challenge this proposition by pointing out that it entails that a world that is (by assumption) entirely just can become infected by injustice even if individuals in that world merely deploy their just holdings as they see fit without trenching on the just holdings of anyone else. Surely anyone who is committed to this entailment is obligated to explain *how* these relevantly innocuous actions can transform a just world into an unjust world.[3] As Nozick puts it:

> Is this new distribution $D_2$, unjust? If so, why? There is *no* question about whether each of the people was entitled to control over the resources they held in $D_1$; because that was the distribution (your favorite) that (for the purposes of argument) we assumed was acceptable ... By what process could such a transfer among two persons give rise to a legitimate claim of distributive justice on a portion of what was transferred, by a third party who had no claim of justice on any holding of the others *before* the transfer? (N: 161–162.)

Nozick's questions are, of course, intended to be rhetorical. He does not expect the pattern theorist to be able to provide an answer. For the only thing the pattern theorist *can* appeal to is the suboptimality of the resulting $D_2$. If the pattern theorist attempts to respond to Nozick by insisting on the non-innocuous character of certain processes that have been involved in the emergence of $D_2$, he abandons his own view that the justice of any distribution is entirely a matter of the degree to which it realizes the right sort of pattern and is not at all a matter of the processes by which it arises.

Pattern theories of distributive justice appeal to us because of what they seem to promise. They seem to promise that, at long last, each person will possess what she has a claim in justice to possess. But a major part of the appeal of this promise derives from our implicit understanding of what it means to at long last be allotted one's just endowment. Nozick's argument takes that implicit understanding to include the expectation that one will be allowed to dispose of one's justly allotted resources as one sees fit and without penalty as long as one's disposition does not preclude others from similarly employing their allotted resources as they see fit. Surely, what makes intuitively satisfying the assignment of certain holdings to individuals *as justly theirs* is the idea that these individuals will then be free, without penalty, to utilize these holdings as they respectively choose (either singularly or in voluntarily formed associations) to advance their values and projects. As Nozick asks about each share assigned under $D_1$, 'what was it for if not to do something with?' Especially since others have also received their just allotment, it is difficult to see how one's cultivation of one's own garden or one's cooperative cultivation of gardens with other consenting adults (which is what we take ourselves to be getting the right to do by way of the institutionalization of $D_1$) could give rise to others having valid complaints in justice against us. The institutionalization of the just $D_1$ is attractive to us because it promises the realization of people's entitlement to employ and dispose of their genuinely just holdings as they see fit. This is why when, subsequent to such employments and dispositions, the pattern theorist points out that the resulting distribution of holdings $D_2$ is unjust (because it can be converted into the better yet $D_3$), this iterated application of the favored pattern seems to violate the promise of its first application. In Hillel

Steiner's apt phrase, the iterated application of any pattern conception of justice 'creates rights to interfere with the rights which it has created'.[4]

So Nozick is actually making two distinct, but interconnected, points against the pattern theorist. First, the friend of pattern is bound to explain, but cannot explain, how quite innocuous actions (indeed, precisely the non-invasive utilitizations of resources the anticipation of which makes a justice-initiating distribution appealing) can inject injustice into a previously just world. Second, the program of the friend of pattern promises us more than the ongoing application of the favored pattern can deliver – precisely because the successive application of the pattern is incompatible with the entitlements to holdings that we expect under the banner of justice in holdings. 'Patterned distributional principles do not give people what entitlement principles do, only better distributed. For they do not give the right to choose what to do with what one has' (N: 167). [5]

In the particular case of Wilt Chamberlain, Nozick asks us to envision Chamberlain having arranged that everyone who enters his home arena to watch him play has to place 25 cents in special boxes whose contents are delivered to Chamberlain. By the end of the season during which these arrangements have been in place, one million fans have happily paid that extra 25 cents and Chamberlain has received US$250,000. (For the sake of simplicity, let us assume that this is the only payment Chamberlain receives.) $D_1$ is the distribution of holdings across the participating fans, non-participating non-fans, and Chamberlain at the start of the season; $D_2$ is the distribution at the end of the season, after those one million voluntary exchanges. The intuition Nozick expects every sensible person to share here is that, if one takes $D_1$ to have been just, then one should take $D_2$ to be just; the only plausible way to challenge the justice of $D_2$ is to challenge the justice of $D_1$. If one rejects this intuition, that is, if one holds that the (seemingly) innocuous exchanges between Chamberlain and the paying fans introduce injustice into the world, one is obligated to explain *how* such actions infect the world with injustice.

Any given pattern theorist who has accepted the justice of this $D_1$ will very likely have to deny the justice of this $D_2$ and, hence, have to explain how these innocuous acts inject injustice into the world. For it will very likely be the case that a portion of Chamberlain's concentrated post-season holdings can effectively be expropriated and redistributed to folks who are too poor to attend NBA games, whereas no effective expropriation and redistribution could have been performed on the dispersed pre-season holdings of Chamberlain's future patrons. When that $D_1$ obtained, there was no other distribution available that friends of equality-leaning patterns favor over $D_1$; but when $D_2$ comes into existence, through the interchange of Wilt and his fans, so also may the possibility of converting that $D_2$ into distribution $D_3$, which more fully satisfies the relevant tilt to equality than does $D_2$ (or $D_1$). When social engineering can achieve such a $D_3$, the equality-leaning pattern theorist who has certified the justice of $D_1$ must assert the injustice of $D_2$. But, in doing so, the pattern theorist obligates himself to perform the unperformable task of explaining how the innocuous interaction of Wilt and the fans injects injustice into $D_2$ and that theorist defaults on the promise that individuals will, without penalty, be free to dispose as they see fit of the holdings assigned under $D_1$.

Before turning to what seems to me to be the strongest challenge to this reconstituted Nozickian argument, I want to address briefly another fairly familiar challenge. One way for the pattern theorist to avoid the whole thrust of the present argument is to avoid condemning $D_2$ as unjust and, thereby, avoid the need to explain how $D_2$ becomes infected with injustice. It may seem that this avoidance can be accomplished by insisting that justice does not concern itself with isolated cases, but rather with a society's basic institutional structure. It may be maintained that society's basic institutional structure cannot be expected to respond to every isolated instance of disparity between what actually obtains and the fullest feasible realization of the pattern that guides the design and operation of that institutional structure. As long as the institutional structure is reasonably well designed and employed to promote the justifying pattern, that structure is just and isolated deviations from the fullest feasible realization of the pattern are *not* unjust.

My response to this challenge is to accept this enhanced focus on basic institutional structure (at least for the sake of argument) as long as it is still recognized that, for the pattern theorist, the justice of the basic structure and its activities still ultimately turns on that structure's propensity to bring about the pattern of holdings that is the ultimate justifying purpose of that basic structure. To this I would simply add that, within a large, complex, and (one presumes) economically dynamic society, the transformantion within the pattern of holdings as that social order moves from society-wide $D_1$ to society-wide $D_2$ by way of millions of individuals deploying, modifying, and exchanging what they possess under $D_1$ will involve much more than isolated departures from the favored profile. The transformation within the profile of holdings will be pervasive and substantial in magnitude. And the disparities between the resulting $D_2$ and the then fullest feasible realization of the justifying pattern, that is, between $D_2$ and $D_3$, will also be pervasive and substantial. So, as this $D_2$ emerges, a pattern-oriented basic institutional structure will have to condemn it as unjust and proceed to require its conversion into something much more like $D_3$. A basic institutional structure that does not intervene to recontour holdings toward $D_3$ will contravene its own justifying purpose. So the shift to a focus on institutional structure and the recognition that such a structure cannot be expected to micro-manage the actual world into the fullest possible realization of the favored pattern does not enable the pattern theorist to avoid the judgment that the $D_2$ that emerges from $D_1$ through those millions of actions and transactions is (or is very likely to be) unjust. Hence, this shift of focus does not enable the pattern theorist to avoid the need to explain how a $D_2$ that emerges from a just $D_1$ by way of individuals freely utilizing their $D_1$ holdings becomes unjust.

## Defending the reconstructed argument

A pattern theorist might well respond to my reconstruction of the 'How Liberty Upsets Patterns' argument by saying, he never promised us gardens to cultivate — at least not gardens over which we would have full liberal ownership. The pattern theorist may say, 'I merely promised that there would be a certain distribution among individuals of *lifetime* income or *lifetime* consumption of goods and services. When I endorsed distribution of holdings $D_1$ at $time_1$, I did so in the anticipation that $D_1$ would be the first phase within a series of distributive phases among individuals such that, when one adds up the holdings each moral subject will have in the whole course of the series, my favorite pattern among individuals' total lifetime holdings will be more fully realized than in any other possible series of distributive phases. Distributive justice calls for such a best realization of the favored pattern within people's lifetime possessions; it does not call for the realization of the favored pattern within each or even within any one distributive phase. Various "interventionist" measures (in particular, various tax and subsidy policies) almost certainly will be an essential part of the plan for achieving this best possible series of distributive phases. What is allotted to individuals in the name of distributive justice is their lifetime distributive shares as they are made possible and shaped by these measures. "Interventions" that are part and parcel of the overall scheme do not contravene the entitlements assigned by justice, but, rather, are the means of sustaining just lifetime shares. Since those interventions are part of the whole scheme for insuring distributive justice, they do not run contrary to anyone's legitimate expectations. They do not come into conflict with any promise made by the pattern theorist.'

The essence of the pattern theorist's response is that the institutionalization of his favored pattern promises people certain streams of income over their lifetimes — streams that will be contoured by certain tax and subsidy policies. Or, perhaps, it would be clearer to say that the pattern theorist offers people a certain income regime, where an income regime consists in certain tax and subsidy policies, including a specification of how the rates of different taxes and subsidies will vary over people's lifetimes as diverse social circumstances vary. Particular individuals are not assured specific flows of income; rather, they are assured that a particular income regime will be in force — a basic institutional structure that is chosen in order to maximally realize some favored pattern of lifetime incomes. A pattern theorist will identify the income regime that will be advanced as just in the following way. He will anticipate how individuals will behave over their lifetimes under each of a number of different sets of tax and subsidy policies and, thereby, anticipate what distribution of lifetime income each of these sets of tax and subsidy policies will yield. He will then pick the income regime that he anticipates will yield the distribution of lifetime income that most fully realizes his favored pattern.[6] For instance, if he is a friend of the difference principle, he will pick the regime that he anticipates will provide a higher long-term income for the least advantaged members of society than he anticipates will be provided by any other regime.[7]

Suppose the pattern theorist's chosen income regime, $R_1$, is institutionalized in anticipation of its yielding a distribution of lifetime income, $LD_1$. The crucial inconvenient facts for the pattern theorist's present response are: (a) it is almost certain that innocuous actions of individuals who conduct themselves entirely in accord with regime $R_1$ will generate distribution $LD_2$, not $LD_1$; and (b) when $LD_2$ is generated, it will almost certainly pervasively and extensively depart from the distribution that, among all the distributions that have then become available, maximally realizes the favored pattern. The reason that $LD_2$, rather than $LD_1$, will almost certainly arise is that many individuals, *in unanticipated ways*, will unilaterally enhance the value of what they produce and are allowed to keep under $R_1$ or what they are allowed to purchase with what they produce and are allowed to keep under $R_1$. In addition, these or many other individuals, *in unanticipated ways*, will engage in mutually beneficial exchange of what they produce and are allowed to keep uner $R_1$.[8] Unless people are effectively prohibited from transforming and exchanging their own just holdings under $R_1$ in accordance with the (non-Stalinist) rules of $R_1$, there will always be many individuals who will find unexpected ways to enhance the value of their holdings by unilateral alteration of those holdings or by mutually agreeable exchange. Furthermore, it is almost certain that, once these unanticipated actions and transactions are performed, the resulting $LD_2$ will depart significantly from the best distribution that has then become available. It is almost certain that any actually produced $LD_2$ will be convertible into another distribution of lifetime income, $LD_3$ that will significantly more realize the favored pattern than does $LD_2$. The reigning pattern theory of justice will, therefore, require that people be subject to a new income regime $R_3$ (a new basic institutional structure) that is designed to yield $LD_3$.[9]

I should emphasize that these pattern-upsetting capitalist acts are not *underground* capitalist acts. The individuals who achieve unexpectedly high incomes act fully in accord with regime $R_1$; this includes their payment of whatever taxes apply to their additional income or wealth under $R_1$. $LD_2$ is the distribution of lifetime incomes that obtains *after* these individuals pay the taxes they owe under $R_1$. That is why, given the supposition that $R_1$ is just, it seems that $LD_2$ must be just — or at least not unjust. More explicitly, if $R_1$ is a just income regime and $LD_2$ arises under $R_1$ by innocuous actions that involve some people making unanticipated gains and no one being rendered worse off, then $LD_2$ is a just (or at least a not unjust) income distribution. The pattern theorist who affirms the justice of $R_1$ but who asserts the injustice of $LD_2$ will be faced with the same puzzles as were posed by Nozick to the theorist who affirms the justice of $D_1$ but rejects the justice of $D_2$. If $R_1$ is a just income regime, then one should be as puzzled about how the unanticipated distribution $LD_2$, which arises under $R_1$ by way of innocuous capitalist acts among solitary or consenting individuals, could be infected with injustice as one should be puzzled about how $D_2$, which arises from a just $D_1$ by some similarly innocuous acts, could be infected with injustice.

Surely, if $R_1$ amounts to the rules of a just distribution game, no one can have any complaint in justice against any resulting $LD_2$ that emerges from individuals acting in ways that are both innocuous and fully in compliance with those rules. If one asserts such a complaint, one must take up the unenviable task of explaining *how* innocuous actions in accord with the rules of a just system give rise to injustice. To tell individuals that they may not retain what they have acquired fully in accord with the rules of a just income regime is, in effect, to rescind that regime; just as to tell people that they may not retain what they transform their just holdings into or what they get in trade for their just holdings is to rescind the assignment of those holdings to those individuals as their just holdings. To tell individuals that they may not retain what they have acquired fully in accord with the rules of a just income regime is, to modify Steiner's quip, to create income regimes that violate the income regimes that one has created.

The point that affirming the justice of $R_1$ strongly pushes one toward affirming the justice of $LD_2$ can be made somewhat more concretely by considering the case of Sally who has a certain expected lifetime income under $R_1$. Suppose that Sally, first, somehow guarantees the other interested parties that she will indeed continue to perform the actions on the basis of which it is expected that this stream of income will accrue to her and, second, sells the rights to that expected income stream to Harry for a lump-sum payment. Let us suppose further that Sally and Harry only engage in this exchange for the sake of the further opportunities they believe it will offer to them. Hence, the exchange itself does not disrupt $LD_1$. But, having got hold of this lump sum, Sally now purchases various materials and in her spare time (not the time she still devotes to her originally anticipated activities) she converts those materials into more valuable objects in ways that impose no loss on anyone else. Even after she pays taxes under $R_1$ on her incremental income, Sally's activities add up to a transformation of $LD_1$ into $LD_2$. (Or, if one objects to the isolated case, we could adjust the story to include lots of other Sally-like people.) If $R_1$ is a just income regime and Sally proceeds in the manner described, it would seem that this resulting $LD_2$ is a just, or at least a not unjust, income distribution.[10] But, of course, if $LD_2$ is a just, or even a not unjust, income distribution, then justice in income distribution cannot be entirely a matter of comportment with some favored pattern of income distribution. The explanation of the justice, or non-injustice, of $LD_2$ will have to invoke the historical fact that $LD_2$ arose under (what has been stipulated as being) a just regime by means of certain innocuous actions. The judgment that $LD_2$ is just will not depend upon the contrary-to-fact determination that, having come into existence, $LD_2$ is the available distribution that most fully realizes the favored pattern.

The steadfast pattern theorist must deny the justice of $LD_2$. Since positing the justice of $R_1$ presses one to the conclusion that $LD_2$ is just, the steadfast pattern theorist has to deny that people have a claim in justice to the basic institutional structure that is regime $R_1$ — just as the pattern theorist has had to deny that people have a claim in justice to $D_1$ in order to deny the justice of $D_2$. The response we have formulated on behalf of the pattern theorist to the 'How Liberty Upsets Patterns' argument is that $D_1$ is not itself just; $D_1$ is merely the first phase of a series of distributions of holdings that, it is hoped, will add up to the fullest realization of his favored pattern. The response we must now formulate on behalf of the still steadfast pattern theorist to my 'Unanticipated Action Upsets Income Regimes' argument is that income regime $R_1$ is not itself just. Institutional structure $R_1$ *itself* is merely the first phase of a series of institutional structures that, it is hoped, will yield over the long term the fullest realization of the favored pattern. (And the later phases cannot be described in advance; if they could be, all the phases would be parts of one mega-regime.)

In order to maintain allegiance to his favored pattern, the pattern theorist has to say that his doctrine never promises people any particular, identifiable, institutionalized income regime. Rather, in the name of distributive justice, people are promised income regimes that will be change periodically (in light of what income streams have come into existence and what new technologies for generating income streams and for redistributing them seem to have been discovered) so as to attempt to produce an optimal long-term distribution. Not only ought people not to count on the particular holdings assigned to them under $D_1$ (or to what they transform those holdings into or get in exchange for them), people ought not to count on what they are said to be entitled to under any particular income regime $R_1$ or even any series of regimes $R_1$-$R_{n-1}$. At most, people can *hope* that there will be some last phase during which an income regime $R_n$ will be instituted that, by correcting for all the errors embodied in previous regimes and taking advantage of the latest technologies of redistribution, will *at last* yield a just distribution of lifetime incomes among them. Or, more precisely, people can at most hope that there will be a final $R_n$ that will yield the best lifetime distribution among those that are still available after all the errors of regimes $R_1$-$R_{n-1}$.

The problem with this final fall-back position for the pattern theorist is that it puts us all in the dark about what our just income claims really are — at least until that final judgment is rendered. We may proceed from one income regime to another, each time doing the best we can to establish a set of rules and policies that will maximally realize the favored pattern across all the contemplated time periods. But we will quickly learn the foolishness of describing the income that anyone receives under any given regime as his just income. For we will quickly learn that social calculations in the not very distant future will very likely reclassify at least some of that income as unjust. No one will be able to count her income chickens, no matter how thoroughly the acquisition of these income chickens has been in accord with the norms of past and present justice-seeking income regimes, until this hoped for final regime has been hatched. Nor, it should be emphasized, will individuals merely be subject to minor adjustments in their lifetime incomes. Which alterations should be made to people's prospective lifetime incomes by the income regime that is presently coming online will depend on complex calculations of social interests. The most reasonable calculations at any given time may very well indicate that the favored pattern of lifetime income will best be served by a new income regime that entirely or substantially eliminates entire categories of income that were protected under previous income regimes.

For example, it is easy to imagine calculations that would seem to reveal that the way to save the social security system and thereby, best serve the favored pattern is to impose a tax of 75 percent on the social security payments of recipients who, aside from these payments, have an annual income of at least US$50,000. Previous income regimes did not recognize the need to save social security in this way, but now our most talented social calculators judge that this tax has to be imposed for the sake of the favored pattern. Indeed, these calculators may now judge that the favored pattern is most promoted by a new regime in which that tax is applied retroactively.[11] Moreover, there is nothing in principle that blocks the new regime, especially if it is that final regime $R_n$, from adjustments of income that on net will move people who had every expectation from their experience of previous regimes of having relatively high lifetime incomes to relatively low lifetime incomes (and vice versa). Such surprising adjustments will be seen to be required by justice if the most up-to-date calculations indicate that they will yield a lifetime distribution of income that significantly more realizes the guiding pattern.

Even our most talented social calculators will (I am contending) be systematically unable to anticipate how people will act within the strictures of the income regimes that they recommend; and they will be unable to anticipate how later social calculators will respond to these acts in their design of new income regimes. That is why the conscientious institution of new income regimes in the ongoing quest for justice in the lifetime distribution of income will frequently have to deprive individuals of what they expected to be their just income or even of previous income that has been viewed as just and will alert people to the fact that their current claims may well be subject to similar abnegation. Indeed, the problem for the steadfast pattern theorist can be restated in terms of legitimate expectations. A just income regime must allow people, through their actions under that regime, to establish various legitimate expectations, for example, to retain the post-tax income that they have earned under the rules of that regime, and must protect rather than defeat the fulfillment of these legitimate expectations. But the protection of these expectations will amount to the sanctioning of distribution $LD_2$ even when our best updated social calculations indicate that $LD_2$ is convertible into a distribution $LD_3$ that will significantly more fully realize the favored pattern. Continued allegiance to the pattern requires disloyalty to the expectations deemed legitimate under the previous applications of the pattern. The prospect of ongoing allegiance to the favored pattern undermines the very formation of legitimate expectations.

In the name of justice the steadfast pattern theorist can offer people an ongoing effort to establish that sequence of regimes that over time seems most likely to yield a fuller realization of the favored pattern than any other (still) available distribution. Yet this effort precludes offering to people currently identifiable distribution-regulating institutions that they can in justice count on as a basis for *their* ongoing projects and endeavors. The steadfast pattern theorist cannot offer to people the *establishment* of a set of just holdings or a just income-regulating structure that will form the basis for their getting on with life through their deployment of their just holdings or their navigation within a system of known just rules. People will not get to live under just circumstances, but rather will continually have to undergo adjustments to what has been said to be their just holdings or just income regime in the name of ever new understandings of how best to realize the cherished pattern. For the steadfast pattern theorist, justice is relentlessly forward looking. However, individuals can be forward looking *under just arrangements* only if justice itself is not relentlessly forward looking.

So let me sum up my rejoinder to the pattern theorist's response to my reconstruction of the 'How Liberty Upsets Patterns' argument. The pattern theorist who turns from time-slice distributions to income regimes must affirm or deny the justice of $R_1$. If he affirms the justice of $R_1$, it looks like he will have to affirm the justice of $LD_2$. And since $LD_2$ will significantly less realize his favored pattern than would $LD_3$ (into which $LD_2$ can be converted), he will have to acknowledge that distributive justice is not entirely a matter of comportment with some sanctified pattern. If, instead, the pattern theorist denies the justice of $R_1$, he will have to say that rather than individuals having claims in justice to any particular income regime and, hence, to what they acquire in accordance with the rules of that regime, they have claims in justice to a periodic readjustment of regimes that, it is hoped, will eventually and cumulatively yield just lifetime distributions. But this ceaseless pursuit of the elusive fullest realization of some favored pattern eliminates (or at least delays until that most longed for final judgment) the fulfillment of people's legitimate expectations. And it eliminates (or at least delays until the era issued in by that final judgment) the establishment of just circumstances.[12] Against the steadfast pattern theorist we can invoke a dictum usually associated with retributive justice rather than distributive justice: justice delayed is justice denied.

## Notes

1 (N : xxx) are page references for Nozick, R. *Anarchy, State, and Utopia* (New York: Basic Books, 1974).
2 Here is another way in which, on any given pattern-based view, injustice can emerge from justice without any morally problematic activity (on the part of those who will be said to have begun to have unjust holdings). Suppose that $D_1$ simply persists from time$_1$ to time$_2$. But in the interim, someone has discovered an effective technique for realizing to a greater yet extent the anointed pattern. For example, if the pattern is significantly egalitarian, the discovery of an effective moral incentive for the most productive (perhaps public initiation into the Productivity Hall of Fame) will make possible a greater downward distribution of holdings from the more productive to the less productive and, hence, a better-yet realization of that egalitarian structure. When this better-yet distribution of holdings becomes possible through the miracles of better techniques of social engineering, the previously just $D_1$ must be condemned as unjust. (Or we must say that what previously *seemed* to be just has now been revealed not to have been just.)
3 The argument here admittedly relies on the intuition that, if $D_1$ is just and $D_2$ arises from $D_1$ via certain actions and $D_2$ is unjust, then some defect in those actions must play a role in explaining the injustice of $D_2$. This intuition would be undercut if we had at hand a convincing argument for some robust pattern principle. For then an advocate of that pattern could say that $D_1$ is just when it obtains because, at that time, it is the fullest available realization of the proven pattern and that $D_2$ is unjust when it obtains because, at that time, it deviates

significantly from the fullest available realizing of the proven pattern and that the quality of the actions that transform $D_1$ into $D_2$ have nothing to do with the injustice of $D_2$. So lurking behind my sharing of the present intuition is my belief that we do not have at hand a convincing argument for any robust pattern principle.

4  Hillel Steiner, 'The Natural Right to the Means of Production', *Philosophical Quarterly* 27 (January 1977): p. 43. As Steiner also points out, the argument of 'How Liberty Upsets Patterns' only undermines *purely* patterned conceptions of justice. The argument does not show any incoherence in a doctrine that combines a pattern for initial holdings with acceptance of what arises by just steps from those initially just holdings. (But, one might argue that once one is partially liberated from pattern worship, even the proposal that initial holdings be patterned will lose its luster.)

5  But, when Nozick makes this remark, he is focused on the special case of pattern theories not allowing one, without penalty, to use one's distributional share for 'the enhancement of another's position'.

6  That such anticipations are pipedreams is the basis for the response that follows. As Scott Arnold reminds me, that 'those setting tax and subsidy policy are exclusively motivated by the desire to do what is just' is another pipedream.

7  Here and over the next several paragraphs, I assume that all lifetimes are temporally coextensive. The fact that there is not one generation in which all lives are temporally coextensive complicates things considerably for the theorist who, out of loyalty to some favored pattern, holds that income regimes should be revised as more information comes in relevant to what income regime will yield the best long-term distribution of income.

8  Other individuals will, in unanticipated ways, unilaterally diminish their holdings under $R_1$.

9  Had these pattern-disrupting, capitalist actions been anticipated, our farsighted pattern theorist would have factored them into the original choice of what income regime should be instituted. Had they been anticipated, income regime $R_3$ (which is $R_1$ plus the procedures for converting $LD_2$ into $LD_3$) would have been adopted. Of course, were it *known* to the relevant individuals that they were living under $R_3$ rather than $R_1$, they might very well *not* engage in the income-enhancing actions that, if they occur, makes $LD_3$ possible. This points to the interesting question of whether a pattern theorist should favor an income regime with *secret* clauses if the secrecy of those clauses makes possible a fuller realization of his favored pattern for the distribution of lifetime income.

10  As is appropriate, this case is an adaptation to income regimes of Nozick's example of the individual in a socialist economy who does some extra work in his spare time with materials assigned to him under the socialist regime (N: 161–162).

11  It will have been highly convenient *not* to have previously anticipated the need for this tax to save social security. For, had this need been previously anticipated (that is, had better-off people recognized that their contributions would not be earning them entitlements, to the projected payments) there would have been much less public support for the establishment of the system.

12  David Hume, as Scott Arnold reminds me, is the most famous advocate of the idea that justice requires known and stable ascriptions of property rights. See, especially, David Hume, *A Treatise on Human Nature* (Oxford: Oxford University Press, 1968), Book III, Part II, Sections I–VI. An alternative expression of the argument of this section is that: (a) justice requires either the 'old property' that consists in rights to particular holdings *or* at least the 'new property' that consists in rights to the operation of known and stable administrative rules; but (b) allegiance to a favored pattern in a world of systematically unanticipated developments precludes the institution of *either* the old or the new property.

# 8 On Rectification in Nozick's Minimal State

Robert E. Litan

In the short time since its publication in 1974, *Anarchy, State, and Utopia*, by Robert Nozick,[1] has been criticized by several authors for the weakness of its libertarian foundations.[2] This essay, however, takes Nozick's libertarian principles seriously and applies them to the single most important issue Nozick admits leaving untreated – the theory of rectification.[3]

The following discussion will advance two central propositions. First, it will be argued that, as practiced, rectification would be limited by Nozick's own "minimal state" principles generally to the correction of wrongs committed during, but not before, an individual's lifetime. In effect, then, initial entitlements would be treated in the same "hands-off" manner in the minimal state as natural assets and cultural background. However, if one remains unconvinced by the case for "limited rectification," the second part of the essay will suggest that nothing in Nozick's exposition precludes a strictly egalitarian distribution of entitlements. That this outcome would be permitted by a libertarian theory should, at the very least, prove surprising to those who are tempted to embrace it.

## The Case for Limited Rectification

Nozick's theory of distributive justice is outlined in his "theory of entitlements." One is entitled to a good or holding under this theory if it has been acquired in accordance with the principles of both justice in acquisition and justice in transfer.

The need for rectification arises in the minimal state when either the principle of justice in acquisition or the principle of justice in transfer is violated. What is not immediately apparent from Nozick's exposition, however, is (1) whether or not a rectification claimant must show a personal link between the alleged injustice and his personal welfare, and (2) if so, what degree of proof is required for such a showing.

These issues can be put into sharper focus by distinguishing between intragenerational and intergenerational rectification procedures. Intragenerational rectification refers to compensation for victims who are alive to collect their rectification awards (or compensation awards arising out of legal actions initiated by the victim's estate). Intergenerational rectification encompasses all injustices and, in theory, ensures that the present distribution of entitlements be that which would have obtained had only the principles of justice in acquisition and justice in transfer been observed throughout history. Quite obviously, the undertaking of intergenerational rectification is a far more ambitious task than rectifying only present injustices.

More important, whatever degree of proof is required, it ordinarily is much more difficult to establish a personal link between alleged injustices and the welfare of the individual rectification claimant for intergenerational than for intragenerational claims. The claimant who is alive is obviously in a much better position to prove that, had an alleged injustice not taken place, he personally would have been better off than the direct or indirect descendant of a dead victim of injustice who was never compensated during his or her lifetime.

As a concrete example, consider the case of two individuals, Black and White, in generation "one," each of whom have one child, Black-son and White-son, respectively, belonging to the "second" generation. Suppose that White during his lifetime violates either the principle of justice in acquisition or justice in transfer in such a manner that Black suffers damage. Clearly, if rectification proceeded during the first generation, all future claims by any descendants of Black for rectification awards would be groundless. The interesting question, however, arises if rectification is not accomplished in the first generation. Does Black-son, as a lineal descendant of Black, have a claim against White-son, the lineal descendant of White?

To illustrate the conceptual difficulties here, imagine the Black has waived his right to the award or has spent it entirely on nondurable goods. Under such circumstances, Black-son would have no claim to it. In the absence of some evidence of what Black would have done with the award had he received it, therefore, Black-son would face an impossible task in attempting to show that by some recognized standard of proof he would have been the beneficiary.[4] Of course, if he could meet such a burden, Nozick would grant him his claim, since as a matter of law Nozick would require White-son to fulfill the unpaid obligation of his ancestor(s) on the theory that property unjustly inherited is not rightfully owned.

Thus, if rectification claimants are required to establish a "sense of personal grievance" (namely, a connection between an alleged injustice and the claimant's personal welfare), then rectification will proceed in Nozick's minimal state only for present injustices and those very few past injustices where plaintiffs can sustain their burdens of proof. In traditional civil actions in the United States today, plaintiffs must ordinarily establish that "more probably than not" their claims are meritorious. But, even under a more lenient standard, it is doubtful, under a rectification scheme where plaintiffs are charged with showing a personal grievance, whether rectification would extend much beyond intragenerational claims.[5]

The foregoing case for limited rectification rests on the view that the rectification plaintiff must establish a personal sense of grievance. If, however, the rectification defendant is charged with proving his personal *right* to a particular set of entitlements, the scope for intergenerational rectification is broadened considerably. Consequently, it is of critical importance in rectification theory who must establish the "personal link" – the plaintiff or the defendant.

Close adherence to the spirit, if not the letter, of Nozick's libertarian theory argues in favor of the initial view that requires plaintiffs to establish their personal link with the wrong(s) in question. A fundamental tenet of the theory is that it takes the anarchist position seriously, and therefore requires an elaborate justification of even a "minimal night-watchman" state. In the language of the law, a presumption exists against the legitimacy of state action.

Discussing the related issue of rights to natural assests, Nozick remarks:

> It is not true, for example, that a person who earns Y (a right to keep a painting he's made, praise for writing *A Theory of Justice*, and so on) only if he's earned (or otherwise deserves) whatever he used (including natural assets) in the process of earning Y. Some of the things he uses he just may *have*, not illegitimately. It needn't be that the foundations underlying desert are themselves deserved, *all the way down*. [p. 225]

The tenor of this discussion is inconsistent with the view that defendants, if challenged by rectification claimants, must prove personal rights to their entitlements. For if each individual is forced by the state to prove historical title for each of his holdings, then a presumption will have been established in favor of the state to take property absent an affirmative showing that title is vested. Thus, only a rule requiring plaintiffs to prove the legitimacy of their rectification claims is consistent with the libertarian foundations of the minimal state.

Under these conditions, therefore, the scope of rectification would be limited, in practice, almost exclusively to actions concerning present injustices. This would, of course, leave the distribution of inherited entitlements largely untouched in each generation. Consequently, just as individuals are, according to Nozick, "entitled" to the natural assets they bring with them into the world (p. 225), the limited rectification procedure would, in all but a few exceptional cases, award entitlements as a matter of right to members of incoming generations to whom property has been properly bequeathed.

As Nozick recognizes, his entitlement theory of natural assets allows the element of chance to govern the distribution of natural assets. But Nozick sees nothing wrong in randomness per se, maintaining that the distributional process, not its result, must be just. The effect of the foregoing arguments for limited rectification should not, therefore, disturb him, since the addition of entitlements to the list of factors to be randomly distributed offends nothing in his conceptual framework.

Nevertheless, it is still puzzling why, in claiming a need for a broader intergenerational rectification policy, Nozick should single out entitlements to property to be governed by the principle of historical determination. Why is it appropriate to trace only the lineage of property, and not genes or family and social background? Why is it just that I should be the product of a relationship between my particular mother and father, both of whom I did not choose to be my procreators? If the answer is that the present generation is bound to live by the free mating choices of prior generations, just as it is bound to live by the free choices of entitlement transfers of prior generations, then what about the products of rape victims or procreative activities where one of the parties did not choose, of his own free will, to be involved (arranged marriages)? Certainly in these cases some doubts must arise about the "justice" of the gene pools that are transmitted to future generations.

More important, the cultural environment one inherits today was influenced by prior property distributions. Thus, while it may be possible to "rectify" the wealth held by the Rockefellers, it would be quite difficult, if not impossible, to "rectify" their social and family background, both of which are products, partial or total, of past property transactions (some of which may have been unjust). Yet, to do nothing to rectify social and family backgrounds is to accept possibly the influence of unjust property transactions on the present distribution of family and social backgrounds.

The foregoing discussion about genes and environment should indicate how truly arbitrary it is to require entitlements alone to submit to rectification. If Nozick is willing to accept the arbitrariness and randomness of the genes and environment of the present-day generation, both of which are either infected by "injustices" of their own (in the case of rape and coerced marriages for genes) or injustices in the realm of entitlements (in the cases of environment and genes), he should not be reluctant to accept the randomness and arbitrariness of inherited entitlements.

Logically, then, it is only appropriate that entitlements be treated in the same fashion as natural assets and cultural background. Either all should submit to the process of historical justification or all should be subject to random determination; there is no justification for singling out entitlements alone for historical examination. Given Nozick's obvious reluctance to pursue a program of rectifying genes and cultural background in addition to entitlements, consistency demands that the principle of randomness govern all three.

## Alternate Rules of Rectification

Suppose, however, that one remains unconvinced by the case presented for limited rectification. In particular, if the burden of proof is placed on individual defendants to justify their rights to their present sets of holdings, under what conditions would one proceed with intergenerational rectification, *knowing that the presence of imperfect information about the past would inevitably lead to mistakes?*

In theory, intergenerational rectification would, under the criteria Nozick outlines, utilize "historical information about previous situations and injustices done in them (as defined by the first two principles of justice and rights against interference), and information about the actual course of events that flowed from these injustices, until the present" to describe a just set of holdings (p. 152). Intergenerational rectification would, then, presumably only be needed once, to bring the initial distribution of entitlements into line with the "just" distribution. Thereafter, intragenerational rectification would be sufficient to correct present wrongs as they occur.

If Nozick's theory of distributive justice is taken seriously, and a broader form of rectification is permissible, determining the "justness" of the present distribution requires an inquiry not only into the justice of all prior transfers, but also into the original acquisitions at some beginning point of time and at subsequent times when groups of men have discovered new, previously uninhabited geographical areas. Compensation is then required for violations of both the principles of justice in acquisition and justice in transfer.[6]

In condensed form, the state which engages in intergenerational rectification would therefore need the following items of information:

(1) Those instances in which the principle of justice in acquisition was violated, the parties committing such violations, the victims, and the amounts of compensation owed.
(2) Those instances in which the principle of justice in transfer was violated, the parties committing such violations, the victims, and the amounts of compensation owed.
(3) The change in the property distribution at time "one" generated by the different capital distribution following compensation.
(4) The alteration of inheritance patterns in all subsequent generations induced by the compensation payments.

In turn, these items would require knowledge of the preferences of all persons throughout time (preferences between goods, between present consumption and saving, and between heirs) and each person's productivity (to compute interest rates tailored to each individual) in order to fix levels of compensation payments at each point in time. Furthermore, as one proceeded to determine the effects of compensation paid at time "one" on future generations, the errors would be multiplicative, growing to enormous levels over time.

Listing the informational requirements should illustrate what Nozick's rectification principle, applied on an intergenerational basis, actually entails. While it is true that the informational burden would be considerably eased if instead of beginning at time "one," the rectification inquiry began in, say, 1800 or 1900, the four essential categories of information would still be required, leaving a gargantuan task for the intergenerational rectifier.

In fact, however, a strict application of the principle of intergenerational rectification would preclude "wiping the slate clean" at arbitrary points of time for the sake of convenience. Instead, it would, in the limit, require an inquiry only into those injustices that occurred in the original acquisitions at the beginning of time and the points in history thereafter when previously unowned land and property were appropriated. For if such injustices were, in fact, significant, then certainly the distribution in all subsequent generations would have been markedly different had compensation been paid for violations of justice in acquisition at the times such violations occurred.[7] In a very real sense, then, historical events between time "one" and the present generation would have little significance for the present-day rectifier, since the course of history would have been different during that long interim period.[8]

Realizing the serious informational problems with inquiries into either injustices in acquisition at some beginning point of time or injustices in transfer at points throughout history, Nozick offers a second-best solution which employs the best estimate of "subjunctive information about what would have occurred" but for the injustices (pp. 152-153). Interestingly, he admits that pattern rules of distribution may serve as a "rough rule of thumb" to supplement this estimation procedure. Thus, if a case can be made that those who are worst-off in present society have the highest probabilities of being the descendants of victims of past injustices, then a rectifier would, in the short run, be justified in employing a Rawlsian-like rule which suggests redistribution in a manner which maximizes the position of those presently worst-off (p. 231).

## Conclusion

The scope of rectification rests on who must prove the personal link with the alleged wrongs, the plaintiff who could be charged with showing how he or she has been personally aggrieved, or the defendant who could be required to prove his personal right to his present set of holdings. Nozick's theory seems to be consistent only with the view that plaintiffs must establish such personal links, implying that rectification in the minimal state should, in all but a few exceptional cases, be limited to intragenerational claims for compensation.

Supposing, however, that intergenerational rectification is pursued, the rule of rectification that is most consistent with Nozick's theory is one in which entitlements are distributed to conform with the means of the "just entitlements probability distributions" of the individuals in society. Depending on what date in history the rectification inquiry commences, this procedure may require entitlements to be redistributed in an egalitarian fashion. Indeed, the egalitarian result can only be avoided if the date at which the rectification inquiry is started is moved close enough to the present to generate meaningful differences in the just entitlements probability distributions of the members of society. And, then, such inegalitarian redistribution can only be legitimately pursued if the characteristics on which the rectification procedure is based are specified with sufficient care.

Nothing in Nozick's theory enables us to determine at what date the rectification inquiry should be started, however. Unfortunately, it is on the resolution of that threshold issue that the results of a broader intergenerational rectification procedure depend. Without an answer to that important issue, however, there can be no theoretical objection to the egalitarian solution. In light of the antilibertarian criticism—much of it imbued with notions of egalitarianism—which Nozick's theory is certain to receive in the next few years, this egalitarian result is paradoxical, to say the least.

## Notes

1. Robert Nozick, *Anarchy, State, and Utopia* (New York, 1974).
2. See Thomas Nagel, "Book Review: Libertarianism Without Foundations," *Yale Law Journal* (November 1975): 136-149; Milton Himmelfarb, "Liberals and Libertarians," *Commentary* (June 1975): 65-70; Hal R. Varian, "Distributive Justice, Welfare Economics, and the Theory of Fairness," *Philosophy and Public Affairs* (Spring 1975): 221-247; and the book review by Brian Barry, *Political Theory* (August 1975): 331-336.
3. See Nozick, p. 152.
4. In the language of David Lyons, Black-son would not acquire a "right" to his award unless he could show that he was the "intended beneficiary." For a full discussion of the rights of beneficiaries, see David Lyons, "Rights, Claimants, and Beneficiaries," *American Philosophical Quarterly* 6 (1969): 173-185, and a response by H.L.A. Hart, "Bentham on Legal Rights," in *Oxford Essays in Jurisprudence*, A.W.B. Simpson, ed. (Oxford, 1973), pp. 171-201.
5. Hal Varian offers another method of weakening Nozick's rectification requirement by attacking the legitimacy of inheritance (Varian, pp. 237-238). For if inheritance itself lacks justification, then there is no link between present and past distributions of entitlements, and therefore there can be no foundation for efforts toward intergenerational rectification. Varian's approach is not pursued here, however, since it can be argued that the right of transfer legitimates inheritance and, second, that the incentive effects of the right to bequeath property may generate more benefits than harms (thereby justifying a resort to the Lockean exception).
6. Presumably, Nozick's criteria for compensation for violations of the principle of justice in acquisition would be the same as for prohibitions of certain risky activities: pay enough compensation to put the victim back at his original level of indifference. Needless to say, the task of determining the amounts of compensation owed to persons long dead for previous injustices, themselves often unknown, would be extremely difficult, if not impossible.
7. If injustices at "time one" were not "significant," then presumably at some point in time transfer injustices achieved a level of significance at which it could be said that the course of subsequent distributions was markedly affected. The argument therefore retains its force under slightly different conditions.
8. Assuming that justice in transfer obtained in subsequent generations, then, the justice of today's distribution depends on the distribution of such abilities among

all of our ancestors throughout history. Given that the distributions of these abilities were random at each stage in history, it follows that today's "just" distribution, too, has been randomly determined. This fortifies the claim made earlier that since Nozick is undisturbed by randomness per se, he should not be bothered by arguments which, in practice, limit his rectification inquiry to intragenerational injustices. See the discussion in the preceding section.

# 9 Justice as Mutual Advantage

## David Gauthier

### Overview of a Theory

What theory of morals can ever serve any useful purpose, unless it can show that all the duties it recommends are also the true interest of each individual?[1] David Hume, who asked this question, seems mistaken; such a theory would be too useful. Were duty no more than interest, morals would be superfluous. Why appeal to right or wrong, to good or evil, to obligation or to duty, if instead we may appeal to desire or aversion, to benefit or cost, to interest or to advantage? An appeal to morals takes its point from the failure of these latter considerations as sufficient guides to what we ought to do. The unphilosophical poet Ogden Nash grasped the assumptions underlying our moral language more clearly than the philosopher Hume when he wrote:

'O Duty!
Why hast thou not the visage of a sweetie or a cutie?'[2]

We may lament duty's stern visage but we may not deny it. For it is only as we believe that some appeals do, alas, override interest or advantage that morality becomes our concern.

But if the language of morals is not that of interest, it is surely that of reason. What theory of morals, we might better ask, can ever serve any useful purpose, unless it can show that all the duties it recommends are also truly endorsed in each individual's reason? If moral appeals are entitled to some practical effect, some influence on our behaviour, it is not because they whisper invitingly to our desires, but because they convince our intellect. Suppose we should find, as Hume himself believes, that reason is impotent in the sphere of action apart from its role in deciding matters of fact.[3] Or suppose we should find that reason is no more than the handmaiden of interest, so that in overriding advantage a moral appeal must also contradict reason. In either case we should conclude that the moral enterprise, as traditionally conceived, is impossible.

To say that our moral language assumes a connection with reason is not to argue for the rationality of our moral views, or of any alternative to them.

Moral language may rest on a false assumption.[4] If moral duties are rationally grounded, then the emotivists, who suppose that moral appeals are no more than persuasive, and the egoists, who suppose that rational appeals are limited by self-interest, are mistaken.[5] But are moral duties rationally grounded? This we shall seek to prove, showing that reason has a practical role related to but transcending individual interest, so that principles of action that prescribe duties overriding advantage may be rationally justified. We shall defend the traditional conception of morality as a rational constraint on the pursuit of individual interest.

Yet Hume's mistake in insisting that moral duties must be the true interest of each individual conceals a fundamental insight. Practical reason is linked to interest, or, as we shall come to say, to individual utility, and rational constraints on the pursuit of interest have themselves a foundation in the interest they constrain. Duty overrides advantage, but the acceptance of duty is truly advantageous. We shall find this seeming paradox embedded in the very structure of interaction. As we come to understand this structure, we shall recognize the need for restraining each person's pursuit of her own utility, and we shall examine its implications for both our principles of action and our conception of practical rationality. Our enquiry will lead us to the rational basis for a morality, not of absolute standards, but of agreed constraints.

We shall develop a theory of morals. Our concern is to provide a justificatory framework for moral behaviour and principles, not an explanatory framework. Thus we shall develop a normative theory. A complete philosophy of morals would need to explain, and perhaps to defend, the idea of a normative theory. We shall not do this. But we shall exemplify normative theory by sketching the theory of rational choice. Indeed, we shall do more. We shall develop a theory of morals as part of the theory of rational choice. We shall argue that the rational principles for making choices, or decisions among possible actions, include some that constrain the actor pursuing his own interest in an impartial way. These we identify as moral principles.

The study of choice begins from the stipulation of clear conceptions of value and rationality in a form applicable to choice situations.[6] The theory then analyses the structure of these situations so that, for each type of structure distinguished, the conception of rationality may be elaborated into a set of determinate conditions on the choice among possible actions. These conditions are then expressed as precise principles of rational behaviour, serving both for prescription and for critical assessment. Derivatively, the principles also have an explanatory role in so far as persons actually act rationally.

The simplest, most familiar, and historically primary part of this study constitutes the core of classical and neo-classical economic theory, which examines rational behaviour in those situations in which the actor knows with certainty the outcome of each of his possible actions. The economist does of course offer to explain behaviour, and much of the interest of her theory depends on its having explanatory applications, but her explanations use a model of ideal interaction which includes the rationality of the actors among its assumptions. Thus economic explanation is set within a normative context. And the role of economics in formulating and evaluating policy alternatives should leave us in no doubt about the deeply prescriptive and critical character of the science.

The economist formulates a simple, maximizing conception of practical rationality, which we shall examine in Chapter II. But the assumption that the outcome of each possible choice can be known with certainty seriously limits the scope of economic analysis and the applicability of its account of reason. Bayesian decision theory relaxes this assumption, examining situations with choices involving risk or uncertainty. The decision theorist is led to extend the economist's account of reason, while preserving its fundamental identification of rationality with maximization.

Both economics and decision theory are limited in their analysis of interaction, since both consider outcomes only in relation to the choices of a single actor, treating the choices of others as aspects of that actor's circumstances. The theory of games overcomes this limitation, analysing outcomes in relation to sets of choices, one for each of the persons involved in bringing about the outcome. It considers the choices of an actor who decides on the basis of expectations about the choices of others, themselves deciding on the basis of expectations about his choice. Since situations involving a single actor may be treated as limiting cases of interaction, game theory aims at an account of rational behaviour in its full generality. Unsurprisingly, achievements are related inversely to aims; as a study of rational behaviour under certainty economic theory is essentially complete, whereas game theory is still being developed. The theory of rational choice is an ongoing enterprise, extending a basic understanding of value and rationality to the formulation of principles of rational behaviour in an ever wider range of situations.

Rational choice provides an exemplar of normative theory. One might suppose that moral theory and choice theory are related only in possessing similar structure. But as we have said, we shall develop moral theory as part of choice theory. Those acquainted with recent work in moral philosophy may find this a familiar enterprise; John Rawls has insisted that the theory of justice is 'perhaps the most significant part, of the theory of rational choice', and John Harsanyi explicitly treats ethics as part of the theory of rational behaviour.[7] But these claims are stronger than their results warrant. Neither Rawls nor Harsanyi develops the deep connection between morals and rational choice that we shall defend. A brief comparison will bring our enterprise into sharper focus.

Our claim is that in certain situations involving interaction with others, an individual chooses rationally only in so far as he constrains his pursuit of his own interest or advantage to conform to principles expressing the impartiality characteristic of morality. To choose rationally, one must choose morally. This is a strong claim. Morality, we shall argue, can be generated as a rational constraint from the non-moral premises of rational choice. Neither Rawls nor Harsanyi makes such a claim. Neither Rawls nor Harsanyi treats moral principles as a subset of rational principles for choice.

Rawls argues that the principles of justice are the objects of a rational choice—the choice that any person would make, were he called upon to select the basic principles of his society from behind a 'veil of ignorance' concealing any knowledge of his own identity.[8] The principles so chosen are not directly related to the making of individual choices.[9] Derivatively, acceptance of them must have implications for individual behaviour, but Rawls never claims that these include rational constraints on individual choices. They may be, in Rawls's terminology, reasonable constraints, but what is reasonable is itself a morally substantive matter beyond the bounds of rational choice.[10]

Rawls's idea, that principles of justice are the objects of a rational choice, is indeed one that we shall incorporate into our own theory, although we shall represent the choice as a bargain, or agreement, among persons who need not be unaware of their identities. But this parallel between our theory and Rawls's must not obscure the basic difference; we claim to generate morality as a set of rational principles for choice. We are committed to showing why an individual, reasoning from non-moral premises, would accept the constraints of morality on his choices.

Although a successful contractarian theory defeats the presumption against morality arising from its conception of rational, independent individuals, yet it should take the presumption seriously. The first conception central to our theory is therefore that of a morally free zone, a context within which the constraints of morality would have no place.[11] The free zone proves to be that habitat familiar to economists, the perfectly competitive market. Such a market is of course an idealization; how far it can be realized in human society is an empirical question beyond the scope of our enquiry. Our argument is that in a perfectly competitive market, mutual advantage is assured by the unconstrained activity of each individual in pursuit of her own greatest satisfaction, so that there is no place, rationally, for constraint. Furthermore, since in the market each person enjoys the same freedom in her choices and actions that she would have in isolation from her fellows, and since the market outcome reflects the exercise of each person's freedom, there is no basis for finding any partiality in the market's operations. Thus there is also no place, morally, for constraint. The market exemplifies an ideal of interaction among persons who, taking no interest in each other's interests, need only follow the dictates of their own individual interests to participate effectively in a venture for mutual advantage. We do not speak of a *co-operative* venture, reserving that label for enterprises that lack the natural harmony of each with all assured by the structure of market interaction.

The perfectly competitive market is thus a foil against which morality appears more clearly. Were the world such a market, morals would be unnecessary. But this is not to denigrate the value of morality, which makes possible an artificial harmony where natural harmony is not to be had. Market and morals share the non-coercive reconciliation of individual interest with mutual benefit.

Where mutual benefit requires individual constraint, this reconciliation is achieved through rational agreement. As we have noted, a necessary condition of such agreement is that its outcome be mutually advantageous; our task is to provide a sufficient condition. This problem is addressed in a part of the theory of games, the theory of rational bargaining, and divides into two issues.[12] The first is the bargaining problem proper, which in its general form is to select a specific outcome, given a range of mutually advantageous possibilities, and an initial bargaining position. The second is then to determine the initial bargaining position. Treatment of these issues has yet to reach consensus, so that we shall develop our own theory of bargaining.

Solving the bargaining problem yields a principle that governs both the process and the content of rational agreement. We shall address this in Chapter V, where we introduce a measure of each person's stake in a bargain—the difference between the least he might accept in place of no agreement, and the most he might receive in place of being excluded by others from agreement. And we shall argue that the equal rationality of the bargainers leads to the requirement that the greatest concession, measured as a proportion of the conceder's stake, be as small as possible. We formulate this as the principle of minimax relative concession. And this is equivalent to the requirement that the least relative benefit, measured again as a proportion of one's stake, be as great as possible. So we formulate an equivalent principle of maximin relative benefit, which we claim captures the ideas of fairness and impartiality in a bargaining situation, and so serves as the basis of justice. Minimax relative concession, or maximin relative benefit, is thus the second conception central to our theory.

If society is to be a co-operative venture for mutual advantage, then its institutions and practices must satisfy, or nearly satisfy, this principle. For if our theory of bargaining is correct, then minimax relative concession governs the *ex ante* agreement that underlies a fair and rational co-operative venture. But in so far as the social arrangements constrain our actual *ex post* choices, the question of compliance demands attention. Let it be ever so rational to agree to practices that ensure maximin relative benefit; yet is it not also rational to ignore these practices should it serve one's interest to do so? Is it rational to internalize moral principles in one's choices, or only to acquiesce in them in so far as one's interests are held in check by external, coercive constraints? The weakness of traditional contractarian theory has been its inability to show the rationality of compliance.

Here we introduce the third conception central to our theory, constrained maximization. We distinguish the person who is disposed straightforwardly to maximize her satisfaction, or fulfil her interest, in the particular choices she makes, from the person who is disposed to comply with mutually advantageous moral constraints, provided he expects similar compliance from others. The latter is a constrained maximizer. And constrained maximizers, interacting one with another, enjoy opportunities for co-operation which others lack. Of course, constrained maximizers sometimes lose by being disposed to compliance, for they may act co-operatively in the mistaken expectation of reciprocity from others who instead benefit at their expense. Nevertheless, we shall show that under plausible conditions, the net advantage that constrained maximizers reap from co-operation exceeds the exploitative benefits that others may expect. From this we conclude that it is rational to be disposed to constrain maximizing behaviour by internalizing moral principles to govern one's choices. The contractarian is able to show that it is irrational to admit appeals to interest against compliance with those duties founded on mutual advantage.[13]

But compliance is rationally grounded only within the framework of a fully co-operative venture, in which each participant willingly interacts with her fellows. And this leads us back to the second issue addressed in bargaining theory—the initial bargaining position. If persons are willingly to comply with the agreement that determines what each takes from the bargaining table, then they must find initially acceptable what each brings to the table. And if what some bring to the table includes the fruits of prior interaction forced on their fellows, then this initial acceptability will be lacking. If you seize the products of my labour and then say 'Let's make a deal', I may be compelled to accept, but I will not voluntarily comply.

We are therefore led to constrain the initial bargaining position, through a proviso that prohibits bettering one's position through interaction worsening the position of another.[14] No person should be worse off in the initial bargaining position than she would be in a non-social context of no interaction. The proviso thus constrains the base from which each person's stake in agreement, and so her relative concession and benefit, are measured. We shall show that it induces a structure of personal and property rights, which are basic to rationally and morally acceptable social arrangements.

The proviso is the fourth of the core conceptions of our theory. Although a part of morals by agreement, it is not the product of rational agreement. Rather, it is a condition that must be accepted by each person for such agreement to be possible. Among beings, however rational, who may not hope to engage one another in a co-operative venture for mutual advantage, the proviso would have no force. Our theory denies any place to rational constraint, and so to morality, outside the context of mutual benefit. A contractarian account of morals has no place for duties that are strictly redistributive in their effects, transferring but not increasing benefits, or duties that do not assume reciprocity from other persons. Such duties would be neither rationally based, nor supported by considerations of impartiality.

To the four core conceptions whose role we have sketched, we add a fifth—the Archimedean point, from which an individual can move the moral world.[15] To confer this moral power, the Archimedean point must be one of assured impartiality—the position sought by John Rawls behind the 'veil of ignorance'. We shall conclude the exposition of our moral theory in Chapter VIII by relating the choice of a person occupying the Archimedean point to the other core ideas. We shall show that Archimedean choice is properly conceived, not as a limiting case of individual decision under uncertainty, but rather as a limiting case of bargaining. And we shall then show how each of our core ideas—the proviso against bettering oneself through worsening others, the morally free zone afforded by the perfectly competitive market, the principle of minimax relative concession, and the disposition to constrained maximization—may be related, directly or indirectly, to Archimedean choice. In embracing these other conceptions central to our theory, the Archimedean point reveals the coherence of morals by agreement.

A contractarian theory of morals, developed as part of the theory of rational choice, has evident strengths. It enables us to demonstrate the rationality of impartial constraints on the pursuit of individual interest to persons who may take no interest in others' interests. Morality is thus given a sure grounding in a weak and widely accepted conception of practical rationality. No alternative account of morality accomplishes this. Those who claim that moral principles are objects of rational choice in special circumstances fail to establish the rationality of actual compliance with these principles. Those who claim to establish the rationality of such compliance appeal to a strong and controversial conception of reason that seems to incorporate prior moral suppositions. No alternative account generates morals, as a rational constraint on choice and action, from a non-moral, or morally neutral, base.

But the strengths of a contractarian theory may seem to be accompanied by grave weaknesses. We have already noted that for a contractarian, morality requires a context of mutual benefit. John Locke held that 'an Hobbist ... will not easily admit a great many plain duties of morality'.[16] And this may seem equally to apply to the Hobbist's modern-day successor. Our theory does not assume any fundamental concern with impartiality, but only a concern derivative from the benefits of agreement, and those benefits are determined by the effects that each person can have on the interests of her fellows. Only beings whose physical and mental capacities are either roughly equal or mutually complementary can expect to find co-operation beneficial to all. Humans benefit from their interaction with horses, but they do not co-operate with horses and may not benefit them. Among unequals, one party may benefit most by coercing the other, and on our theory would have no reason to refrain. We may condemn all coercive relationships, but only within the context of mutual benefit can our condemnation appeal to a rationally grounded morality.

Moral relationships among the participants in a co-operative venture for mutual advantage have a firm basis in the rationality of the participants. And it has been plausible to represent the society that has emerged in western Europe and America in recent centuries as such a venture. For Western society has discovered how to harness the efforts of the individual, working for his own good, in the cause of ever-increasing mutual benefit.[17] Not only an explosion in the quantity of material goods and in the numbers of persons, but, more important, an unprecedented rise in the average life span, and a previously unimaginable broadening of the range of occupations and activities effectively accessible to most individuals on the basis of their desires and talents, have resulted from this discovery.[18] With personal gain linked to social advance, the individual has been progressively freed from the coercive bonds, mediated through custom and education, law and religion, that have characterized earlier societies. But in unleashing the individual, perhaps too much credit has been given to the efficacy of market-like institutions, and too little attention paid to the need for co-operative interaction requiring limited but real constraint.[19] Morals by agreement then express the real concern each of us has in maintaining the conditions in which society can be a co-operative venture.

But if Locke's criticism of the scope of contractarian morality has been bypassed by circumstances that have enabled persons to regard one another as contributing partners to a joint enterprise, changed circumstances may bring it once more to the fore. From a technology that made it possible for an ever-increasing proportion of persons to increase the average level of well-being, our society is passing to a technology, best exemplified by developments in medicine, that make possible an ever-increasing transfer of benefits to persons who decrease that average.[20] Such persons are not party to the moral relationships grounded by a contractarian theory.

Beyond concern about the scope of moral relationships is the question of their place in an ideal human life. Glaucon asked Socrates to refute a contractarian account of justice, because he believed that such an account must treat justice as instrumentally valuable for persons who are mutually dependent, but intrinsically disvaluable, so that it 'seems to belong to the form of drudgery'.[21] Co-operation is a second-best form of interaction, requiring concessions and constraints that each person would prefer to avoid. Indeed, each has the secret hope that she can be successfully unjust, and easily falls prey to that most dangerous vanity that persuades her that she is truly superior to her fellows, and so can safely ignore their interests in pursuing her own. As Glaucon said, he who 'is truly a man' would reject moral constraints.[22]

A contractarian theory does not contradict this view, since it leaves altogether open the content of human desires, but equally it does not require it. May we not rather suppose that human beings depend for their fulfilment on a network of social relationships whose very structure constantly tempts them to misuse it? The constraints of morality then serve to regulate valued social relationships that fail to be self-regulating. They constrain us in the interests of a shared ideal of sociability.

Co-operation may then seem a second-best form of interaction, not because it runs counter to our desires, but because each person would prefer a natural harmony in which she could fulfil herself without constraint. But a natural harmony could exist only if our preferences and capabilities dovetailed in ways that would preclude their free development. Natural harmony would require a higher level of artifice, a shaping of our natures in ways that, at least until genetic engineering is perfected, are not possible, and were they possible, would surely not be desirable. If human individuality is to bloom, then we must expect some degree of conflict among the aims and interests of persons rather than natural harmony. Market and morals tame this conflict, reconciling individuality with mutual benefit.

## Notes

1. See David Hume, *An Enquiry concerning the Principles of Morals*, sect. ix, pt. ii, in L. A. Selby-Bigge (ed.), *Enquiries concerning Human Understanding and concerning the Principles of Morals*, 3rd edn. (Oxford, 1975), p. 280.
2. Ogden Nash, 'Kind of an Ode to Duty', *I Wouldn't Have Missed It: Selected Poems of Ogden Nash* (Boston, 1975), p. 141.
3. See David Hume, *A Treatise of Human Nature*, bk. ii, pt. iii, sect. iii, ed. L. A Selby-Bigge (Oxford, 1888), pp. 413–18.
4. Thus one might propose an error theory of moral language; for the idea of an error theory, see J. L. Mackie, *Ethics: Inventing Right and Wrong* (Harmondsworth, Middx., 1977), ch. 1, esp. pp. 35, 48–9.
5. The idea that moral appeals are persuasive is developed by C. L. Stevenson; see *Ethics and Language* (New Haven, 1944), esp. chs. vi, ix.
6. Our sketch of rational choice owes much to J. C. Harsanyi; see 'Advances in Understanding Rational Behavior', in *Essays on Ethics, Social Behavior, and Scientific Explanation* (Dordrecht, 1976), pp. 89–98, and 'Morality and the theory of rational behaviour', in A. Sen and B. Williams (eds.), *Utilitarianism and beyond* (Cambridge, 1982), pp. 42–4.
7. J. Rawls, *A Theory of Justice* (Cambridge, Mass., 1971), p. 16; J. Harsanyi, 'Morality and the theory of rational behaviour', p. 42.
8. See Rawls, p. 12.
9. See ibid., p. 11; 'the principles ... are to assign basic rights and duties and to determine the division of social benefits.' Principles for individuals are distinguished from the principles of justice; see p. 108.
10. See Rawls's distinction of 'the Reasonable' and 'the Rational', in 'Kantian Constructivism in Moral Theory', *Journal of Philosophy* 77 (1980), pp. 528–30.
11. This is the theme of ch. IV, below. See also my earlier discussion in 'No Need for Morality: The Case of the Competitive Market', *Philosophic Exchange* 3, no. 3 (1982), pp. 41–54.
12. For references to the literature on rational bargaining, see notes 12–14 to ch. V, below.
13. This conclusion rests on a reinterpretation of the maximizing conception of rationality, which we develop in ch. VI, below; see especially the opening paragraph of 3. 1.
14. For the idea of the proviso, see note 1 to ch. VII, below.
15. For the idea of an Archimedean point, see Rawls, *A Theory of Justice*, pp. 260–5.
16. Locke MS, quoted in J. Dunn, *The Political Thought of John Locke* (Cambridge, 1969), pp. 218–19.
17. We offer no explanation of this discovery. There seems no reason to suppose that it resulted from deliberate search.
18. For the increase in average life span, see N. Eberstadt, 'The Health Crisis in the U.S.S.R.', *New York Review of Books* 28, no. 2 (1981), p. 23. For the broadening in the range of accessible occupations, note that 'As late as 1815 three-quarters of its [Europe's] population were employed on the land...', *The Times Concise Atlas of World History*, ed. G. Barraclough (London, 1982), p. 82.
19. Thus the idea of economic man as an unlimited appropriator comes to dominate social thought. The effects of this conception are one of the themes of my 'The Social Contract as Ideology', *Philosophy and Public Affairs* 6 (1977), pp.130–64.
20. The problem here is not care of the aged, who have paid for their benefits by earlier productive activity. Life-extending therapies do, however, have an

ominous redistributive potential. The primary problem is care for the handicapped. Speaking euphemistically of enabling them to live productive lives, when the services required exceed any possible products, conceals an issue which, understandably, no one wants to face. Without focusing primarily on these issues, I endeavour to begin a contractarian treatment of certain health care issues in 'Unequal Need: A Problem of Equity in Access to Health Care', *Securing Access to Health Care: The Ethical Implications of Differences in the Availability of Health Services*, 3 vols., President's Commission for the Study of Ethical Problems in Medicine and Biomedical and Behavioral Research (Washington, 1983), vol. 2, pp. 179–205.
21 *Republic*, 358a, trans. A. Bloom (New York, 1968), p. 36.
22 ibid., 359b, p. 37.

# 10 A Critique of Justice as Reciprocity

Allen Buchanan

## Justice as Reciprocity: A Radical Challenge

There is a strain of thought in the history of ethics that surfaces from time to time in the work of powerful thinkers and that threatens to shatter the basic conceptual framework within which our legal system and commonsense morality formulate the problems of justice. This idea may be called *justice as reciprocity*. While taking several forms, it has more often appeared as a disturbing challenge to orthodox thinking and practice concerning justice than as a systematically developed theory in its own right. In Hume it is the speculation that creatures otherwise like us but powerless to harm us can at most hope to be treated mercifully, but cannot expect to be treated justly.[1] It is at least strongly suggested by Epicurus's thesis that justice is founded solely on mutual gain and that for this reason animals, as beings from whom one can benefit without reciprocating, are not within the scope of justice.[2] In David Gauthier's recent influential book *Morals by Agreement*, justice as reciprocity is the view that not only relations of distributive justice but moral relations generally, at least so far as they are rationally justifiable, obtain only among those who are (or at least can be) net contributors to the cooperation.[3] Both the capacity to contribute and the capacity to harm may be thought of as *strategic* capacities insofar as an individual can use them to influence the behavior of other rational, purely self-interested agents. Justice as reciprocity makes the ascription of rights depend only upon the possession of either or both of these strategic capacities.

The idea to be explored, then, is that distributive justice (if not the whole of justice, or even of morality) is founded solely on reciprocity, or, more precisely, that an individual has a right to a share of social resources (or moral rights of any kind) *only* if that individual contributes or at least can contribute to the cooperative surplus.[4] I will concentrate on the contribution variant of justice as reciprocity rather than on Hume's reciprocal threat capacity variant, but most of what I will have to say about the former will apply to the latter as well. Justice as reciprocity in both variants clashes both with commonsense morality, according to which it makes perfectly good sense to say that a person who is unable to contribute to the social surplus can be treated justly or unjustly, and with some of our most fundamental legal institutions, which extend basic rights to all persons, regardless of their ability to contribute.[5]

## Justice as Self-interested Reciprocity and Justice as Fair Reciprocity

There are two quite different versions of the contribution variant of justice as reciprocity. The first, of which Gauthier's work may be the clearest example, conceives of the project as that of grounding justice (and morality in general) in the rational self-interest of the individual. We may call it *justice as self-interested reciprocity*. For Gauthier the reason for restricting rights to potential contributors is quite apparent: if being just is to be rational, then it must be rational *for the individual* to be just, and for it to be rational for the individual, it must be *to the individual's advantage*. The specific form the argument takes in Gauthier's work is this: Agreement on and compliance with principles specifying rights to shares of social wealth (and moral principles generally) is rational because it is the outcome of a rational bargain. Simply put, those who cannot make a contribution (indeed, a net contribution) to the cooperative surplus are entitled to nothing because they have nothing to offer, nothing with which to bargain.

The second version grounds justice in a particular conception of fairness: Each person who benefits from the contributions of others in a cooperative enterprise in which that person participates owes something to those other contributors, and they, for the same reason, owe something to the individual, but only insofar as that individual is a contributor. This version may be called *justice as fair reciprocity*. Unlike the self-interest version, justice as fair reciprocity does not (or at least need not attempt to) found justice (or morality in general) on rationality as individual utility-maximization.[6]

What is common to both versions of justice as reciprocity is what may be called *the reciprocity thesis*: the claim that only those who do (or at least can) make a contribution to the cooperative surplus have rights to social resources. The implications of the reciprocity thesis for the treatment of severely disabled persons are as disturbing as they are obvious. If, for whatever reason, an individual is never capable of being a contributor to the cooperative surplus, then that individual has no right to social resources whatsoever—not even the most minimal support—even in an affluent society. The clearest case would be that of a person who from birth was so severely and permanently incapacitated that he could not contribute. I wish to emphasize that justice as reciprocity is committed to the position that *persons* who are not able to contribute have no rights to social resources, even if they could clearly benefit significantly from them. Thus justice as reciprocity is much stronger and more austere than the view that human beings who are not persons or who are persons but could not benefit significantly from resources have no right to them (for example, permanently unconscious individuals).[7]

Justice as reciprocity is to be contrasted with what I shall call *subject-centered* conceptions of justice. According to subject-centered conceptions, basic rights to resources are grounded not in the individual's strategic capacities but rather in other features of the individual herself—her needs or non-strategic capacities. The term 'subject-centered' seems apt since it serves to emphasize that moral status depends upon features of the individual herself other than her power to affect others for good or for ill. As we shall see, different examples of subject-centered justice ascribe rights or moral status based on different features of the individual. What they have in common is the independence of basic moral status from the ability to harm or to contribute. In contrast, in justice as reciprocity, an individual's needs and non-strategic capacities count for nothing: it is *only* the individual's ability to benefit others through cooperation (or, in Hume's case, to harm others) that grounds her rights and the corresponding obligations of others toward her.

The harsh counterintuitiveness of justice as reciprocity should not be underestimated by confusing it with a much more limited and less controversial thesis about the generation of special rights through voluntary participation in cooperative schemes. The most limited and plausible thesis is that in certain voluntary cooperative enterprises only those who contribute to the creation of a joint product have a just claim to a share of it. This thesis, of course, is quite compatible with the view that an individual may have a general right to some minimal share of social resources—at least where dire scarcity does not prevail—simply because he possesses certain fundamental human needs, capacities, or interests, or simply because he is a person, even if he is unable to contribute to any of the cooperative enterprises of society. Justice as reciprocity is a much more comprehensive view. Its claim is not that special rights *can* be generated by mutually beneficial cooperative schemes, but rather that it is *only* in this fashion that rights can be grounded: unless an individual can contribute he has *no* rights to social resources. The more limited thesis states only that *if* the individual does contribute, his contribution gives him a right to a share of the surplus. This more limited thesis is consistent both with the claim that those who cannot contribute have rights that are not grounded in reciprocity and with the thesis that noncontributors have no rights whatsoever.

Justice as reciprocity, then, in both its fairness and self-interest variants, is a truly radical and severe view. In denying that noncontributors have any distributive rights at all, it rejects out of hand current debates about the *extent* of the rights of severely handicapped persons, since virtually all parties to these controversies share the assumption that there are some subject-centered rights, disagreeing only upon their scope and limits. If justice as reciprocity is extended to all rights, not just rights of distributive justice, it is even more radical and, one is tempted to say, even more inhumane. If, as Gauthier believes, all moral rights, including the so-called negative rights to refrain from injuring and killing, are rationally ascribable only to potential contributors to social wealth, then we violate no rights if we choose to use noncontributors in experiments on the nature of pain or for military research on the performance of various designs of bullets when they strike human tissue, slaughter them for food, or bronze them to make lifelike statues.[8]

If justice as reciprocity were understood as the thesis that *actual* (not just potential) contribution is a necessary condition for having rights, it would have even more startling implications—for example, that not just the severely handicapped but all normal children, prior to the age at which they make net contributions to the cooperative surplus, have no rights. Because I believe that the *potential* contribution interpretation of justice as reciprocity is the more plausible and because this is the version that has actually been advanced, most forcefully by Gauthier, I shall concentrate on it. We shall see, however, that whether an individual is even a potential contributor depends in part upon social choices concerning institutional design and that this simple fact has profound and disturbing implications for justice as reciprocity.

## The Conceptual and Normative Poverty of Justice as Reciprocity

The problems with justice as reciprocity run still deeper. It is not simply that justice as reciprocity conflicts sharply with some of our most basic principled judgments about justice. Another important comparative disadvantage of justice as reciprocity is that it fails to render intelligible some of the most serious and perplexing questions concerning the justice or injustice of *basic frameworks of social cooperation* and the *distributive effects of choosing one cooperative framework over another*.

Whether or not an individual is a potential contributor will depend not only upon whether she has the minimal cognitive capacities and capacities for agency necessary for personhood, but also upon whether she possesses whatever capacities are required for effective participation under the rules of that particular cooperative scheme. These rules and the cooperative schemes they constitute will vary from society to society. To be a contributor in a society in which cooperation is an extremely complex and intricate process, one will require capacities that exceed those that would suffice in a much simpler cooperative arrangement. *Being able to contribute is relative to a cooperative framework.* Yet, clearly, what sort of cooperative framework we are to have is, within natural and cultural limits, a matter of human decision. And for this reason we can and do evaluate cooperative frameworks *from the standpoint of justice.*

In our society the rules of social cooperation are quite complex and demanding—so much so that large numbers of persons, including minors and the retarded, are classified as incompetent, not simply for this or that particular task, but, as it were, globally. In being deemed incompetent, these individuals are barred from a wide range of activities, including the making of contracts, the acquisition and disposition of property, marriage (in some cases), and so on. Being "incompetent" is, in other words, a significant social liability that limits one's ability to engage in various forms of cooperation. In a simpler (or at least different) cooperative arrangement, say, that of a traditional peasant village, many of these "incompetents" might be full-fledged, active participants in social cooperation.[9]

Different cooperative arrangements may demand different skills, not just different levels of excellence of the same skills. For example, mild retardation combined with dyslexia might render an individual incompetent in a highly literate society in which basic social cooperation required the mastery of sophisticated rules and techniques for processing and issuing written instructions, agreements, and contracts. Yet these same characteristics might not constitute a significant handicap in a hunting-and-gathering society.

The minimum level of skills that a society determines is necessary for an individual to be ascribed competence as a general status, as well as *which* skills it selects, will have profound effects on individuals, depending on whether they happen to fall above or below the threshold. Further, in classifying some individuals as incompetent—and thereby barring them from important forms of social cooperation—we may not be operating solely from paternalistic motives. That is, we may be excluding them not in order to protect them from mishaps they might suffer if they tried to participate in activities beyond their capacities, but in order to enjoy for ourselves the greater benefits that more complex cooperative interactions can yield, while preventing the discoordination and interference that would be introduced if the less capable were allowed to participate in the game. After all, if our motives were exclusively paternalistic, we, the more capable, might well choose a simpler cooperative game in order to extend participation rights to a larger number of people.[10]

Only if extending access to the cooperative framework to those not competent to play the more complex game would increase overall productivity would it be in the self-regarding interest of the more competent to do so. But surely this will not always or even generally be the case, especially if there is a considerable spread in the distribution of talents among the population. Sometimes there will be genuine conflicts of interest as to the choice of a cooperative framework. To set the threshold of skills and capacities that determines who shall be able to participate in social cooperation is to take a stand on whose interests should count more, those of the more capable or those of the less capable, and this is surely a question of justice.

Given that the capacity to be a contributor is socially determined, then it is clear that questions of justice arise not only with respect to relations among contributions but also at the deeper level of what sort of cooperative institutions we ought to have, insofar as the character of these institutions will determine in part who can contribute. But if this is so, then justice as reciprocity, because it is blind to the prior question of which cooperative institutions will produce *just conditions for membership in the class of contributors*, is a radically incomplete and, to that extent, defective conception of justice. Justice as reciprocity can at best yield an account of what those who happen to be able to contribute in a given scheme of cooperation owe one another. It can shed no light whatsoever on the question of whether the scheme of cooperation unjustly excludes some persons from participating.

## Notes

1. David Hume, *Enquiries concerning Human Understanding and concerning the Principles of Morals*, ed. L. A. Selby-Bigge and P. H. Nidditch, 3d ed. (Oxford: Clarendon Press, 1975), pp. 190–91.
2. Epicurus suggests a view of justice as reciprocity in his *Kuriai Doxai* (or "Key Doctrines"). See, for example, Key Doctrine 32: "Nothing is just or unjust in relation to those creatures which were unable to make contracts over not harming one another and not being harmed"; and Key Doctrine 33: "Justice was never anything *per se*, but a contract regularly arising at some place or other in people's dealings with one another, over not harming or being harmed" (*The Hellenistic Philosophers*, trans. A. A. Long and D. N. Sedley [Cambridge: Cambridge University Press, 1987], p. 127).

    For an interpretation of Epicurus as a proto-Hobbesian in his thinking on justice see Nicholas Denyer, "The Origins of Justice," in *Syzetesis*, ed. Gaetano Macchiaroli (Naples: Biblioteca della Parola del Passato, 1982), 2: 133–52. This interpretation is shared by Cyril Bailey, *The Greek Atomists and Epicurus* (Oxford: Clarendon Press, 1928).
3. David Gauthier, *Morals by Agreement* (Oxford: Clarendon Press, 1986). In chap. I Gauthier summarizes his theory and draws the explicit conclusion that it gives no moral standing to those who are not contributors to the cooperative surplus: "From a technology that made it possible for an ever-increasing proportion to increase the average level of well-being, our society is passing to a technology, best exemplified by developments in medicine, that make[s] possible an ever-increasing transfer of benefits to persons who decrease that average. Such persons are not party to the moral relationships grounded by a contractarian theory" (p. 18). As we shall see later, the last statement is misleading. It would be more accurate to say that those who do not or cannot make a contribution to the social surplus are not within the scope of morality according to any contractarian theory that is an example of justice (or morality) as reciprocity. This leaves open the possibility, explored later in this article, that not all contractarian theories are examples of justice as reciprocity. Gauthier makes it clear that he espouses a version of what I call justice as reciprocity in a number of other places in his book, but the most extended discussion of the implications of this view is found in the passage on the purple people and the green people (pp. 282–87). This passage is examined in some detail later in this article, but its main point is simple: if the purple people have nothing to gain from the greens or can gain from them without having to contribute to their well-being, then what the purples do to the greens is not subject to moral constraints.
4. The cooperative surplus consists of the net supply of good (and services) that arise from cooperation. I will generally use the words *justice* and *rights* interchangeably, since nothing in the argument hangs on the distinction between them. The discussion could easily be recast, however, in a way that is consistent with the view that justice is not exclusively or primarily a matter of rights. The central idea to be explored is the thesis that being within the scope of justice (or of morality in general) depends upon being able to contribute to the cooperative surplus (or, in Hume's case, being able to harm others).
5. In the American legal system, all persons are recognized as having the same basic common law and constitutional rights, and all are protected by statute law. Although there is some disagreement over the legal concept of a person, the disagreement concerns the status of fetuses, not whether the ability to contribute (or threat capacity) is a necessary condition for personhood under the law.

6 Especially in his more recent work, Rawls makes it clear that his theory is not a version of justice as self-interested reciprocity. For Rawls the task of the theorist of justice is not to derive principles of justice or our obligation to comply with them from rational self-interest. See, e.g., "Kantian Constructivism in Moral Theory: The Dewey Lectures 1980," *Journal of Philosophy* 77 (1980): 515–72, and "Justice as Fairness: Political not Metaphysical," *Philosophy & Public Affairs* 14, no. 3 (Summer 1985): 223–51. It might be tempting to classify Rawls as a proponent of justice as fair reciprocity because of his characterization of the parties to the Original Position and his way of framing the problem of justice. He says that the parties are *fully participating contributors to social cooperation* (not simply members of society) and that the problem of justice is to find principles by which to distribute the burdens and benefits of cooperation *among such contributors* (not among members of society in general) ("Kantian Constructivism," p. 546). In his later work, however, Rawls founds the characterization of the hypothetical choice situation and hence the principles chosen from it on a normative ideal of persons as free and equal. It seems to be his considered view that it is beings who possess these properties who are within the scope of justice, regardless of whether they are contributors to the cooperative surplus. Rawls confirmed this interpretation in a conversation with the author. His theory appears to be a Kantian version of what I call subject-centered justice.

In a very illuminating discussion Brian Barry argues that both Rawls and Hume (inconsistently) hold two (types of) theories of justice: justice as mutual advantage and justice as impartiality (Brian Barry, *A Treatise on Social Justice, Volume 1: Theories of Justice* [Berkeley: University of California Press, 1989], chaps. 5 and 6). Barry's distinction overlaps with but is not the same as mine between justice as reciprocity and subject-centered (or nonstrategic) justice (see Section IV of this article). Justice as mutual advantage corresponds to what I have called the rational self-interest variant of justice as reciprocity. Justice as impartiality is the thesis that principles of justice are to be chosen from a point of view that is impartial, where impartiality excludes the influence of bargaining advantages on the choice of principles. Justice as impartiality is not identical to subject-centered justice because the former assumes that principles of justice are the objects of a collective choice or contract, whereas the latter does not assume that principles of justice are the objects of an agreement of any sort.

7 Gauthier acknowledges that his theory has implications that clash with our intuitions about the moral status of severely handicapped persons: "The problem here is not care of the aged, who have paid for their benefits by earlier productive activity.... The primary problem is care for the handicapped" (*Morals by Agreement*, p. 18 n. 30).

8 There is at least one moral principle that, according to Gauthier, is not the outcome of a rational bargain among contributors to the cooperative surplus but rather is a prior constraint on the bargaining process itself: the Lockean Proviso. Gauthier notes that this principle, properly understood, expresses "a constraint on acquisition as a proviso that simultaneously licenses and limits the exclusive rights of individuals to objects and powers. Its effect is to afford each person a sphere of exclusive control by forbidding others from interfering with certain of his activities" (*Morals by Agreement*, p. 201). The Proviso forbids worsening others' conditions (in certain ways) and, as interpreted by Gauthier, includes a prohibition against coercion in the pre-bargaining state of nature (p. 192). Thus it might seem that for Gauthier the Proviso is an exception not only to the statement that principles of morality are the outcome of a rational bargain but also to the thesis that the scope of morality includes only those who are contributors, who have

something with which to bargain. This, however, would be misinterpretation. Gauthier bases the Proviso on what he takes to be the requirements of a stable bargain, arguing that any bargain that originated from a state of nature in which the Proviso was not satisfied would be unstable and that rational bargainers, seeing that this was the case, would not make a bargain under those conditions. Thus, the basis of the Proviso is that "it is rational for utility-maximizers to accept [it] as constraining their natural interaction and their individual endowments, in so far as they anticipate beneficial social interactions with their fellows" (pp. 192–93). The Proviso is a constraint that "moralizes and rationalizes the state of nature ... only insofar as we conceive of the state of nature as giving way to" social cooperation for mutual advantage (p. 193). Since the Proviso is binding only insofar as it is required for a rational bargain among contributors, it follows that it applies only to the interaction of potential contributors. But, if so, then it is not an exception to the thesis of justice as reciprocity.
9   Daniel Wikler, "Paternalism and the Mildly Retarded," in *Paternalism*, ed. Rolf E. Sartorius (Minneapolis: University of Minnesota Press, 1983), pp. 91–92.
10  Ibid.

# Part Three: Communitarianism

# Introduction

Central to the liberal morality is the belief that individual rights should be given a high priority. This sentiment is evident in the priority Rawls gives to the first principle of justice and Nozick's appeal to the thesis of self-ownership. The emphasis liberals place on individual rights has given rise to a distinct criticism that dominated many of the debates in political theory in the 1980s and 1990s – communitarianism. The 'liberal/communitarian' debate covers a varied range of issues and theorists and there is no simple contrast between liberalism and communitarianism. Two of the excerpts reproduced in this part are from the prominent communitarian critics Michael Sandel and Michael Walzer, while the third excerpt is from a liberal critic of communitarianism – Will Kymlicka. Sandel and Walzer challenge distinct aspects of contemporary liberal theory. In *Liberalism and the Limits of Justice* and *Democracy's Discontent* Sandel examines the conception of the self implicit in contemporary liberalism. Sandel calls this conception of the self the 'unencumbered (or voluntarist) conception of the self'. This vision of the self, argues Sandel, informs the public philosophy of contemporary American politics. Sandel labels this public philosophy the procedural republic. He claims:

> The political philosophy by which we live is a certain version of liberal political theory. Its central idea is that government should be neutral toward the moral and religious views its citizens espouse. Since people disagree about the best way to live, government should not affirm in law any particular vision of the good life. Instead, it should provide a framework of rights that respects persons as free and independent selves, capable of choosing their own values and ends. Since this liberalism asserts the priority of fair procedures over particular ends, the public life it informs might be called the procedural republic. (Sandel, 1996: 4)

The procedural republic is ill-equipped, argues Sandel, to deal with the two fears that define the anxiety of contemporary American politics – the fear of losing control of the forces that govern our lives and the fear that the moral fabric of community is eroding. Sandel is critical of the neutralist aspirations of liberals such as Rawls. First, there are many cases where the state simply cannot remain neutral. Sandel gives the example of abortion, an issue that deeply divides many Americans. Whatever decision the government makes regarding abortion it cannot be neutral with respect to the underlying moral and religious controversy. If, for example, the government grants women the right to abortion then the government is making a judgement about the claim made by many religious people that abortion is morally tantamount to murder. The judgement in this case is that the belief that life begins at conception is wrong. This is what happened in *Roe v. Wade* (1973) when the American Supreme Court struck down a Texas law against abortion. Despite the Court's attempt to take a neutral stance on the contentious issue of when life begins, its decision to strike down the Texas law meant that it took a stance on exactly that issue. *Roe v. Wade* supported the judgement that life does not begin at conception. The government simply cannot resolve an issue such as abortion without engaging in moral and religious controversy.

In addition to not always being possible, Sandel also argues that state neutrality has costly consequences. The aspiration for neutrality is one that has emerged over the last 50 years in American constitutional law and this is evident in a number of judicial decisions ranging from the separation of church and school to restrictions on hate speech and pornography. Sandel points to the failed attempts to prevent the harm of group defamation as evidence of how prevalent the unencumbered conception of the self is in contemporary American constitutional law. The court's handling of the Skokie controversy of 1977–78 illustrates this point. The controversy concerned the freedom of a neo-Nazi group to march through Skokie, Illinois, a predominantly Jewish community. The municipal ordinances that prohibited the dissemination of materials inciting hatred based on race, national origin or religion were declared unconstitutional. Part of the rationale for rejecting such restrictions, claims Sandel, stems from the court's acceptance of the liberal view of the self.

> ... on the liberal conception of the person, the highest respect is the self-respect of a self independent of its aims and attachments. However much I prize the esteem of others, the respect that counts cannot conceivably be injured by a slur against the racial or religious groups to which I happen to belong. For the unencumbered self, the grounds of self-respect are antecedent to any particular ties or attachments, and so beyond the reach of an insult to "my people". (Sandel, 1996: 82)

The controversy over Indianapolis anti-pornography law also illustrates this point. The 1984 Indianapolis ordinance sought to restrict pornography on the grounds that it degraded women and undermined civic equality and the ordinance was invalidated by the courts. A central justification behind the law, articulated by feminists like Catharine MacKinnon, was that pornography is an intrinsic harm because it shapes our understanding of the relations between the sexes. But this emphasis on the social nature of communication is at odds with the liberal conception of the self. Persons are, according to the liberal view, autonomous agents and choose their own identity. Autonomous agents who choose their own ends and values are not susceptible to the intrinsic harms that underlie the justification of the Indianapolis ordinance.

When the doctrine of state neutrality is utilised to protect racists, neo-Nazis or violent pornographic depictions, as it has in decisions in American constitutional law, it neglects the realities of many situated selves who are members of historically subordinated groups. Furthermore, it also prevents political communities from acting democratically to realise important goods. This is why Sandel claims that it gives rise to a public philosophy that has costly consequences.

In the excerpt from 'Liberal Individualism and Liberal Neutrality' Kymlicka clarifies what the ideal of neutrality amounts to and why liberals argue in favour of it. He distinguishes between neutrality in the *consequences* of government policy and neutrality in the *justification* of government policy. It is the latter, argues Kymlicka, that liberals defend. Furthermore, Kymlicka does not believe that the charge that liberal neutrality is premised on 'individualism' is very fruitful. Liberals and communitarians, he argues, have both failed to learn an important lesson taught by the other side. Communitarians are right, he argues, 'to insist that we examine the history and structure of a particular culture' (Kymlicka, 1989: 902). But communitarians also tend to ignore the fact that our cultural traditions tend to have exclusionary histories and thus we should not base a politics of the common good on such ends and practices. The liberal doctrine of neutrality thus has some potential in terms of inspiring a public philosophy that is more inclusive.

Like Sandel, Michael Walzer's communitarian critique also focuses on American politics but Walzer's concern is not with the conception of the self liberalism invokes nor with the ideal of state neutrality. Walzer takes issue with the methodology many contemporary liberals invoke when constructing a theory of justice. His argument is radically pluralistic and he rejects the universalist aspirations of liberals who seek to construct a theory of justice that can be applied universally to all cultures. Justice, argues Walzer, is a human construction and thus we cannot arrive at answers to the difficult questions justice raises if we conceive of justice in a way that ignores the particularist claims that are bound to arise when one considers the history, culture and membership of different societies. We cannot derive principles of justice from an abstract thought experiment which asks what principles rational persons would choose if they knew nothing of their situation except that they desired an abstract set of primary goods. Each community creates its own social goods and thus what each community thinks should be justly distributed will vary from culture to culture. What members of hierarchies and caste societies value is very different from what members of liberal democratic societies value. Furthermore, even within one community there will be a plurality of principles to regulate the plurality of goods. There aren't one or two fundamental principles that govern the regulation of all social goods. The principle that is appropriate for these different goods is determined by the social meaning of the good in question. How we should distribute health care or education, for example, will depend on what we take these goods to mean. We do not begin with abstract principles and then simply apply them to these goods.

In addition to criticising the universalist aspirations of liberalism, Walzer puts forth his own positive theory of distributive justice – what he calls 'complex equality'. Each social good represents a distinct sphere of justice and complex equality obtains when:

> no citizen's standing in one sphere or with regard to one social good can be undercut by his standing in some other sphere, with regard to some other good. Thus, citizen X may be chosen over citizen Y for political office, and then the two of them will be unequal in the sphere of politics. But they will not be unequal generally so long as X's office gives him no advantages over Y in any other sphere – superior medical care, access to better schools for his children, entrepreneurial opportunities, and so on. (Walzer, 1983: 19)

Complex equality is contrasted with the system of simple equality. The latter seeks to equally distribute (or more widely share) some dominant good, like money. But complex equality can permit inequalities in social goods. What complex equality resists is the convertibility of social goods, so that a good like money cannot be converted into better medical care or better education. Complex equality requires that the distinct distributive spheres be autonomous. Domination occurs when possession of one social good or set of goods is allowed to be transferred into an advantage in another sphere and thus complex equality is necessary to rule out domination.

**References**

Kymlicka, Will. 'Liberal Individualism and Liberal Neutrality', *Ethics*, Vol. 99(4), 1989: 883-905.
Sandel, Michael. *Democracy's Discontent*. (Cambridge, Mass.: Harvard University Press, 1996).
Walzer, Michael. *Spheres of Justice*. (New York: Basic Books, 1983).

# 11 The Procedural Republic and the Unencumbered Self

## Michael J. Sandel

Political philosophy seems often to reside at a distance from the world. Principles are one thing, politics another, and even our best efforts to "live up" to our ideals typically founder on the gap between theory and practice.[1]

But if political philosophy is unrealizable in one sense, it is unavoidable in another. This is the sense in which philosophy inhabits the world from the start; our practices and institutions are embodiments of theory. To engage in a political practice is already to stand in relation to theory.[2] For all our uncertainties about ultimate questions of political philosophy—of justice and value and the nature of the good life—the one thing we know is that we live *some* answer all the time.

In this essay I will try to explore the answer we live now, in contemporary America. What is the political philosophy implicit in our practices and institutions? How does it stand, as philosophy? And how do tensions in the philosophy find expression in our present political condition?

It may be objected that it is a mistake to look for a single philosophy, that we live no "answer," only answers. But a plurality of answers is itself a kind of answer. And the political theory that affirms this plurality is the theory I propose to explore.

### The Right and the Good

We might begin by considering a certain moral and political vision. It is a liberal vision, and like most liberal visions gives pride of place to justice, fairness, and individual rights. Its core thesis is this: a just society seeks not to promote any particular ends, but enables its citizens to pursue their own ends, consistent with a similar liberty for all; it therefore must govern by principles that do not presuppose any particular conception of the good. What justifies these regulative principles above all is not that they maximize the general welfare, or cultivate virtue, or otherwise promote the good, but rather that they conform to the concept of *right*, a moral category given prior to the good, and independent of it.

This liberalism says, in other words, that what makes the just society just is not the *telos* or purpose or end at which it aims, but precisely its refusal to choose in advance among competing purposes and ends. In its constitution and its laws, the just society seeks to provide a framework within which its citizens can pursue their own values and ends, consistent with a similar liberty for others.

The ideal I've described might be summed up in the claim that the right is prior to the good, and in two senses: The priority of the right means first, that individual rights cannot be sacrificed for the sake of the general good (in this it opposes utilitarianism), and second, that the principles of justice that specify these rights cannot be premised on any particular vision of the good life. (In this it opposes teleological conceptions in general.)

This is the liberalism of much contemporary moral and political philosophy, most fully elaborated by Rawls, and indebted to Kant for its philosophical foundations.[3] But I am concerned here less with the lineage of this vision than with what seem to me three striking facts about it.

First, it has a deep and powerful philosophical appeal. Second, despite its philosophical force, the claim for the priority of the right over the good ultimately fails. And third, despite its philosophical failure, this liberal vision is the one by which we live. For us in late twentieth century America, it is our vision, the theory most thoroughly embodied in the practices and institutions most central to our public life. And seeing how it goes wrong as philosophy may help us to diagnose our present political condition. So first, its philosophical power; second, its philosophical failure; and third, however briefly, its uneasy embodiment in the world.

But before taking up these three claims, it is worth pointing out a central theme that connects them. And that is a certain conception of the person, of what it is to be moral agent. Like all political theories, the liberal theory I have described is something more than a set of regulative principles. It is also a view about the way the world is, and the way we move within it. At the heart of this ethic lies a vision of the person that both inspires and undoes it. As I will try to argue now, what make this ethic so compelling, but also, finally, vulnerable, are the promise and the failure of the unencumbered self.

## Kantian Foundations

The liberal ethic asserts the priority of right, and seeks principles of justice that do not presuppose any particular conception of the good.[4] This is what Kant means by the supremacy of the moral law, and what Rawls means when he writes that "justice is the first virtue of social institutions."[5] Justice is more than just another value. It provides the framework that *regulates* the play of competing values and ends; it must therefore have a sanction independent of those ends. But it is not obvious where such a sanction could be found.

Theories of justice, and for that matter, ethics, have typically founded their claims on one or another conception of human purposes and ends. Thus Aristotle said the measure of a *polis* is the good at which it aims, and even J.S. Mill, who in the nineteenth century called "justice the chief part, and incomparably the most binding part of all morality," made justice an instrument of utilitarian ends.[6]

This is the solution Kant's ethic rejects. Different persons typically have different desires and ends, and so any principle derived from them can only be contingent. But the moral law needs a *categorical* foundation, not a contingent one. Even so universal a desire as happiness will not do. People still differ in what happiness consists of, and to install any particular conception as regulative would impose on some the conceptions of others, and so deny at least to some the freedom to choose their *own* conceptions. In any case, to govern ourselves in conformity with desires and inclinations, given as they are by nature or circumstance, is not really to be *self*-governing at all. It is rather a refusal of freedom, a capitulation to determinations given outside us.

According to Kant, the right is "derived entirely from the concept of freedom in the external relationships of human beings, and has nothing to do with the end which all men have by nature [i.e., the aim of achieving happiness] or with the recognized means of attaining this end."[7] As such, it must have a basis prior to all empirical ends. Only when I am governed by principles that do not presuppose any particular ends am I free to pursue my own ends consistent with a similar freedom for all.

But this still leaves the question of what the basis of the right could possibly be. If it must be a basis prior to all purposes and ends, unconditioned even by what Kant calls "the special circumstances of human nature,"[8] where could such a basis conceivably be found? Given the stringent demands of the Kantian ethic, the moral law would seem almost to require a foundation in nothing, for any empirical precondition would undermine its priority. "Duty!" asks Kant at his most lyrical, "What origin is there worthy of thee, and where is to be found the root of thy noble descent which proudly rejects all kinship with the inclinations?"[9]

His answer is that the basis of the moral law is to be found in the *subject*, not the object of practical reason, a subject capable of an autonomous will. No empirical end, but rather "a subject of ends, namely a rational being himself, must be made the ground for all maxims of action."[10] Nothing other than what Kant calls "the subject of all possible ends himself" can give rise to the right, for only this subject is also the subject of an autonomous will. Only this subject could be that "something which elevates man above himself as part of the world of sense" and enables him to participate in an ideal, unconditioned realm wholly independent of our social and psychological inclinations. And only this thoroughgoing independence can afford us the detachment we need if we are ever freely to choose for ourselves, unconditioned by the vagaries of circumstance.[11]

Who or what exactly *is* this subject? It is, in a certain sense, *us*. The moral law, afterall, is a law we give *ourselves*; we don't *find* it, we *will* it. That is how it (and we) escape the reign of nature and circumstance and merely empirical ends. But what is important to see is that the "we" who do the willing are not "we" qua particular persons, you and me, each for ourselves—the moral law is not up to us as individuals—but "we" qua participants in what Kant calls "pure practical reason," "we" qua participants in a transcendental subject.

Now what is to guarantee that I *am* a subject of this kind, capable of exercising pure practical reason? Well, strictly speaking, there *is* no guarantee; the transcendental subject is only a possibility. But it is a possibility I must *presuppose* if I am to think of myself as a free moral agent. Were I wholly an empirical being, I would not be capable of freedom, for every exercise of will would be conditioned by the desire for some object. All choice would be heteronomous choice, governed by the pursuit of some end. My will could never be a first cause, only the effect of some prior cause, the instrument of one or another impulse or inclination. "When we think of ourselves as free," writes Kant, "we transfer ourselves into the intelligible world as members and recognize the autonomy of the will."[12] And so the notion of a subject prior to and independent of experience, such as the Kantian ethic requires, appears not only possible but indispensible, a necessary presupposition of the possibility of freedom.

How does all of this come back to politics? As the subject is prior to its ends, so the right is prior to the good. Society is best arranged when it is governed by principles that do not presuppose any particular conception of the good, for any other arrangement would fail to respect persons as being capable of choice; it would treat them as objects rather than subjects, as means rather than ends in themselves.

We can see in this way how Kant's notion of the subject is bound up with the claim for the priority of right. But for those in the Anglo-American tradition, the transcendental subject will seem a strange foundation for a familiar ethic. Surely, one may think, we can take rights seriously and affirm the primacy of justice without embracing the *Critique of Pure Reason*. This, in any case, is the project of Rawls.

He wants to save the priority of right from the obscurity of the transcendental subject. Kant's idealist metaphysic, for all its moral and political advantage, cedes too much to the transcendent, and wins for justice its primacy only by denying it its human situation. "To develop a viable Kantian conception of justice," Rawls writes, "the force and content of Kant's doctrine must be detached from its background in transcendental idealism" and recast within the "canons of a reasonable empiricism."[13] And so Rawls' project is to preserve Kant's moral and political teaching by replacing Germanic obscurities with a domesticated metaphysic more congenial to the Anglo-American temper. This is the role of the original position.

## From Transcendental Subject to Unencumbered Self

The original position tries to provide what Kant's transcendental argument cannot—a foundation for the right that is prior to the good, but still situated in the world. Sparing all but essentials, the original position works like this: It invites us to imagine the principles we would choose to govern our society if we were to choose them in advance, before we knew the particular persons we would be—whether rich or poor, strong or weak, lucky or unlucky—before we knew even our interests or aims or conceptions of the good. These principles—the ones we would choose in that imaginary situation—are the principles of justice. What is more, if it works, they are principles that do not presuppose any particular ends.

What they *do* presuppose is a certain picture of the person, of the way we must be if we are beings for whom justice is the first virtue. This is the picture of the unencumbered self, a self understood as prior to and independent of purposes and ends.

Now the unencumbered self describes first of all the way we stand toward the things we have, or want, or seek. It means there is always a distinction between the values I *have* and the person I *am*. To identify any characteristics as *my* aims, ambitions, desires, and so on, is always to imply some subject "me" standing behind them, at a certain distance, and the shape of this "me" must be given prior to any of the aims or attributes I bear. One consequences of this distance is to put the self *itself* beyond the reach of its experience, to secure its identity once and for all. Or to put the point another way, it rules out the possibility of what we might call *constitutive* ends. No role or commitment could define me so completely that I could not understand myself without it. No project could be so essential that turning away from it would call into question the person I am.

For the unencumbered self, what matters above all, what is most essential to our personhood, are not the ends we choose but our capacity to choose them. The original position sums up this central claim about us. "It is not our aims that primarily reveal our nature," writes Rawls, "but rather the principles that we would acknowledge to govern the background conditions under which these aims are to be formed ... We should therefore reverse the relation between the right and the good proposed by teleological doctrines and view the right as prior."[14]

Only if the self is prior to its ends can the right be prior to the good. Only if my identity is never tied to the aims and interests I may have at any moment can I think of myself as a free and independent agent, capable of choice.

This notion of independence carries consequences for the kind of community of which we are capable. Understood as unencumbered selves, we are of course free to join in voluntary association with others, and so are capable of community in the cooperative sense. What is denied to the unencumbered self is the possibility of membership in any community bound by moral ties antecedent to choice; he cannot belong to any community where the self *itself* could be at stake. Such a community—call it constitutive as against merely cooperative—would engage the identity as well as the interests of the participants, and so implicate its members in a citizenship more thoroughgoing than the unencumbered self can know.

For justice to be primary, then, we must be creatures of a certain kind, related to human circumstance in a certain way. We must stand to our circumstance always at a certain distance, whether as transcendental subject in the case of Kant, or as unencumbered selves in the case of Rawls. Only in this way can we view ourselves as subjects as well as objects of experience, as agents and not just instruments of the purposes we pursue.

The unencumbered self and the ethic it inspires, taken together, hold out a liberating vision. Freed from the dicates of nature and the sanction of social roles, the human subject is installed as sovereign, cast as the author of the only moral meanings there are. As participants in pure practical reason, or as parties to the original position, we are free to construct principles of justice unconstrained by an order of value antecedently given. And as actual, individual selves, we are free to choose our purposes and ends unbound by such an order, or by custom or tradition or inherited status. So long as they are not unjust, our conceptions of the good carry weight, whatever they are, simply in virtue of our having chosen them. We are, in Rawls' words, "self-originating sources of valid claims."[15]

This is an exhilarating promise, and the liberalism it animates is perhaps the fullest expression of the Enlightenment's quest for the self-defining subject. But is it true? Can we make sense of our moral and political life by the light of the self-image it requires? I do not think we can, and I will try to show why not by arguing first within the liberal project, then beyond it.

## Justice and Community

We have focused so far on the foundations of the liberal vision, on the way it derives the principles it defends. Let us turn briefly now to the substance of those principles, using Rawls as our example. Sparing all but essentials once again, Rawls' two principles of justice are these: first, equal basic liberties for all, and second, only those social and economic inequalities that benefit the least-advantaged members of society (the difference principle).

In arguing for these principles, Rawls argues against two familiar alternatives—utilitarianism and libertarianism. He argues against utilitarianism that it fails to take seriously the distinction between persons. In seeking to maximize the general welfare, the utilitarian treats society as a whole as if it were a single person; it conflates our many, diverse desires into a single system of desires, and tries to maximize. It is indifferent to the distribution of satisfactions among persons, except insofar as this may affect the overall sum. But this fails to respect our plurality and distinctness. It uses some as means to the happiness of all, and so fails to respect each as an end in himself. While utilitarians may sometimes defend individual rights, their defense must rest on the calculation that respecting those rights will serve utility in the long run. But this calculation is contingent and uncertain. So long as utility is what Mill said it is, "the ultimate appeal on all ethical questions,"[16] individual rights can never be secure. To avoid the danger that their life prospects might one day be sacrificed for the greater good of others, the parties to the original position therefore insist on certain basic liberties for all, and make those liberties prior.

If utilitarians fail to take seriously the distinctness of persons, libertarians go wrong by failing to acknowledge the arbitrariness of fortune. They define as just whatever distribution results from an efficient market economy, and oppose all redistribution on the grounds that people are entitled to whatever they get, so long as they do not cheat or steal or otherwise violate someone's rights in getting it. Rawls opposes this principle on the ground that the distribution of talents and assets and even efforts by which some get more and others get less is arbitrary from a moral point of view, a matter of good luck. To distribute the good things in life on the basis of these differences is not to do justice, but simply to carry over into human arrangements the arbitrariness of social and natural contingency. We deserve, as individuals, neither the talents our good fortune may have brought, nor the benefits that flow from them. We should therefore regard these talents as common assets, and regard one another as common beneficiaries of the rewards they bring. "Those who have been favored by nature, whoever they are, may gain from their good fortune only on terms that improve the situation of those who have lost out... In justice as fairness, men agree to share one another's fate."[17]

This is the reasoning that leads to the difference principle. Notice how it reveals, in yet another guise, the logic of the unencumbered self. I cannot be said to deserve the benefits that flow from, say, my fine physique and good looks, because they are only accidental, not essential facts about me. They describe attributes I *have*, not the person I *am*, and so cannot give rise to a claim of desert. Being an unencumbered self, this is true of *everything* about me. And so I cannot, as an individual, deserve anything at all.

However jarring to our ordinary understandings this argument may be, the picture so far remains intact; the priority of right, the denial of desert, and the unencumbered self all hang impressively together.

But the difference principle requires more, and it is here that the argument comes undone. The difference principle begins with the thought, congenial to the unencumbered self, that the assets I have are only accidentally mine. But it ends by assuming that these assets are therefore *common* assets and that society has a prior claim on the fruits of their exercise. But this assumption is without warrant. Simply because I, as an individual, do not have a privileged claim on the assets accidentally residing "here," it does not follow that everyone in the world collectively does. For there is no reason to think that their location in society's province or, for that matter, within the province of humankind, is any *less* arbitrary from a moral point of view. And if their arbitrariness within *me* makes them ineligible to serve *my* ends, there seems no obvious reason why their arbitrariness within any particular society should not make them ineligible to serve that society's ends as well.

To put the point another way, the difference principle, like utilitarianism, is a principle of sharing. As such, it must presuppose some prior moral tie among those whose assets it would deploy and whose efforts it would enlist in a common endeavor. Otherwise, it is simply a formula for using some as means to others ends, a formula this liberalism is committed to reject.

But on the cooperative vision of community alone, it is unclear what the moral basis for this sharing could be. Short of the constitutive conception, deploying an individual's assets for the sake of the common good would seem an offense against the "plurality and distinctness" of individuals this liberalism seeks above all to secure.

If those whose fate I am required to share really are, morally speaking, *others*, rather than fellow participants in a way of life with which my identity is bound, the difference principle falls prey to the same objections as utilitarianism. Its claim on me is not the claim of a constitutive community whose attachments I acknowledge, but rather the claim of a concatenated collectivity whose entanglements I confront.

What the difference principle requires, but cannot provide, is some way of identifying those *among* whom the assets I bear are properly regarded as common, some way of seeing ourselves as mutually indebted and morally engaged to begin with. But as we have seen, the constitutive aims and attachments that would save and situate the difference principle are precisely the ones denied to the liberal self; the moral encumbrances and antecedent obligations they imply would undercut the priority of right.

What, then, of those encumbrances? The point so far is that we cannot be persons for whom justice is primary, and also be persons for whom the difference principle is a principle of justice. But which must give way? Can we view ourselves as independent selves, independent in the sense that our identity is never tied to our aims and attachments?

I do not think we can, at least not without cost to those loyalties and convictions whose moral force consists partly in the fact that living by them is inseparable from understanding ourselves as the particular persons we are—as members of this family or community or nation or people, as bearers of that history, as citizens of this republic. Allegiances such as these are more than values I happen to have, and to hold, at a certain distance. They go beyond the obligations I voluntarily incur and the "natural duties" I owe to human beings as such. They allow that to some I owe more than justice requires or even permits, not by reason of agreements I have made but instead in virtue of those more or less enduring attachments and commitments that, taken together, partly define the person I am.

To imagine a person incapable of constitutive attachments such as these is not to conceive an ideally free and rational agent, but to imagine a person wholly without character, without moral depth. For to have character is to know that I move in a history I neither summon nor command, which carries consequences nonetheless for my choices and conduct. It draws me closer to some and more distant from others; it makes some aims more appropriate, others less so. As a self-interpreting being, I am able to reflect on my history and in this sense to distance myself from it, but the distance is always precarious and provisional, the point of reflection never finally secured outside the history itself. But the liberal ethic puts the self beyond the reach of its experience, beyond deliberation and reflection. Denied the expansive self-understandings that could shape a common life, the liberal self is left to lurch between detachment on the one hand, and entanglement on the other. Such is the fate of the unencumbered self, and its liberating promise.

## The Procedural Republic

But before my case can be complete, I need to consider one powerful reply. While it comes from a liberal direction, its spirit is more practical than philosophical. It says, in short, that I am asking too much. It is one thing to seek constitutive attachments in our private lives; among families and friends, and certain tightly knit groups, there may be found a common good that makes justice and rights less pressing. But with public life—at least today, and probably always—it is different. So long as the nation-state is the primary form of political association, talk of constitutive community too easily suggests a darker politics rather than a brighter one; amid echoes of the moral majority, the priority of right, for all its philosophical faults, still seems the safer hope.

This is a challenging rejoinder, and no account of political community in the twentieth century can fail to take it seriously. It is challenging not least because it calls into question the status of political philosophy and its relation to the world. For if my argument is correct, if the liberal vision we have considered is not morally self-sufficient but parasitic on a notion of community it officially rejects, then we should expect to find that the political practice that embodies this vision is not *practically* self-sufficient either—that it must draw on a sense of community it cannot supply and may even undermine. But is that so far from the circumstance we face today? Could it be that through the original position darkly, on the far side of the veil of ignorance, we may glimpse an intimation of our predicament, a refracted vision of ourselves?

How does the liberal vision—and its failure—help us make sense of our public life and its predicament? Consider, to begin, the following paradox in the citizen's relation to the modern welfare state. In many ways, we in the 1980s stand near the completion of a liberal project that has run its course from the New Deal through the Great Society and into the present. But notwithstanding the extension of the franchise and the expansion on individual rights and entitlements in recent decades, there is a widespread sense that, individually and collectively, our control over the forces that govern our lives is receding rather than increasing. This sense is deepened by what appear simultaneously as the power and the powerlessness of the nation-state. One the one hand, increasing numbers of citizens view the state as an overly intrusive presence, more likely to frustrate their purposes than advance them. And yet, despite its unprecedented role in the economy and society, the modern state seems itself disempowered, unable effectively to control the domestic economy, to respond to persisting social ills, or to work America's will in the world.

This is a paradox that has fed the appeals of recent politicians (including Carter and Reagan), even as it has frustrated their attempts to govern. To sort it out, we need to identify the public philosophy implicit in our political practice, and to reconstruct its arrival. We need to trace the advent of the procedural republic, by which I mean a public life animated by the liberal vision and self-image we've considered.

The story of the procedural republic goes back in some ways to the founding of the republic, but its central drama begins to unfold around the turn of the century. As national markets and large-scale enterprise displaced a decentralized economy, the decentralized political forms of the early republic became outmoded as well. If democracy was to survive, the concentration of economic power would have to be met by a similar concentration of political power. But the Progressives understood, or some of them did, that the success of democracy required more than the centralization of government; it also required the nationalization of politics. The primary form of political community had to be a recast on a national scale. For Herbert Croly, writing in 1909, the "nationalizing of American political, economic, and social life" was "an essentially formative and enlightening political transformation." We would become more of a democracy only as we became "more of a nation ... in ideas, in institutions, and in spirit."[18]

This nationalizing project would be consummated in the New Deal, but for the democratic tradition in America, the embrace of the nation was a decisive departure. From Jefferson to the populists, the party of democracy in American political debate had been, roughly speaking, the party of the provinces, of decentralized power, of small-town and small-scale America. And against them had stood the party of the nation—first Federalists, then Whigs, then the Republicans of Lincoln—a party that spoke for the consolidation of the union. It was thus the historic achievement of the New Deal to unite, in a single party and political program, what Samuel Beer has called "liberalism and the national idea."[19]

What matters for our purpose is that, in the twentieth century, liberalism made its peace with concentrated power. But it was understood at the start that the terms of this peace required a strong sense of national community, morally and politically to underwrite the extended involvements of a modern industrial order. If a virtuous republic of small-scale, democratic communities was no longer a possibility, a national republic seemed democracy's next best hope. This was still, in principle at least, a politics of the common good. It looked to the nation, not as a neutral framework for the play of competing interests, but rather as a formative community, concerned to shape a common life suited to the scale of modern social and economic forms.

But this project failed. By the mid- or late twentieth century, the national republic had run its course. Except for extraordinary moments, such as war, the nation proved too vast a scale across which to cultivate the shared self-understandings necessary to community in the formative, or constitutive sense. And so the gradual shift, in our practices and institutions, from a public philosophy of common purposes to one of fair procedures, from a politics of good to a politics of right, from the national republic to the procedural republic.

## Our Present Predicament

A full account of this transition would take a detailed look at the changing shape of political institutions, constitutional interpretation, and the terms of political discourse in the broadest sense. But I suspect we would find in the *practice* of the procedural republic two broad tendencies foreshadowed by its philosophy: first, a tendency to crowd out democratic possibilities; second, a tendency to undercut the kind of community on which it nonetheless depends.

Where liberty in the early republic was understood as a function of democratic institutions and dispersed power,[20] liberty in the procedural republic is defined in opposition to democracy, as an individual's guarantee against what the majority might will. I am free insofar as I am the bearer of rights, where rights are trumps.[21] Unlike the liberty of the early republic, the modern version permits—in fact even requires—concentrated power. This has to do with the universalizing logic of rights. Insofar as I have a right, whether to free speech or a minimum income, its provision cannot be left to the vagaries of local preferences but must be assured at the most comprehensive level of political association. It cannot be one thing in New York and another in Alabama. As rights and entitlements expand, politics is therefore displaced from smaller forms of association and relocated at the most universal form—in our case, the nation. And even as politics flows to the nation, power shifts away from democratic institutions (such as legislatures and political parties) and toward institutions designed to be insulated from democratic pressures and hence better equipped to dispense and defend individual rights (notably the judiciary and bureaucracy).

These institutional developments may begin to account for the sense of powerlessness that the welfare state fails to address and in some ways doubtless deepens. But it seems to me a further clue to our condition recalls even more directly the predicament of the unencumbered self—lurching, as we left it, between detachment on the one hand, the entanglement on the other. For it is a striking feature of the welfare state that it offers a powerful promise of individual rights, and also demands of its citizens a high measure of mutual engagement. But the self-image that attends the rights cannot sustain the engagement.

As bearers of rights, where rights are trumps, we think of ourselves as freely choosing, individual selves, unbound by obligations antecedent to rights, or to the agreements we make. And yet, as citizens of the procedural republic that secures these rights, we find ourselves implicated willy-nilly in a formidable array of dependencies and expectations we did not choose and increasingly reject.

In our public life, we are more entangled, but less attached, than ever before. It is as though the unencumbered self presupposed by the liberal ethic had begun to come true—less liberated than disempowered, entangled in a network of obligations and involvements unassociated with any act of will, and yet unmediated by those common identifications or expansive self-definitions that would make them tolerable. As the scale of social and political organization has become more comprehensive, the terms of our collective identity have become more fragmented, and the forms of political life have outrun the common purpose needed to sustain them.

Something like this, it seems to me, has been unfolding in America for the past half-century or so. I hope I have said at least enough to suggest the shape a fuller story might take. And I hope in any case to have conveyed a certain view about politics and philosophy and the relation between them—that our practices and institutions are themselves embodiments of theory, and to unravel their predicament is, at least in part, to seek after the self-image of the age.

## Notes

1 An excellent example of this view can be found in Samuel Huntington, *American Politics: The promise of Disharmony* (Cambridge: Harvard University Press, 1981). See especially his discussion of the "ideals versus institutions" gap, pp. 10-12, 39-41, 61-84, 221-262.
2 See, for example, the conceptions of a "practice" advanced by Alasdair MacIntyre and Charles Taylor. MacIntyre, *After Virtue* (Notre Dame: University of Notre Dame Press, 1981), pp. 175-209. Taylor, "Interpretation and the Sciences of Man," *Review of Metaphysics* 25, (1971) pp. 3-51.
3 John Rawls, *A Theory of Justice* (Oxford: Oxford University Press, 1971). Immanuel Kant, *Groundwork of the Metaphysics of Morals*, trans. H. J. Paton. (1785; New York: Harper and Row, 1956). Kant, *Critique of Pure Reason*, trans. Norman Kemp Smith (1781, 1787; London: Macmillan, 1929). Kant, *Critique of Practical Reason*, trans. L. W. Beck (1788; Indianapolis: Bobbs-Merrill, 1956). Kant, "On the Common Saying: 'This May Be True in Theory, But It Does Not Apply in Practice,'" in Hans Reiss, ed., *Kant's Political Writings* (1793; Cambridge: Cambridge University Press, 1970). Other recent versions of the claim for the priority of the right over good can be found in Robert Nozick, *Anarchy, State, and Utopia* (New York: Basic Books, 1974); Ronald Dworkin, *Taking Rights Seriously* (London: Duckworth, 1977); Bruce Ackerman, *Social Justice in the Liberal State* (New Haven: Yale University Press, 1980).

4 This section, and the two that follow, summarize arguments developed more fully in Michael Sandel, *Liberalism and the Limits of Justice* (Cambridge: Cambridge University Press, 1982).
5 Rawls (1971), p. 3.
6 John Stuart Mill, *Utilitarianism*, in *The Utilitarians* (1893; Garden City: Doubleday, 1973), p. 465. Mill, *On Liberty*, in *The Utilitarians*, p. 485 (Originally published 1849).
7 Kant (1793), p. 73.
8 Kant (1785), p. 92.
9 Kant (1788), p. 89.
10 Kant (1785), p. 105.
11 Kant (1788), p. 89.
12 Kant (1785), p. 121.
13 Rawls, "The Basic Structure as Subject," *American Philosophical Quarterly* (1977), p. 165.
14 Rawls (1971), p. 560.
15 Rawls, "Kantian Constructivism in Moral Theory," *Journal of Philosophy* 77 (1980), p. 543.
16 Mill (1849), p. 485.
17 Rawls (1971), pp. 101-102.
18 Croly, *The Promise of American Life* (Indianapolis: Bobbs-Merrill, 1965), pp. 270-273.
19 Beer, "Liberalism and the National Idea," *The Public Interest*, Fall (1966), pp. 70-82.
20 See, for example, Laurence Tribe, *American Constitutional Law* (Mineola: The Foundation Press, 1978), pp. 2-3.
21 See Ronald Dworkin, "Liberalism," in Stuart Hampshire, ed., *Public and Private Morality* (Cambridge: Cambridge University Press, 1978), p. 136.

# 12 Liberal Individualism and Liberal Neutrality

Will Kymlicka

## Defining Liberal Neutrality

What sort of neutrality is present, or aspired to, in Rawls's theory? Raz distinguishes two principles which he believes are present, and inadequately distinguished, in liberal writings on neutrality. One, which Raz calls "neutral political concern," requires that the state seek to help or hinder different life-plans to an equal degree—that is, government action should have neutral consequences. The other, which Raz calls the "exclusion of ideals," allows that government action may help some ways of life more than others but denies that government should act in order to help some ways of life over others. The state does not take a stand on which ways of life are most worth living, and the desire to help one way of life over another is precluded as a justification of government action. The first requires neutrality in the consequences of government policy; the second requires neutrality in the justification of government policy. I will call these two conceptions consequential and justificatory neutrality, respectively.

Which conception does Rawls defend? Raz argues that Rawls endorses consequential neutrality,[1] and some of Rawls's formulations are undoubtedly consistent with that interpretation. But there are two basic tenets of Rawls's theory which show that he could not have endorsed consequential neutrality. First, respect for civil liberties will necessarily have nonneutral consequences. Freedom of speech and association allow different groups to pursue and advertise their way of life. But not all ways of life are equally valuable, and some will have difficulty attracting or maintaining adherents. Since individuals are free to choose between competing visions of the good life, civil liberties have nonneutral consequences—they create a marketplace of ideas, as it were, and how well a way of life does in this market depends on the kinds of goods it can offer to prospective adherents. Hence, under conditions of freedom, satisfying and valuable ways of life will tend to drive out those which are worthless and unsatisfying.

Rawls endorses such a cultural marketplace, despite its nonneutral consequences. Moreover, the prospect that trivial and degrading ways of life fare less well in free competition is not something he regrets or views as an unfortunate side effect. On the contrary, the liberal tradition has always endorsed civil liberties precisely because they make it possible "that the worth of different modes of life should be proved practically."[2]

Consequential neutrality is also inconsistent with Rawls's explanation of the role of "primary goods." They are supposed to be employable in the pursuit of diverse conceptions of the good. But not all ways of life have the same costs, and so an equal distribution of resources will have nonneutral consequences. Those who choose expensive ways of life—valuing leisure over work, or champagne over beer—will get less welfare out of an equal bundle of resources than will people with more modest tastes. This is unlike an equality of welfare scheme, in which those with expensive tastes would be subsidized by others in order to achieve equality of welfare. On an equality of welfare scheme, resources would be unequally distributed so that every way of life is equally helped, no matter how expensive—those who wish beer get enough money for beer, those who wish champagne get enough money for champagne.

Rawls favors equality of resources, despite its nonneutral consequences and, indeed, because it prohibits excess demands on resources by those with expensive desires:

> It is not by itself an objection to the use of primary goods that it does not accommodate those with expensive tastes. One must argue in addition that it is unreasonable, if not unjust, to hold people responsible for their preferences and to require them to make out as best they can. But to argue this seems to presuppose that citizens' preferences are beyond their control as propensities or cravings which simply happen. Citizens seem to be regarded as passive carriers of desires. The use of primary goods, however, relies on a capacity to assume responsibility for our ends. This capacity is part of the moral power to form, to revise, and rationally to pursue a conception of the good.... In any particular situation, then, those with less expensive tastes have presumably adjusted their likes and dislikes over the course of their lives to the income and wealth they could reasonably expect; and it is regarded as unfair that they now should have less in order to spare others from the consequences of their lack of foresight or self-discipline.[3]

Since individuals are responsible for forming "their aims and ambitions in the light of what they can reasonably expect," they recognize that "the weight of their claims is not given by the strength or intensity of their wants and desires."[4] Those people who have developed expensive tastes in disregard of what they can reasonably expect have no claim to be subsidized by others, no matter how strongly felt those desires are.[5]

So the two fundamental components of liberal justice—respect for liberty and fairness in the distribution of material resources—both preclude consequential neutrality. However ambiguous his terminology is, Rawls has to be interpreted as endorsing justificatory neutrality.[6] As Rawls puts it, government is neutral between different conceptions of the good, "not in the sense that there is an agreed public measure of intrinsic value or satisfaction with respect to which all these conceptions come out equal, but in the sense that they are not evaluated at all from a social standpoint."[7] The state does not justify its actions by reference to some public ranking of the intrinsic value of different ways of life, for there is no public ranking to refer to. This kind of neutrality is consistent with the legitimate nonneutral consequences of cultural competition and individual responsibility. Indeed, and I'll return to this point, one might think that good ways of life are most likely to establish their greater worth, and individuals are most likely to accept responsibility for the costs of their choices, when the state is constrained by justificatory neutrality—that is, when individuals cannot "use the coercive apparatus of the state to win for themselves a greater liberty or larger distributive share on the grounds that their activities are of more intrinsic value."[8]

## Evaluating the Neutrality Debate

I have argued that liberal neutrality is not excessively individualistic, either in terms of the way it conceives the content of people's ends, or in the way that people evaluate and pursue those ends. Of course neutrality may be indefensible for other reasons. Neutrality requires a certain faith in the operation of nonstate forums and processes for individual judgement and cultural development, and a distrust of the operation of state forums and processes for evaluating the good. Nothing I have said so far shows that this optimism and distrust are warranted. Indeed, just as critics of neutrality have failed to defend their faith in political forums and procedures, so liberals have failed to defend their faith in nonstate forums and procedures. The crucial claims have not been adequately defended by either side.

In fact, it is hard to avoid the conclusion that each side in the neutrality debate has failed to learn the important lesson taught by the other side. Despite centuries of liberal insistence on the importance of the distinction between society and the state, communitarians still seem to assume that whatever is properly social must become the province of the political. They have not confronted the liberal worry that the all-embracing authority and coercive means which characterize the state make it a particularly inappropriate forum for the sort of genuinely shared deliberation and commitment that they desire. Despite centuries of communitarian insistence on the historically fragile and contingent nature of our culture, and the need to consider the conditions under which a free culture can arise and sustain itself, liberals still tend to take the existence of a tolerant and diverse culture for granted, as something which naturally arises and sustains itself, the ongoing existence of which is therefore simply assumed in a theory of justice. Hegel was right to insist that a culture of freedom is a historical achievement, and liberals need to explain why the cultural marketplace does not threaten that achievement either by failing to connect people in a strong enough way to their communal practices (as communitarians fear), or conversely, by failing to detach people in a strong enough way from the expectations of existing practices and ideologies (as Habermas fears). A culture of freedom requires a mix of both exposure and connection to existing practices, and also distance and dissent from them. Liberal neutrality may provide that mix, but that is not obviously true, and it may be true only in some times and places. So both sides need to give us a more comprehensive comparison of the opportunities and dangers present in state and nonstate forums and procedures for evaluating the good.

While both sides have something to learn from the other, that is not to say that the truth is somewhere in between the two. I cannot provide here the sort of systematic comparison of the empirical operation of state and nonstate forums and procedures that is required for a proper defense of neutrality, but I want to suggest a few reasons why state perfectionism would have undesirable consequences for our society. I will assume, for the moment, that the public ranking of the value of different ways of life which a perfectionist state appeals to would be arrived at through the collective political deliberation of citizens, rather than through the secret or unilateral decisions of political elites.

What are the consequences of having a collectively determined ranking of the value of different conceptions of the good? One consequence is that more is at stake when people publicly formulate and defend their conception of the good. If people do not advance persuasive arguments for their conception of the good, then a perfectionist state may take action which will make their way of life harder to maintain. In a liberal society with a neutral state, on the other hand, people who cannot persuade others of the value of their way of life will lose out in the competition with other conceptions of the good being advanced in the cultural marketplace, but they will not face adverse state action.

Why is that an undesirable consequence? In principle, it is not undesirable—it may simply intensify the patterns of cultural development, since the pros and cons of different ways of life might be revealed more quickly under the threat of state action than would occur in the cultural marketplace, where people are sometimes reluctant to confront opposing values and arguments. However, I believe that state perfectionism would in fact serve to distort the free evaluation of ways of life, to rigidify the dominant ways of life, whatever their intrinsic merits, and to unfairly exclude the values and aspirations of marginalized and disadvantaged groups within the community.

First, state perfectionism raises the prospect of a dictatorship of the articulate and would unavoidably penalize those individuals who are inarticulate. But being articulate, in our society, is not simply an individual variable. There are many culturally disadvantaged groups whose beliefs and aspirations are not understood by the majority. Recent immigrants are an obvious example whose disadvantage is partly unavoidable. But there are also groups which have been deliberately excluded from the mainstream of American society, and whose cultural disadvantage reflects prejudice and insensitivity. The dominant cultural practices of our community were defined by one section of the population—that is, the male members of the upper classes of the white race—and were defined so as to exclude and denigrate the values of subordinate groups. Members of these excluded groups—women, blacks, Hispanics—have been unable to get recognition for their values from the cultural mainstream and have developed (or retained) subcultures for the expression of these values, subcultures whose norms, by necessity, are incommensurable with those of the mainstream. It is unfair to ask them to defend the value of their way of life by reference to cultural standards and norms that were defined by and for others. Even where these historical factors are absent, the majority is likely to use state perfectionism to block valuable social change that threatens their preferred cultural practices. This cultural conservatism need not be malicious—the majority may simply not see the value of cultural change, partly due to incomprehension, partly from fear of change.

State perfectionism would also affect the kinds of arguments given. Minority groups whose values conflict with those of the majority often put a high value on the integrity of their practices and aim at gaining adherents from within the majority slowly, one by one. But where there is state perfectionism, the minority must immediately aim at persuading the majority, and so they will describe their practices in such a way as to be most palatable to the majority, even if that misdescribes the real meaning and value of the practice, which often arose precisely in opposition to dominant practices. There would be an inevitable tendency for minorities to describe and debate conceptions of the good in terms of dominant values, which then reinforces the cultural conservatism of the dominant group itself.

In these and other ways, the threats and inducements of coercive power would distort rather than improve the process of individual judgment and cultural development. Some of these problems also arise in the cultural marketplace (i.e., penalizing the inarticulate, social prejudice). Insensitivity and prejudice will be problems no matter which model we choose, since both models reward those groups who can make their way of life attractive to the mainstream. But state perfectionism intensifies these problems, since it dictates to minority groups when and how they will interact with majority norms, and it dictates a time and place—political deliberation over state policy—in which minorities are most vulnerable. State neutrality, on the other hand, gives culturally disadvantaged groups a greater ability to choose the time and place in which they will confront majority sensitivities and to choose an audience with whom they are most comfortable. There will always be an imbalance in the interaction between culturally dominant and subordinate groups. State neutrality ensures that the culturally subordinate group has as many options as possible concerning that interaction, and that the costs of that imbalance for the subordinate groups are minimized. State perfectionism, I think, does just the opposite.

Some of these problems could be avoided if the public ranking of ways of life was determined by political elites, insulated from popular debate and prejudice. Indeed, an enlightened and insulated political elite could use state perfectionist policies to promote the aims and values of culturally disadvantaged groups. Just as the Supreme Court is supposed to be more able to protect the rights of disadvantaged groups because of its insulation from political pressures, so an insulated political elite may be able to give a fairer hearing to minority values than they get in the cultural marketplace. But this raises troubling questions about accountability and the danger of abuse (after all, if majority groups are insensitive to minority aspirations, why won't they elect leaders who are similarly insensitive?). And, in any event, why shouldn't the aim of the political elite be to counteract the biases of the cultural marketplace, which affect the public evaluation of all minority values, rather than deciding for themselves which minority values are worth promoting? Using state power to counteract biases against minority values may be legitimate, not because of a general principle of perfectionism, but because of a general principle of redressing biases against disadvantaged groups.

These are some of the reasons why liberals distrust state perfectionism for our society.[9] Communitarians are right to insist that we examine the history and structure of a particular culture, but it is remarkable how little communitarians themselves undertake such an examination of our culture. They wish to use the ends and practices of our cultural tradition as the basis for a politics of the common good, but they do not mention that these practices were historically defined by a small segment of the population, nor do they discuss how that exclusionary history would affect the politicization of debates about the value of different ways of life. If we look at the history of our society, surely liberal neutrality has the great advantage of its potential inclusiveness, its denial that marginalized and subordinate groups must fit into the historical practices, the "way of life," which have been defined by the dominant groups. Forcing subordinate groups to defend their ways of life, under threat or promise of coercive power, is inherently exclusive. Communitarians simply ignore this danger and the cultural history which makes it so difficult to avoid.[10]

## Notes

1 Joseph Raz, *The Morality of Freedom* (Oxford: Oxford University Press, 1986), p. 117.
2 J. S. Mill, *On Liberty*, ed. David Spitz (New York: Norton, 1975), p. 54.
3 John Rawls, "Social Unity and Primary Goods," in *Utilitarianism and Beyond*, ed. Amartya Sen and Bernard Williams (Cambridge: Cambridge University Press, 1982), pp. 168–69; see also Rawls, "Fairness to Goodness," *Philosophical Review* 84 (1975): 553.
4 John Rawls, "Kantian Constructivism in Moral Theory: The Dewey Lectures 1980," *Journal of Philosophy* 77 (1980): 545.
5 This principle of responsibility is also central to Dworkin's equality of resources scheme: the cost to others of the resources we claim should "figure in each person's sense of what is rightly his and in each person's judgment of what life he should lead, given that command of justice" (Ronald Dworkin, "What Is Equality? Part 2," *Philosophy and Public Affairs* 10 [1981]: 289). Indeed, Dworkin's

scheme does a better job than Rawls's difference principle of distinguishing the costs that people are responsible for from the costs that are an unchosen part of people's circumstances. Some people argue that an accurate assessment of individual responsibility requires going beyond either primary goods or equality of resources to "equal opportunity for welfare" (Richard Arneson, "Equality and Equal Opportunity for Welfare," *Philosophical Studies* 55 [1989]: 79–95), or "equal access to advantage" (G. A. Cohen, "On the Currency of Egalitarian Justice," *Ethics*, in this issue). While these critiques of Rawls's account of primary goods are important, they are not moves away from justificatory neutrality.

6   Although I cannot argue the point here, I believe that the other major statements of liberal neutrality must similarly be interpreted as endorsing justificatory neutrality—e.g., Bruce Ackerman, *Social Justice in the Liberal State* (New Haven, Conn.: Yale University Press, 1980), pp. 11, 61; Charles Larmore, *Patterns of Moral Complexity* (Cambridge: Cambridge University Press, 1987), chap. 3, esp. pp. 44–47; Ronald Dworkin, "Liberalism," in *Public and Private Morality*, ed. Stuart Hampshire (Cambridge: Cambridge University Press, 1978), p. 127, and *A Matter of Principle* (London: Harvard University Press, 1985), p. 222; Robert Nozick, *Anarchy, State, and Utopia* (New York: Basic, 1974), pp. 272–73 (for an extended exegetical discussion of these passages, see David Knott, *Liberalism and the Justice of Neutral Political Concern* [D.Phil. thesis, Oxford University, 1989], chap. 2). Hence, I will be using "liberal neutrality" and "justificatory neutrality" interchangeably. It is quite possible that "neutrality" is not the best word to describe the policy at issue. Rawls himself has avoided the term until recently because of its multiple and often misleading meanings—e.g., neutrality in its everyday usage usually implies neutral consequences (John Rawls, "The Priority of Right and Ideas of the Good," *Philosophy and Public Affairs* 17 [1988]: 260, 265; cf. Raz, chap. 5). He has instead used the term "priority of the right over the good." But that too has multiple and misleading meanings, since it is used by Rawls to describe both the affirming of neutrality over perfectionism, and the affirming of deontology over teleology. These issues need to be kept distinct, and neither, viewed on its own, is usefully called a matter of the "priority of the right"; see my "Rawls on Teleology and Deontology," *Philosophy and Public Affairs* 17 (1988): 173–90, for a critique of Rawls's usage of "priority of the right." Given the absence of any obviously superior alternative, I will continue to use the term "neutrality."

7   Rawls, "Social Unity," p. 172; cf. Rawls, *A Theory of Justice* (London: Oxford University Press, 1971), p. 94.

8   Rawls, *Theory of Justice*, p. 329.

9   There are other reasons for opposing state perfectionism. I have been discussing the difficulty of finding acceptable procedures for formulating a public ranking of different ways of life. There are also difficulties about how the state should go about promoting its preferred ways of life, once those are identified. Even if the state can be relied on to come up with an accurate ranking and can get people to pursue the right ways of life, it may not be able to get people to pursue them *for the right reasons*. Someone who acts in a certain way in order to avoid state punishment, or to gain state subsidies, is not guided by an understanding of the genuine value of the activity (Jeremy Waldron "Autonomy and perfectionism in Raz's *The Morality of Freedom*," *Southern California Law Review*, 62, (1989); Loren Lomasky, *Persons, Rights and the Moral Community* (Oxford: Oxford University Press, 1987), pp. 253–54). This criticism is important and precludes various coercive and manipulative forms of perfectionism, but it does not preclude short-term state intervention designed to introduce people to valuable ways of life. One way to get

people to pursue something for the right reasons is to get them to pursue it for the wrong reasons and hope they will then see its true value. This is not inherently unacceptable, and it occurs often enough in the cultural marketplace. Hence a comprehensive defense of neutrality may need to focus on a prior stage of state perfectionism—i.e., the problems involved in formulating a public ranking of conceptions of the good.

10 On the exclusionary tendencies of communitarianism, see Amy Gutmann, "Communitarian Critics of Liberalism," *Philosophy and Public Affairs* 14 (1985): 318–22; Don Herzog, "Some Questions for Republicans," *Political Theory* 14 (1986): 481–90; H. Hirsch, "The Threnody of Liberalism: Constitutional Liberty and the Renewal of Community," *Political Theory* 14 (1986): 435–38; Nancy Rosenblum, *Another Liberalism: Romanticism and the Reconstruction of Liberal Thought* (Cambridge, Mass.: Harvard University Press, 1987), pp. 178–81.

# 13 Complex Equality

## Michael Walzer

### Pluralism

Distributive justice is a large idea. It draws the entire world of goods within the reach of philosophical reflection. Nothing can be omitted; no feature of our common life can escape scrutiny. Human society is a distributive community. That's not all it is, but it is importantly that: we come together to share, divide, and exchange. We also come together to make the things that are shared, divided, and exchanged; but that very making—work itself—is distributed among us in a division of labor. My place in the economy, my standing in the political order, my reputation among my fellows, my material holdings: all these come to me from other men and women. It can be said that I have what I have rightly or wrongly, justly or unjustly; but given the range of distributions and the number of participants, such judgments are never easy.

The idea of distributive justice has as much to do with being and doing as with having, as much to do with production as with consumption, as much to do with identity and status as with land, capital, or personal possessions. Different political arrangements enforce, and different ideologies justify, different distributions of membership, power, honor, ritual eminence, divine grace, kinship and love, knowledge, wealth, physical security, work and leisure, rewards and punishments, and a host of goods more narrowly and materially conceived—food, shelter, clothing, transportation, medical care, commodities of every sort, and all the odd things (paintings, rare books, postage stamps) that human beings collect. And this multiplicity of goods is matched by a multiplicity of distributive procedures, agents, and criteria. There are such things as simple distributive systems—slave galleys, monasteries, insane asylums, kindergartens (though each of these, looked at closely, might show unexpected complexities); but no full-fledged human society has ever avoided the multiplicity. We must study it all, the goods and the distributions, in many different times and places.

There is, however, no single point of access to this world of distributive arrangements and ideologies. There has never been a universal medium of exchange. Since the decline of the barter economy, money has been the most common medium. But the old maxim according to which there are some things that money can't buy is not only normatively but also factually true.

What should and should not be up for sale is something men and women always have to decide and have decided in many different ways. Throughout history, the market has been one of the most important mechanisms for the distribution of social goods; but it has never been, it nowhere is today, a complete distributive system.

Similarly, there has never been either a single decision point from which all distributions are controlled or a single set of agents making decisions. No state power has ever been so pervasive as to regulate all the patterns of sharing, dividing, and exchanging out of which a society takes shape. Things slip away from the state's grasp; new patterns are worked out—familial networks, black markets, bureaucratic alliances, clandestine political and religious organizations. State officials can tax, conscript, allocate, regulate, appoint, reward, punish, but they cannot capture the full range of goods or substitute themselves for every other agent of distribution. Nor can anyone else do that: there are market coups and cornerings, but there has never been a fully successful distributive conspiracy.

And finally, there has never been a single criterion, or a single set of interconnected criteria, for all distributions. Desert, qualification, birth and blood, friendship, need, free exchange, political loyalty, democratic decision: each has had its place, along with many others, uneasily coexisting, invoked by competing groups, confused with one another.

In the matter of distributive justice, history displays a great variety of arrangements and ideologies. But the first impulse of the philosopher is to resist the displays of history, the world of appearances, and to search for some underlying unity: a short list of basic goods, quickly abstracted to a single good; a single distributive criterion or an interconnected set; and the philosopher himself standing, symbolically at least, at a single decision point. I shall argue that to search for unity is to misunderstand the subject matter of distributive justice. Nevertheless, in some sense the philosophical impulse is unavoidable. Even if we choose pluralism, as I shall do, that choice still requires a coherent defense. There must be principles that justify the choice and set limits to it, for pluralism does not require us to endorse every proposed distributive criteria or to accept every would-be agent. Conceivably, there is a single principle and a single legitimate kind of pluralism. But this would still be a pluralism that encompassed a wide range of distributions. By contrast, the deepest assumption of most of the philosophers who have written about justice, from Plato onward, is that there is one, and only one, distributive system that philosophy can rightly encompass.

Today this system is commonly described as the one that ideally rational men and women would choose if they were forced to choose impartially, knowing nothing of their own situation, barred from making particularist claims, confronting an abstract set of goods.[1] If these constraints on knowing and claiming are suitably shaped, and if the goods are suitably defined, it is probably true that a singular conclusion can be produced. Rational men and women, constrained this way or that, will choose one, and only one, distributive system. But the force of that singular conclusion is not easy to measure. It is surely doubtful that those same men and women, if they were transformed into ordinary people, with a firm sense of their own identity, with their own goods in their hands, caught up in everyday troubles, would reiterate their hypothetical choice or even recognize it as their own. The problem is not, most importantly, with the particularism of interest, which philosophers have always assumed they could safely—that is, uncontroversially—set aside. Ordinary people can do that too, for the sake, say, of the public interest. The greater problem is with the particularism of history, culture, and membership. Even if they are committed to impartiality, the question most likely to arise in the minds of the members of a political community is not, What would rational individuals choose under universalizing conditions of such-and-such a sort? But rather, What would individuals like us choose, who are situated as we are, who share a culture and are determined to go on sharing it? And this is a question that is readily transformed into, What choices have we already made in the course of our common life? What understandings do we (really) share?

Justice is a human construction, and it is doubtful that it can be made in only one way. At any rate, I shall begin by doubting, and more than doubting, this standard philosophical assumption. The questions posed by the theory of distributive justice admit of a range of answers, and there is room within the range for cultural diversity and political choice. It's not only a matter of implementing some singular principle or set of principles in different historical settings. No one would deny that there is a range of morally permissible implementations. I want to argue for more than this: that the principles of justice are themselves pluralistic in form; that different social goods ought to be distributed for different reasons, in accordance with different procedures, by different agents; and that all these differences derive from different understandings of the social goods themselves—the inevitable product of historical and cultural particularism.

## A Theory of Goods

Theories of distributive justice focus on a social process commonly described as if it had this form:

*People distribute goods to (other) people.*

Here, "distribute" means give, allocate, exchange, and so on, and the focus is on the individuals who stand at either end of these actions: not on producers and consumers, but on distributive agents and recipients of goods. We are as always interested in ourselves, but, in this case, in a special and limited version of ourselves, as people who give and take. What is our nature? What are our rights? What do we need, want, deserve? What are we entitled to? What would we accept under ideal conditions? Answers to these questions are turned into distributive principles, which are supposed to control the movement of goods. The goods, defined by abstraction, are taken to be movable in any direction.

But this is too simple an understanding of what actually happens, and it forces us too quickly to make large assertions about human nature and moral agency—assertions unlikely, ever, to command general agreement. I want to propose a more precise and complex description of the central process:

*People conceive and create goods, which they then distribute among themselves.*

Here, the conception and creation precede and control the distribution. Goods don't just appear in the hands of distributive agents who do with them as they like or give them out in accordance with some general principle.[2] Rather, goods with their meanings—because of their meanings—are the crucial medium of social relations; they come into people's minds before they come into their hands; distributions are patterned in accordance with shared conceptions of what the goods are and what they are for. Distributive agents are constrained by the goods they hold; one might almost say that goods distribute themselves among people.

Things are in the saddle
And ride mankind.[3]

But these are always particular things and particular groups of men and women. And, of course, we make the things—even the saddle. I don't want to deny the importance of human agency, only to shift our attention from distribution itself to conception and creation: the naming of the goods, and the giving of meaning, and the collective making. What we need to explain and limit the pluralism of distributive possibilities is a theory of goods. For our immediate purposes, that theory can be summed up in six propositions.

1. All the goods with which distributive justice is concerned are social goods. They are not and they cannot be idiosyncratically valued. I am not sure that there are any other kinds of goods; I mean to leave the question open. Some domestic objects are cherished for private and sentimental reasons, but only in cultures where sentiment regularly attaches to such objects. A beautiful sunset, the smell of new-mown hay, the excitement of an urban vista: these perhaps are privately valued goods, though they are also, and more obviously, the objects of cultural assessment. Even new inventions are not valued in accordance with the ideas of their inventors; they are subject to a wider process of conception and creation. God's goods, to be sure, are exempt from this rule—as in the first chapter of Genesis: "and God saw every thing that He had made, and, behold, it was very good" (1:31). That evaluation doesn't require the agreement of mankind (who might be doubtful), or of a majority of men and women, or of any group of men and women meeting under ideal conditions (though Adam and Eve in Eden would probably endorse it). But I can't

think of any other exemptions. Goods in the world have shared meanings because conception and creation are social processes. For the same reason, goods have different meanings in different societies. The same "thing" is valued for different reasons, or it is valued here and disvalued there. John Stuart Mill once complained that "people like in crowds," but I know of no other way to like or to dislike social goods.[4] A solitary person could hardly understand the meaning of the goods or figure out the reasons for taking them as likable or dislikable. Once people like in crowds, it becomes possible for individuals to break away, pointing to latent or subversive meanings, aiming at alternative values—including the values, for example, of notoriety and eccentricity. An easy eccentricity has sometimes been one of the privileges of the aristocracy: it is a social good like any other.

2. Men and women take on concrete identities because of the way they conceive and create, and then possess and employ social goods. "The line between what is me and mine," wrote William James, "is very hard to draw."[5] Distributions can not be understood as the acts of men and women who do not yet have particular goods in their minds or in their hands. In fact, people already stand in a relation to a set of goods; they have a history of transactions, not only with one another but also with the moral and material world in which they live. Without such a history, which begins at birth, they wouldn't be men and women in any recognizable sense, and they wouldn't have the first notion of how to go about the business of giving, allocating, and exchanging goods.

3. There is no single set of primary or basic goods conceivable across all moral and material worlds—or, any such set would have to be conceived in terms so abstract that they would be of little use in thinking about particular distributions. Even the range of necessities, if we take into account moral as well as physical necessities, is very wide, and the rank orderings are very different. A single necessary good, and one that is always necessary—food, for example—carries different meanings in different places. Bread is the staff of life, the body of Christ, the symbol of the Sabbath, the means of hospitality, and so on. Conceivably, there is a limited sense in which the first of these is primary, so that if there were twenty people in the world and just enough bread to feed the twenty, the primacy of bread-as-staff-of-life would yield a sufficient distributive principle. But that is the only circumstance in which it would do so; and even there, we can't be sure. If the religious uses of bread were to conflict with its nutritional uses—if the gods demanded that bread be baked and burned rather than eaten—it is by no means clear which use would be primary. How, then, is bread to be incorporated into the universal list? The question is even harder to answer, the conventional answers less plausible, as we pass from necessities to opportunities, powers, reputations, and so on. These can be incorporated only if they are abstracted from every particular meaning—hence, for all practical purposes, rendered meaningless.

4. But it is the meaning of goods that determines their movement. Distributive criteria and arrangements are intrinsic not to the good-in-itself but to the social good. If we understand what it is, what it means to those for whom it is a good, we understand how, by whom, and for what reasons it ought to be distributed. All distributions are just or unjust relative to the social meanings of the goods at stake. This is in obvious ways a principle of legitimation, but it is also a critical principle.[6] When medieval Christians, for example, condemned the sin of simony, they were claiming that the meaning of a particular social good, ecclesiastical office, excluded its sale and purchase. Given the Christian understanding of office, it followed—I am inclined to say, it necessarily followed—that office holders should be chosen for their knowledge and piety and not for their wealth. There are presumably things that money can buy, but not this thing. Similarly, the words *prostitution* and *bribery*, like *simony*, describe the sale and purchase of goods that, given certain understandings of their meaning, ought never to be sold or purchased.

5. Social meanings are historical in character; and so distributions, and just and unjust distributions, change over time. To be sure, certain key goods have what we might think of as characteristic normative structures, reiterated across the lines (but not all the lines) of time and space. It is because of this reiteration that the British philosopher Bernard Williams is able to argue that goods should always be distributed for "relevant reasons"— where relevance seems to connect to essential rather than to social meanings.[7] The idea that offices, for example, should go to qualified candidates—though not the only idea that has been held about offices—is plainly visible in very different societies where simony and nepotism, under different names, have similarly been thought sinful or unjust. (But there has been a wide divergence of views about what sorts of position and place are properly called "offices."). Again, punishment has been widely understood as a negative good that ought to go to people who are judged to deserve it on the basis of a verdict, not of a political decision. (But what constitutes a verdict? Who is to deliver it? How, in short, is justice to be done to accused men and women? About these questions there has been significant disagreement.) These examples invite empirical investigation. There is no merely intuitive or speculative procedure for seizing upon relevant reasons.

6. When meanings are distinct, distributions must be autonomous. Every social good or set of goods constitutes, as it were, a distributive sphere within which only certain criteria and arrangements are appropriate. Money is inappropriate in the sphere of ecclesiastical office; it is an intrusion from another sphere. And piety should make for no advantage in the marketplace, as the marketplace has commonly been understood. Whatever can rightly be sold ought to be sold to pious men and women and also to profane, heretical, and sinful men and women (else no one would do much business). The market is open to all comers; the church is not. In no society, of course, are social meanings entirely distinct. What

happens in one distributive sphere affects what happens in the others; we can look, at most, for relative autonomy. But relative autonomy, like social meaning, is a critical principle—indeed, as I shall be arguing throughout this book, a radical principle. It is radical even though it doesn't point to a single standard against which all distributions are to be measured. There is no single standard. But there are standards (roughly knowable even when they are also controversial) for every social good and every distributive sphere in every particular society; and these standards are often violated, the goods usurped, the spheres invaded, by powerful men and women.

## Dominance and Monopoly

In fact, the violations are systematic. Autonomy is a matter of social meaning and shared values, but it is more likely to make for occasional reformation and rebellion than for everyday enforcement. For all the complexity of their distributive arrangements, most societies are organized on what we might think of as a social version of the gold standard: one good or one set of goods is dominant and determinative of value in all the spheres of distribution. And that good or set of goods is commonly monopolized, its value upheld by the strength and cohesion of its owners. I call a good dominant if the individuals who have it, because they have it, can command a wide range of other goods. It is monopolized whenever a single man or woman, a monarch in the world of value—or a group of men and women, oligarchs—successfully hold it against all rivals. Dominance describes a way of using social goods that isn't limited by their intrinsic meanings or that shapes those meanings in its own image. Monopoly describes a way of owning or controlling social goods in order to exploit their dominance. When goods are scarce and widely needed, like water in the desert, monopoly itself will make them dominant. Mostly, however, dominance is a more elaborate social creation, the work of many hands, mixing reality and symbol. Physical strength, familial reputation, religious or political office, landed wealth, capital, technical knowledge: each of these, in different historical periods, has been dominant; and each of them has been monopolized by some group of men and women. And then all good things come to those who have the one best thing. Possess that one, and the others come in train. Or, to change the metaphor, a dominant good is converted into another good, into many others, in accordance with what often appears to be a natural process but is in fact magical, a kind of social alchemy.

No social good ever entirely dominates the range of goods; no monopoly is ever perfect. I mean to describe tendencies only, but crucial tendencies. For we can characterize whole societies in terms of the patterns of conversion that are established within them. Some characterizations are simple: in a capitalist society, capital is dominant and readily converted into prestige and power; in a technocracy, technical knowledge plays the same part. But it isn't difficult to imagine, or to find, more complex social arrangements. Indeed, capitalism and technocracy are more complex than their names imply, even if the names do convey real information about the most important forms of sharing, dividing, and exchanging. Monopolistic control of a dominant good makes a ruling class, whose members stand atop the distributive system—much as philosophers, claiming to have the wisdom they love, might like to do. But since dominance is always incomplete and monopoly imperfect, the rule of every ruling class is unstable. It is continually challenged by other groups in the name of alternative patterns of conversion.

Distribution is what social conflict is all about. Marx's heavy emphasis on productive processes should not conceal from us the simple truth that the struggle for control of the means of production is a distributive struggle. Land and capital are at stake, and these are goods that can be shared, divided, exchanged, and endlessly converted. But land and capital are not the only dominant goods; it is possible (it has historically been possible) to come to them by way of other goods—military or political power, religious office and charisma, and so on. History reveals no single dominant good and no naturally dominant good, but only different kinds of magic and competing bands of magicians.

The claim to monopolize a dominant good—when worked up for public purposes—constitutes an ideology. Its standard form is to connect legitimate possession with some set of personal qualities through the medium of a philosophical principle. So aristocracy, or the rule of the best, is the principle of those who lay claim to breeding and intelligence: they are commonly the monopolists of landed wealth and familial reputation. Divine supremacy is the principle of those who claim to know the word of God: they are the monopolists of grace and office. Meritocracy, or the career open to talents, is the principle of those who claim to be talented: they are most often the monopolists of education. Free exchange is the principle of those who are ready, or who tell us they are ready, to put their money at risk: they are the monopolists of movable wealth. These groups—and others, too, similarly marked off by their principles and possessions—compete with one another, struggling for supremacy. One group wins, and then a different one; or coalitions are worked out, and supremacy is uneasily shared. There is no final victory, nor should there be. But that is not to say that the claims of the different groups are necessarily wrong, or that the principles they invoke are of no value as distributive criteria; the principles are often exactly right within the limits of a particular sphere. Ideologies are readily corrupted, but their corruption is not the most interesting thing about them.

## Tyranny and Complex Equality

I want to argue that we should focus on the reduction of dominance—not, or not primarily, on the break-up or the constraint of monopoly. We should consider what it might mean to narrow the range within which particular goods are convertible and to vindicate the autonomy of distributive spheres.

But this line of argument, though it is not uncommon historically, has never fully emerged in philosophical writing. Philosophers have tended to criticize (or to justify) existing or emerging monopolies of wealth, power, and education. Or, they have criticized (or justified) particular conversions—of wealth into education or of office into wealth. And all this, most often, in the name of some radically simplified distributive system. The critique of dominance will suggest instead a way of reshaping and then living with the actual complexity of distributions.

Imagine now a society in which different social goods are monopolistically held—as they are in fact and always will be, barring continual state intervention—but in which no particular good is generally convertible. As I go along, I shall try to define the precise limits on convertibility, but for now the general description will suffice. This is a complex egalitarian society. Though there will be many small inequalities, inequality will not be multiplied through the conversion process. Nor will it be summed across different goods, because the autonomy of distributions will tend to produce a variety of local monopolies, held by different groups of men and women. I don't want to claim that complex equality would necessarily be more stable than simple equality, but I am inclined to think that it would open the way for more diffused and particularized forms of social conflict. And the resistance to convertibility would be maintained, in large degree, by ordinary men and women within their own spheres of competence and control, without large-scale state action.

This is, I think, an attractive picture, but I have not yet explained just why it is attractive. The argument for complex equality begins from our understanding—I mean, our actual, concrete, positive, and particular understanding—of the various social goods. And then it moves on to an account of the way we relate to one another through those goods. Simple equality is a simple distributive condition, so that if I have fourteen hats and you have fourteen hats, we are equal. And it is all to the good if hats are dominant, for then our equality is extended through all the spheres of social life. On the view that I shall take here, however, we simply have the same number of hats, and it is unlikely that hats will be dominant for long. Equality is a complex relation of persons, mediated by the goods we make, share, and divide among ourselves; it is not an identity of possessions. It requires then, a diversity of distributive criteria that mirrors the diversity of social goods.

### Notes

1 See John Rawls, *A Theory of Justice* (Cambridge, Mass., 1971); Jürgen Habermas, *Legitimation Crisis*, trans. Thomas McCarthy (Boston, 1975), esp. p. 113; Bruce Ackerman, *Social Justice in the Liberal State* (New Haven, 1980).
2 Robert Nozick makes a similar argument in *Anarchy, State, and Utopia* (New York, 1974), pp. 149–50, but with radically individualistic conclusions that seem to me to miss the social character of production.

3   Ralph Waldo Emerson, "Ode," in *The Complete Essays and Other Writings*, ed. Brooks Atkinson (New York 1940), p. 770.
4   John Stuart Mill, *On Liberty* in *The Philosophy of John Stuart Mill*, ed. Marshall Cohen (New York, 1961), p. 255. For an anthropoligical account of liking and not liking social goods, see Mary Douglas and Baron Isherwood, *The World of Goods* (New York, 1979).
5   William James, quoted in C.R. Snyder and Howard Fromkin, *Uniqueness: The Human Pursuit of Difference* (New York, 1980), p. 108.
6   Aren't social meanings, as Marx said, nothing other than "the ideas of the ruling class," "the dominant material relationships grasped as ideas"? I don't think that they are ever only that or simply that, though the members of the ruling class and the intellectuals they patronize may well be in a position to exploit and distort social meanings in their own interests. When they do that, however, they are likely to encounter resistance, rooted (intellectually) in those same meanings. A people's culture is always a joint, even if it isn't an entirely cooperative, production; and it is always a complex production. The common understanding of particular goods incorporates principles, procedures, conceptions of agency, that the rulers would not choose if they were choosing *right now*—and so provides the terms of social criticism. The appeal to what I shall call "internal" principles against the usurpations of powerful men and women is the ordinary form of critical discourse.
7   Bernard Williams, *Problems of the Self: Philosophical Papers, 1956-1972* (Cambridge, England, 1973), pp. 230-49 ("The Idea of Equality"). This essay is one of the starting points of my own thinking about distributive justice. See also the critique of Williams's argument (and of an earlier essay of my own) in Amy Gutmann, *Liberal Equality* (Cambridge, England, 1980), chap. 4.

# Part Four: Republicanism

# Introduction

In recent years some political philosophers have turned to the republican tradition of political thought as a way of offering a more viable and attractive public philosophy.[1] Philip Pettit (1997) calls this recent development the 'republican turn'. Contemporary political thinkers have found past republican thinkers such as Cicero, Machiavelli, and Thomas Jefferson inspiring for a number of reasons. Some find the emphasis past thinkers place on active citizenship and civic virtue a welcome alternative to the 'rights-oriented' conception of justice endorsed by contemporary liberals. Thus republicanism does share, to some extent, the concerns of communitarianism. Republicanism also shares some of the concerns of liberalism. Pettit, for example, is a republican political theorist who believes that liberalism and republicanism do share common ground. Both share the 'presumption that it is possible to organise a viable state and a viable civil society on a basis that transcends many religious and related divides' (Pettit, 1997: 8). But what separates liberalism from republicanism, according to Pettit, is the conception of freedom they endorse:

> ...liberalism has been associated over the two hundred years of its development, and in most of its influential varieties, with the negative conception of freedom as the absence of interference, and with the assumption that there is nothing inherently oppressive about some people having dominating power over others, provided they do not exercise that power and are not likely to exercise it. This relative indifference to power or domination has made liberalism tolerant of relationships in the home, in the workplace, in the electorate and elsewhere, that the republican must denounce as paradigms of domination and unfreedom. (Pettit, 1997: 8-9)

Appealing to the republican political tradition, Pettit defends a third conception[2] of freedom – freedom as non-domination (or antipower). Freedom as non-domination is distinct from both negative and positive freedom. Domination is exemplified by the relationship between master and slave.

> Such a relationship means, at the limit, that the dominating party can interfere on an arbitrary basis with the choices of the dominated: can interfere, in particular, on the basis of an interest or an opinion that need not be shared by the person affected. The dominating party can practice interference, then, at will and with impunity: they do not have to seek anyone's leave and they do not have to incur any scrutiny or penalty. (Pettit, 1997: 22)

Someone dominates another when they have the *capacity to interfere, on an arbitrary basis,* in *certain choices that the other is in a position to make* (Pettit, 1997: 52). To be free, according to Pettit, means that one is not dominated by another. This does not mean that a person will necessarily have 'self-mastery', as entailed by the positive conception of liberty. Pettit believes that adopting this third conception of liberty would increase social radicalism and make us less sceptical about the possibilities of rectifying those complaints by recourse to state action.

Freedom as non-domination is different from non-interference in two important respects. First, the former maintains that you can have domination without interference. Domination does not require that there actually be interference in one's choices before we deem the situation unjust. Consider, for example, the institution of the family in an unjust patriarchal society. Suppose that the laws of this society grant a husband rights over his wife as if she were his property. He is thus free to beat her, for example, without fear of punishment from the state. This legal structure would obviously permit men to dominate women. But suppose there is a wife who has a just husband and he does not interfere in the decisions of his wife. He permits her to make her own decisions regarding her occupation, education, etc. and tells her that he will not treat her as his property even though he is legally entitled to do that. In this case it would appear that the husband's actions respect the freedom of his wife and thus if his attitude was shared by all husbands in this society then the freedom of women would not actually be undermined by their unjust legal structure. If no one is interfering in the choices of women then there is no violation of their freedom.

But freedom as non-domination would characterise this society as unfree, even though no one is actually interfering with the choices of women. Freedom as non-domination does not require there to be *actual* interference before domination can occur. In the case just described the husbands *could* interfere, on an arbitrary basis, and they would not incur any scrutiny or penalty for such interference. The fact that you might have a just husband who does not actually interfere in this way does not eliminate domination because your freedom is contingent upon your husband's just disposition. If he were to change his mind then he could prevent his wife from doing what she wants. When a husband has this unequal capacity to interfere in the choices of his wife her freedom is undermined. Freedom as non-domination is distinct from freedom as non-interference in that the former does not require *actual interference* to take place before it can characterise a situation as a violation of freedom.

The second way in which Pettit distinguishes these two conceptions of freedom is that, for freedom as non-domination, you can have interference without it being a violation of freedom. Interference alone is not enough to qualify as domination. For Pettit, the interference must also be *arbitrary* in order for it to represent domination. Take, for example, a policy that makes it a criminal offence to practice a certain religion. According to negative liberty this policy would be a violation of freedom as it interferes with the religious freedom of the individual. The fact that there is interference is enough to warrant our classifying this policy as one that violates freedom. But freedom as non-domination asks a further question – what is the justification of this policy? If that justification is arbitrary (for example, perhaps the majority of people in our society believe that this religion is heresy) then freedom as non-domination would also condemn this policy as unjust because it is domination. But there will be policies that interfere but do not do so on an arbitrary basis. Take, for example, seat belt laws. According to freedom as non-interference these laws violate our freedom as they interfere in our decisions about how we prefer to travel. But freedom as non-domination will not necessarily characterise such laws as violating our freedom. Granted there is interference in this case we must also ask if such laws are arbitrary. If one believes that legitimate concerns about public safety are

# Introduction

the basis of seat belt laws and that such an aim is not arbitrary then such laws could be defended on republican grounds as being consistent with freedom.

The message Pettit wants to convey to liberals is that they should not always wait for interference before they characterise a practice or policy as unjust nor should they always characterise interference as being antithetical to freedom. Pettit believes that freedom as non-domination is compatible with a diverse number of concerns, ranging across environmentalism and feminism to socialism and multiculturalism.

In the second excerpt in this part Alan Patten suggests that the republican emphasis on public service and civic virtue is not in fact an improvement on liberal political theory. Patten identifies five distinct criticisms which Quentin Skinner has raised against liberalism in his reflections on the republican tradition. These are:

1. Liberalism's Commitment to the 'Invisible Hand' Doctrine
2. Liberalism's Commitment to the Priority of Rights over Duties
3. Liberalism's Defective Conception of Law
4. Liberalism's Hostility to Utilitarianism
5. The Misunderstanding of Negative Liberty.

Patten argues against each of these five points, thus suggesting that instrumental republicanism 'does not represent an improvement upon the liberal attitude towards citizenship and civic virtue, because it fails to identify any philosophically interesting disagreement between the two positions' (Patten, 1996: 36).

The third and final excerpt in this part is from James Bohman's article 'Cosmopolitan Republicanism: Citizenship, Freedom and Global Political Authority'. As Bohman notes, cosmopolitanism and republicanism are taken to have contrasting or even conflicting normative aspirations. The abstract and universalist aspirations of cosmopolitanism seem to be at odds with the 'thick' conception of citizenship that is typically endorsed by republican political theorists. But Bohman argues that these two traditions are compatible and that 'a republican understanding of world citizenship is the best and most feasible cosmopolitan ideal of freedom under current circumstances – understood as freedom from domination and servitude' (Bohman, 2001: 4). The position Bohman defends is called 'cosmopolitan republicanism'. The republican emphasis on freedom from domination has been premised on a strong nation state. Such a state is taken to be the proper location for the kind of political identity republican freedom presupposes. Bohman argues that, due to globalisation, the nation state may no longer be able to enjoy the prominent role republicans give it. The nation state may 'no longer be the primary mechanism for the constitution and authorization of political authority; it increasingly fails, in Weber's terms, to possess, exercise, and organize exclusive authority over its own territory and thus to protect the liberty of its citizens from subjection and domination' (Bohman, 2001: 9).

Bohman considers how the uncertainty of authority that has arisen in the era of globalisation might be resolved. The ideal of freedom requires a political community that goes beyond the nation state. Many of the issues Bohman addresses, such as the importance of deliberation, are ones we shall further explore in Chapters 20, 21 and 22. What is distinctive about Bohman's analysis of these issues in this article is his grounding of cosmopolitan concerns in republican aspirations. His argument is a good example of how political theorists should not be constrained by labels but be willing to combine the appealing features of those political traditions they feel best encapsulate a formative public philosophy that can meet the different challenges we now face.

## Notes

1 See Skinner (1978, 1983, 1984), Sunstein (1990, 1993a, 1993b), Sandel (1996), Pettit (1997) and Dagger (1997).
2 The second conception of freedom is 'positive liberty'. See Berlin (1997).

## References

Berlin, Isaiah. 'Two Concepts of Liberty'. In P. Pettit and R. Goodin (eds) *Contemporary Political Philosophy* (Oxford: Blackwell Publishers, 1997).
Bohman, James. 'Cosmopolitan Republicanism: Citizenship, Freedom and Global Political Authority', *The Monist*, 84(1), 2001: 3-21.
Dagger, Richard. *Civic Virtues* (Oxford: Oxford University Press, 1997).
Patten, Alan. 'The Republican Critique of Liberalism', *British Journal of Political Science*, 26, 1996: 25-44.
Pettit, Philip. *Republicanism* (Oxford: Oxford University Press, 1997).
Sandel, Michael. *Democracy's Discontent* (Cambridge, Mass.: Harvard University Press, 1996).
Skinner, Quentin. *The Foundations of Modern Political Thought*, 2 volumes (Cambridge: Cambridge University Press, 1978).
────── 'Machiavelli on the Maintenance of Liberty', *Politics*, 18, 1983: 3-15.
────── 'The Idea of Negative Liberty'. In R. Rorty, J. B. Schneewind, and Q. Skinner (eds) *Philosophy in History* (Cambridge: Cambridge University Press, 1984).
Sunstein, Cass. *After The Rights Revolution: Reconceiving the Regulatory State* (Cambridge, Mass.: Harvard University Press, 1990).
────── *The Partial Constitution* (Cambridge, Mass.: Harvard University Press, 1993a).
────── *Democracy and the Problem of Free Speech* (New York: Free Press, 1993b).

# 14 Freedom as Antipower

## Philip Pettit

### Freedom

Contemporary political thinkers, certainly contemporary liberals, divide into those on the right, who say that only liberty (perhaps equal liberty) matters—whether it matters in a consequentialist or nonconsequentialist way—and those on the left, who argue that the state should be concerned not just with liberty (or equal liberty) but also with the fortunes of the worst off, with overall satisfaction of needs, with material equality, or something of the kind. But however deep this division between them, the broad range of contemporary thinkers appear to defend a conception of liberty as actual noninterference: to be free is not to suffer compulsion by force, coercion by threat, or manipulation by background stage setting; it is to enjoy the fact of noninterference.

This conception of liberty as noninterference probably derives from Hobbes. "A Free-Man," he wrote in *Leviathan*, "is he, that in those things, which by his strength and wit he is able to do, is not hindred to doe what he has a will to."[1] People are hindered and rendered strictly unfree, for Hobbes, only so far as they are physically coerced. But he allows that there is also a sense in which people are rendered unfree by bonds that coerce by threat, not by physical means: these are "made to hold, by the danger, though not by the difficulty of breaking them."[2] To be free in the full sense, then, is not to suffer either coercion of the body or coercion of the will: not to suffer interference of either of these two broad kinds.

There are two characteristic marks of the conception of freedom as noninterference. The first is that under this approach the interference of a nonsubjugating authority impacts on the liberty of the people affected—although, no doubt, with aggregate, long-term benefit—even if the interference involved is just the constitutional imposition of a fair but (necessarily) coercive rule of law. As Berlin writes in paraphrase of the approach: "Law is always a 'fetter,' even if it protects you from being bound in chains that are heavier than those of the law, say, arbitrary despotism or chaos."[3] Bentham was emphatic on the point: "As against the coercion applicable by individual to individual, no liberty can be given to one man but in proportion as it is taken away from another. All coercive laws, therefore, and in particular all laws creative of liberty, are as far as they go abrogative of liberty.'"[4] John Rawls indicates that he too shares this understanding of liberty when he writes: "Liberty can be restricted only for the sake of liberty";[5] the assumption is that law always does represent a restriction, however benign, of liberty.[6]

The second characteristic mark of the conception of freedom as noninterference is that while it represents even nonsubjugating interference as a deprivation of liberty, it finds nothing hostile to liberty in a form of subjugation that does not involve any actual interference. There is nothing about the traditional, unconstrained relation of employer to employee or husband to wife, for example, that raises questions in the ledger book of liberty, nothing, at any rate, in the absence of actual or expected compulsion, coercion, manipulation, or whatever. The fact that the relation puts one party under the power of the other does nothing, in itself, to affect the liberty of the weaker person.

But suppose we move away from the opposition to bare interference in terms of which contemporary thinkers tend to understand freedom. Suppose we take up the older opposition to servitude, subjugation, or domination as the key to construing liberty. Suppose we understand liberty not as noninterference but as antipower. What happens then?

Unsurprisingly, we find ourselves with a conception of freedom under which the two marks of the dominant contemporary approach are reversed. If freedom is opposed to subjugation, then the introduction of constitutional authority does not, as such, constitute an abrogation of liberty, for it need not itself involve subjugation or domination: it does not essentially involve anyone's having the capacity to interfere arbitrarily in another's affairs. Under any rule of law, those in the parliament, those in the administration, and those in the judiciary have special powers of coercion, but if the powers are regulated in a constitutional manner, then they do not give the authorities power over people in the distinctive sense associated with subjugation. The authorities may be more or less productive of antipower, depending on how well they cope with existing patterns of domination and depending on how wide the range of antipower is that they allow. But provided they are truly constitutional in character—a big proviso, indeed—they relate to freedom as antipower in quite a different way from how they must be seen to relate to freedom as noninterference: they do not represent an abrogation, even an abrogation that is benign in the long term, of that freedom.[7]

If freedom is construed as antipower rather than noninterference, then we do not have to see the rule of law, and more generally of constitutional authority, as itself an abrogation of liberty. But the construal of freedom as antipower has exactly the contrary effect on judgments about asymmetric relations such as those that have traditionally obtained between employers and employees, husbands and wives, and parents and children. Contemporary thinkers tend to see no loss of liberty here—they may see other deficits, of course—given that there is no actual interference. But if liberty is opposed to subjugation in the first place, then, even in the absence of actual interference, these relationships are often going to represent paradigms of unfreedom. The powerful employer, husband, or parent who can interfere arbitrarily in certain ways subjugates the employee, wife, or child. Even if no interference actually occurs, even if no interference is particularly likely—say, because the employee, wife, or child happens to be very charming—the existence of that relationship and that power means that freedom fails. The employee, wife, or child is at the mercy of the employer, husband, or parent, at least in some respects, at least in some measure, and to that extent they live in a condition of servitude.

There is a nice balance, then, in the relationship between the idea of freedom as noninterference and the idea of freedom as antipower. The first conception is anxious about the authority-freedom connection and relaxed on the authority-power linkage. The second is relaxed about authority and anxious about power, in particular, anxious about the informal sort of power that is not subject to constitutional check. But these are very abstractly drawn contrasts between the two conceptions of freedom. What are their concrete implications? I shall try to answer the question by mentioning some of the implications that mattered in the historical development of the ideals.[8]

The first contrast may suggest that freedom as noninterference is, in this respect, the more challenging and demanding ideal. But a little reflection shows that this is not so. One of the reasons the new conception of freedom appealed to Hobbes is that he could use it to argue against the republican line that properly constituted authority establishes freedom where despotic authority destroys it; he could argue that since all laws are *pro tanto* destructive of liberty, there is no difference of kind between what the laws of republican Lucca do in regard to liberty, for example, and what the laws of Constantinople—or indeed the laws of Leviathan—do in this way.[9] "Whether a Commonwealth be Monarchicall, or Popular, the Freedome is still the same."[10] Sir Robert Filmer adopted this antirepublican argument for his own authoritarian purposes,[11] but those who espoused liberty in the seventeenth and eighteenth centuries generally followed James Harrington in rejecting it. Harrington argued against Hobbes that freedom is freedom by the law, not freedom from the law, and that "whereas the greatest bashaw is a tenant, as well of his head as of his estate, at the will of his lord, the meanest Lucchese that hath land is a freeholder of both."[12]

The Hobbesian approach was rejected with particular force by the champions and defenders of the American Revolution. These thinkers insisted recurrently that freedom and slavery are opposites, both for individuals and for peoples, and that freedom requires an absence of exposure to the arbitrary interference of others, in particular, the absence of exposure guaranteed under a proper rule of law.[13] As Richard Price put the point in a remark already quoted: "Individuals in private life, while held under the power of masters, cannot be denominated free, however equitably and kindly they may be treated."[14] Joseph Priestley used this point to argue that the American colonists were in danger of being "reduced to a state of as complete servitude, as any people of which there is an account in history. For by the same power, by which the people of England can compel them to pay one penny, they may compel them to pay the last penny they have. There will be nothing but arbitrary imposition on the one side, and humble petition on the other."[15]

The opponents of the likes of Priestley and Price reintroduced the Hobbesian idea of freedom as noninterference and used it to debunk the case for American independence. Jeremy Bentham made what he thought was "a kind of discovery" that liberty is nothing more than the absence of coercion;[16] he urged on the basis that all government is in some measure an invasion of liberty and maintained that defenders of the American cause were confused and simplistic in thinking there was any great difference between how British and American subjects fared in this regard.[17] Lord North's pamphleteer, John Lind, hammered the argument home against Price. Following Bentham, Lind stressed that liberty is negative—the absence of coercion, physical or moral—and that all government and legal power reduces people's liberty in the same way, whether it is exercised in a constrained or unconstrained fashion. "Dreadful as this power may be, let me ask you, Sir, if this same power is not exercised by the same persons over all the subjects who reside in all the other parts of this same empire?—It is."[18]

What does this historical debate show about the first contrast between our two conceptions of liberty? In a word, whereas freedom as noninterference is consistent with the benign dictator—the sort of benign dictator that the British government may have represented for American colonists—freedom as antipower is not. Embrace the notion of freedom as antipower, and it becomes essential for the enjoyment of freedom that government is subject to proper, constitutional control: the sort of control that guards against arbitrary power. Richard Price thought that such control necessarily required voting power, whereas Joseph Priestley did not; while he strongly favored the extension of the franchise, he argued that there might be control enough if the colonies were in the same position as Britain and "the persons who impose the tax upon others, impose it upon themselves at the same time."[19] The important point in common between them is that those in power should not be able to interfere at will and with impunity in the affairs of citizens; their power over others should not be a power of arbitrary interference.

The second contrast between freedom as noninterference and freedom as antipower is that the first is consistent with a relationship of domination, provided the dominating party does not actually interfere with the dominated, whereas of course the second conception is not: the subjugation of individuals renders them unfree, "however equitably and kindly they may be treated." The concrete implications of this contrast are fairly obvious. If a society is committed to the realization of freedom as antipower, then it is going to have to do something about the conditions of women and employees: certainly, it is going to have to transform the conditions of women and employees such as they were in the eighteenth and nineteenth centuries. If a society is committed to the realization of freedom as noninterference, on the other hand, that need not be so: women and employees may be left in relationships of subjugation, provided the overall probability of interference is reduced as far as possible. It doesn't matter if the husband or employer is given a power of interference, provided interference is suitably improbable.[20]

Those who traditionally defended freedom as antipower would not have been particularly troubled by the radical implications of the ideal for women and servants. For them, it would have been axiomatic that freedom as antipower could only be realized for an elite constituency of propertied males. The point is obvious in Harrington's remark: "The man that cannot live upon his own must be a servant; but he that can live upon his own may be a freeman."[21] It was fast becoming common wisdom in the late eighteenth century, however, that all human beings were equal, and the growing assumption of equality would have made the ideal of freedom as antipower seem more and more radical. The combination of the assumption and the ideal would have supported the idea, in the early socialist phrase, that employment was "wage-slavery," as it would have supported the description of marriage as the "white-slave code."[22]

Just a decade or so after the exchanges between defenders and opponents of American independence, William Paley set the tone for later discussions of liberty when he argued in defense of, roughly, the Benthamite conception of freedom. He acknowledged that common discourse embodied a different notion of liberty: "This idea places liberty in security; making it to consist not merely in an actual exemption from the constraint of useless and noxious laws and acts of dominion, but in being free from the danger of having such hereafter imposed or exercised."[23] But he argued that the ideal in question is extremely—and, to Paley's eye, excessively—demanding: "Those definitions of liberty ought to be rejected, which, by making that essential to civil freedom which is unattainable in experience, inflame expectations that can never be gratified, and disturb the public content with complaints, which no wisdom or benevolence of government can remove."[24] Paley does not make clear how the ideal of liberty as security, liberty as antipower, proves to be excessively demanding. But it is quite plausible that he may have been thinking, as others certainly were,[25] of the implications of the ideal for the position of women and servants in society.

I hope that these historical remarks may serve to illustrate the concrete implications of the two contrasts that I drew between the non-established ideal of liberty as noninterference and what I see as the older ideal of liberty as antipower.

Freedom as noninterference is open to the benign dictator model of the state, since all law, even nondictatorial law, involves an abrogation of such freedom, and it is tolerant of relationships of domination, since domination need not mean interference. Freedom as noninterference can be made available, then, even to someone in a position of extreme dependence and deference, a position in which they are not able to command the respect of others, even if they are lucky enough to receive it.

Freedom as antipower, on the other hand, requires a specific sort of law and polity in which the powers that be are denied possibilities of arbitrary interference, and if it is to be a universally enjoyed ideal, it requires attention to the patterns of domination associated with such contexts as marriage and the workplace. To return to a theme that we have emphasized earlier, freedom as antipower represents a status, psychological as well as social, that is inconsistent with any suggestion of living at another's mercy or acting by another's grace and favor. As Priestley wrote,[26] in an unhappily (and unnecessarily) sexist vein, "A sense of political and civil liberty, though there should be no great occasion to exert it in the course of a man's life, gives him a constant feeling of his own power and importance; and is the foundation of his indulging a free, bold, and manly turn of thinking, unrestrained by the most distant idea of control."[27]

I end on a note of advocacy. The ideal of freedom as noninterference which contemporary liberal theorists espouse is less challenging, so it now appears, than the older ideal of freedom as antipower which it displaced; this may be why left-of-center liberals invoke other values like equality or justice as supplements to the more traditional goal of liberty. But there is no reason in principle why liberals should not embrace the older ideal instead of the newer. The most characteristic feature of liberal doctrine is the search for a universalist and neutralist brief to give the state, a brief involving equal concern with all and a brief that can recommend itself across a wide range of the moral and religious positions that flourish in contemporary, pluralist societies. And that aspiration is quite consistent with the ideal of freedom as antipower.

Consider the constituency of people who do not despair of pluralist society and who are content that the state should look to the wellbeing of individuals, without favoring any particular gender, race, or class. Who among these is likely to dismiss the value of freedom as antipower? Such freedom is going to recommend itself to them as something that has the status of a primary good:[28] no matter what else you seek, at least in a pluralist society, the enjoyment of freedom as antipower will almost certainly facilitate the search. There is every reason, then, why liberals should be sympathetic to the exploration of how far the state might be organized around the promotion of freedom as antipower, every reason why they should want to investigate what this brief would imply for state institutions and whether the implications are congenial from the standpoint of independent moral and other commitments.

## Notes

1 Thomas Hobbes, *Leviathan*, ed. C. B. Macpherson (Harmondsworth: Penguin, 1968), p. 262.
2 Ibid., p. 264.
3 Isaiah Berlin, *Two Concepts of Liberty* (Oxford: Oxford University Press, 1958), p. 8.

4  Jeremy Bentham, 'Anarchical Fallacies,' in *The Works of Jeremy Bentham*, ed. J. Bowring (Edinburgh, 1843), vol. 2.
5  John Rawls, *A Theory of Justice* (Oxford: Oxford University Press, 1971), p. 302.
6  Skinner, 'Machiavelli on the Maintenance of Liberty,' pp. 12–13.
7  What of the situation of the convicted offender who is subjected to some penalty? Does the punishment mean an assault on that person's liberty? I mentioned already that those in prison may indeed be subjugated by the warders. But doesn't imprisonment invariably involve subjugation? For the record, no, although making this point is not necessarily to approve of imprisonment (see John Braithwaite and Philip Pettit, *Not Just Deserts: A Republican Theory of Criminal Justice* (Oxford: Oxford University Press, 1990)). Prisoners may be deprived of antipower, in the sense of being given only a reduced scope for its enjoyment, but that does not mean that they are necessarily subjugated by anyone. They do not enjoy antipower over any significant range of choice, but that does not mean that they have to suffer domination.
8  I am greatly indebted to Quentin Skinner for having drawn my attention, in connection with the idea of freedom as antipower, to the work of Priestley, Price, and Paley. His forthcoming study of English traditions of liberty should introduce us properly to the development of the idea of freedom among such writers.
9  Quentin Skinner, 'Thomas Hobbes on the Proper Signification of Liberty,' *Transactions of the Royal Historical Society* 40 (1990): 121–51.
10  Hobbes, p. 266.
11  Sir Robert Filmer, *'Patriarcha' and Other Writings*, ed. J. P. Sommerville (Cambridge: Cambridge University Press, 1991), p. 275.
12  James Harrington, *The Commonwealth of Oceana and A System of Politics*, ed. J. G. A. Pocock (Cambridge: Cambridge University Press, 1992), p. 20.
13  Bernard Bailyn, *The Ideological Origins of the American Revolution* (Cambridge, Mass.: Harvard University Press, 1967); John Reid, *The Concept of Liberty in the Age of the American Revolution* (Chicago: University of Chicago Press, 1988).
14  Richard Price, *Political Writings*, ed. D.O. Thomas (Cambridge: Cambridge University Press, 1991), p. 77.
15  Joseph Priestley, *Political Writings*, ed. P. N. Miller (Cambridge: Cambridge University Press, 1993), p. 140.
16  Douglas G. Long, *Bentham on Liberty* (Toronto: University of Toronto Press, 1977), p. 54.
17  Ibid., pp. 53–54. One source from which Bentham may have absorbed Hobbesian ideas on liberty is the protoutilitarian Abraham Tucker. In his anxiety to argue that people may be free while living under 'the domination of Providence,' Abraham Tucker (*The Light of Nature Pursued*, 3d ed. [London: Tegg & Son, 1834], chap. 26) followed Hobbes (although not by name) in equating freedom with the absence of active coercion. Tucker did not extend this idea of freedom, however, into the political sphere; his interests lay elsewhere.
18  John Lind, *Three Letters to Dr. Price* (London: Payne, 1776), pp. 16–18.
19  Priestley, p. 141.
20  For a comparison between this probability-based concern and the sort of concern that the advocate of liberty as antipower will have—a concern at the very fact that arbitrary interference is possible and know to be possible—see Philip Pettit, *The Common Mind: An Essay on Psychology, Society and Politics* (New York: Oxford University Press, 1993), pp. 316–19, 'Negative Liberty.'

21 Harrington, p. 269.
22 Carole Pateman, *The Sexual Contract* (Cambridge: Polity, 1988), pp. 67, 123.
23 William Paley, *The Principles of Moral and Political Philosophy*, vol. 4 of Collected Works (London: Rivington, 1825), p. 357.
24 Ibid., p. 359.
25 Lind, pp. 40, 156.
26 Priestley, p. 36.
27 See Baron de Montesquieu, *The Spirit of the Laws*, ed. D.W. Carrithers (Berkeley: University of California Press, 1977), p. 202; Ch. Wirszubski, *Libertas as a Political Ideal at Rome* (Oxford: Oxford University Press, 1968), p. 159: Price, p. 85.
28 Rawls.

# 15 The Republican Critique of Liberalism

## Alan Patten

### Skinner's Formulation of Instrumental Republicanism

There are sufficiently important differences between Skinner's and Taylor's accounts of instrumental republicanism to warrant examining their views separately. So let me start with Skinner's formulation. Republicans, according to Skinner, are above all committed to the ideal of a 'free state'. A free state, like a free individual, is one which is not subject to constraints, but which is able to act according to its own will, that is, according to the general will of all of the members of the community.[1] As Skinner sees it, republicans value free states for two distinct kinds of reasons. First, free states tend to be better than unfree ones at accumulating wealth and civic greatness. Secondly, and more importantly for Skinner's account, free states are better at guaranteeing the personal liberties of their citizens than are unfree ones.[2] The personal liberties which republicans have in mind here are some of the familiar negative liberties cherished by liberals: they include, for instance, personal security and the political liberties. To possess these liberties, as Skinner puts it, 'is simply to be unconstrained from pursuing whatever goals we may happen to set ourselves'.[3]

Free states, republicans assume, break down easily into unfree ones because of the negligence and indifference of their citizens. When this happens, the negative liberties cherished by liberals and republicans are in danger of being lost. This sets up the central republican problem, which is to identify the conditions under which a society can maintain the institutions of its freedom, despite this tendency to corruption.[4]

Republicans address this problem by exploring various different arrangements and policies which help to preserve liberty, typically including the rule of law and some form of democratic self-government.[5] The *distinctive* claim made by republicans – the claim which they think takes them beyond the liberal tradition – emphasizes the role of political participation and civic virtue. It is a necessary condition of the maintenance of a free state, they argue, that its citizens be politically active and motivated by a high degree of civic virtue.[6] Unless citizens participate actively in political life, they will allow their institutions to stagnate and corrupt and will eventually lose them. Moreover, this participation is only likely if citizens are motivated by commitment to the common good and a high degree of civic virtue, rather than by self-interest. Purely self-interested citizens will prefer to attend only to their private affairs and to free ride on the public activity of others.

Let us call citizens who are politically active, and motivated by a high degree of civic virtue, 'good citizens'. The next question that Skinner turns to concerns the conditions under which individuals can be relied upon to become and remain good citizens.[7] Here republicans emphasize the importance of social institutions in moulding individuals into citizens: it is a necessary condition of individuals becoming and remaining good citizens, republicans think, that their social institutions imbue them with certain attitudes and dispositions.[8] The qualities of the good citizen are not something which individuals are naturally born with. They must be nourished and fostered by education, by the everyday customs and practices of the culture, and, where necessary, by the threat of sanctions and the strict regulation of personal conduct.

Putting these claims together, then, we can see that, so far, Skinner's republicanism consists in a commitment to the ideal of negative liberty and an empirical analysis of the conditions under which this ideal might be realized. Republicans think that negative liberty is a worthwhile ideal – but not one which it is easy to realize. They argue that it can only be realized if individuals are good citizens, and that means that they must participate actively in the political life of their community and be motivated by a high degree of civic virtue. This participation and virtue, in turn, are only found where social institutions inculcate individuals with the right sorts of attitudes and dispositions.

From this analysis of the conditions of the maintenance of a free state, Skinner draws several important normative conclusions. He concludes, first of all, that individuals have a duty to participate actively in politics.[9] The exact reasoning behind this conclusion is never spelt out explicitly, but it seems to be something like the following. Since we all have reason to live in a free society, and whoever wills the end, wills the necessary means to that end, then, if the republican analysis sketched above is correct, we all have reason to participate actively in politics. To the extent that the end of living in a free society has priority over our other ends, our reason to participate in politics takes on a similar priority and we can say that it is a *duty*.[10] As it stands, this deduction of a duty of participation will not do, of course, because it ignores the familiar problem that no *particular* individual's participation is strictly necessary for the maintenance of liberty. I do not see how it is possible to negotiate this difficulty, except perhaps by appealing to fairness, or by embedding the argument in a more Kantian moral framework, which has recourse to an 'original position' or other similar device.[11]

The second normative conclusion which republicans draw from their analysis of the conditions of liberty is a recommendation that social and political institutions be shaped and modified so as to encourage individuals to acquire the civic virtue which will ensure that they conscientiously fulfil their duties of political participation.¹² Although republicans are pessimistic about the prospects of establishing and maintaining a free state, they deny that it is a matter which is entirely outside of human control. Human beings can shape and modify their own social institutions, and these institutions, in turn, can imbue individuals with the virtuous attitudes and dispositions that are required to preserve liberty. Because liberty depends on citizenship and public service, it becomes imperative that social institutions be constructed so as to foster and encourage these values.

## Skinner's Objections and Liberal Rejoinders

Having given a rough sketch of Skinner's instrumental republicanism, I want now to explore the objections to contractarian liberalism which Skinner thinks are implied by his account. I shall identify five different objectives to liberalism which Skinner draws from his reflections on the republican tradition. Since the republican analysis consists in part in a set of empirical hypotheses concerning the maintenance of a free society, one might expect Skinner's differences with liberalism to be empirical in character.¹³ However, with the possible exception of the first objection, this does not seem to be the case. What Skinner's different objections have in common instead is the philosophical claim that contractarian liberals' commitment to some particular doctrine or idea makes it impossible for them to take seriously the republican analysis of the maintenance of liberty. In each case, I argue that the objection fails: in the case of objections (i), (iii) and (v), liberals are not committed to the doctrine or idea in question: whereas in the case of objections (ii) and (iv), they are, but this does not inhibit them from taking seriously Skinner's republican analysis.

### (i) Liberalism's Commitment to the 'Invisible Hand' Doctrine

Skinner charges that contractarian liberals – and here he mentions Rawls in particular – have come to rely upon a complacent 'invisible hand' doctrine of how individual liberty can be maintained. According to this view, 'if we all pursue our own enlightened self-interest ... the outcome will in fact be the greatest good of the community as a whole'.¹⁴

Reflection on the republican tradition shows us that the problem with this invisible hand doctrine is that it forgets the fragility of free institutions and, in particular, the need for civic virtue which this fragility occasions. It ignores the fundamental insight of instrumental republicanism, which is that individuals must have certain duties and virtues, and attitudes and dispositions, if their institutions are to avoid corruption and decline. Liberalism's commitment to the invisible hand doctrine helps explain its hostility to the goods of citizenship and public service.

This objection, however, runs foul of two different doctrines which Rawls expounds in *A Theory of Justice*. The first is his doctrine of the sense of justice: Rawls argues that a condition of the possibility of a just society is that citizens possess an effective sense of justice and, in particular, a highest-order desire to abide by the principles of justice.[15] Without this other-regarding motivation, the basic liberties cannot be maintained. One of the strengths of his theory, Rawls thinks, is that it can explain how citizens would come to acquire this sense of justice. A republican might choose to take issue with this explanation, but this would be quite different from the objection that Rawls is committed to an invisible hand doctrine.

The second doctrine is that of the natural duty of justice. Parties to the original position, Rawls argues, would rationally choose to be constrained by a duty to support and further just institutions.[16] This duty regulates, for instance, their compliance with the law, their decisions about participation in politics, and their voting behaviour.

Both of these points contradict Skinner's 'invisible hand' reading. The reason why the sense of justice is so important for Rawls is exactly because a just social system is not like a self-regulating market in which every agent can purse his or her own interest.[17] Moreover, parties to the original position choose to be bound by the duty to support and further just institutions precisely because they recognize the fragility of free and just institutions – precisely, that is, because they recognize the naivety of the invisible hand doctrine. I conclude that, if instrumental republicanism offers an improvement on the liberal understandings of active citizenship and civic virtue, it is not because liberalism is committed to an invisible hand doctrine.

### (ii) Liberalism's Commitment to the Priority of Rights over Duties

A further objection made by Skinner is that contemporary liberals – and here he specifically mentions Dworkin – mistakenly give priority to rights over duties. According to Skinner, contractarians think that 'we must first seek to erect around ourselves a cordon of rights treating these as "trumps" and insisting on their priority over any calls of social duty'.[18] On the republican view, by contrast,

> to insist on rights as trumps ... is simply to proclaim our corruption as citizens. It is also to embrace a self-destructive form of irrationality. Rather we must take our duties seriously, and instead of trying to evade anything more than 'the minimum demands of social life' we must seek to discharge our public obligations as whole-heartedly as possible.[19]

The contractarian insistence on the primacy of rights forces them to neglect the instrumental republican idea that a commitment to liberty enjoins us virtuously to pursue certain determinate ends of public service and political participation. Contractarians forget that an ethic of rights, without a corresponding ethic of social duties, cannot form the basis of a self-sustaining system of free institutions and practices.

The problem with this objection is that Skinner is conflating two different senses in which rights can have priority over duties. On one view, rights can be said to have priority if and only if they have justificatory primacy in moral argument: the suggestion is that a good argument for some arrangement or action is one which appeals, ultimately, to the protection or advancement of rights. This is the view that Dworkin had in mind when he said that our political morality ought to be right-based rather than goal-based or duty-based.[20] Given the close connection between rights and negative liberties, it is hard to see how Skinner can disagree. The republican view, on Skinner's reconstruction of it, is not a duty-based theory, according to Dworkin's categories, but a right-based, or better yet a 'liberty-based', one.

The second sense in which rights might have priority over duties is if it is typically the case that the rights that we have are such that we never, or *hardly* ever, have any social duties. This is clearly the view that Skinner wants to criticize, but it is not a view that is implied by Dworkin's argument. Dworkin allows that we may have social duties, so long as they are right-based, that is, are ultimately justified not by goals or duties, but by the preservation and protection of rights.[21] As Dworkin points out, this makes such duties purely 'instrumental', but then this 'instrumental' view of duty is exactly what is on offer in Skinner's reconstruction of classical republicanism. Thus I can find no relevant difference between Skinner's position and Dworkin's and conclude that the objection fails. Contractarianism's insistence on the primacy of rights does not prevent it from taking seriously the concerns raised by instrumental republicans.

### (iii) Liberalism's Defective Conception of Law

Another criticism that Skinner draws from his reflections on the republican tradition is that contractarians operate with a defective conception of law. They agree with republicans that the coercive powers of the law are required to safeguard individual liberty. But they mistakenly think that 'the law preserves our liberty essentially by coercing other people'.[22] For republicans, by contrast, 'the law preserves our liberty not merely by coercing others, but also by directly coercing each one of us into acting in a particular way'.[23] The contractarian conception of law, Skinner implies, inhibits them from endorsing the republican conclusion that a legitimate function of the law may be to coerce and cajole us into doing that which is necessary for the maintenance of our own liberty.

As examples of such a use of the law, Skinner mentions the republican doctrine of a balance of powers in the constitution and their policy of using the law to encourage citizens to fight courageously on behalf of their community. Directed against modern contractarians, the objection fails, however, because writers like Rawls endorse similar policies and on similar grounds. Rawls argues that a procedure of majority rule can legitimately be restricted by the 'mechanisms of constitutionalism', including the separation of powers, if such an arrangement has the best consequences for the complete system of liberty.[24] Likewise, he thinks that conscription may be justified if it is necessary to protect a just community against hostile powers likely to remove its liberties.[25] In short, Rawls does not operate with the defective conception of law that Skinner associates with contractarianism: for Rawls, a legitimate function of the law may be to coerce us into doing that which is necessary for the maintenance of our own liberty.

### (iv) Liberalism's Hostility to Utilitarianism

A fourth argument made by Skinner is that liberalism's hostility to utilitarianism prevents it from taking seriously the republican insight that a commitment to the common good is a necessary condition for the realization of a free society.[26] Skinner notes, for instance, that Rawls affirms the priority of individual liberty over all utilitarian considerations, including, he thinks, any kind of appeal to what Skinner calls the 'general welfare'. As a result of this, Skinner concludes, Rawls is unable to sanction the kinds of limitations on individual liberty that are recommended by the republican view in the name of the common good, since these are essentially appeals to the general welfare. Rawls cannot allow that individuals should be required to participate in political life, because this would be to violate his own strictures against general welfare arguments for restricting liberty. Since Rawlsian justice 'requires the maximizing of individual liberty,' Skinner argues, 'the basic duty of the state must be to keep its own demands upon its citizens to an agreed minimum'.[27]

Skinner is correct to say that Rawls refuses to sanction limitations on individual liberty which are justified only on utilitarian grounds. For Rawls, it would be irrational for a party to the original position to choose to sacrifice his own liberties solely for the sake of greater benefits for *others*. Skinner is wrong to think, however, that this argument prevents Rawls from requiring the kinds of duties of citizenship, and commitment to the common good, that republicans cherish. In considering whether to impose upon themselves these duties, parties to the original position can take into consideration not only the benefits to others, but also the benefits to themselves, that these duties will help secure. The importance of the latter sort of benefit is implicitly conceded by Skinner himself: a failure to embrace our civic duties, he aruges, is 'simply a failure of rationality, an inability to recognize that *our own liberty* depends on committing ourselves to a life of virtue and public service'.[28] I conclude that, as with liberalism's attitude towards rights, law and the invisible hand, its anti-utilitarianism does not prevent it from taking seriously the concerns raised by instrumental republicans.[29]

## (v) The Misunderstanding of Negative Liberty

An overarching concern of several of Skinner's articles is to analyse the relationship between negative liberty and two historically important propositions about liberty. The first of these propositions is that liberty is only realized through the pursuit, by individuals, of certain determinate ends and activities. The second is that it can make sense, under some conditions, to talk of forcing someone to be free.[30]

Skinner thinks that one tradition of thinking about negative liberty, which he identifies with contractarianism, rejects both of these propositions about liberty as incoherent. For contractarianism, negative liberty consists in an *absence* of external constraints on what one is able to do and thus seems entirely opposed to any suggestion that one only enjoys freedom in pursuing certain determinate ends and activities, let alone any claim that one can be forced or coerced into freedom.

Skinner argues, however, that the republican view shows that there is a much closer connection between negative liberty, public service, and perhaps even coercion, than contractarians have been willing to admit. As we have seen, republicans draw from their analysis of the conditions of liberty the normative conclusion that individuals have a duty to participate actively in politics: in this sense, a commitment to negative liberty does privilege certain determinate ends and activities as especially rational for individuals to pursue. Given the tendency for our institutions of liberty to decline, and given the way in which virtue and participation work against this tendency, it is crucial that we recognize our duties of participation. To ignore this would be to lapse into corruption.

Republicans warn, moreover, that human beings often fail to be rational. For this reason, as we have seen, they conclude that it may be necessary for social institutions to exercise coercion in order to preserve liberty. In this sense, it is coherent both to hold a negative conception of liberty and to allow that it may occasionally be necessary to force someone to be free.

So Skinner's claim, then, is that contractarians have misunderstood the nature and implications of their own central ideal – negative liberty. This misunderstanding inhibits liberals from taking seriously the republican warnings about the maintenance of liberty.

A first point to note about this argument is that there is an important ambiguity in the formulation of the two propositions about liberty. It is ambiguous whether they are making *constitutive* or *instrumental* claims about liberty. Do republicans want to say that the fulfilment of their civic duties is a condition that agents must satisfy if they are to count as being free? And are they claiming that agents still count as being free even when they are being forced or coerced? These would be constitutive claims about liberty. Or do the two propositions simply refer to certain enabling conditions, the satisfaction of which can lead to agents being free in some different sense that is assumed to be understood?

It seems clear from his discussion that Skinner is *not* making constitutive claims about liberty.[31] This would be to abandon the commitment to negative liberty that his republican view takes as its starting point. Rather, I take Skinner's point to be that contractarian liberals have themselves been confused by the ambiguity into leaping from a denial of the two constitutive claims about liberty to a rejection of the two instrumental claims.

What Skinner's objection boils down to, then, is the assertion that liberals have wrongly dismissed two instrumental claims about liberty, claims which the republican view shows to be plausible. I hope that my discussion of Skinner's other objections is sufficient to show that this assertion cannot be defended. Liberals can and do allow that the maintenance of liberty rests on the kinds of conditions which republicans emphasize. In particular, they agree that liberty cannot be maintained unless individuals have a sense of justice and recognize a duty to support just institutions. And they join republicans in thinking that the coercive powers of the law may occasionally need to be employed to ensure that individuals do what is required to preserve their own liberty. This is not to deny that liberals and republicans may disagree about what specific policy prescriptions might be necessary for the preservation of liberty; it is only to suggest that they do not disagree at the level of philosophical abstraction at which Skinner's critique operates.[32]

I conclude that Skinner's formulation of instrumental republicanism does not represent an improvement upon the liberal attitude towards citizenship and civic virtue, because it fails to identify any philosophically interesting disagreement between the two positions. Nothing in liberalism's attitude to the invisible hand, rights, law, the common good, or liberty itself, prevents it from endorsing the instrumental republican understanding of the importance of public service and citizenship. To the contrary, liberals like Rawls explicitly assume – with republicans – that we must have a sense of justice, that we have duties to support just political institutions and the legal arrangements may help ensure that we do not throw away our own liberty.

## Notes

1. Skinner, 'Republican Ideal of Liberty', p. 301.
2. Skinner, 'Republican Ideal of Liberty', p. 301–2.
3. Skinner, 'Republican Ideal of Liberty', p. 302.
4. Skinner, 'Republican Ideal of Liberty', p. 302.
5. Skinner, 'Republican Ideal of Liberty', p. 302–3.
6. Skinner, 'Republican Ideal of Liberty', p. 303.
7. Skinner, 'Republican Ideal of Liberty', p. 304.
8. Skinner, 'Republican Ideal of Liberty', p. 305–6.
9. Skinner, 'Republican Ideal of Liberty', p. 307–8.
10. Skinner hints at such an argument in 'Republican Ideal of Liberty', pp. 304 and 308.
11. It is possible that Skinner has something like this in mind, but then it is misleading of him to characterize corruption (the tendency to ignore the claims of our

community) as 'simply a failure of rationality, an inability to recognize that our own liberty depends on committing ourselves to a life of virtue and public service', 'Republican Ideal of Liberty', p. 304. The use of the words 'our' and 'ourselves' makes this claim about the preservation of liberty crucially ambiguous. If he means each of us separately, then the claim seems mistaken: it is false that any particular individual's liberty depends on committing himself or herself to 'a life of virtue and public service'. If, however, he literally means 'our' and 'ourselves', the claim about liberty may well be true, but then corruption hardly seems like a *simple* failure of rationality. Rather it looks like a failure either of collective rationality or of individual rationality with a normative component built in.

12 Skinner, 'Republican Ideal of Liberty', pp. 305–7.
13 For a fascinating attempt to test some of the republican hypotheses empirically, see Robert D. Putnam, with Robert Leonardi and Raffaella Y. Nanetti, *Making Democracy Work: Civic Traditions in Modern Italy* (Princeton, NJ: Princeton University Press, 1993), especially chap. 4.
14 Skinner, 'Republican Ideal of Liberty', p. 304.
15 Rawls, *A Theory of Justice*, pp. 454–8, 474 and 493.
16 Rawls, *A Theory of Justice*, pp. 333–7.
17 As Rawls puts it in discussing the 'economic theory of democracy', 'since no system of constitutional checks and balances succeeds in setting up an invisible hand that can be relied upon to guide the process to a just outcome, a public sense of justice is to some degree necessary' (*A Theory of Justice*, p. 493).
18 Skinner, 'Republican Ideal of Liberty', p. 307.
19 Skinner, 'Republican Ideal of Liberty', p. 307.
20 Ronald Dworkin, *Taking Rights Seriously* (London: Duckworth, 1977), pp. 169–72. In his recent Tanner Lecture, 'Foundations of Liberal Equality', Dworkin appears to repudiate the right-basedness of political morality in favour of a more goal-based view.
21 See the comments on 'codes of conduct', *Taking Rights Seriously*, p. 172.
22 Skinner, 'Republican Ideal of Liberty', p. 305.
23 Skinner, 'Republican Ideal of Liberty', p. 305.
24 Rawls, *A Theory of Justice*, pp. 229–30. The 'balance of powers' and the 'separation of powers' are, of course, distinct sorts of constitutional arrangements, but the distinction does not seem relevant to Skinner's argument nor to my attempt to rebut it.
25 Rawls, *Theory of Justice*, p. 380.
26 This argument is made by Skinner in 'On Justice, the Common Good, and the Priority of Liberty'.
27 Skinner, 'On Justice, the Common Good, and the Priority of Liberty', p. 215.
28 Skinner, 'Republican Ideal of Liberty', p. 304 (emphasis added).
29 Rawls's recent work makes it especially clear that he does not wish to abandon notions of the common good. See, in particular, *Political Liberalism*, Lecture, V, Section 7.
30 See Skinner, 'Republican Ideal of Liberty', pp. 294–5.
31 Skinner, 'Republican Ideal of Liberty', p. 302.
32 It is difficult to say whether Skinner thinks that contractarians and republicans would disagree about concrete policies and legislation, because we are told very little by Skinner about republican policy prescriptions. Some republican policies *might* include: (a) compulsory voting; (b) extending the idea of jury service into other domains; (c) encouraging the creation of neighbourhood councils and committees which take part in the political life of the community; (d) national

service; (e) an education system which inculcates the virtues of the good citizen and a degree of patriotic allegiance; (f) prohibiting insults to the flag and national anthem; (g) subsidizing patriotic festivals and rites; or (h) establishing and preserving a certain social and cultural environment in the polity so as to secure maximal patriotic allegiance. Liberals might well balk at some of these proposals (in part, for reasons I discuss in Section 5 below), but not, as Skinner maintains, because they cannot, in principle, endorse the republican argument. I am grateful to an anonymous referee for suggesting to me some of the possible practical implications of instrumental republicanism.

# 16 Cosmopolitan Republicanism

## James Bohman

Cosmopolitanism and republicanism are both inherently political ideals. In most discussions, they are taken to have contrasting, if not conflicting, normative aspirations (Sandel 1996; Miller 1998). Cosmopolitanism is "thin" and abstractly universal, unable to articulate the basis for a "thick" citizenship in a republican political community. This commonly accepted way of dividing up the conceptual and political terrain is, however, increasingly misleading in the age of the global transformation of political authority. Rather than centered on community, republicanism is in the first instance an ideal of political liberty in terms of which one is free to the extent that one is not subordinated to others. To be free is not to live under the power of some master, but rather to live as an equal in "a free state" (Skinner 1995, 25). According to the republican ideal of freedom, the purpose of the political community is to maintain and promote the equal freedom of its citizens in this sense (Skinner 1997; Pettit, 1997). Hardly a community in either the universalist or the particularist sense, the international society of states at best satisfies Berlin's demand for a "maximum degree of noninterference compatible with the minimum demands of social life" (Berlin 1969, 161).

As an ideal of proper political order, cosmopolitanism is subject to a variety of interpretations. Cosmopolitanism could seek to protect the rights of individuals or to maximize the freedom of sovereign states to act as their citizens would choose. As opposed to such moral and liberal interpretations, cosmopolitanism is now perhaps better understood as an ideal of citizenship, particularly if it is understood in light of the republican ideal of self-governance and freedom from tyranny. What it means to be "a citizen of the world" would then be open to a variety of different interpretations of the democratic ideal, including a republican one in which each person is free to the extent that he or she can participate as an equal in a world political community of self-governing citizens. I call such an understanding of free self-governance and active world citizenship "cosmopolitan republicanism." Cosmopolitan republicanism argues that a liberal cosmopolitanism aimed solely at the moral status of individuals independent of political institutions is inadequate.

My argument here is that such a republican understanding of world citizenship is the best and most feasible cosmopolitan ideal of freedom under current circumstances—understood as freedom from domination and servitude. Republicanism demands that citizens are sovereign to the extent that they are able collectively to authorize (rather than merely to influence) such uses of public power in their public deliberation. This self-governance over the authority to incur obligations can no longer solely be realized in the form that republicanism has classically favored: the territorially and culturally bounded city-states or nation states. Cosmopolitan republicanism answers the following question: how is it that freedom from tyranny and subordination can remain a viable political ideal, even if the state as a homogenous and territorially bounded political community can no longer effectively realize or maintain such freedom? What is the necessarily cosmopolitan substitute when "living in a free state" is no longer a sufficient guarantee for the absence of tyranny and subordination?

Even if cosmopolitanism is consistent with the republican ideal of freedom and citizenship, it will still take some further argument to show why republicanism is the best current interpretation of cosmopolitanism. Cosmopolitanism is indeed opposed to those forms of republicanism that are linked to another political ideal: nationalism, whether liberal or illiberal. Because being a citizen of a free state places one in a particular set of obligations and ties of solidarity, republicanism has been a communitarian ideal. In light of such relationships, cosmopolitanism might appear as "thin" and "abstract" as Toulmin, Walzer and Guttman have argued it is (Guttman 1993; Walzer 1987; Toulmin 1990). Indeed, the original context of Diogenes' assertion that "I am a citizen of the world" was just such a fallacy of composition: Diogenes was concerned to deny the validity of *any* local obligations, such as the duty to pay taxes, since the duties of the cosmopolitan citizen must only be universal ones. Republican cosmopolitanism must reconcile elements of each of the opposing sides: it demands a *universalist* civic framework within which people act as citizens by bringing to bear their *particular* interests, identities and perspectives on common governance and problem-solving. It asks of new forms of cosmopolitan governance not how they aggregate or represent various interests. Rather, it is concerned with the worth of political liberty for those whom it governs once they are regarded as world citizens.

The nation state may no longer be the primary mechanism for the constitution and authorization of political authority; it increasingly fails, in Weber's terms, to possess, exercise, and organize exclusive authority over its own territory and thus to protect the liberty of citizens from subjection and domination. Whether or not they entail the strong thesis that the nation state has come to an end, most accounts of globalization show the ways in which global interactions across a variety of domains and exogenous influences from many different sources weaken the nation state's capacities to regulate activities within its borders. The very policies pursued to deal with these new exigencies, such as the active denationalization of new international legal regimes with the full cooperation of nation-state authorities, further widen the gap between citizens and those who exercise public power. Why is global authority now becoming less transparent and responsive to citizens? If that is the case, what is the place of citizenship outside of national borders? The specific republican strategies for effective citizenship, such as constitutional constraints, may have to be rethought and extended in this context.

Let me briefly mention three constraining effects of the extent and intensity of contemporary globalization on the governing capacities of current democratic institutions. These trends do not mean that the nation state has no role in citizenship, but only that it cannot be the sole location for the exercise of significant political rights and liberties. First, globalization challenges authority and citizenship based on a well-defined and bounded political community. Such boundaries are now more porous than ever with the movement of peoples, goods and information at an unprecedented pace and scale. Besides new conflicts, such interactions decrease the autonomy of many political decisions, as political communities are increasingly vulnerable to external influences. Even if states have not entirely lost their *de jure* sovereignty, they have increasingly lost some of their *de facto* independence, that is, their capacity to control processes through laws and policies directed to activities in their borders. Third, besides the porousness of boundaries, globalization has also lessened the scope of formal, national political authority in crucial domains. The relation of ruler and ruled has in some domains been replaced by legally unregulated and often anonymous relations of authority between agents and principals, experts and their clients, who (like the IMF and other international and often private regulatory regimes) set the terms of cooperation in a domain of interaction even for nation states as political actors.

## World Citizenship, Sovereignty and Accountability

Given the pervasiveness of agency at the international level and its tendency to expand non-democratic authority, how might a political community beyond the nation state solve the uncertainty of authority so as to promote the ideal of freedom? As the problem of agency shows, issues of sovereignty and accountability are directly related to problems of freedom and control. Both the freedom and control of citizens are necessary for a robust freedom from subjection and for democratic accountability. In this section, I argue that accountability (or reasons-responsiveness) demands the sovereignty of world citizens. In the next, I return to the problem of the extent of control. Freedom on a republican account is non-domination; it is "freedom from arbitrary authority and hierarchy," whether they are political or non-political in form. Democratic control is always limited by its own respect for freedom. Put positively, it is best understood as "the capacity to demand accountability" and is thus the responsiveness of institutions or agents to the reasons of citizens. Whatever uncertainty there is in such responsiveness, it must only be the inherent uncertainty as to why reasons fail or prevail in a democracy (Przeworski 1991, 40).

A more direct argument for the reasons-responsiveness of authority as a form of control has to do with the nature of freedom and authorization in large, pluralistic democracies. Under such circumstances authorization is neither the direct control of those affected, nor even their actual consent. These sorts of control are already inapplicable to most large-scale constitutional democracies, and there are often advantages in making even indirect control difficult to achieve (as in impeaching judges or changing basic constitutional provisions). Following Amartya Sen, we might distinguish between "effective freedom" and "freedom as control" (Sen 1992, 87). This distinction is useful particularly in public and institutional contexts where it seems unlikely that we could claim that citizens must exercise agency over all decisions that affect them. Effective freedom requires only that decisions be made for reasons that citizens would choose even if they do not have operational control over policies. This seems to demand too little since citizens need not exercise any control at all so long as citizens would have chosen what authorities chose without their influence or input.

The republican answer to the question of control concerns its ideal of self-governance by citizens. The presence of agency relations, a social fact of modern and complex societies, does not necessarily violate its ideal of social freedom as non-domination. Rather than direct control or explicit consent for all decisions, such freedom is violated when citizens are not able to exercise control as a collective body in a specific respect: with regard to incurring obligations. In order for freedom as non-domination to apply to all citizens, additional control is required for obligations. It must be at least possible for citizens to avoid unwanted obligations as the consequence of decisions by their agents (Scanlon 1999, 260). Such control requires effective democratic activity, either in the form of effective contestation or effective deliberation. Citizens are thus free from the domination of arbitrary power in the following way: either they are able to refuse obligations, or they are able to participate directly in the procedures of deliberation that authorize collectively binding decisions.

So far, the main argument for the sovereignty of world citizens has been a negative and empirical one: without such freedom and accountability there is no check to the power exercised on a similar scale by hierarchies based on agency relations. Such citizenship is the only available check on "the slow decline into guardianship" that Dahl argues already is occurring in the nation state with all its liberal protections. Dahl, liberal nationalists, and others have raised the following suspicion for all such cosmopolitan remedies: Why are they democratic? Dahl argues that the problem with cosmopolitan democracy is that "one cannot decide from within democratic theory what constitutes the proper unit of democracy" (Dahl 1987, 103; against Dahl, see Hurley 1999, 373). In contrast to this exogenous view of the proper boundaries of democracy (of which liberal nationalism is one variety), republican cosmopolitanism is committed to an endogenous view that democratic values do bear upon such jurisdictional questions. The second objection is that international organizations can never be democratic, since in them "delegation has become so extensive as to move the political system beyond the democratic threshold" (Dahl 1999, 21). In the remainder of this section I shall provide an answer to the first objection. The second objection is exactly correct for the international system as it stands today in which the delegated authorities of states delegate their authority to agents, who in turn hold them accountable to financial markets. I argue that on a republican conception such second-order accountability must be replaced by more collective, direct and deliberative authorization. This sort of authorization in turn requires that cosmopolitan citizens (and not their delegates) define themselves as the principals and thus do the authorizing.

My first defense of cosmopolitan institutions is normative and republican; my reply to the second objection argues that republican citizenship rather than representative institutions ought to be the central feature of cosmopolitan democracy. Both suggest that the exogenous view of the boundaries inevitably produces a new and unacceptable form of political subordination, the tyranny of citizens over non-citizens. The current nation-state system lacks the ability to assure sufficient representativeness in global decision-making and remains the basis for a pervasive and deep distinction between those who make global judgments and decisions and those who have neither exit options nor effective voice.

Two interrelated considerations tell against Dahl's argument about the exogenous character of the unit of democracy. The first is egalitarian. Consider Walzer's arguments for granting citizenship to guest workers who immigrate to a bounded political community, usually a nation state. Walzer argues that the exclusion of guest workers from political life and civil rights after a reasonable interval becomes a tyranny. The determination of aliens or guests by an exclusive band of citizens is not communal freedom, but oppression; it is to "claim territorial jurisdiction and rule over people with whom they share a territory. Indeed the rule of citizens over non-citizens is probably the most common form of tyranny in human history" (Walzer 1983, 62). Such a political community admits outsiders on terms that make them vulnerable to domination, since they are subject entirely to the beneficence of the members of the host community. This sort of dependency is equally true for those who have been incorporated in processes of globalization without their voluntary cooperation. Thus, Walzer's argument extends beyond territorial citizenship to any exclusion from effective influence that is *ipso facto* an arbitrary and thus tyrannous form of authority.

The egalitarian argument then says that citizenship is required for those who are involuntarily incorporated into processes of globalization over which they have no voice. The second argument concerns the loss of freedom in non-voluntary inclusion. In effect, the very encompassing and global character of many economic, legal and political processes that together make up globalization broadly understood are not just non-voluntary. They entail the imposition of unresponsive judgments upon all those for there is no exit option, at least one that is not extremely costly (as many governments have found out). As James Tobin points out, "equity requires democracy when exit is infeasible or very costly" (Tobin 1999, 37). The lack of both exit and voice is certainly met for most of the private regulatory regimes of the global economy (including environmental protection). Thus, basic democratic commitments to exit and voice, and republican commitments to eliminating nonvoluntary exclusion and inclusion, demand that citizenship be exercised beyond the boundaries of the nation state.

If the *de jure* sovereignty and *de facto* independence of liberal nation states are now substantially weakened and replaced by agent/principal hierarchies, then it would seem that without such citizenship many areas of social life that affect us most would be entirely out of the domain of democratic control. It is then with good reason that many now wonder about the emergence of a "neo-feudalism" of multiple sources of authority. Such neo-feudal order would be non-democratic, to the extent that it results in differentiated sovereignty without differentiated citizenship (Bull 1977, 254). Cosmopolitan citizenship establishes the latter to limit the hierarchies of the former: it establishes voice for the processes of globalization from which there is no feasible exit.

## Cosmopolitan Citizenship: Contestation or Deliberation?

In the previous section, I discussed cosmopolitan republican citizenship as a way to defend an ideal of social freedom that is directly challenged by the reversal of control in agency relations that has been typical of globalization. I argued that the creation of such citizenship beyond the nation state is the appropriate response to the fact that states no longer provide for adequate exit and voice in globalization. In a word, globalization increasingly produces domination, new global power and authority that elide current political practices of promoting freedom. It would seem unlikely, then, that international institutions constituted by agency could be influenced at all except through the nation state. Democratic nation states have provided a location for some participation in global decision-making by citizens, to the extent that robust civil rights and freedom of expression, voting, and "tertiary democratic activities" of public criticism and contestation have extended such opportunities for political influence to global public spheres. Given such protections, some forms of contestation and public monitoring may have some influence on some agency hierarchies. As large protests during the 1999 WTO meetings in Seattle show, the effectiveness of such strategic pressure from the public sphere does not extend to many core regulatory regimes in which the reversal of agency has occurred. How might citizens not only influence such regimes by symbolic protests within the boundaries of nation-state politics and begin to make them responsive to their public deliberation?

There are two generally republican answers to this question, one weaker and one stronger. The first says that influence can *only* take the form of challenge and contestation. Democratic reform would entail extending such public spheres and transnational civil society that follow from it (Dryzek 1996, chapter 4). The second says that while that may be all that can be expected in the case of minimal influence, fully democratic institutions and sovereign citizenship sufficient for accountability both require wider opportunities for effective deliberation. While the minimal position seems to take into account the fact that there is no unified collective will of the people that can be appealed to in the cosmopolitan context, the latter seems to be required for citizens to go beyond the dependence on independent authority that is the hallmark of the tyranny without voice or exit that I criticized in the last section. The second and less well-explored option is a republican cosmopolitanism that equal standing makes citizens sovereign. According to the republican view, citizens do not merely contest or challenge authority ("countersteer" or "speak truth to power"), but directly shape and collectively authorize it in public deliberation. Depending on circumstances, republican citizenship could be indirectly contestatory or directly deliberative, located primarily in the public sphere or in institutions as well. In the face of problems of scale, pace and complexity, republican cosmopolitan citizenship demands a "directly deliberative" collective authorization of the exercise of public power (Cohen and Sabel 1998). The problem is to show why such an ideal is feasible under conditions of globalization even as citizenship based solely on bounded community is less and less effective in preserving freedom.

In the absence of strong international judicial and legislative institutions or anything like a global will of the people organized by representation to which to appeal, cosmopolitan citizenship may very well be exercised primarily in public contestation. This form of political influence is certainly public, but primarily occurs through transnational civil society organized around specific sorts of issues or problems. It may even sometimes be deliberative; but it is still deliberative polyarchy, in which different interests and voices attempt to influence the formation and structure of various more or less informal regimes. The problem is that it may also be insufficiently democratic, since it cannot compensate for differing capacities for organization among groups that often become regularized patterns of influence over more formal institutions. Groups in civil society may themselves become agents, as NGOs have become experts in various kinds of monitoring. For such forms of indirect control to be exercised and new agency relations avoided, it will be necessary that citizen activity become more directly deliberative and participatory in shaping the policies and rules that agents carry out. Such strategic control by "citizen-principals" is only a form of guidance control or countersteering that mobilized publics can exercise through protest and contestation. It occurs when the principals find ways to reconstitute their identity as citizens independently from the boundaries of culturally and territorially bounded communities. We might think of this expansion of rights of participation as realigning social and cultural boundaries in order to "loosen the grip of specialization on authority" and make its control an object of contestation (White 1985, 209).

The very facts that make the contestation an attractive mechanism also tell against it as a complete model of cosmopolitan citizenship. While complexity and pluralism make it hard to see how the global will of the people could be expressed and then institutionally implemented, it is also hard to see how contestation alone is democratic when opportunities for influence are unevenly distributed. Contestation alone tends toward a strategic orientation to such authority, leading to trading off group interests in exchange for continued cooperation and control. Thus, the emphasis on contestation in the current exercise of cosmopolitan citizenship is best viewed primarily as a corrective mechanism that can be employed when democratic authority has broken down and been reversed. Non-domination as an ideal requires that citizens directly participate in the terms of the constitution and operation of authority. This means that democratic accountability must have a directly deliberative component: that is, citizens must have effective deliberative input in the operational control of democratic regulatory institutions to the extent that they generate collectively binding obligations. The process of deliberation of sovereign citizens to whom institutions are responsive then becomes *collectively* authoritative.

Besides such arguments from effectiveness, directly deliberative forms of cosmopolitan democracy are normatively superior in light of ideals of equal citizenship. In comparison, current arrangements are the worst of all possible worlds: they have the worst features of agency (unaccountability) and of the territorial state (uniform policies executed with little direct input). Given this combination of regulatory failures, such practices of agency are most likely to violate conditions of freedom as non-domination. The directness of deliberation allows citizens to participate in formulating cooperative conditions of agency that all can accept; it provides best for citizen sovereignty as the ability to demand an account from agents and other delegated forms of authority. Directness also permits the introduction of local variation through responsiveness to direct participation of a variety of citizens in shaping institutional rules and policies. Deliberativeness introduces features that are complementary to direct, local participation. It permits higher-order coordination and the diffusion of successful policies, as well as testing of the larger and often unintended impact of local decisions upon other locales and constituencies. More than merely legitimating and strategically influencing, cosmopolitan citizens are free from the domination of agents only if they authorize and delimit hierarchy by their direct and deliberative participation in decisions that set the terms of their shared obligations.

## Conclusion

I began the last section with a disjunction: contestation or deliberation? I have argued that contestation alone is insufficient, even if it is all that is feasible in the absence of democratically organized institutions that offer opportunities for deliberation and participation. Without reasons-responsive institutions, citizens can only hope indirectly to influence decisions by means of public strategic actions; this sort of activity is typical of transnational civil society, evident in human-rights and environmental NGOs and other civil society organizations. In order for a more strongly republican form of cosmopolitan citizenship to be realized, a number of further conditions must be fulfilled. The most important is the emergence of a robust set of international institutions, especially an international judiciary. If cosmopolitan institutions are democratic, then obligations incurred by participating in them will be constantly tested and revised by public deliberation. Such democratic activity should enhance rather than reduce national democracy. Indeed, citizen sovereignty functions in part as a principle favoring the pluralism of democratic forms of life.

## References

Berlin, Isaiah. 1969. *Four Essays on Liberty*. Oxford: Oxford University Press.
Bull, Hedley. 1977. *The Anarchical Society*. London: Macmillan.
Cohen, Joshua and Charles Sabel. 1998. "Directly-Deliberative Polyarchy," in *Private Governance, Democratic Constitutionalism and Supranationalism*, 3–30. Florence: European Commission.
Dahl, Robert. 1987. *Democracy and Its Critics*. New Haven, CT: Yale University Press.
———. 1999. "Can International Organizations Be Democratic? A Skeptic's View," in *Democracy's Edges*, ed. I. Shapiro and C. Hacker-Cordon, 19–36. Cambridge: Cambridge University Press.
Dryzek, John. 1996. *Democracy in Capitalist Times*. Oxford: Oxford University Press.
Guttman, Amy. 1993. "The Challenge of Multiculturalism in Political Ethics," *Philosophy and Public Affairs* 22, 171–206.
Hurley, Susan. 1999. "Rationality, Democracy and Leaky Boundaries," in *Democracy's Edges*, ed. I. Shapiro and C. Hacker-Cordon, 273–94. Cambridge: Cambridge University Press.
Miller, Richard. 1998. "Cosmopolitan Respect and Patriotic Concern," *Philosophy and Public Affairs* 27, 202–24.
Pettit, Philip. 1997. *Republicanism: A Theory of Freedom and Government*. Oxford: Oxford University Press.
Przeworski, Adam. 1991. *Democracy and the Market*. Cambridge: Cambridge University Press.
Sandel, Michael. 1996. *Democracy's Discontent*. Cambridge, MA: Harvard University Press.
Scanlon, T. M. 1999. *What We Owe Each Other*. Cambridge, MA: Harvard University Press.
Sen, Amartya. 1992. *Inequality Reexamined*. Cambridge, MA: Harvard University Press.
Skinner, Quentin. 1995. "The Paradoxes of Political Liberty," in *Equal Freedom*, ed. S. Darwall, 15–38. Ann Arbor, MI: University of Michigan Press.
———. 1997. *Liberty Before Liberalism*. Cambridge: Cambridge University Press.
Tobin, James. 1999. "A Comment on Dahl's Skepticism,' in *Democracy's Edges*, ed. I. Shapiro and C. Hacker-Cordon, 37–40. Cambridge: Cambridge University Press.

Toulmin, Stephen. 1990. *Cosmopolis: The Hidden Agenda of Modernity.* Chicago: University of Chicago Press.

Walzer, Michael. 1983. *Spheres of Justice.* New York: Basic Books.

——. 1987. *Interpretation and Social Criticism.* Cambridge, MA: Harvard University Press.

White, Harrison. 1985. "Agency as Control," in *Principal and Agents*, ed. J. Pratt and R. Zeckhauser, 187-212. Cambridge, MA: Harvard Business School Press.

# Part Five: Feminism

# Introduction

As a political theory feminism covers a wide range of distinct issues and concerns. Some feminists align themselves with liberalism whilst others see liberalism as a thoroughly patriarchal ideology and thus they construct their normative theories in response to what they take the deficiencies of liberalism to be. Depending on which version of feminism one endorses, feminism may or may not be compatible with liberalism or other normative theories, such as communitarianism, republicanism or multiculturalism. What makes a political theory 'feminist' is the emphasis it places on eliminating the oppression of women. Thus a liberal feminist believes that a liberal framework of rights, correctly conceived, could put an end to the subordination of women whilst a socialist feminist believes that class exploitation and gender exploitation are interconnected and thus the latter could not be achieved without eliminating the former.

We begin this part with Susan Okin's critique of the public/private dichotomy, a dichotomy which Okin takes to be fundamental to liberalism. This dichotomy maintains that a division should be drawn between the 'public' world of political life and the 'private' life of the family and our personal relations. Liberals tend to focus primarily, if not exclusively, on the former, thus suggesting that the demands of justice only apply to things like the constitution or the market but not to the family. Of course liberals will argue that there are good reasons why they defend the public/private distinction. The distinction is often invoked so as to oppose the repressive measures of an authoritarian state. The government should not, liberals will argue, tell you whom to marry, how to raise your kids, or what religion you should practice. Such interventions are illegitimate because they invade the private realm liberals believe must be protected if we are to respect our autonomy.

But feminism challenges the public/private dichotomy. Feminists such as Okin invoke the slogan 'the personal is political' and argue that the public/private dichotomy obscures the inequalities between men and women. A truly humanist conception of justice, argues Okin, must challenge the public/private dichotomy and ask – how just is gender? Gender is 'the deeply entrenched institutionalization of sexual difference' (Okin, 1989: 6). Gender is a social construction. This means that many of the differences that exist between men and women are socially imposed differences as opposed to strictly biological differences. It is a biological fact that only women can give birth. But this biological difference does not justify the other ways in which women are different from men. For example, that women, and not men, typically have to sacrifice their careers if they want to be a parent and that it is women who do most of the unpaid domestic labour in the home. By saying that a humanist theory of justice must ask – how just is gender? – Okin means that we must consider these socially imposed vulnerabilities. If we claim that the family is part of the 'private' realm that is beyond the concerns of justice then we will ignore the oppression of women.

In the first excerpt Okin argues that the personal is political in four respects. These are:

1. Power, a distinguishing feature of the political, can exist within the family.
2. The domestic sphere itself is the result of political decisions.
3. Domestic life is where most of our early socialisation takes place.
4. The division of labour within most families raises psychological as well as practical barriers against women in all other spheres.

The just society, argues Okin, would be a society where one's sex is just as irrelevant as one's eye colour when it comes to social structures and practices. The existing inequalities between men and women stem largely from the fact that the family remains an unjust institution, one that imposes unequal burdens on women and makes them vulnerable. By invoking the slogan 'the personal is political' feminists hope to inspire a public philosophy that takes more seriously the inequalities that exist between the sexes.

The second excerpt in this part is from the feminist Iris Marion Young who, in *Justice and the Politics of Difference*, argues that liberalism cannot adequately deal with difference. Young argues that it is a mistake to reduce social justice to redistribution, as egalitarian-liberals such as Rawls and Dworkin tend to do. Young identifies two problems with what she calls the 'distributive paradigm'. The first problem is that 'it tends to focus thinking about social justice on the allocation of material goods such as things, resources, income and wealth, or on the distribution of social positions, especially jobs. This focus tends to ignore the social structure and institutional context that often help determine distributive patterns' (Young, 1990: 5). Young provides some examples to illustrate this concern. She considers the case of a large employer that decides to close its plant in a small city. Such an action will have a devastating impact on the small community as the plant employs a large portion of the city's workers. This example raises concerns that go beyond those of the distributive paradigm, argues Young. What is at stake in this example is not simply a concern about the justice of material distributions but the justice of decision-making power and procedures. The just remedy in situations like this might not entail achieving a certain distributive pattern but giving the workers and community the option of taking over and operating the plant themselves.

Young argues that injustices in the division of labour and of cultural imagery and symbols are further examples that cannot be subsumed within the distributive paradigm. Media stereotyping of women and ethnic minorities, for example, raise concerns that are not primarily about the distribution of income or resources. The differences between social groups are brought to the fore by making the concepts of domination and oppression, and not distribution, the central concern of justice. Young argues that 'where social group differences exist and some groups are privileged while others are oppressed, social justice requires explicitly acknowledging and attending to those group differences in order to undermine the oppression' (Young, 1990: 3).

The second shortcoming of the distributive paradigm, argues Young, is that even when distributive theorists extend the demands of justice to non-material social goods (for example, rights, opportunities, self-respect) by doing so they mistakenly ascribe material-like properties to goods that do not have these properties. By doing this liberals obscure the institutional and social bases of these values. Take, for example, rights. Young asks:

## Introduction

What can it mean to distribute rights that do not refer to resources or things, like the right of free speech, or the right of trial by jury? We can conceive of a society in which some persons are granted these rights while others are not, but this does not mean that some people have a certain 'amount' or 'portion' of a good while others have less. Altering the situation so that everyone has these rights, moreover, would not entail that the formerly privileged group gives over some of its right of free speech or trial by jury to the rest of society's members, on analogy with a redistribution of income. (Young, 1990: 25)

By invoking the language of distribution liberal theories of justice focus more on end-state patterns (for example, the difference principle, equality of resources) rather than attending to social processes. But the injustices of social processes are not brought to the fore if we adopt the pattern orientation of the distributive paradigm. Young argues that two social conditions define injustice – oppression and domination. The former involves the institutional constraint on self-development and the latter the institutional constraint on self-determination (Young, 1990: 37).

Young believes that by making the concepts of oppression and domination the focus of a theory of justice one can inspire a liberating public philosophy, one that can appeal to diverse radical movements ranging from feminism to movements for Blacks, Latinos, American Indians, poor people, lesbians, old people and the disabled. Such a public philosophy does not seek to eliminate group differences, as the liberal ideals of equal treatment and impartiality attempt to do. It is both unrealistic and undesirable to attempt to eliminate group differences. Justice in a group-differentiated society, argues Young, 'demands social equality of groups, and mutual recognition and affirmation of group differences. Attending to group-specific needs and providing for group representation both promotes that social equality and provides the recognition that undermines cultural imperialism' (Young, 1990: 191). This emphasis on recognition is an issue which will come up again in the chapter on multiculturalism.

Feminists such as Young do not take the theory of liberalism as the sole object of their critique. In the excerpt in this part Young considers the ideal of community, an ideal that has led to the rise of communitarianism. Young criticises the notion of community on both philosophical and practical grounds. The ideal of community 'presumes subjects who are present to themselves and presumes subjects can understand one another as they understand themselves' (Young, 1986: 1–2). Thus by invoking the ideal of community one denies difference between subjects. In place of the value of community Young advocates the normative ideal of political emancipation. 'A model of the unoppressive city offers an understanding of social relations without domination in which persons live together in relations of mediation among strangers with whom they are not in community' (Young, 1986: 2).

In the final excerpt in this part Nancy Fraser examines Young's conceptions of oppression, social group and 'five faces of oppression'. Fraser rejects Young's wholesale endorsement of the politics of difference. Fraser argues that some oppressions are rooted in political economy whilst others are rooted in culture. Exploitation, marginalisation and powerlessness are rooted in the former whilst cultural imperialism and violence are rooted in culture. By considering some real-world applications that concern different cases of oppressed groups, such as working-class nonprofessionals, women, and African-Americans, Fraser argues that the politics of difference is not globally applicable.

> In some cases, such as that of nonprofessional workers, it is simply askew of the nature of the group and its oppression. In other cases, in contrast, such as gays and lesbians, the politics of difference is absolutely crucial for remedying oppression. The hardest cases, of course, are those, such as gender and 'race,' in which both redistribution and recognition are required to overcome a complex of oppression that is multiple and multiply-rooted. (Fraser, 1995: 179)

Fraser concludes her article by contrasting four possible attitudes towards 'difference'. She defends the position that there are different kinds of difference. Some differences should be eliminated, others should be universalised, and some should be enjoyed. Fraser opposes a politics of difference that is wholesale and undifferentiated.

## References

Fraser, Nancy. 'Recognition or Redistribution? A Critical Reading of Iris Young's *Justice and the Politics of Difference*', *The Journal of Political Philosophy*, Vol. 3(2), 1995: 166–180.

Okin, Susan. *Justice, Gender and the Family*. (New York: Basic Books, 1989).

Young, Iris Marion. 'The Ideal of Community and the Politics of Difference', *Social Theory and Practice*, 12(1), 1986: 1–26.

—— *Justice and the Politics of Difference*. (Princeton: Princeton University Press, 1990).

# 17 The Public/Private Dichotomy

## Susan Moller Okin

### The Personal as Political

"The personal is political" is the central message of feminist critiques of the public/domestic dichotomy. It is the core idea of most contemporary feminism. Though many of those who fought in the nineteenth and early twentieth centuries for suffrage and for the abolition of the oppressive legal status of wives were well aware of the connections between women's political and personal dominations by men, few pre-1960s feminists questioned women's special role in the family. While arguing for equal rights, such as the vote or access to education, most accepted the prevailing assumption that women's close association with and responsibility for the care of the family was natural and inevitable.

The earliest claims that the personal is political came from those radical feminists of the 1960s and 1970s who argued that, since the family was at the root of women's oppression, it must be "smashed."[1] The anti-family nature of some early radical feminism has been exaggerated and exploited both by antifeminists and by those who have been termed "conservative" or "backlash" feminists. They have focused on it in order to attack all, or all but their own version, of feminism.[2] But most contemporary feminists, while critiquing the gender-structured family, have not attacked all varieties of family. Many advocate that "family" be defined so as to include any intimately connected and committed group, specifically endorsing homosexual marriage; most, certainly, refuse to accept that the choice must be between accepting women's double burden and abolishing the family. We refuse to give up on the institution of the family, and refuse to accept the division of labor between the sexes as natural and unchangeable. More and more, as the extent to which gender is a social construction has become understood, feminists have come to recognize how variable are the potential forms and practices of family groups. The family is in no way inevitably tied to its gender structure, but until this notion is successfully challenged, and nontraditional groupings and divisions of labor are not only recognized but encouraged, there can be no hope of equality for women in either the domestic or the public sphere.

Thus feminists have turned their attention to the politics of what had previously been regarded—and, as I have shown, still is seen by most political theorists—as paradigmatically *non*political. That the personal sphere of sexuality, of housework, of child care and family life *is* political became the underpinning of most feminist thought. Feminists of different political leanings and in a variety of academic disciplines have revealed and analyzed the multiple interconnections between women's domestic roles and their inequality and segregation in the workplace, and between their socialization in gendered families and the psychological aspects of their oppression. We have strongly and persistently challenged the long-standing underlying assumption of almost all political theories: that the sphere of family and personal life is so separate and distinct from the rest of social life that such theories can justifiably assume but ignore it.

As my argument so far has made clear, however, these feminist arguments have not been acknowledged by most contemporary political theorists writing about justice. In discussing some of the central feminist arguments about the essentially political nature of personal life and of the family in particular, I shall establish that domestic life needs to be just and to have its justice reinforced by the state and its legal system. In the circumstances of the division of labor that is practiced within the vast majority of households in the United States today, women are rendered vulnerable by marriage and especially by motherhood, and there is great scope for unchecked injustice to flourish.

The interconnections between the domestic and the nondomestic aspects of our lives are deep and pervasive. Given the power structures of both, women's lives are far more detrimentally affected by these interconnections than are men's. Consider two recent front-page stories that appeared on subsequent days in the *New York Times*. The first was about a tiny elite among women: those who work as lawyers for the country's top law firms.[3] If these women have children with whom they want to spend any time, they find themselves off the partnership track and instead, with no prospects of advancement, on the "mommy track." "Nine-to-five" is considered part-time work in the ethos of such firms, and one mother reports that, in spite of her twelve-hour workdays and frequent work on weekends, she has "no chance" of making partner.[4] The article fails to mention that these women's children have fathers, or that most of the men who work for the same prestigious law firms also have children, except to report that male lawyers who take parental leave are seen as "wimp-like." The sexual division of labor in the family, even in these cases where the women are extremely well qualified, successful, and potentially influential, is simply assumed.[5]

The next day's *Times* reported on a case of major significance for abortion rights, decided by a Federal Appeals Court in Minnesota.[7] The all-male panel of judges ruled 7 to 3 that the state may require a woman under eighteen years who wishes to obtain an abortion to notify *both* her parents—even in cases of divorce, separation, or desertion—or to get special approval from a state judge. The significance of this article is amplified when it is juxtaposed with the previous one. For it shows us how it is that those who rise to the top in the highly politically influential profession of law are among those who have had the least experience of all in raising children. There is a high incidence of recruitment of judges from those who have risen to partnership in the most prestigious law firms. Other judges are often drawn from the equally highly competitive field of academic law, which also places its greatest demands (those of the tenure hurdle) on lawyers during the child-rearing years, and therefore discriminates against those who participate in parenting. Those who are chosen, therefore, would seem to be those least well informed to make decisions about abortion, especially in cases involving relations between teenage girls and their parents. Here we find a systematically built-in absence of mothers (and presumably of "wimp-like" participating fathers, too) from high-level political decisions concerning some of the most vulnerable persons in society—women, disproportionately poor and black, who become pregnant in their teens, and their future children. It is not hard to see here the ties between the supposedly distinct public and domestic spheres.

This is but one example of what feminists mean by saying that "the personal is political," sometimes adding the corollary "the political is personal." It is because of this claim, of course, that the family became and has remained central to the politics of feminism and to feminist theory. Contemporary feminism poses a significant challenge to the long-standing and still-surviving assumption of political theories that the sphere of family and personal life is sharply distinct from the rest of social and political life, that the state can and should restrain itself from intrusion into the domestic sphere, and that political theories can therefore legitimately ignore it. In contrast, both challenging and aiming to restructure the public/domestic dichotomy are fundamental to the feminist enterprise.

I must point out here what many feminists who challenge the traditional dichotomy of public and domestic do *not* claim, especially because it is a claim that some do make.[8] Challenging the dichotomy does not necessarily mean denying the usefulness of a concept of privacy or the value of privacy itself in human life. Nor does it mean denying that there are *any* reasonable distinctions to be made between the public and domestic spheres. It does not mean, to many feminists, including myself, a simple or a total *identification* of the personal and the political. Carol Pateman, Linda Nicholson, and Mary O'Brien, for example, all distance themselves from the literal interpretation that some radical feminists give to "the personal is political," and I agree with them in not accepting a complete overlapping or identification of the two. Anita Allen's recent book, *Uneasy Access*, is a feminist argument based on women's often unfulfilled need for personal privacy.[9] Both the concept of privacy and the existence of a personal sphere of life in which the state's authority is very limited are essential. However, such a sphere can be just and secure only if its members are equals, and if those who must be temporarily regarded as unequal—children—are protected from abuse. "How political *is* the personal?" and "*In what ways* is the personal political and is the political personal?" are important questions within feminist argument.[10]

My discussion about the politics of marriage contributes to this argument. Here, I shall lay out four major flaws in the dichotomy between "private" domestic life and "public" life in the marketplace or politics, as it is currently drawn or assumed in theories of justice. These constitute, in other words, four respects in which the personal is political.

First, what happens in domestic and personal life is not immune from the dynamic of *power*, which has typically been seen as the distinguishing feature of the political. Power within the family, whether that of husband over wife or of parent over child, has often not been recognized as such, either because it has been regarded as natural or because it is assumed that, in the family, altruism and the harmony of interests make power an insignificant factor. This seems to be tacitly assumed by most contemporary theorists of justice, given their neglect of intrafamilial relations. But the notion that power in its crassest form, physical violence, is not a factor in family life is a myth that has been exposed during the last century and increasingly exposed in the last two decades. As has now become well known, wife abuse, though still seriously underreported, is not an uncommon phenomenon. According to a 1976 national survey, it is estimated that between 1.8 and 5.7 million women in the United States are beaten each year in their homes. A recent government study of marital violence in Kentucky found that 4 percent of women living with a male partner had been kicked or bitten, struck with a fist or an object, beaten up, or either threatened or attacked with a knife or gun during the previous year. Nine percent reported this degree of physical abuse at some time in the past from the man they lived with, and some estimates of actual incidence are far higher. Thirty percent of all female murder victims in 1986 were killed by their husbands or boyfriends, compared with 6 percent of male victims killed by wives or girlfriends.[11]

People are far more tolerant of physical abuse of a woman by a man when they believe she is his wife or girlfriend than otherwise. This is probably due in part to the fact that violence used to be a legally sanctioned part of male dominance in the patriarchal family. The privacy that early liberal theorists claimed for the "individuals" they wrote about was the power of patriarchs; it was taken for granted that husbands and fathers should have power over their wives and children, including the right to "chastise" them physically. Until recently, though in principle no longer legally sanctioned, violence within families was in practice ignored; the police and the courts were loath to "intervene" in ostensibly "private" familial disputes. In the late nineteenth and early twentieth centuries, child abuse was "discovered". And in the 1970s and 1980s, partly as a result of the feminist and children's rights movements that originated in the 1960s, wife abuse has been "discovered" and child abuse "rediscovered." Family violence is now much less sanctioned or ignored that in the past; it is becoming recognized as a serious problem that society must act on. There is now no doubt that family violence, as it affects both wives and children, is closely connected with differentials of power and dependency between the sexes. It is certainly impossible to claim, in the face of current evidence, that the family is private and nonpolitical because power is an insignificant factor in it. In addition to physical force, there are subtler, though no less important, modes of power that operate within families, some of which will be discussed in the next chapter. As feminists have pointed out, in many respects the notion that state intervention in the family should be minimized has often served to reinforce the power of its economically or physically more powerful members. The privacy of home can be a dangerous place, especially for women and children.[12]

The second problem with the public/domestic dichotomy is that, as feminist historians and lawyers have shown, to the extent that a more private, domestic sphere does exist, its very existence, the limits that define it, and the types of behavior that are acceptable and not acceptable within it all result from political decisions.[13] If there *were* a clear sphere from which the state refrained from intruding, that sphere would have to be defined, and its definition would be a political issue. But in fact, the state has not just "kept out of" family life. In innumerable ways, the state determines and enforces the terms of marriage. For hundreds of years, the common law deprived women of their legal personhood upon marriage. It enforced the rights of husbands to their wives' property and even to their wives' bodies, and made it virtually impossible for women to divorce or even to live separately from their husbands. Long after married women gained rights over their own property and the possibility of divorce, as we have seen, marriage has remained a peculiar contract, a preformed status contract whose terms have been enforced in innumerable ways. Courts have refused to allow wives to trade or forgo their rights to support, but have also refused to "intrude" into the family to enforce any specific level of support; few jurisdictions recognize marital rape; and married women have been "compelled, by law, to perform housework without pay [and] the obligation cannot be altered."[14] In addition, until the "divorce revolution" of the last two decades, the terms of divorce strongly reinforced traditional sex roles within marriage, by means of rewards and punishments. As Lenore Weitzman wrote in 1985, "the common law assumption that the husband was the head of the family remained firmly embodied in statute and case law until the last decade."[15]

There is a whole other dimension, too, to the state's pervasive regulation of family life. Historically, the law closed off to women most means of making a living wage. Until very recently, women have been legally denied rights routinely exercised by men in the spheres of work, marketplace, and politics, on the grounds that the exercise of such rights would interfere with the performance of their domestic responsibilities. All of this obviously reinforced the patriarchal structure of marriage, but the myth of the separation of the public and the domestic, of the political from the personal, was sustained throughout. Even now that most of the explicit legal disabilities of women have been done away with, the state has a direct hand in regulating family life in such crucial areas as marriage, divorce, and child custody. Who can marry whom, who is legally the child of whom, on what grounds marriages can be dissolved, and whether both spouses or only one must consent to their dissolution, are all directly determined by legislation. In turn, such laws themselves and how they are applied can have a critical impact on how people live their domestic lives, and thence a cyclical effect on their entire lives.

As Frances Olsen has pointed out with great clarity and perceptiveness, the very notion that the state has the option to intervene or not to intervene in the family is not only mythical but meaningless. In many ways "the state is responsible for the background rules that affect people's domestic behaviors." The law does not on the one hand legitimize any and all kinds of behavior within the family—murder being the most obvious example. But neither does it regulate the behavior of family members toward each other in the same way that in regulates the behavior of strangers; for example, parents can "ground" their children as a means of discipline, or enlist the state's help in restraining children who run away. Children cannot sue their parents (as others could) for kidnapping them on such occasions and, as Olsen says, "the staunchest opponents of state intervention in the family will insist that the state reinforce parents' authority over their children." "Because the state is deeply implicated in the formation and functioning of families," she argues, "it is nonsense to talk about whether the state does or does not intervene in the family."[16] On the vital question of divorce, for example, would "nonintervention" mean allowing divorce, or not allowing it? Making a divorce difficult or easy to acquire? The issue is not whether, but *how* the state intervenes. The myth that state intervention in the family is an option allows those who support the status quo to call it "nonintervention" and to label policies that would alter it—such as the provision of shelters for battered wives—"intervention." This language takes the focus off more pertinent questions such as whether the policy in question is equitable or prevents harm to the vulnerable.[17]

The third reason it is invalid to assume a clear dichotomy between a nonpolitical sphere of family life and a public or political sphere is that domestic life is where most of our early socialization takes place. Feminist scholarship has contributed much to our understanding of how we *become* our gendered selves. Psychoanalytic and other psychologically based theories have explained how gender is reproduced specifically through gendered parenting. One of the earliest of such theories of development (though still highly influential, on account of its persuasiveness) is that of Nancy Chodorow. She argues, building on object-relations theory, that a child's experience of individuation—separating from the caregiver with whom he or she is at first psychologically fused—is a very different experience for those of the same sex as the nurturer than it is for those of the other sex.[18] In a gender-structured society like ours, where primary nurturers are almost always mothers (and, if not, other females), this makes for a sexually differentiated developmental path for girls and for boys. The psychological task of identification with the same-sexed parent is very different for girls, for whom the mother (or female surrogate) is usually present, than for boys, for whom the parent to identify with is often absent for long periods of the day, engaged in tasks the child has no concrete knowledge of. Chodorow argues that, as a result, the personality characteristics in girls and women that make them more psychologically connected with others, more likely to choose nurturing and to be regarded as especially suited for it—and those in men that lead them to a greater need and capacity for individuation and orientation toward achieving "public" status—can be explained by the assignation of primary parenting within the existing gender structure. Thus mothering itself is "reproduced" in girls. Once we admit the idea that significant differences between women and men are *created* by the existing division of labor within the family, it becomes increasingly obvious just how political an institution the family is.

Moreover, the connections between domestic life and the rest of life are accentuated by the fact that the complete answer to the question of why women are primary parents cannot be arrived at by looking solely at the family and at the psychology of gender development. A large part of the answer is to be found in the sex segregation of the workplace, where the great majority of women are still concentrated in low-paid, dead-end occupations. This fact makes it economically "rational" in most two-parent families for the mother to be the primary child rearer, which continues the cycle of gender.

A fourth respect in which "the personal is political" and the public/domestic dichotomy breaks down is that division of labor within most families raises psychological as well as practical barriers against women in all other spheres. In liberal democratic politics, as well as in most workplace situations, speech and argument are often recognized as crucial components of full participation. Michael Walzer, for example, writes: "Democracy is...*the political way* of allocating power...What counts is argument among the citizens. Democracy puts a premium on speech, persuasion, rhetorical skill. Ideally, the citizen who makes the most persuasive argument...gets his way."[19] Women, however, are often handicapped by being deprived of any authority in their speech. As one recent feminist analysis has diagnosed the problem, it is not "that women have not learned how to be in authority," but rather "that authority currently is conceptualized so that female voices are excluded from it."[20] This results, to a large extent, from the fact that women's public and private personae are inextricably linked in the minds of many men and is exacerbated by the fact that women are often represented in token numbers, both in influential positions in the workplace and on authoritative political bodies. One example of this is the sex bias in the nation's courtrooms, which has been increasingly well documented during the last few years. It affects judicial attitudes toward women as defendants, plaintiffs, victims, and lawyers, with consequent effects on sentencing, treatment of domestic-violence and rape victims, alimony and child support awards, and damage awards.[21] Sometimes women in the public sphere are simply not seen or heard. Sometimes we are seen and heard only insofar as we make ourselves seem as much as possible like men. Sometimes we are silenced by being demeaned or sexually harassed. And sometimes what we say is silenced or distorted because we have projected onto us the personae of particularly important women (especially their mothers) in the intrapsychic lives of men.

All of these handicaps, which women carry with them from the sexual division of labor at home to the outside spheres of life, certainly do not make it easy for us to make transitions back and forth between them. Because of the past and present division of labor between the sexes, for women especially, the public and the domestic are in many ways *not* distinct, separate realms at all. The perception of a sharp dichotomy between them depends on the view of society from a traditional male perspective that tacitly assumes different natures and roles for men and women. It cannot, therefore, be maintained in a truly humanist theory of justice—one that will, for the first time, include all of us.

## Notes

1  The unique argument of Shulamith Firestone went further. She argued that equality between the sexes could occur only with the attainment and use of techniques of artificial reproduction. See *The Dialectic of Sex* (New York: Morrow, 1971).

2  See Judith Stacey, "Are Feminists Afraid to Leave Home? The Challenge of Conservative Profamily Feminism," in *What Is Feminism? A Re-examination*, ed. Juliet Mitchell and Ann Oakley (New York: Pantheon, 1986).

3  "Women in the Law Say Path Is Limited by 'Mommy Track,'" *New York Times*, August 9, 1988, pp. A1 and A15. See also Felice N. Schwartz, "Management Women and the New Facts of Life," *Harvard Business Review* 89, no. 1 (1989); and her response to critics in "The 'Mommy Track' Isn't Anti-Woman," *New York Times*, March 22, 1989, p. A27.

4  On the career barriers faced by lawyers who are mothers, see also Valerie Lezin and Sherrill Kushner, "Yours, Mine and Hours" in *Barrister* (publication of the Young Lawyers' Division, American Bar Association) (Spring 1986).

5  That many dual-career couples themselves make this assumption is confirmed by other recent research. See, for example, Hertz, *More Equal Than Others*, chaps. 4 and 5.

\* Felice Schwartz, too, in a recent controversial article at first assumes the traditional division of parenting labor between the sexes, even when both parents are high-powered professionals. She justifies this by saying that "the one immutable, enduring difference between men and women is maternity," in which she includes everything from the anticipation of motherhood through the psychological adjustment to having a child to child rearing. But a few lines later, seemingly in total contradiction with this, she acknowledges that "today, in the developed world, the only role still uniquely gender related is childbearing." She adds that though "men and women are still socialized to perform their traditional roles...certainly both men and women are capable of the full range of behavior." Thus what starts out as immutable becomes by the next paragraph almost entirely alterable. The *reasons* that, as Schwartz reports, "some 90% of executive men but only 35% of executive women have children by the age of 40" and that her article focuses on executives who are mothers rather than all those who are parents, can be discerned only if one tries to understand the interrelation of the public and the domestic spheres.[6]

6  Schwartz, "Management Women," pp. 66–67, 69.

7 "Curbs for Minors Seeking Abortion Upheld on Appeal," *New York Times*, August 9, 1988, p. A1.
8 Alison Jaggar says that both radical and socialist feminists argue for total abolition of the distinction between public and private, while liberal feminists argue for a narrower definition of the private sphere. *Feminist Politics and Human Nature* (Totowa, N.J.: Rowman and Allanheld, 1983), pp. 145, 254. I am not convinced that the correlation can be drawn so clearly.
9 Pateman, "Feminist Critiques," pp. 297–98; Linda J. Nicholson, *Gender and History: The Limits of Social Theory in the Age of the Family* (New York: Columbia University Press, 1986); Mary O'Brien, *The Politics of Reproduction* (London: Routledge & Kegan Paul, 1981), p. 193; Anita L. Allen, *Uneasy Access: Privacy for Women in a Free Society* (Totowa, N.J.: Rowman and Allanheld, 1988).
10 Nicholson, *Gender and History*, pp. 19–20.
11 *Report to the Nation on Crime and Justice*, 2nd ed. (Washington, D.C.: Government Printing Office, March 1988), p. 33; *A Survey of Spousal Violence Against Women in Kentucky* (Washington, D.C.: Law Enforcement Assistance Administration, 1979), cited by Barbara Bergmann, *The Economic Emergence of Women* (New York: Basic Books, 1986), p. 205; *Age, Sex, Race and Ethnic Origin of Murder Victims, 1986*, U.S. Department of Justice Uniform Crime Reports (Washington, D.C.: Government Printing Office, July 1987), p. 11.
12 On the history of family violence and its connections with the traditional division of labor and dependence of wives, see Linda Gordon, *Heroes of Their Own Lives* (New York: Viking, 1988), esp. chaps. 8 and 9, and Elizabeth Pleck, *Domestic Tyranny* (New York: Oxford University Press, 1987), esp. chap. 10. On issues of power differentials and family privacy, see Gordon, *Heroes of Their Own Lives*, chap. 9; Martha Minow, "We the Family: Constitutional Rights and American Families," *The American Journal of History* 74, no. 3 (1987); Susan Moller Okin, "Gender, the Public and the Private," in *Political Theory Today*, ed. David Held (Oxford: Polity Press, 1991); and Nikolas Rose, "Beyond the Public/Private Division: Law, Power and the Family," *Journal of Law and Society* 14, no. 1 (1987).
13 See Olsen, "The Myth of State Intervention"; Minow, "We the Family"; and Nicholson, *Gender and History*, esp. introduction and part 3.
14 Sylvia Law and Nadine Taub, "Constitutional Considerations and the Married Woman's Obligation to Serve," unpublished ms. quoted in Weitzman, *The Marriage Contract*, p. 65; see also Weitzman, chap. 3 passim, on the wife's legal responsibility for domestic service and its consequences.
15 Lenore J. Weitzman, *The Divorce Revolution: The Unexpected Social and Economic Consequences for Women and Children in America* (New York: The Free Press, 1985), p. 2 and chap. 1 passim. See also Weitzman, *The Marriage Contract*, where she notes "the extent to which the traditional coverture-inspired model of marriage still persists despite major social and economic changes in the position of women in our society" (p. 6).
16 Olsen, "The Myth of State Intervention," p. 837.
17 Ibid., pp. 842, 861–64.
18 Nancy Chodorow, "Family Structure and Feminine Personality," in *Woman, Culture, and Society*, ed. M. Z. Rosaldo and Louise Lamphere (Stanford: Stanford University Press, 1974); idem, *The Reproduction of Mothering: Psychoanalysis and the Sociology of Gender* (Berkeley: University of California Press, 1978). For related arguments, see also Isaac Balbus, *Marxism and Domination* (Princeton: Princeton University Press, 1982); Dorothy Dinnerstein, *The Mermaid and the Minotaur: Sexual Arrangements and Human Malaise* (New York: Harper & Row, 1976).

19  Walzer, *Spheres of Justice*, p. 304. Cf. Benjamin Barber, *Strong Democracy* (Berkeley: University of California Press, 1984), pp. 173–78. Though he starts by stating that "at the heart of strong democracy is talk," Barber's discussion is unusual in its emphasis on the fact that listening is just as important a part of "talk" as speaking, and that the "potential for empathy and affective expression" is as crucial as is eloquence or creativity. Thus Barber's approach is less biased in favor of traditionally masculine and away from traditionally feminine qualities than is usual in such discussions of political speech.

20  Kathleen Jones, "On Authority: Or, Why Women Are Not Entitled to Speak," in *Authority Revisited*, ed. J. Roland Pennock and John W. Chapman (New York: New York University Press, 1987).

21  Arizona, Massachusetts, New Jersey, New York, Rhode Island, and other states have established task forces to investigate and work toward elimination of sex and race bias in their courts. See, for example, Lynn Hecht Schafran and Norma J. Wikler, *Task Forces on Gender Bias in the Courts: A Manual for Action* (available from the Foundation for Women Judges, Washington, D.C.), and *Special Focus: Gender Bias in the Court System*, 1986 Annual Meeting of the American Bar Association, New York, August 10, 1986; also annual reports of the various state task forces.

# 18 The Ideal of Community and the Politics of Difference

## Iris Marion Young

Radical theorists and activists often appeal to an ideal of community as an alternative to the oppression and exploitation they argue characterize capitalist patriarchal society. Such appeals often do not explicitly articulate the meaning of the concept of community, but rather tend to evoke an affective value. Even more rarely do those who invoke an ideal of community as an alternative to capitalist patriarchal society ask what it presupposes or implies, or what it means concretely to institute a society that embodies community. I raise a number of critical questions about the meaning, presuppositions, implications and practical import of the ideal of community.

As in all conceptual reflection, in this case there is no universally shared concept of community, but only particular articulations that overlap, complement, or sit at acute angles to one another.[1] I shall rely on the definitions and expositions of a number of writers for examples of conceptualizations about community as a political ideal. All these writers share a critique of liberal individualist social ontology, and most think democratic socialism is the best principle of social organization. I claim acceptance for my analysis only within this general field of political discourse, though I suspect that much of the conceptual structure I identify applies to an ideal of community that might be appealed to by more conservative or liberal writers.

I criticize the notion of community on both philosophical and practical grounds. I argue that ideal of community participates in what Derrida calls the metaphysics of presence or Adorno calls the logic of identity, a metaphysics that denies difference. The ideal of community presumes subjects who are present to themselves and presumes subjects can understand one another as they understand themselves. It thus denies the difference between subjects. The desire for community relies on the same desire for social wholeness and identification that underlies racism and ethnic chauvinism, on the one hand, and political sectarianism on the other.

Insofar as the ideal of community entails promoting a model of face-to-face relations as best, it devalues and denies difference in the form of temporal and spatial distancing. The ideal of a society consisting of decentralized face-to-face communities is undesirably utopian in several ways. It fails to see that alienation and violence are not a function of mediation of social relations, but can and do exist in face-to-face relations. It implausibly proposes a society without the city. It fails to address the political question of the relations among face-to-face communities.

The ideal of community, finally, totalizes and detemporalizes its conception of social life by setting up an opposition between authentic and inauthentic social relations. It also detemporalizes its understanding of social change by positing the desired society as the complete negation of existing society. It thus provides no understanding of the move from here to there that would be rooted in an understanding of the contradictions and possibilities of existing society.

I propose that instead of community as the normative ideal of political emancipation, that radicals should develop a politics of difference. A model of the unoppressive city offers an understanding of social relations without domination in which persons live together in relations of mediation among strangers with whom they are not in community.

## Denial of Difference as Time and Space Distancing

Many political theorists who put forward an ideal of community specify small group, face-to-face relations as essential to the realization of that ideal. Peter Manicas expresses a version of the ideal of community that includes this face-to-face specification.

> Consider an association in which persons are in face-to-face contact, but where the relations of persons are not mediated by "authorities," sanctified rules, reified bureaucracies or commodities. Each is prepared to absorb the attitudes, reasoning and ideas of others and each is in a position to do so. Their relations, thus, are open, immediate and reciprocal. Further, the total conditions of their social lives are to be conjointly determined with each having an equal voice and equal power. When these conditions are satisfied and when as a result, the consequences and fruits of their associated and independent activities are perceived and consciously become an object of individual desire and effort, then there is a democratic community.[2]

Roberto Unger argues that community requires face-to-face interaction among members within a plurality of contexts. To understand other people and to be understood by them in our concrete individuality, we must not only work together, but play together, take care of children together, grieve together, and so on.[3] Christian Bay envisions the good society as founded upon small face-to-face communities of direct democracy and many sided interaction.[4] Michael Taylor specifies that in a community relations among members must be direct and many-sided. Like Manicas, he asserts that relations are direct only when they are unmediated by representatives, leaders, bureaucrats, state institutions or codes.⁵ While Gould does not specify face-to-face relations as necessary for community, some of her language suggests that community can only be realized in such face-to-face relations. In the institutionalization of democratic socialism, she says, "social combination now becomes the *immediate* subjective relations of mutuality among individuals. The relations again become *personal* relations as in the precapitalist stage, but no longer relations of domination and no longer mediated, as in the second stage, by external objects."⁶

I take there to be several problems with the privileging of face-to-face relations by theorists of community. It presumes an illusory ideal of unmediated social relations, and wrongly identifies mediation with alienation. It denies difference in the sense of time and space distancing. It implies a model of the good society as consisting of decentralized small units which is both unrealistic and politically undesirable. And finally, it avoids the political question of the relation among the decentralized communities.

All the writers cited above give primacy to face-to-face presence because they claim that only under those conditions can the social relations be *immediate*. I understand them to mean several things by social relations that are immediate. They are direct, personal relations, in which each understands the other in her or his individuality. This is an extension of the ideal of mutual understanding I have criticized in the previous section. Immediacy also here means relations of co-presence in which persons experience a simultaneity of speaking and hearing, and are in the same space, that is, have the possibility to move close enough to touch.⁷

This ideal of the immediate presence of subjects to one another, however, is a metaphysical illusion. Even a face-to-face relation between two is mediated by voice and gesture, spacing and temporality. As soon as a third person enters the interaction the possibility arises of the relation between the first two being mediated through the third, and so on. The mediation of relations among persons by the speech and actions of still other persons is a fundamental condition of sociality. The richness, creativity, diversity and potential of a society expand with growth in the scope and means of its media, linking persons across time and distance. The greater the time and distance, however, the greater the number of persons who stand between other persons.

The normative privileging of face-to-face relations in the ideal of community seeks to suppress difference in the sense of the time and space distancing of social processes, which material media facilitate and enlarge. Such an ideal dematerializes its conception of interaction and institutions. For all social interaction takes place over time and across space. Social desire consists in the urge to carry meaning, agency, and the effects of agency, beyond the moment and beyond the place. As laboring subjects we separate the moment of production from the moment of consumption. Even societies confined to a limited territory with few institutions and a small population devise means of their members communicating with one another over distances, means of maintaining their social relationships even though they are not face to face. Societies occupy wider and wider territorial fields and increasingly differentiate their activity in both space, time and function, a movement that of course accelerates and takes on qualitatively specific form in modern industrial societies.[8]

I suggest that there are no conceptual grounds for considering face-to-face relations more pure, authentic social relations than relations mediated across time and distance. For both face-to-face and non-face-to-face relations are mediated relations, and in both there is as much the possibility of separation and violence as there is communication and consensus. Theorists of community are inclined to privilege face-to-face relations, I suggest, because they wrongly identify mediation and alienation.

By alienation, I mean a situation in which persons do not have control either over their actions, the conditions of their action, or the consequences of their action, due to the intervention of other agents.[9] Social mediation is a condition for the possibility of alienation in this sense; media make possible the intervention of agents between the conditions of a subject's action and the action, or between a subject's action and its consequences. Thus media make domination and exploitation possible. In modern society the primary structures creating alienation and domination are bureaucracy and commodification of all aspects of human activity, including and especially labor. Both bureaucracy and commodification of social relations depend on complex structures of mediation among a large number of persons.

That mediation is a necessary condition of alienation, however, does not entail the reverse implication: that only by eliminating structures of mediation do we eliminate alienation. If temporal and spatial distancing are basic to social processes, and if persons always mediate between other persons to generate social networks, then a society of immediacy is impossible. While mediation may be a necessary condition for alienation, it is not sufficient. Alienation is that specific process of mediation in which the actions of some serve the ends of others without reciprocation and without being explicit, and this requires coercion and domination.

By positing a society of immediate face-to-face relations as ideal, community theorists generate a dichotomy between the "authentic" society of the future and the "inauthentic" society we live in, which is characterized only by alienation, bureaucratization, and degradation. Such a dichotomization between the inauthentic society we have and the authentic society of community, however, detemporalizes our understanding of social change. On this understanding social change, revolution, consists in the complete negation of this society and the establishment of the truly good society. In her scheme of social evolution, Gould conceives of "the society of the future" as the negated sublation of capitalist society. This understands history not as temporal process, but as divided into two static structures: the before of alienated society and the after of community.

The projection of the ideal of community as the radical other of existing society denies difference in the sense of the contradictions and ambiguities of social life. Instead of dichotomizing the pure and the impure into two stages of history or two kinds of social relations, a liberating politics should conceive the social process in which we move as a multiplicity of actions and structures which cohere and contradict, some of them exploitative and some of them liberating. The polarization between the impure, inauthentic society we live in and the pure, authentic society we seek to institute, detemporalizes the process of change, because it fails to articulate how we move from one to the other. If institutional change is possible at all, it must begin from intervening in the contradictions and tensions of existing society. No telos of the final society exists, moreover; society understood as a moving and contradictory process implies that change for the better is always possible and always necessary.

The requirement that genuine community embody face-to-face relations, when taken as a model of the good society, carries a specific vision of social organization. Since the ideal of community demands that relations between members be direct and many-sided, the ideal society is composed of small locales, populated by a small enough number of persons so that each can be personally acquainted with all the others. For most writers this implies that the ideal social organization is decentralized, with small-scale industry and local markets. Each community aims for economic self-sufficiency, and each democratically makes its own decisions about how to organize its working and playing life.

I do not doubt the desirability of small groups in which individuals have personal acquaintance with one another and interact in a plurality of contexts. Just as the intimacy of living with a few others in the same household has unique dimensions that are humanly valuable, so existing with others in communities of mutual friendship has specific characteristics of warmth and sharing that are humanly valuable. Furthermore, there is no question that capitalist patriarchal society discourages and destroys such communities of mutual friendship, just as it squeezes and fragments families. In our vision of the good society we surely wish to include institutional arrangements that would nurture the specific experience of mutual friendship which only relatively small groups interacting in a plurality of contexts can produce. Recognizing the specific value of such face-to-face relations, however, is quite a different matter from proposing them as the organizing principle of a whole society.

Such a model of the good society as composed of decentralized, economically self-sufficient face-to-face communities functioning as autonomous political entities is both wildly utopian and undesirable. To bring it into being would require dismantling the urban character of modern society, a gargantuan physical overhaul of living space, workplaces, places of trade and commerce. A model of a transformed better society must in some concrete sense begin from the concrete material structures that are given to us at this time in history, and in the United States these are large-scale industry and urban centers. The model of society composed of small communities is not desirable, at least in the eyes of many. If we take seriously the way many people live their lives today, it appears that people enjoy cities, that is, places where strangers are thrown together.

One final problem arises from the model of face-to-face community taken as a political goal. This model of the good society as usually articulated leaves completely unaddressed the question of how such small communities are to relate to one another. Frequently the ideal projects a level of self-sufficiency and decentralization which suggests that proponents envision few relations among the decentralized communities except those of friendly visits. But surely it is unrealistic to assume that such decentralized communities need not engage in extensive relations of exchange of resources, goods and culture. Even if one accepts the notion that a radical restructuring of society in the direction of a just and humane society entails people living in small democratically organized units of work and neighborhood, this has not addressed the important political question: how will the relations among these communities be organized so as to foster justice and prevent domination? When we raise this political question the philosophical and practical importance of mediation reemerges. Once again politics must be conceived as a relationship of strangers who do not understand one another in a subjective and immediate sense, relating across time and distance.

## City Life and the Politics of Difference

I have claimed that radical politics must begin from historical givens, and conceive radical change not as the negation of the given, but rather as making something good from many elements of the given. The city, as a vastly populated area with large-scale industry and places of mass assembly, is for us a historical given, and radical politics must begin from the existence of modern urban life. The material surroundings and structures available to us define and presuppose urban relationships. The very size of populations in our society and most other nations of the world, coupled with a continuing sense of national or ethnic identity with millions of other people, all support the conclusion that a vision of dismantling the city is hopelessly utopian.

Starting from the given of modern urban life is not simply necessary, moreover, it is desirable. Even for many of those who decry the alienation, massification and bureaucratization of capitalist patriarchal society, city life exerts a powerful attraction. Modern literature, art and film have celebrated city life, its energy, cultural diversity, technological complexity, and the multiplicity of its activities. Even many of the most staunch proponents of decentralized community love to show visiting friends around the Boston, or San Francisco or New York in which they live, climbing up towers to see the glitter of lights and sampling the fare at the best ethnic restaurants. For many people deemed deviant in the closeness of the face-to-face community in which they lived, whether "independent" women or socialists or gay men and lesbians, the city has often offered a welcome anonymity and some measure of freedom.[10] To be sure, the liberatory possibilities of capitalist cities have been fraught with ambiguity.

Yet I suggest that instead of the ideal of community we begin from our positive experience of city life to form a vision of the good society. Our political ideal is the unoppressive city. In sketching this ideal, I assume some material premises. We will assume a productivity level in the society that can meet everyone's needs, and a physical urban environment that is cleaned up and renovated. We will assume, too, that everyone who can work has meaningful work and those who cannot are provided for with dignity. In sketching this ideal of city life, I am concerned to describe the city as a *kind of relationship* of people to one another, to their own history and one another's history. Thus by "city" I am not referring only to those huge metropolises that we call cities in the U.S. The kinds of relationship I describe obtain also ideally in those places we call "towns," where perhaps 10 or 20 thousand people live.

As a process of people's relating to one another, city life embodies difference in all the senses I have discussed in this essay. The city obviously exhibits the temporal and spatial distancing and differentiation I have argued the ideal of community seeks to collapse. On the face of the city environment lies its history and the history of the individuals and groups that have dwelt within it. Such physical historicity, as well as the functions and groups that live in the city at any given time, create its spatial differentiation. The city as a network and sedimentation of discretely understood places, such as particular buildings, parks, neighborhoods, and as a physical environment offers changes and surprises in transition from one place to another.

The temporal and spatial differentiation that mark the physical environment of the city produce an experience of aesthetic *inexhaustibility.* Buildings, squares, the twists and turns of streets and alleys, offer an inexhaustible store of individual spaces and things, each with unique aesthetic characteristics. The juxtaposition of incongruous styles and functions that usually emerge after a long time in city places contributes to this pleasure in detail and surprise. This is an experience of difference in the sense of always being inserted. The modern city is without walls; it is not planned and coherent. Dwelling in the city means always having a sense of beyond, that there is much human life beyond my experience going on in or near these spaces, and I can never grasp the city as a whole.

City life thus also embodies difference as the contrary of the face-to-face ideal expressed by most assertions of community. City life is the "being-together" of strangers. Strangers encounter one another, either face to face or through media, often remaining strangers and yet acknowledging their contiguity in living and the contributions each makes to the others. In such encountering people are not "internally" related, as the community theorists would have it, and do not understand one another from within their own perspective. They are externally related, they experience each other as other, different, from different groups, histories, professions, cultures, which they do not understand.

The public spaces of the city are both an image of the total relationships of city life and a primary way those relationships are enacted and experienced. A public space is a place accessible to anyone, where people engage in activity as individuals or in small groups. In public spaces people are aware of each other's presence and even at times attend to it. In a city there are a multitude of such public spaces, streets, restaurants, concert halls, parks. In such public spaces the diversity of the city's residents come together and dwell side by side, sometimes appreciating one another, entertaining one another, or just chatting, always to go off again as strangers. City parks as we now experience them often have this character.

City life implies a social inexhaustibility quite different from the ideal of the face-to-face community in which there is mutual understanding and group identification and loyalty. The city consists in a great diversity of people and groups, with a multitude of subcultures and differentiated activities and functions, whose lives and movements mingle and overlap in public spaces. People belong to distinct groups or cultures, and interact in neighborhoods and workplaces. They venture out from these locales, however, to public places of entertainment, consumption and politics. They witness one another's cultures and functions in such public interaction, without adopting them as their own. The appreciation of ethnic foods or professional musicians, for example, consists in the recognition that these transcend the familiar everyday world of my life.

In the city strangers live side by side in public places, giving to and receiving from one another social and aesthetic products, often mediated by a huge chain of interactions. This instantiates social relations as difference in the sense of an understanding of groups and cultures that are different, with exchanging and overlapping interactions that do not issue in community, yet which prevent them from being outside of one another. The social differentiation of the city also provides a positive inexhaustibility of human relations. The possibility always exists of becoming acquainted with new and different people, with different cultural and social experience; the possibility always exists for new groups to form or emerge around specific interests.

The unoppressive city is thus defined as openness to unassimilated otherness. Of course, we do not have such openness to difference in our current social relations. I am asserting an ideal, which consists in a politics of difference. Assuming that group differentiation is a given of social life for us, how can the relationships of group identities embody justice, respect and the absence of oppression? The relationship among group identities and cultures in our society is blotted by racism, sexism, xenophobia, homophobia, suspicion and mockery. A politics of difference lays down institutional and ideological means for recognizing and affirming differently identifying groups in two basic senses: giving political representation to group interests and celebrating the distinctive cultures and characteristics of different groups.[11]

Many questions arise in proposing a politics of difference. What defines a group that deserves recognition and celebration? How does one provide representation to group interests that avoids the mere pluralism of liberal interest groups? What are institutional forms by which the mediations of the city and the representation of its groups in decision making can made democratic? These questions, as well as many others, confront the ideal of the unoppressive city. They are not dissimilar from questions of the relationships that ought to exist among communities. They are questions, however, which appeal to community as the ideal of social life appears to repress or ignore. Some might claim that a politics of difference does express what the ideal of community ought to express, despite the meaning that many writers give the concept of community. Fred Dallmayr, for example, reserves the term community for just this openness toward unassimilated otherness, designating the more totalistic understandings of social relations I have criticized as either "communalism" or "movement."

> As opposed to the homogeneity deliberately fostered in the movement, the communitarian mode cultivates diversity—but without encouraging willful segregation or the repressive preponderance of one of the social subsectors. ... Community may be the only form of social aggregation which reflects upon, and makes room for, otherness or the reverse side of subjectivity (and inter-subjectivity) and thus for the play of difference—the difference between ego and Other and between man and nature.[12]

In the end it may be a matter of stipulation whether one chooses to call such politics as play of difference "community." Because most articulations of the ideal of community carry the urge to unity I have criticized, however, I think it is less confusing to use a term other than community rather than to redefine the term. Whatever the label, the concept of social relations that embody openness to unassimilated otherness with justice and appreciation needs to be developed. Radical politics, moreover, must develop discourse and institutions for bringing differently identified groups together without suppressing or subsuming the differences.[13]

## Notes

1. I examine community specifically as a normative ideal designating how social relations ought to be organized. There are various non-normative uses of the term community to which my analysis does not apply. Sociologists engaged in community studies, for example, usually use the term to mean something like "small town" or "neighborhood," and use the term primarily in a descriptive sense. The questions raised apply to community understood only as a normative model of ideal social organization. See Jessie Bernard, *The Sociology of Community*, (Glenview: Scott, Foresman and Co., 1973), for a summary of different sociological theories of community in its non-normative senses.
2. Peter Manicas, *The Death of State*, (New York: C.P. Putnam and Sons, 1974), p. 247.
3. Roberto Unger, *Knowledge and Politics* (New York: The Free Press, 1975), pp. 262–63.
4. Christian Bay, *Strategies of Political Emancipation*, (South Bend: Notre Dame Press, 1981), Chapters 5 and 6.
5. Michael Taylor, *Community, Anarchy and Liberty*, (Cambridge: Cambridge University Press, 1982), pp. 27–28.
6. Carol Gould, *Marx's Social Ontology* (Cambridge: MIT Press, 1978), p. 26.
7. Derrida discusses the illusory character of this ideal of immediate presence of subjects to one another in community in his discussions of Lévi-Strauss and Rousseau. See *Of Grammatology*, pp. 101–40.

8   See Anthony Giddens, *Central Problems in Social Theory* (Berkeley: University of California Press, 1979), pp. 198–233.
9   For a useful account of alienation, see Richard Schmitt, *Alienation and Class*, (Cambridge, MA: Schenkman Publishing Co., 1983), especially Chapter 5. In this book Schmitt, like many other of the writers I have cited, takes community to stand as the negation of the society of alienation. Unlike those writers discussed in this section, however, he does not take face-to-face relations as a condition of community. To the degree that he makes a pure/impure distinction, and exhibits the desire for unity I have criticized, however, the critique articulated here applies to Schmitt's appeal to the ideal of community.
10  Marshall Berman presents a fascinating account of the attractions of city life in *All that Is Solid Melts Into Air*, (New York: Simon and Schuster, 1982). George Shulman points to the open-endedness of city life as contrasted with the pastoral vision of community in 'The Pastoral Idyll of Democracy,' in *Democracy* 3 (1983): 43–54; for a similar critique, see David Plotke, "Democracy, Modernization, and Democracy," *Socialist Review* 14 (March–April 1984): 31–56.
11  In my previously cited paper, "Impartiality and the Civic Public," I formulate some ideals of a heterogeneous public life; I have developed further some principles of a politics of difference in "Elements of a Politics of Difference," paper presented at the North American Society for Social Philosophy, Colorado Springs, August 1985.
12  Fred Dallmayr, *Twilight of Subjectivity: Contributions to a Post-Structuralist Theory of Politics* (Ameherst, MA: University of Massachusetts Press, 1981), pp. 142–43.
13  I am grateful to David Alexander, Ann Ferguson, Roger Gottlieb, Peter Manicas, Peter Onuf, Lucius Outlaw, Michael Ryan, Richard Schmitt, Ruth Smith, Tom Wartenburg, and Hugh Wilder for helpful comments on earlier versions of this paper.

# 19 Recognition or Redistribution?

## Nancy Fraser

The "struggle for recognition" has become the paradigmatic form of political conflict in the late twentieth century. Demands for "recognition of difference" fuel struggles of groups mobilized under the banners of nationality, ethnicity, "race," gender, and sexuality. In these "post-socialist" conflicts, group identity supplants class interest as the chief medium of political mobilization. Cultural domination supplants exploitation as the fundamental injustice. And cultural recognition displaces socio-economic redistribution as the remedy for injustice and the goal of political struggle.

That, of course, is not the whole story. Struggles for recognition occur in a world of exacerbated material inequality—in income and property ownership; in access to paid work, education, health care and leisure time; but also more starkly in caloric intake and exposure to environmental toxicity, hence in life expectancy and rates of morbidity and mortality. Material inequality is on the rise in most of the world's countries—in the United States and in Haiti, in Sweden and in India, in Russia and in Brazil. It is also increasing globally, across the line that divides North from South.

How, then, should we view the eclipse of a socialist imaginary centered on "interest," "exploitation," and "redistribution"? And what should we make of the rise of a new political imaginary centered on notions of "identity," "difference," "cultural domination," and "recognition"? Does this shift represent a lapse into "false consciousness"? Or does it, rather, redress the culture-blindness of a materialist paradigm rightfully discredited by the collapse of Soviet Communism?

If neither of those alternatives seems adequate to the times, then perhaps a third approach is advisable. We might see ourselves as presented with a new intellectual and practical task: that of developing a *critical* theory of recognition, one which identifies and defends only those versions of the politics of difference that coherently synergize with the politics of redistribution.

Political theorists are only beginning to approach this task. Until recently, theorists of distributive justice simply ignored identity politics, apparently assuming that it represented false consciousness. And theorists of recognition likewise ignored distribution, as if the problematic of cultural difference had nothing to do with that of social equality. Both groups, in sum, tended to evade the crucial questions of the day: What is the relationship between redistribution and recognition? Do these constitute two distinct conceptions of justice, belonging to two distinct theoretical paradigms? Or can both be accommodated within a single comprehensive theory? On the practical-political plane, moreover, do struggles for recognition work against struggles for redistribution? Or can both be pursued simultaneously without mutual interference?

Iris Marion Young's 1990 book, *Justice and the Politics of Difference*, has the merit of inviting such questions.[1] Not that she herself poses them in precisely these terms, to be sure. But Young's book is unusual in that it aspires to be "bifocal." It seeks to explicate a theory of justice that encompasses claims of both redistribution and recognition, of both equality and difference, of both culture and political economy. On this ground alone it represents an important step forward in political theory.

Integrating recognition and redistribution in a single theory is no easy task, however. And Young's effort is not free of difficulties. In what follows, I shall examine the unresolved tensions between the cultural and political-economic dimensions of her framework. By identifying some ambiguities in several of her core conceptions, I shall show that she unselfconsciously mixes elements of the two paradigms, without however successfully integrating them. Because she has not thought through the relations between them, moreover, the two paradigms interfere with one another. The difficulties become especially serious, I contend, when Young seeks to defend a wholesale, undifferentiated and uncritical version of the politics of difference; for this version is at odds with her own professed commitment to the politics of redistribution.

My discussion proceeds in six parts. In the first, I present the general contours of Young's "bifocal" concern with culture and political economy. Then, in sections two, three and four, I examine her conceptions of oppression, social group and the "five faces of oppression" respectively. Next, in section five, I consider some real-world applications. I conclude, finally, in section six, by rejecting Young's wholesale endorsement of the politics of difference and by proposing a more differentiated alternative.

## The Predominance of Recognition in a Bifocal Schema

Young herself does not use the terms "recognition" and "redistribution." In fact, she claims to reject the sort of categorical dualism that would divide issues of justice in this way; she prefers an alternative five-fold classification of oppressions that purports to bypass the distinction between culture and political economy. Moreover, Young explicitly criticizes what she calls the "distributive paradigm" of justice; and she supposes that her framework supersedes it.

Nevertheless, a bifocal interest in recognition and redistribution runs throughout *Justice and the Politics of Difference*. Young's account of oppression encompasses both injustices rooted in political economy, such as exploitation, and also injustices rooted in culture, such as "cultural imperialism." She thus follows contemporary "post-socialist" social-movement thought in giving considerable attention to culture. Yet she refuses to follow those extreme culturalists who would jettison altogether a focus on political economy. She insists, rather, on maintaining a "quasi-socialist" interest in that problematic as well. Indeed, it is this dual focus, this interest in both recognition and redistribution, that marks the innovation, and the promise, of her book.

Thus, Young's critique of "the distributive paradigm" should not be taken entirely at face value. In my view, this critique is ambiguous and confused. In one aspect, it recapitulates the Marxian objection to approaches that focus exclusively on end-state patterns of allocation among individuals of tangible goods and positions, such as income and jobs or offices, while neglecting the underlying structural processes that produce them. Here the target is "the standpoint of distribution," as opposed to "the standpoint of production." In another aspect, however, Young recapitulates Amartya Sen's objection to approaches that focus on the distribution of commodities, as opposed to capabilities, thereby casting people as passive consumers instead of as agents.[2] Here the critique is aimed, not at distribution *per se*, but at distribution of the wrong goods. In a third aspect, finally, Young's critique is aimed precisely at approaches, like Sen's, that treat nontangibles such as capabilities as foci and objects of distribution. Here the target is "reification."

No matter how we resolve these ambiguities, the important point is this: none of Young's objections to "the distributive paradigm" constitutes a persuasive argument against approaches that assess the justice of social arrangements in terms of how they distribute economic advantages and disadvantages. Although made from the "standpoint of distribution," such judgments need not entail that remedies for injustice be limited to such measures as equalizing income through redistributive taxation. Instead, they can provide good reasons for condemning the underlying "basic structure" of a society and for seeking its wholesale transformation. Young herself makes such judgments throughout her book. In so doing, she generally follows Sen in defining economic advantage and disadvantage in terms of capabilities. This, however, puts her squarely inside the distributive paradigm, broadly conceived, her qualms about reification notwithstanding. Nor could she escape that paradigm with respect to socio-economic justice, finally, by opposing its extension to issues of cultural justice as well. Rather, as I shall show, she effectively adds a second, recognition problematic alongside it. Despite Young's explicit caveats, then, redistribution remains relevant to *Justice and the Politics of Difference*.

If redistribution represents an implicit presence in Young's book, then recognition constitutes its gravitational center. The recognition paradigm undeniably dominates the book, reflecting Young's identification with contemporary new social movements. Her stated aim is, in fact, to explicate, and defend, the theory of justice that is implicit in the political practice of movements such as feminism, gay and lesbian liberation, and anti-racism. What is distinctive about these movements, as she presents them, is their view of the dominant culture as a locus of oppression, their rejection of the "ideal of assimilation," and their demand for the recognition of difference. Theorizing cultural recognition is therefore central to the project of Young's book.

Accordingly, Young mounts a challenge to theories that would exclude the domain of culture from the scope of justice. She makes a compelling case for the view that the dominant images, symbolic associations, and interpretations of a culture may denigrate and degrade some social groups; they may even find expression in unconscious and preconscious reactions of bodily aversion in everyday life in ways that constitute serious harm. Culture, therefore, may be oppressive and unjust. No theory of justice can with justice ignore it.

Young also follows contemporary movements in defending the "politics of difference." By this she means a "cultural revolution" in which social group differences cease to be viewed as deviations from a single norm and are seen, rather, as cultural variations. Far from seeking to abolish such differences, then, Young aims to preserve and affirm them. This politics of difference is so central to her vision that it appears in the title of her book. It is her distinctive politics of recognition.

Despite her continuing interest in the politics of redistribution, then, Young's primary focus is the politics of recognition. She returns to the latter again and again, in virtually every chapter of the book. By contrast, her treatment of political economy is somewhat cursory. To be sure, at least three of the five forms of oppression that Young identifies are based in political economy, but that domain receives only one chapter-length elaboration—namely, in the chapter that criticizes "the myth of merit" and the division between task-defining and task-executing labor. Virtually every other chapter, in contrast, focuses primarily on cultural oppression and its remedy, the "politics of difference."

The dominance of the cultural paradigm over the political-economy paradigm is not merely a matter of length of treatment, however. It can also be read in some of Young's central categorical conceptions, as indeed can some unresolved tensions between the cultural and the political-economic dimensions of her framework.

## Defining Oppression

Consider, first, Young's general definition of oppression as "the institutional constraint on self-development" (37). To be oppressed, in her view, is to be inhibited from "developing and exercising one's capacities and expressing one's experience" (37). More elaborately: "Oppression consists in systematic institutional processes which prevent some people from learning and using satisfying and expansive skills in socially recognized settings, or institutional processes which inhibit people's ability to play and communicate with others or to express their feelings and perspectives on social life in contexts where others can listen" (38).

There are many interesting and attractive features of this definition. The focus on capacities, for example, provides a welcome corrective to approaches that focus on resource distribution and implicitly posit people as inactive consumers. As I noted, this point recalls Amartya Sen's argument in *Commodities and Capabilities*.

For present purposes, however, I want to focus on something else: the two-pronged or bipartite character of the definition, the way in which it turns one of its two faces toward problems of culture and the other toward problems of political economy. The cultural face of the definition is captured in the clauses that concern constraints on "expressing one's experience," and processes "which inhibit people's ability to play and communicate with others or to express their feelings and perspectives on social life in contexts where others can listen." These clauses define oppression as inhibited expression and communication, rooted in a lack of cultural recognition. The political-economic face, in contrast, appears in the clauses about constraints on "developing and exercising one's capacities," and "systematic institutional processes which prevent some people from learning and using satisfying and expansive skills in socially recognized settings." These clauses define oppression as inhibited development of expansive skills, rooted in inequities in the division of labor.

Here, then, we see Young's dual focus on redistribution and recognition. She has sought to yoke culture and political economy together under a single, albeit bipartite, definition of oppression. But the two sides are not adequately integrated with one another. And the definition contains an unresolved tension. The cultural dimension of the definition suggests that the capacities and abilities of oppressed people are essentially undamaged and intact; they suffer chiefly from misrecognition and undervaluation of their group-specific modes of cultural expression. The political-economy face, in contrast, suggests that certain skill-developing capacities and abilities of the oppressed are stunted or unrealized; they suffer from lack of opportunity to grow, learn and enhance their skills in socially valued work. The cultural face of the definition, then, is a problem of undervaluation; the political-economic face, in contrast, is a problem of underdevelopment.

These two understandings of oppression are clearly in tension with one another. And the tension has significant political consequences. Arrangements that positively affirm the culture of oppressed groups constitute a plausible remedy for the cultural face of oppression. But they are far less plausible as a remedy for the political-economic face. To remedy that face of oppression, opportunities for self-development are required. Recognition of cultural difference, in sum, is no substitute for redistribution. In some cases, we shall see, it could interfere with the latter.

Young appears not to notice this problem. But it surfaces repeatedly throughout her book. Not just oppression, but also other key conceptions, evince a bipartite structure. In them, too, as we shall see, cultural and political-economic elements are unself-consciously mixed, but not successfully integrated with one another. Consequently, those conceptions, too, manifest theoretical tensions, which ultimately call into question Young's politics of difference.

## Defining a Social Group

Consider, as another example, Young's conception of a social group. Groups, according to her, are the entities that suffer oppression. Individuals are oppressed in virtue of belonging to oppressed groups. Groups, moreover, are prior to individuals in that they are constitutive of individual identities. Groups in Young's sense, then, are neither aggregates, which are classified externally by an observer on the basis of objective similarities, nor voluntary associations, which individuals might join or not join, without any shifts in their identities. Rather, in Young's words: "a social group is a collective of persons differentiated from at least one other group by *cultural forms, practices, or ways of life*. Members of a group have a specific affinity with one another *because of their similar experience or way of life*, which prompts them to associate with one another more than with those not identified with the group, or in a different way" (43, my emphasis). Elsewhere: "a social group is a collective of people who have affinity with one another *because of a set of practices or way of life*. They differentiate themselves from or are differentiated by at least one other group *according to these cultural forms*" (186, my emphasis).[3]

This conception, too, has many attractive features. For example, it neatly bypasses all the dilemmas associated with the standard Marxian distinction between the class-in-itself, defined by its objective structural position, and the class-for-itself, defined as the group's accurate subjective awareness of its objective position. Young's idea of an affinity group is reducible neither to an objective position nor to its reflection in consciousness. Rather, it is a lived sense of connection and differentiation.

How, then, does group differentiation arise? On what precisely is lived affinity based? In the passages quoted above, Young refers alternatively to "cultural forms," "ways of life," "similar experiences," and "sets(s) of practices." These expressions, although somewhat vague, suggest that groups may be formed in a variety of different ways and on a multiplicity of different bases. Elsewhere in her book, in fact, Young elaborates several different scenarios. She notes that in some cases the affinities that comprise a social group arise simply as a result of shared cultural forms; an example is an ethnic group. In other cases, however, Young claims that group affinities can arise as a result of people's shared position in the division of labor; here, interestingly, she mentions gender as an example. In still other cases, finally, she suggests that group affinities may arise even in the absence of a shared culture or a shared position in the division of labor, as the result of a shared experience of hostility from the outside. This sort of group affinity is constituted when members of another group brand people as "Other" from without and proceed to oppress them; here Young cites the example of assimilated German Jews under Nazism.

Once again, we find that Young invokes a single conception to cover both cultural and political-economic phenomena. Her notion of a social group, too, is bipartite. It encompasses both those modes of collectivity, such as ethnicity, that are rooted in culture alone, and also those modes of collectivity, such as class, that are rooted in political economy. Young apparently sees no need to maintain such distinctions. For our purposes, however, it will be useful to avoid collapsing them, at least until we have had a chance to interrogate them.

Let me therefore introduce the following terminology: Insofar as group affinity rests on shared cultural forms, I shall call the result "a culture-based group." Insofar as affinity rests on shared position in the division of labor, in contrast, I shall call the result "a political-economy-based group." To repeat: the best familiar model for the culture-based group is the ethnic group. The best model for the political-economy-based group, in contrast, is class, especially the lived experience of social class theorized by Pierre Bourdieu as "class habitus," which is not limited to the classes recognized by Marxism.[4] In Young's framework, as we saw, this distinction disappears. Nevertheless, insofar as it encompasses both culture-based groups and political-economy-based groups, her conception of a social group is bipartite.

The bipartite character of Young's conception is simultaneously appealing and troubling. The appeal is the attraction of parsimony—the possibility that a single conception might encompass several disparate modes of collectivity. The difficulty is the possibility that it might not do justice to them all. It could be the case, for example, that important conceptual distinctions will be lost if we assimilate genders, "races," ethnic groups, sexualities, nationalities, and social classes to the single model of the affinity group. It could also be the case that one of these modes of collectivity will implicitly predominate, that its distinctive characteristics will be projected as characteristics of all social groups, and that other modes of collectivity will be distorted.

This does in fact happen in the course of Young's argument. She implicitly privileges the culture-based social group. As a result, the ethnic group surreptitiously becomes the paradigm not only for such collectivities as Jews, Arab-Americans, and Asian-Americans, where it is clearly apt, but also for such collectivities as gays and lesbians, women, African Americans, old people, people with disabilities, Native Americans, and working-class people, where it distorts.

This, too, has unfortunate political consequences. The politics of difference embraced by Young is a vision of emancipation especially suited to the situation of ethnic groups. Where the differences in question are those of ethnic cultures, it is prima facie plausible to consider that justice would be served by affirming them and thereby fostering cultural diversity. Where, in contrast, cultural differences are linked to differentially desirable locations in the political economy, a politics of difference may be misplaced. There justice may require precisely undermining group differentiation by, for example, restructuring the division of labor. In that case, redistribution could obviate the need for recognition.

It is true, of course, that modelling the character of oppressed groups on ethnicity fits the self-understanding of many of the new social movements Young supports. Thus, in settling on such a conception, she has succeeded in her professed aim of articulating the implicit theories of such groups. At the same time, however, to the extent that these movements may misunderstand themselves, she risks reproducing their self-misunderstandings. In noting this, I mean to signal a broader unease with a theoretical stance that could be too closely identified with its subjects to be critical of their self-understandings.

Equally troubling, there is something specifically, and even quintessentially, American about this way of understanding collectivities. Where else but in the United States does ethnicity so regularly eclipse class, nation and party? This, of course, is not an indefeasible criticism of Young's concept of a social group, but it should give one pause about its applicability.

## Five Faces of Oppression

I have already noted that Young disclaims the sort of categorial dualism I have been at pains to uncover in her book. Instead, she proposes a five-part classification of oppressions, which purports to scramble the distinction between culture and political economy. In this section, I examine her classificatory schema in order to show that it, too, is implicitly bipartite.

Young's classification of oppressions is perhaps the most interesting part of her book. With this classification she aims to circumvent painful and unproductive squabbles among oppressed groups as to whose oppression is "primary" and whose merely "secondary," whose, therefore, should be prioritized in political struggle and whose should be put on the back-burner. Her inspired move is to reconceptualize what it means to theorize oppression. Instead of classifying oppressions in terms of who suffers them, and thus, distinguishing such varieties as sexism, racism, ableism and homophobia, she classifies different types of capacity-inhibition. Only then will she ask which groups suffer which kind(s) of oppression? This approach generates five distinct "faces" or forms of oppression, which may attach to groups singly or in various combinations or permutations. Each of the five is a sufficient condition for calling a group oppressed; none is a necessary condition.

Very briefly, the five forms of oppression identified by Young are:

1. *Exploitation*, defined as a structural relation whereby some people exercise their capacities under the control of others, according to the purposes and for the benefit of others, thereby systematically augmenting the power of the others. Exploitation in Young's view is not restricted to Marxian class

relations. It also occurs in gender-specific and race-specific forms, in unpaid activities as well as in paid work[5]. The remedy for exploitation, according to Young, is radical restructuring of both political economy and culture.

2. *Marginalization*, defined as the condition of expulsion or exile from the system of labor and from useful participation in social life. Those who suffer marginalization, according to Young, include the racially marked underclass, the old, youth, the disabled, and single mothers and their children. The harm of this oppression includes not only material deprivation but also curtailment of citizenship rights and loss of opportunities for developing and exercising capacities in socially recognized ways. The remedy is political-economic restructuring.

3. *Powerlessness*, defined as the condition of having power exercised over one by others without oneself exercising power in turn; hence, having to take orders but never oneself giving them; occupying a position in the division of labor that affords little opportunity to develop and exercise skills; and being subject as a result to disrespectful treatment because of low occupational status; being viewed, moreover, as lacking "respectability." This oppression is, according to Young, suffered by nonprofessional workers. Its remedy is radical restructuring of the division of labor to eliminate the division between task-defining and task-executing work.

4. *Cultural imperialism*, defined as the universalization and establishment as the norm of the dominant group's experience and culture, which has the result of rendering invisible the oppressed group's perspective, while simultaneously stereotyping that group as Other. Cultural imperialism is suffered by women, African Americans, Native Americans, gays and lesbians, and many other social groups in contemporary society. The best remedy for this form of oppression, according to Young, is "the politics of difference," or attention to and affirmation of social group differences.

5. *Violence*, defined as susceptibility to systematic, albeit random, irrational, unconsciously motivated, and socially tolerated attacks on group members' persons and property. Included here are physical attacks, to be sure, but also harassment, intimidation and ridicule. Violence, according to Young, is closely related to cultural imperialism. Many groups that suffer the latter also suffer the former, for example, gays and lesbians, Jews, African Americans, Latinos and women. The remedy for it, too, is cultural revolution: changes in the images, stereotypes, and the mundane gestures of everyday life wherein oppressed people meet aversive reactions to their bodily presence.

Each of these five definitions of the forms of oppression is extremely interesting and deserves some individual attention. Here, however, I shall consider only the general configuration. Young presents the five as distinct faces of oppression, and she declines to explore possible connections among them. We may note, however, that they fall broadly into two groups. Exploitation, marginalization and powerlessness are rooted in political economy; they involve inhibition of the sort of self-development that Young believes comes from meaningful, skill-enhancing and socially valued work. Cultural imperialism and violence, in contrast, are said by Young to be rooted in culture; they involve inhibition with respect to expression and communication.

Here, then, is another bipartite schema. Some oppressions (exploitation, marginalization and powerlessness) are rooted in political economy; others (cultural imperialism and violence) are rooted in culture. Again, Young herself does not make this distinction. But for my purposes it will be useful to develop it. Let me therefore introduce the following terminology: those instances of oppression that are rooted in political economy I shall call "economically-rooted oppressions." Those that are rooted in culture, in contrast, I shall call "culturally-rooted oppressions."

Each of these two broad categories of oppressions has its own proper broad category of remedy. The remedy for the culturally-rooted oppressions of cultural imperialism and violence, according to Young, is cultural revolution. This means breaking down the idea of a single universal set of cultural norms and affirming cultural pluralism and difference. The principal remedy for the economically-rooted oppressions, on the other hand, is radical restructuring of the division of labor. This includes eliminating the division between, for example, task-defining and task-executing work and providing socially valued, skin-enhancing activities for all.

Each of these remedies seems well-suited to redress its respective oppressions—assuming that we follow Young's characterizations. But there is a potentially harmful tension between them. Whereas the remedy for the culturally-rooted oppressions promotes group differentiation, the remedy for the economically-rooted oppressions may undermine it. In some cases, consequently, the effects of the two remedies will be contradictory.

The problem becomes evident when we take a closer look at the oppressions of cultural imperialism and violence. As we saw, Young's definitions suggested that both of them were culturally rooted and, hence, best remedied by the politics of difference. This, however, begs the question.

Consider, first, that Young's account of cultural imperialism contains an important ambiguity. She defines this oppression as the universalization of the particular culture of the dominant group. But she does not specify the grounds of that group's dominance. One possibility, of course, is that its dominance consists precisely in the fact that its culture is universalized; in that case, cultural imperialist oppression would be culturally rooted. Another possibility, however, is that the group's dominance arises in some other way, such as through political-economic superordination, which then provides the basis for the universalization of its culture; in that case, cultural imperialist oppression would be economically rooted.[6] In the first case, moreover, affirmation of cultural difference is a plausible remedy for oppression. In the second case, however, political-economic restructuring is necessary. In that case, consequently, the politics of difference could be counterproductive, as it tends to preserve those group differences that redistribution could well undermine. Recognition, in sum, could work against redistribution.

Analogous problems arise with respect to the oppression of violence. As we saw, violence in Young's definition is closely linked to cultural imperialism as it is said to be fostered by cultural othering. It, too, is thus open to ambiguity. In some instances, oppressive violence may be linked to autonomous processes of cultural othering; violence against gays is an example. In other cases, however, violence may be fostered by forms of cultural othering that are themselves in turn rooted in political economy; the lynching of Blacks in the Jim Crow South is an example. In still other cases, finally, oppressive violence may flow directly out of political-economic oppression, with little or no intermediary cultural othering; violence against (ethnically-majoritarian) unionizing and striking workers is an example. It follows that oppressive violence is not always best remedied by recognizing cultural difference. While clearly appropriate in the case of violence against gays, the politics of difference may be counterproductive in the case of violence against strikers, where the primary need is redistribution. The case of lynching is more complicated, I think, as both recognition and redistribution are needed. Yet is is still true that they stand in tension with one another, and that the first can interfere with the second.

## Applications

The preceding discussion suggests that the politics of difference may be less globally applicable than Young thinks. To illustrate the multiplicity of possibilities here, let us consider some real-world applications that concern different cases of oppressed groups.

First, take the case of working-class nonprofessionals. In Young's account, they suffer primarily the oppression of powerlessness, although presumably also that of exploitation. As a consequence of powerlessness, moreover, they are said to develop a class habitus or affinity that marks them as lacking "respectability." Here, then, is an oppressed group whose existence and whose oppression are both rooted in political economy. Is the politics of difference apposite?

In my view the answer is no. This is because it is unlikely that an affinity group based on the shared experience of powerlessness and non-respectability would survive as a group in the event that its economic oppression were remedied via redistribution. Suppose, for example, that the division of labor between task-defining work and task-executing work were abolished. In that case, all jobs would encompass both sorts of work, and the class division between professionals and nonprofessionals would be abolished. Cultural affinities that differentiate professionals from nonprofessionals would probably wither away as well, since they appear to have no other basis of existence. Thus, a politics of redistribution that successfully combatted the political-economic oppression of powerlessness would effectively destroy the group as a group, much as Marx claimed that the task of the proletariat was to abolish itself as a class. The politics of difference, in contrast, would not contribute to overcoming oppression in this case. Instead it would interfere with the pursuit of redistribution.

Consider, second, the case of women as an oppressed group. It is doubtful to me that women really do constitute a group in Young's sense of a felt connection of shared experience or affinity. Yet gender is unquestionably a structural principle of the division of labor, and as such it disadvantages women as a group. Let us consider, therefore, the effects of a restructured division of labor on women as an oppressed group. Let us assume, further, that a long-term feminist goal is to subvert the existing gender division of labor, and not merely to elevate the standing of women within it, hence to establish a radical redistribution. Now, if the gender division of labor were effectively abolished, would gender-distinct cultural affinities survive? And if not, is the politics of difference an appropriate remedy for the oppression of women?

This case seems less clear-cut than the previous one. Gender affinities, if indeed they exist, could have additional bases beyond their basis in the division of labor, for example, in socialization, in culture, even in bodily experiences, such as menstruation. Thus, even a successful politics of redistribution might not abolish women as a group. They could still be culturally constructed as different from men and be denigrated and oppressed on that basis. Thus, a politics of difference could be in order here. This raises a further dilemma, however. The struggle to remedy women's cultural oppression by affirming women's "difference" on the model of ethnicity might militate against the struggle to abolish the gender division of labor, which entails decreasing the social salience of gender. The first, after all, calls attention to and exaggerates, if it does not performatively create, gender difference. The second, in contrast, would minimize such difference, if not abolish it altogether.

Consider, finally, the case of African Americans. This case seems different yet again. There is little reason to think that abolishing the racial division of labor would entail the disappearance of the affinity group, since that group has an independent cultural basis. A more likely result would be the transformation of a subordinate racialized caste into an ethnic group. And this would be historically new, since African Americans, like Native Americans, have never been allowed to be just another ethnic group.

What these examples show, I think, is that disadvantaged social collectivities differ from one another importantly—both in their bases of differentiation and also in the roots of their oppression. In some cases, political-economic restructuring seems certain to entail group dedifferentiation, while in others it clearly does not. In still other cases, by contrast, the implications are harder to predict.

If this is right, then the politics of difference is not globally applicable. In some cases, such as that of nonprofessional workers, it is simply askew of the nature of the group and its oppression. In other cases, in contrast, such as gays and lesbians, the politics of difference is absolutely crucial for remedying oppression. The hardest cases, of course, are those, such as gender and "race," in which both redistribution and recognition are required to overcome a complex of oppression that is multiple and multiply-rooted. The difficulty here stems from the real tensions and interferences that arise when one tries both to affirm and to abolish difference simultaneously. A glib and global endorsement of the politics of difference will not help us solve this problem. For that, we need to face the problem squarely and to develop a *critical* theory of recognition.

## Conclusion: Toward a Differentiated Politics of Difference and a Critical Theory of Recognition

We have seen that the "politics of difference" is less globally applicable than Young thinks. In the case of some groups and some oppressions, such a politics is clearly apposite. In the case of others, however, such a politics may be counterproductive, since their oppressions may be better combatted precisely by undermining the conditions of existence that differentiate the group as a group. Classes, subordinated sexualities, genders, subordinate racialized castes and ethnic groups represent conceptually distinct kinds of collectivities. Not all of them are suitable vehicles for "the politics of difference." (Nor of course are what we might call "bad groups," such as neo-Nazi skinheads, who are certainly oppressed in Young's terms, since they suffer marginalization and cultural imperialism, but whose "differences" we do not wish to affirm.)

One might accept what I have said so far and still defend the broader applicability of the politics of difference. One might maintain that even where this politics is not a tenable long-term goal, it is indispensable as a transitional strategy. One might claim, for example, that this politics promotes group solidarity and thus is a necessary condition for the possibility of any sort of political struggle whatsoever.

It is certainly true that one cannot stand up for oneself when one is crippled by self-hatred. But it does not follow that affirming one's difference in Young's sense is the only or best way of overcoming internalized self-hatred. Here the history of second-wave feminism is instructive. The radical consciousness-raising of the late 1960s and early 1970s helped heal wounds, forge solidarity and galvanize struggle. But it was a far cry from the sort of cultural feminism in vogue today, which celebrates the traditional feminine. It is far from clear, moreover, that the latter really does foster solidarity of the sort that coheres with the long-term goal of debinarizing gender. It seems rather to have led to fractiousness and hurt by affirming traits specific to white middle class heterosexual women and by promoting repressive forms of "correctness."

Young counterposes her ideal of the politics of difference to what she calls "the assimilationist ideal," which, she argues, perpetuates oppression. But are these really the only two possibilities? My argument suggests they are not. In order to convey a sense of additional possibilities, let me conclude by contrasting four possible attitudes towards "difference."

1. The first is the one Young calls humanism: it is the view that the differences that members of oppressed groups evince are precisely the damages of oppression or the lies that rationalize them. Difference, in other words, is an artifact of oppression, as in the stunting of skills and capacities. The proper political response is to abolish it. This is essentially the position of Catharine MacKinnon with respect to gender difference.

2. A second position on difference is sometimes called cultural nationalism. Within feminism, it has been called (by Young) gynocentrism; within anti-racist politics, it has been called "Afrocentrism." It is the view that the differences that members of oppressed groups evince are marks of their cultural superiority over their oppressors. These differences, like feminine nurturance or Native American connection to the land, merit revaluation. But this does not mean that they should be celebrated as differences. On the contrary, they should be universalized and extended to those who currently manifest inferior traits such as competitiveness and instrumentalism. This position can be represented by Sonya Johnson and some (mis)interpreters of Carol Gilligan.

3. A third position views difference as cultural variation. This is the view that the differences manifested by members of different groups are neither superiorities nor interiorities but simply variations. They should neither be eliminated nor universalized but rather affirmed as differences; they are valuable as expressions of human diversity. This is Young's position.

4. A fourth position, which is the one I wish to commend, is that there are different kinds of differences. Some differences are of type 1 and should be eliminated; others are of type 2 and should be universalized; still others are of type 3 and should be enjoyed. This position implies that we can make judgments about which differences fall into which categories. It also implies that we can make normative judgments about the relative value of alternative norms, practices and interpretations, judgments which could lead to conclusions of inferiority, superiority and equivalent value. It militates against any politics of difference that is wholesale and undifferentiated. Put differently, it entails a different—and differentiated—politics of difference.

Such a differentiated view of difference would be an important contribution to a critical theory of recognition. It would help us to identify, and defend, only those versions of the politics of difference that coherently synergize with the politics of redistribution. This is the sort of approach we need in order to meet the challenges of our time. The task is to integrate the egalitarian ideals of the socialist paradigm with whatever is genuinely emancipatory in the paradigm of recognition.

## Notes

1. Iris Marion Young, *Justice and the Politics of Difference* (Princeton, N.J.: Princeton University Press, 1990); citations to this volume will appear in the text as page numbers in parentheses.

2   See, for example, Amartya Sen, *Commodities and Capabilities* (Amsterdam: North-Holland, 1985).
3   Young also gives another definition: "What makes a group a group is a social process of interaction and differentiation in which some people come to have a particular affinity with one another. My affinity group in a given social situation comprises those *people with whom I feel most comfortable, who are more familiar.* Affinity names the manner of *sharing assumptions, affective bonding, and networking* that recognizably differentiates groups from one another ..." (172, my emphasis).
4   For class habitus, see, for example, Pierre Bourdieu, *Distinction: A Social Critique of the Judgement of Taste*, trans. Richard Nice (Cambridge, Mass.: Harvard University Press, 1984).
5   For an account that uses game-theoretical tools to construct a conception of exploitation that applies to gender as well as class, see Alan Carling, *Social Division* (London: Verso, 1991).
6   There are other possibilities as well. A group's dominance could also be rooted in numerical superiority, military superiority, and/or political domination, any of which could then give rise to its cultural dominance. For the sake of simplicity, I leave aside these other possibilities here.

# Part Six:
# Deliberative Democracy

# Introduction

Contemporary liberal theory has been dominated by debates about distributive justice. Different principles have been endorsed by different theorists. For example, Rawls defends his two principles of justice and Gauthier the principle of minimax relative concession. But, as became evident in Part five on feminism, many political theorists have questioned the distributive paradigm that has dominated contemporary liberal theory. The readings in this part focus on another theory which also questions the dominance of the distributive paradigm – *deliberative democracy*. Since the early 1990s the so-called 'deliberative turn' (Dryzek, 2000) in democratic theory has preoccupied debates concerning the relation between democracy and social justice, a relation that was marginalised by the distributive paradigm. Ian Shapiro describes the gulf that existed between theorists of democracy and justice:

> It would be going too far to say that theoreticians of democracy and justice speak past one another, but there has been little systematic attention by political theorists to the ways in which considerations about democracy and justice are or should be mutually related. This relative inattention seems partly to have sprung from optimism among many justice theorists about what armchair reflection should be expected to deliver, a driving conviction that what is just in the distribution of social goods can be settled as a matter of speculative theory. (Shapiro, 1999: 3)

If the demands of justice can be established by invoking the principles chosen in the original position, or the requirements of minimax relative concession, the thesis of self-ownership or by resolving the 'equality of what?' debate, then what is the role of democratic politics? If we can arrive at the correct answer to what laws and policies are legitimate *independently* of any real democratic processes then it seems that the latter are superfluous. As Shapiro notes, many political theorists 'take it for granted that there is a correct answer to the question of what principles of justice we ought to affirm; that Rawls, Ronald Dworkin, Robert Nozick, Amartya Sen, or someone else will eventually get it right' (Shapiro, 1999: 3). But if we believe that the demands of justice and the practices of a democratic polity are inextricably linked then the ideal of democracy must enjoy more prominence in our theorising than it does in the distributive paradigm of contemporary liberalism.

We often invoke the ideal of democracy in many different contexts, both political and nonpolitical. Associations or committees may seek to resolve certain decisions 'democratically'. This usually entails deciding the issue by a show of hands and being bound by the majority decision. When applied to a political association this popular understanding of democracy requires that all citizens be entitled to an equal vote and that the will of the majority rules. Deliberative democrats defend a version of democratic theory that goes against the so-called 'aggregative model' of democracy. According to this model of democracy, decision-making processes ought simply to aggregate the preferences of citizens in choosing public officials and parties. An outcome is thus just, according to this account of democracy, if it mirrors the preferences of the majority of people. Young describes how the aggregative model conceives of democratic processes of policy formation:

> Individuals in the polity have varying preferences about what they want government institutions to do. They know that other individuals also have preferences, which may or may not match their own. Democracy is a competitive process in which political parties and candidates offer their platforms and attempt to satisfy the largest number of people's preferences. Citizens with similar preferences often organize interest groups in order to try to influence the actions of parties and policy-makers once they are elected. Individuals, interest groups, and public officials each may behave strategically, adjusting the orientation of their pressure tactics or coalition-building according to their perceptions of the activities of competing preferences. (Young, 2000: 19)

According to the aggregative model of democracy citizens participate in the decision-making process by making their preferences known, primarily through voting, and thereby increasing the chances that such preferences will guide public policy. Voting is thus conceived of as the *primary* political act. But deliberative democrats reject this narrow conception of participation. To fully participate in the decision-making process one must participate in *authentic deliberation*, not simply express one's preferences. Such deliberation requires participants to seek to reach a *consensus* among free and equal participants. To participate in this discursive practice is quite different from participating in the decision-making process of the aggregative model of democracy. Deliberative democrats characterise participation in the democratic process as a *transformative* process. 'Through the process of public discussion with a plurality of differently opinioned and situated others, people often gain new information, learn of different experiences of their collective problems, or find that their own initial opinions are founded on prejudice or ignorance, or that they have misunderstood the relation of their own interests to others' (Young, 2000: 26). In the first excerpt in this part Young identifies four normative ideals which are logically related in the deliberative model. These are: inclusion, political equality, reasonableness, and publicity.

Joshua Cohen claims that 'the fundamental idea of democratic legitimacy is that the authorisation to exercise state power must arise from the collective decisions of the members of a society who are governed by that power' (Cohen, 1996: 95). By equating legitimacy with the outcome of an actual democratic process the deliberative democrat rejects the idea that the content of the law should be premised on substantive principles that are independent of such a process (for example, Rawls's two principles of justice). Jürgen Habermas, for example, claims that 'all contents, no matter how fundamental the action form involved may be, must be made to depend on real discourses (or advocatory discourses conducted as substitutes for them)' (Habermas, 1990: 94). According to Habermas's democratic principle the only test for the legitimacy of laws is a procedural test. 'Statutory legitimacy hangs solely on whether a law has been enacted in the correct way, not on whether it fulfils some antecedently specified substantive normative criteria for goodness or rightness' (Zurn, 2002: 510). For proceduralists like Habermas there are no legitimate principles that are independent of the democratic process as the latter is the only source of legitimacy. Elaborating on why he advocates a proceduralist view Habermas claims:

# Introduction

> The *democratic process* bears the entire burden of legitimation. It must simultaneously secure the private and public autonomy of legal subjects. This is so because individual private rights cannot be adequately formulated, let alone politically implemented, if those affected have not first engaged in public discussions to clarify which features are relevant in treating typical cases alike or different, and then mobilized communicative power for the consideration of their newly interpreted needs. The proceduralist understanding of law thus privileges the communicative presuppositions and procedural conditions of democratic opinion- and will-formation as the sole source of legitimation. (Habermas, 1996, 450)

Some deliberative democrats reject the purely procedural account of deliberative democracy. Gutmann and Thompson, for example, argue that the ideal of deliberative democracy includes both substantive and procedural principles. In the second excerpt in this part entitled 'Deliberative Democracy Beyond Process' Gutmann and Thompson argue that deliberative democratic theory can and should go beyond process. They focus in particular on the principle of reciprocity, a principle that expresses neither purely procedural nor purely substantive values. They illustrate this point by considering the National Institute for Clinical Excellence (NICE), a new institute that was created by the British Government in 1999. Recognising that the National Health Service (NHS) could not fund all the health needs of its citizens, the British Government hoped to make the difficult decisions regarding health care provisions more public and deliberative by creating NICE, which would provide assessments of treatments and clinical guidelines. NICE came under fire from the House of Commons which is itself a deliberative forum. The defenders of NICE appealed to substantive standards to defend NICE's decision as a purely procedural justification was not sufficient. It was not enough to say that these decisions were made in a public and deliberative manner.

In the last contribution in this part John Dryzek considers the difficulties deliberative democrats have dealing with what he calls the problem of 'large scale'. Modern democratic states consist of millions, even hundreds of millions, of people. Is it thus realistic to talk about citizens deliberating with one another and searching for a consensus on complex and contentious issues? Dryzek considers and criticises the different ways deliberative democrats have attempted to resolve this issue. He argues that the idea of legitimacy needs to be detached from a head count of reflectively consenting individuals. Dryzek then constructs a conception of discursive democracy that recognises that the public sphere is at any time home to constellations of discourses. Discursive legitimacy is secured, argues Dryzek, 'to the degree that collective outcomes are responsive to the balance of competing discourses in the public sphere, to the extent that this balance is itself subject to dispersed and competent control' (Dryzek, 2001: 652).

## References

Cohen, Joshua. 'Procedure and Substance in Deliberative Democracy'. In S. Benhabib (ed.), *Democracy and Difference* (Princeton, NJ: Princeton University Press, 1996).

Dryzek, John. *Deliberative Democracy and Beyond: Liberals, Critics, and Contestations.* (Oxford: Oxford University Press, 2000).

Dryzek, John. 'Legitimacy and Economy in Deliberative Democracy', *Political Theory*, 29(5), 2001: 651–69.

Habermas, Jürgen. *Moral Consciousness and Communicative Action*. (Cambridge, Mass: MIT Press, 1990).

—— *Between Facts and Norms: Contributions to a Discourse Theory of Law and Democracy*. (Cambridge, Mass: MIT Press, 1996).

Shapiro, Ian. *Democratic Justice*. (New Haven and London: Yale University Press, 1999).

Young, Iris Marion. *Inclusion and Democracy*. (Oxford: Oxford University Press, 2000).

Zurn, Christopher. 'Deliberative Democracy and Constitutional Review', *Law and Philosophy*, 21, 2002: 467–542.

# 20 The Deliberative Model

## Iris Marion Young

The model of democracy as a process of aggregating preferences does loosely describe some aspects of democratic process in the world today, and also expresses the way many political actors think about democracy. Not only political scientists and economists, but many journalists, politicians, and citizens, implicitly share the assumptions of this model that ends and values are subjective, non-rational, and exogenous to the political process. Consequently, they believe that democratic politics is nothing other than a competition between private interests and preferences. The operation of liberal democratic politics corresponds to these assumptions. Voting—the expressing of preferences among a list of candidates or referendum choices—is the primary political act. The democratic process consists in various groups putting out their interests and competing for those votes. Such a mass plebiscite process treats citizens as atomized, privately responding to itemized opinion poll questions.[1]

Even in our imperfect democracies, however, another model of democracy lies in the shadows. Wherever the democratic impulse emerges, many people associate democracy with open discussion and the exchange of views leading to agreed-upon policies. In parliamentary discussions participants often claim that theirs is the most just and reasonable proposal. Most democracies contain other institutions and practices of political discussion and criticism in which participants aim to persuade one another of the rightness of their positions.

Contemporary political theorists usually call this alternative model deliberative democracy. A number of important theories of deliberative democracy have appeared in recent years, sparking a renewed interest in the place of reasoning, persuasion, and normative appeals in democratic politics.[2] In the deliberative model democracy is a form of practical reason. Participants in the democratic process offer proposals for how best to solve problems or meet legitimate needs, and so on, and they present arguments through which they aim to persuade others to accept their proposals. Democratic process is primarily a discussion of problems, conflicts, and claims of need or interest. Through dialogue others test and challenge these proposals and arguments. Because they have not stood up to dialogic examination, the deliberating public rejects or refines some proposals. Participants arrive at a decision not by determining what preferences have greatest numerical support, but by determining which proposals the collective agrees are supported by the best reasons. This model of democratic processes entails several normative ideals for the relationships and dispositions of deliberating parties, among them inclusion, equality, reasonableness, and publicity. These ideals are all logically related in the deliberative model.

*Inclusion.* On this model a democratic decision is normatively legitimate only if all those affected by it are included in the process of discussion and decision-making. This simple formulation opens many questions about the way in which they are affected, and how strongly; it might be absurd to say that everyone affected by decisions in any trivial way ought to be party to them. To limit this question somewhat, we can say that 'affected' here means at least that decisions and policies significantly condition a person's options for action. As an ideal, inclusion embodies a norm of moral respect. Persons (and perhaps other creatures) are being treated as means if they are expected to abide by rules or adjust their actions according to decisions from where determination their voice and interests have been excluded. When coupled with norms of political equality, inclusion allows for maximum expression of interests, opinions, and perspectives relevant to the problems or issues for which a public seeks solutions.

*Political equality.* As a normative ideal, democracy means political equality. Not only should all those affected be nominally included in decision-making, but they should be included on equal terms. All ought to have an equal right and effective opportunity to express their interests and concerns.[3] All also ought to have equal effective opportunity to question one another, and to respond to and criticize one another's proposals and arguments. The ideal model of deliberative democracy, that is, promotes free and equal opportunity to speak. This condition cannot be met, however, without a third condition of equality, namely freedom from domination. Participants in an ideal process of deliberative democracy must be equal in the sense that none of them is in a position to coerce or threaten others into accepting certain proposals or outcomes.

While I have distinguished the terms 'inclusion' and 'political equality' in order to specify their normative import, for the rest of this book when I refer to a norm of inclusion I shall understand it to entail the norm of political equality. In real political conflict, when political actors and movements protest exclusion and demand greater inclusion, they invariably appeal to ideals of political equality and do not accept token measures of counting people in. When discussion is inclusive, in this strong sense, it allows the expression of all interests, opinions, and criticism, and when it is free from domination, discussion participants can be confident that the results arise from good reasons rather than from fear or force or false consensus. This confidence can be maintained, however, only when participants have a disposition to be reasonable.

*Reasonableness.* In the context of the model of deliberative democracy, I take reasonableness to refer more to a set of dispositions that discussion participants have than to the substance of people's contributions to debate. Reasonable people often have crazy ideas; what makes them reasonable is their willingness to listen to others who want to explain to them why their ideas are incorrect or inappropriate. People who think they know more or are better than others are sometimes too quick to label the assertions of others as irrational, and thereby try to avoid having to engage with them. Since reasonable people often disagree about what proposals, actions, groundings, and narratives are rational or irrational, judging too quickly is itself often a symptom of unreasonableness.

Reasonable people enter discussion to solve collective problems with the aim of reaching agreement. Often they will not reach agreement, of course, and they need to have procedures for reaching decisions and registering dissent in the absence of agreement. Reasonable people understand that dissent often produces insight, and that decisions and agreements should in principle be open to new challenge. While actually reaching consensus is thus not a requirement of deliberative reason, participants in discussion must be *aiming* to reach agreement to enter the discussion at all. Only if the participants believe that some kind of agreement among them is possible in principle can they in good faith trust one another to listen and aim to persuade one another.

Thus reasonable participants in democratic discussion must have an open mind. They cannot come to the discussion of a collective problem with commitments that bind them to the authority of prior norms or unquestionable beliefs.[4] Nor can they assert their own interests above all others' or insist that their initial opinion about what is right or just cannot be subject to revision. To be reasonable is to be willing to change our opinions or preferences because others persuade us that our initial opinions or preferences, as they are relevant to the collective problems under discussion, are incorrect or inappropriate. Being open thus also refers to a disposition to listen to others, treat them with respect, make an effort to understand them by asking questions, and not judge them too quickly. A reasonable respectful process of discussion exhibits deliberative uptake; when some speak, others acknowledge the expression in ways that continue the engagement.[5]

*Publicity.* The conditions of inclusion, equality, and reasonableness, finally, entail that the interaction among participants in a democratic decision-making process forms a public in which people hold one another accountable.[6] A public consists of a plurality of different individual and collective experiences, histories, commitments, ideals, interests, and goals that face one another to discuss collective problems under a common set of procedures. When members of such a public speak to one another, they know they are answerable to that plurality of others; this access that others have to their point of view makes them careful about expressing themselves. This plural public-speaking context requires participants to express themselves in ways accountable to all those plural others. They must try to explain their particular background experiences, interests, or proposals in ways that others can understand, and they must express reasons for their claims in ways that others recognize could be accepted, even if in fact they disagree with the claims and reasons. Even when they address a particular group with a particular history, as is usually the case, they speak with the reflective idea that third parties might be listening.[7] For the content of an expression to be public does not entail that it *is* immediately understood by all, or that the principles to which argument appeals *are* accepted by all, but only that the expression aims in its form and content to be understandable and acceptable. Deliberative exchange thus entails expressions of puzzlement or disagreement, the posing of questions, and answering them.

## The Adequacy of the Deliberative Model

Though both models rely on the actual experience of democracy, the deliberative model is more adequate to the set of commitments than bring us to value democratic practice than is the aggregative. The latter model responds primarily to democracy's purpose as a protection against tyranny and the ability of individuals and groups to promote and protect their interests in politics and policy. The deliberative model responds to these purposes, but also corresponds to other purposes people express for valuing democracy, such as promoting cooperation, solving collective problems, and furthering justice.

The interactive aspect of this model accounts for its greater comprehensiveness. In the deliberative model political actors not only express preferences and interests, but they engage with one another about how to balance these under circumstances of inclusive equality. Because this interaction requires participants to be open and attentive to one another, to justify their claims and proposals in terms acceptable to all, the orientation of participants moves from self-regard to an orientation towards what is publicly assertable. Interests and preferences continue to have a place in the processes of deliberative democracy, but not as given and exogenous to the process. Most proponents of deliberative democracy emphasize that this model conceptualizes the process of democratic discussion as not merely expressing and registering, but as *transforming* the preferences, interests, beliefs, and judgements of participants. Through the process of public discussion with a plurality of differently opinioned and situated others, people often gain new information, learn of different experiences of their collective problems, or find that their own initial opinions are founded on prejudice or ignorance, or that they have misunderstood the relation of their own interests to others'.[8]

I endorse the basic outlines of the model of deliberative democracy as I have formulated them here. It is the best way to think about democracy from the point of view of an interest in a politics of inclusion and promoting greater justice. Some formulations of the model should be criticized, however, and the model also needs refinement in several respects in order to a serve a theory of inclusive democratic process.

## Notes

1  On the idea of and for a critique of plebiscite democracy, see James Fishkin, *The Voice of the People* (New Haven: Yale University Press, 1991).
2  Among the writers whom I include as theorists of deliberative democracy are Joshua Cohen, 'Deliberation and Democratic Legitimacy', in Alan Hamlin and Philip Pettit (eds.), *The Good Polity* (London: Blackwell, 1989); Thomas Spragens, *Reason and Democracy* (Durham, NC: Duke University Press, 1990); Benjamin Barber, *Strong Democracy* (Berkeley: University of California Press, 1984); Cass R. Sunstein, *The Partial Constitution* (Cambridge, Mass.: Harvard University Press, 1993), esp. ch. 8; Frank Michelman, 'Traces of Self-Government', *Harvard Law Review*, 100 (1986), 4–77; Jane Mansbridge, 'A Deliberative Theory of Interest Representation', in Mark P. Patracca (ed.), *The Politics of Interest: Interest Groups Transformed* (Boulder, Colo., Westview Press, 1992); John Dryzek, *Discursive Democracy* (Cambridge: Cambridge University Press, 1990); James Bohman, *Public Deliberation* (Cambridge, Mass.: MA: MIT Press, 1996); Fishkin, *The Voice of the People*; Jürgen Habermas, *Between Facts and Norms* (Cambridge, Mass.: MIT Press, 1996); Amy Gutmann and Dennis Thompson, *Democracy and Disagreement* (Cambridge, Mass.: Harvard University Press, 1996); Thomas Christiano, *The Rule of the Many* (Boulder, Colo.: Westview Press, 1996), esp. ch. 3; David Ingram, *Reason, History and Politics* (Albany: State University of New York Press, 1995).
3  For a comprehensive theory of political equality in the deliberative mode, see Charles Beitz, *Political Equality* (Princeton: Princeton University Press, 1990).
4  Cohen, 'Deliberation and Democratic Legitimacy', 22–3.
5  Of deliberative theorists, Bohman has made the most of this idea of uptake; *Public Deliberation*, 58–9, 116–18.
6  Publicity and accountability are the core of Amy Gutmann and Dennis Thompson's conception of deliberation. See *Democracy and Disagreement*.
7  See Jodi Dean, *Solidarity of Strangers* (Berkeley: University of California Press, 1994). Dean develops an idea of a universalist open relation of solidarity among particular group members, where they are united by their relation to a 'hypothetical third'. Some writers put this publicity condition in terms of Kantian universalizability, but I think that this is a mistake, because it removes the discourse from its situatedenss. See Bohman, *Public Deliberation*, 35–47.
8  Most deliberative theorists thematize this transformative aspect of discursive interaction. See e.g. Barber, *Strong Democracy*, 136–58; Jane Mansbridge, 'Self-Interest and Political Transformation', in George E. Marcus and Russell L. Hanson (eds.), *Reconsidering the Democratic Public* (University Park: Pennsylvania State University Press, 1993).

# 21 Deliberative Democracy Beyond Process

## Amy Gutmann and Dennis Thompson

Theories of deliberative democracy consist of a set of principles that are intended to establish fair terms of political cooperation in a democratic society. Some theorists believe that the principles should refer only to the process of making political decisions in government or civil society.[1] The principles of deliberative democracy, they argue, should not prescribe the content of the laws, but only the procedures (such as equal suffrage) by which laws are made and the conditions (such as free political speech) necessary for the procedures to work fairly. These theorists, whom we call pure proceduralists, insist that democratic theory should not incorporate substantive principles such as individual liberty or equal opportunity beyond what is necessary for a fair democratic process. They do not deny that substantive principles such as freedom of religion, nondiscrimination or basic health care are important, but they wish to keep these principles out of their democratic theories.

We argue that this effort to keep democratic theory procedurally pure fails, and that any adequate theory must include substantive as well as procedural principles. Our own theory, presented in *Democracy and Disagreement*, offers one such approach: it includes substantive principles (such as basic liberty and fair opportunity) that extend fairness to persons (for the sake of reciprocity, mutual respect, or fairness itself). Principles of basic liberty and fair opportunity can be defended on many substantive grounds; in that book we argue from a widely recognized principle of reciprocity or mutual justification among persons who are bound by the laws of a democracy.

But our argument here does not depend on accepting the whole theory in that book, or even the specific grounds of reciprocity on which we base the principles. We wish to maintain here that, on a wide range of available grounds, democratic principles must be substantive as well as procedural. A democratic theory that shuns substantive principles for the sake of remaining purely procedural sacrifices an essential value of democracy itself: its principles cannot claim to treat citizens in the way that free and equal persons should be treated—whether fairly, reciprocally, or with mutual respect—in a democratic society in which laws bind all equally.

Pure proceduralists make two kinds of arguments against including substantive principles—one from moral authority and the other from political authority. The argument from moral authority holds that the moral judgment of democratic citizens, not democratic theorists, should determine the content of laws. A theory that contains substantive principles improperly pre-empts the moral authority of citizens. The argument from political authority maintains that substantive principles similarly pre-empt the political sovereignty of citizens, which should be exercised not through hypothetical theoretical reasoning but through actual democratic decision-making. A theory that contains substantive principles unduly constrains the democratic decision-making process, including the process of deliberation itself.

We dispute both of these arguments and defend the inclusion of substantive principles in a theory of deliberative democracy. We agree with those theorists who point out that mere procedures such as majority rule cannot justify outcomes that are unjust according to substantive principles. But these theorists usually neglect the substantive value in the procedures, and assume that an outcome is justified if it is just according to their substantive principles.

In any case, our main argument against pure proceduralism is not the same as the standard objection that procedures can produce unjust outcomes, though we accept this objection. We also argue for including substantive principles in a democratic theory for another, generally neglected reason. Such principles should be included so that the theory can explicitly recognize that both substantive and procedural principles are subject to contestation in similar ways. A critical claim in our defense of a deliberative democratic theory that is both procedural and substantive is that the principles are to be treated as morally and politically provisional. This provisionality gives deliberation part of its point. Both procedural and substantive principles are systematically open to revision in an ongoing process of moral and political deliberation. If the principles are understood in this way, the usual objections against including substantive principles lose their force. The provisional status of all its principles thus constitutes a distinctive strength of deliberative democratic theory, and at the same time offers deliberative democrats an effective response to those who would exclude substantive principles from democratic theory.

Although we concentrate here on showing the problems with the form of pure proceduralism that justifies political outcomes by procedural criteria only, our general criticisms also apply against any attempt to segregate procedural and substantive principles in separate theories. Theorists who judge outcomes partly by substantive principles of justice are still pure proceduralists (with respect to their democratic theories) if they assume that the democratic procedures can be justified without reference to some of the same substantive values expressed by their principles of justice. Our argument is intended to show that this kind of sharp separation between procedural and substantive principles and theories is not sustainable.

To illustrate some of the major points in the argument for including both procedural and substantive principles in a deliberative democratic theory, we use a case involving deliberation about health care in the United Kingdom. In 1999, the British Government created a new body, the National Institute for Clinical Excellence (NICE), which is to provide assessments of treatments and clinical guidelines for use by the National Health Service (NHS).[2] The impetus for the new Institute came from the widespread recognition that the NHS could not fund care for all health needs, and needed to find a way to make its difficult decisions in a more public and deliberative manner. By creating a deliberative decision-making body, which includes both expert and lay members, the British Government may also have hoped that it could defuse some of the controversy about the hard choices that had to be made. But not surprisingly, shortly after its creation, NICE itself came under criticism in another deliberative forum—the House of Commons. Together these moments of deliberation—the proceedings of NICE and the Commons debate about NICE—are more appropriate for our purposes than cases from the US. They involve an attempt to institutionalize nationwide deliberation about health care priorities in a way that the US has tried only in certain states. Also, the deliberation takes place in a nation in which principles of justice in health care come closer to being satisfied than in the US, and therefore poses a greater challenge to our claim that such principles are necessary in any adequate theory of deliberative democracy. If a theory needs substantive principles when applied to health care in the UK, then a fortiori it should need them when applied to similar issues in the US.

## Why Reciprocity Requires Substantive Principles

The practice of deliberation is an ongoing activity or reciprocal reason-giving, punctuated by collectively binding decisions. It is a process of reaching mutually binding decisions on the basis of mutually justifiable reasons. Because the reasons have to be mutually justifiable, the process presupposes some principles with substantive content. It is possible, and sometimes desirable, to distinguish procedural and substantive aspects of principles and theories, but to turn these distinctions into separate principles or distinct theories is to distort both the theory and practice of (deliberative) democracy. Although for convenience we refer to principles and theories as procedural and substantive, strictly speaking democratic principles and theories have both procedural and substantive dimensions, and approaches that force a sharp division are misleading.

The principle of reciprocity itself expresses neither purely procedural nor purely substantive values. A reciprocal perspective is both procedural and substantive because mutual justification cannot proceed without appealing to reasons that refer to both procedures of government and substance of laws, often at the same time. Even philosophers like Stuart Hampshire who seek to exclude substantive justice completely from their procedural political theories acknowledge the need for some substantive values—such as "common decency"—in the very concept of justice.[3] Hampshire says justice is "primarily procedural"—not entirely so.[4] Like other philosophers who want to be pure proceduralists, he never says what constitutes the correct set of procedural principles, and why people who remain subject to tyrannical rule should settle for only procedural principles if they permit tyranny.

At a minimum, no one would seriously dispute that justifications should recognize some values expressed by substantive principles such as liberty and opportunity. It would hardly be sufficient for NICE to justify a decision to deny prescription drugs to West Indian immigrants on the grounds that they are not white. Even—or especially—if a large majority of British citizens would accept such reasoning, the justification would not satisfy any adequate standard of reciprocity. Nor would it be any more acceptable to deny prescription drugs to a disadvantaged minority on the grounds that they agreed with the conclusion. They might have agreed simply because they had less power than the groups that prevailed and had no better alternative in a bargaining situation.

To see more clearly why reciprocity requires substantive principles, we might further imagine a situation in which the process of decision-making itself was fair in the sense that the bargaining power of the parties was equitable, but in which the reasoning of the decision-makers was prejudiced (or could only be reasonably interpreted as based on prejudice) against West Indian immigrants or another disadvantaged minority group. The prejudiced reasoning then yields an outcome—supported by the vast majority—that denies critical health care to the disadvantaged minority. This outcome could not be justified on grounds of reciprocity, even if the procedures by which it was reached were otherwise completely fair. The justification for the outcome does not treat members of the minority group as worthy of a justification that they could reasonably accept. Alternatively, one might say that the prejudiced reasoning denies members of the minority group the status of free and equal persons. Given the nature of the reasoning, this would be so no matter how fair the process of decision-making itself might otherwise be.

We can see the principle of reciprocity in action, and the mixture of procedural and substantive values it implies, in the debate about NICE in the House of Commons. The debate had hardly begun when an MP (who is also a physician) challenged the idea that NICE or anyone else has the moral or political authority to ration health care. Another MP responded, saying that rationing was necessary and therefore justifiable: "sometimes some treatments are not available when they would benefit patients or populations, because there simply are not the resources to provide all those treatments on the NHS." Although the debate at first seemed to turn on issues about the legitimacy of the process (who has the authority to decide), most critics (as well as most defenders of the Government) agreed that NICE represented an improvement as far as process was concerned. Most recognized that the new decision-making process is preferable to the old, and much superior to the less deliberative process that prevails in the US.

The challenge instead was directed against the substance of NICE's decision in its first review of a drug. NICE had recommended against the NHS's funding the new anti-flu drug Relenza.[5] The critics worried that this decision would be a precedent that would justify NICE's recommending against funding of other more expensive and effective new drugs, such as beta interferon (which treats the symptoms of multiple sclerosis). The critics argued that decisions denying coverage are likely to deprive less advantaged patients of life-enhancing and life-saving treatments that more advantaged patients receive, and that this unequal opportunity cannot be justified. It leaves the less fortunate without the health care and the life chances that, if any citizens enjoy, then all should be entitled to.[6] They appealed to substantive principles, not simply to a claim that the process was unfair, or even that it was not deliberative.

Defenders of NICE's decision rightly realized that they needed to justify the substance of the decision because the deliberative process in which NICE had engaged (and in which they were engaging in the Commons debate) could not in itself be a sufficient justification of the decision. They explicitly invoked substantive standards to defend NICE's decision. They argued, for example, that the decision not to fund Relenza would not adversely affect the basic life chances of any citizen, not even patients who are at high risk of complications from influenza. They called for more research on the effects of Relenza on high-risk patients, and suggested that if there were evidence of Relenza's benefit in reducing the serious secondary complications of influenza in such patients, then they would support NHS funding. Their arguments, whether correct on the merits, were entirely in order, and if correct they were also necessary to justify their conclusion. That they were necessary cannot readily be accommodated in a democratic theory that limits itself to procedural considerations only.

An obvious but no less important virtue of a theory that does not limit itself to procedural principles is that it has no problem with asserting that what the majority decides, ever after full deliberation, is wrong. Within a deliberative theory, one should be able to condemn majority tyranny on substantive grounds: one should be able to say that a majority acts wrongly if it violates basic liberty by denying health care on grounds of race, gender, or poverty. Or suppose that the majority, following perfectly deliberative procedures, decides to institute a practice of compulsory organ donation. On a purely procedural conception of deliberative democracy, this law would be justified. If a deliberative theory includes substantive principles such as basic liberty which protect bodily integrity, democrats would be able to object to such a law, without abandoning their commitment to deliberative democracy.

Democrats of course may be mistaken when they assert claims based on substantive principles either because they draw incorrect implications from a correct principle or because they rely on an indefensible principle. Perhaps compulsory organ donation does not violate basic liberty, or perhaps this particular principle of basic liberty is flawed. Our argument for including substantive principles—based on reciprocity—not only allows for both kinds of mistake; it also incorporates into the theory itself the insight that democratic theorists and citizens may be mistaken about both procedural and substantive principles. Deliberation explicitly deals with the likelihood of mistaken views about principles and their implications by considering the principles of a theory to be provisional, and therefore subject to ongoing deliberation. To point out the possibility of being mistaken about substantive principles is therefore not an argument against including such principles within a deliberative democratic theory.

The conclusions of purely procedural theories sometimes converge with the claims of the substantive standards that reciprocity requires. For example, a procedural theory of democracy may say that racial discrimination in voting is not justified because it excludes a class of human beings from citizenship, and this violates the procedural requirements of democracy, which demand the enfranchisement of all adult persons. This procedural reason is fine as far as it goes. But it does not go far enough in establishing why such discrimination is not justified. Democratic theorists should be able to object that racial discrimination (for example, in the provision of health care by a for-profit Health Maintenance Organization) is not justified even if democratic citizenship or no other process values are at stake. Majority tyranny is objectionable on substantive, not only procedural, grounds.

Moreover, this kind of objection should be capable of being made from *within* a deliberative democratic theory. After all, democracy has never meant merely majority rule. Denying basic liberties and opportunities by racially discriminatory policies is either the result of state action or can be remedied by state action, and any such action or inaction requires a justification that could reasonably be accepted by those whose liberties and opportunities are denied. This is a direct implication of the basic requirement of reciprocity. The requirement to give such a justification—to invoke substantive principles in the public forum to justify a mutually binding law or policy—is therefore not an incidental feature of deliberative democracy. The substantive principles are integral to the deliberative process itself.

To say that the principles are integral to the process is not to deny that they may be justifiable outside of that process. Like any theorist of justice (or citizen making a claim about justice), deliberative democrats may put forward principles for consideration which they regard as justifiable—and which indeed may be correct, but simply not yet justified as laws. Deliberative theorists try to justify their substantive principles in a number of familiar ways, some just like those used by any theorist. We justify the substantive principles such as basic liberty in *Democracy and Disagreement*, first and foremost, on their own terms—by identifying core values, convictions, and paradigmatic cases where no one would reasonably deny that they were violated (for example, discrimination on grounds of race). Then by analogy and other forms of reasoning, we try to thicken and extend the principles to apply to more controversial cases. This is also how much of actual political deliberation proceeds.

Certainly, these substantive principles might be rejected, and perhaps even reasonably rejected, in a deliberative process that satisfies the procedural conditions of deliberative democracy. But a precisely parallel argument can be made about procedural principles. Procedural principles may also be rejected by a deliberative democracy (and so may a purely procedural conception of deliberative democracy). Pure proceduralists do not have access to some moral basis, which our conception lacks, on which to claim that the procedural constraints that they recommend for a constitutional deliberative democracy are correct or authoritative.

Some critics who object to including substantive principles in a deliberative democratic theory are themselves not pure proceduralists with respect to justice. They agree that justice requires the protection of basic liberties and opportunities, including perhaps even access to adequate health care. But they still insist that the subject matter of *democratic* theories should be kept distinct from questions of distributive justice. They are pure proceduralists with respect to democracy, but not justice. Democracy, they imply, is supposed to tell us how to decide when we do not agree on what is just; we should not confuse matters by combining principles of justice with the procedures for deciding disputes about those principles.

This argument is not so much substantive as it is definitional: democracy (including deliberative democracy) *means* fair procedures, not right outcomes. The critics cannot rely on ordinary usage or the history of modern democratic theory, because representative democracy has rarely been characterized as exclusively procedural. Ordinary usage of a concept as complex as democracy is enormously varied, as are the conceptions of democracy found in modern democratic theory. And democratic practice itself is full of debates about substantive principles. Why then strain so hard to exclude them from the definition of democracy?

The reason cannot be that democratic theory is somehow internally inconsistent if it contains substantive as well as procedural principles. To be sure, the more principles a theory contains, the more likely there are to be conflicts among them. And including both substantive and procedural principles certainly increases the potential for conflict. But democratic politics itself is rife with conflict among principles, and a democratic theory that tries to insulate itself from that conflict by limiting the range of principles it includes is likely to be less relevant for recognizing and resolving the disagreements that democracies typically confront. When the disagreements mix substantive and procedural values as so many do in actual democratic practice, theorists who artificially segregate substance and procedure in separate theories of justice and democracy are prone to distort the role of both.

Some pure proceduralists may wish to keep out substantive principles because they are contestable, and democracy is supposed to be a means of resolving disagreement among contestable principles such as basic liberty.

But the content of principles that are more procedural, such as majority rule or public accountability, are also contestable. A purely procedural theory does not avoid fundamental disagreement: conflicts among procedural principles are no less severe than among substantive principles. For example, in the debate in Commons about NICE's decision to deny coverage for beta interferon, the MP from North Wiltshire implicitly raised a basic procedural question—to what extent does democratic control require local autonomy—when he argued that his constituents should have access to the drug. He objected that—because of the relative autonomy of regions—some citizens in other parts of the country could get beta interferon from the NHS while his constituents could not. This is "a terrible tragedy for constituents such as mine, who could be prescribed beta interferon if they lived in Bath or Oxford, but not in Wiltshire."[7]

The political debates over health care rationing that are occurring not only in the UK but also in almost every contemporary democracy clearly reveal the need to consider both procedures and outcomes in judging democratic justice. At stake are both the conditions under which these decisions are made and their content. Do the decision-making bodies bring together representatives of all the people who are most affected by the decisions? Are the representatives accountable to all their constituents? These procedural questions cannot be answered in the context of these debates without also asking: to what extent is the substance of the decisions justifiable to all the people who are bound by them? To exclude substantive criteria—such as liberty and opportunity—that judge the justice of decisions would be morally arbitrary and incomplete according to deliberative democracy's own premise of reciprocity. (To exclude substantive criteria would also be morally arbitrary and incomplete according to other premises that are often identified as fundamental to deliberative democracy, such as free and equal personhood or mutual respect).

To affirm that a democratic theory should include substantive principles does not of course commit one to any particular set of principles. In *Democracy and Disagreement*, we propose a set of principles that are both substantive and procedural, and present arguments for their inclusion as part of the constitution of a deliberative democracy.[8] The arguments we present are intended to be part of a deliberative process itself, and in fact include fragments from actual deliberations. For example, we argue that laws or policies that deprive individuals of the basic opportunities necessary for making choices among good lives cannot be mutually justified as a principle of reciprocity requires. The basic opportunities typically include adequate health care, education, security, work, and income, and are necessary for living a decent life and having the ability to make choices among good lives. We therefore would include a principle of basic opportunity as part of any adequate theory of deliberative democracy.

Critics who object that this principle is not mutually justifiable or that other principles of equality are more mutually justifiable are effectively accepting the idea that democratic theory should include substantive principles.

Even while challenging the content of the principles, they are nevertheless accepting that the terms of the argument should be reciprocal. Such challenges are welcome by the terms of the theory itself, which asks for reasons that can be publicly assessed by all those who will be bound by them.[9] This kind of challenge can then become part of the continuing deliberative process. The reason that such a challenge fits within the terms of a deliberative theory itself is that the principles of the theory per se have a morally and politically provisional status.

Deliberative democratic theory can and should go beyond process. It can consistently incorporate both substantive and procedural principles. It should go beyond process for many reasons that we have suggested, but above all because its core principle—reciprocity—requires substantive as well as procedural principles. Reciprocity is widely accepted as a core principle of democracy, but even those democrats who do not emphasize this principle argue from ideals such as free and equal personhood, mutual respect or avoidance of majority tyranny, which like reciprocity require both substantive and procedural principles to justify the laws that democracies adopt.

Deliberative democratic theory is better prepared to deal with the range of moral and political challenges of a robust democratic politics if it includes both substantive and procedural principles. It is well equipped to cope with the conflict between substantive and procedural principles because its principles are to varying degrees morally and politically provisional. Deliberative democratic theory can avoid usurping the moral or political authority of democratic citizens—and yet still make substantive judgments about the laws they enact—because it claims neither more, nor less, than provisional status for the principles it defends.

## Notes

1. As Jürgen Habermas writes, "All contents, no matter how fundamental the action norm involved may be, must be made to depend on real discourses (or advocatory discourses conducted as substitutes for them)". "Discourse ethics," *Moral Consciousness and Communicative Action*, trans. Christian Lenhardt and Shierry Weber Nicholsen (Cambridge, Mass.: M.I.T. Press, 1993), p. 94. For comments and other citations, see our discussion in Amy Gutmann and Dennis Thompson, *Democracy and Disagreement* (Cambridge, Mass.: Harvard University Press, 1996), pp. 17–18. Other theorists who would also be more inclined to limit deliberative democracy to process considerations and are therefore critical of including substantive principles in its theory include: Jack Knight, "Constitutionalism and deliberative democracy" *Deliberative Politics*, ed. Stephen Macedo (New York: Oxford University Press, 1999), pp. 159–69; Cass Sunstein, "Agreement without theory," ibid., pp. 147–8; and Iris Marion Young, "Justice, inclusion, and deliberative democracy," ibid., pp. 151–8. For our reply, see Gutmann and Thompson, "Democratic disagreement," ibid., pp. 261–8.
2. See statements by NICE's newly appointed director Michael Rawlins: Richard Horton, "NICE: a step forward in the quality of NHS care," *The Lancet*, 353

(March 27, 1999), 1028–9, and Gavin Yamey, "Chairman of NICE admits that its judgments are hard to defend," *British Medical Journal*, 319 (November 6, 1999), 1222.
3. Stuart Hampshire, *Innocence and Experience* (Cambridge, Mass.: Harvard University Press, 1989), p. 112.
4. Ibid.
5. See "NICE appraisal of Zanamivir (Relenza)." For some of the reaction, see Moore, "U.K. rebuffs Glaxo on new flu drug." The Food and Drug Administration approved Relenza for use in the US despite a 13–4 vote of an outside panel of experts recommending against approval. Some critics believe that the drug has been overprescribed during the current flu season. See Sheryl Gay Stolberg, "F.D.A. warns of overuse of 2 new drugs against flu," *New York Times* (Jan. 13, 2000), p. A 18.
6. As one MP put it in the Commons debate: "When we talk about rationing of NHS treatments, we aren't saying no one in the UK has them. What we are saying is that they aren't available to poor people. The rich and those who can afford it can get these treatments privately" (House of Commons Debate, November 10, 1999).
7. House of Commons Debate, November 10, 1999. Also see Jo Lenaghan, "The rationing debate: Central government should have a greater role in rationing decisions," *British Medical Journal*, 314 (March 29, 1997), 967–71.
8. Gutmann and Thompson, *Democracy and Disagreement*, pp. 199–229.
9. Not so welcome are other critics—those who reject the aim of giving substantive content to the claims of reciprocity or who reject the very standard of reciprocity. But neither are their claims cogent. Having rejected the idea of mutual justification, they are hard-pressed to explain how they can justify at all imposing coercive laws and policies on citizens who morally disagree with them. See section III below, and Gutmann and Thompson, *Democracy and Disagreement*, pp. 352–3.

# 22 Legitimacy and Economy in Deliberative Democracy

## John S. Dryzek

### The Competing Claims of Legitimacy and Economy

Deliberative democracy, though the dominant theme in recent democratic theory, remains on the face of it impossible—at least to the degree it is cast as an account of democratic legitimacy. Yet this is how the theory arrived in Joshua Cohen's classic formulation, and this is still the claim at the theory's core: that outcomes are legitimate to the extent they receive reflective assent through participation in authentic deliberation by all those subject to the decision in question.[1] As Seyla Benhabib puts it, "Legitimacy in complex democratic societies must be thought to result from the free and unconstrained deliberation *of all* about matters of common concern" (emphasis added).[2] The essence of deliberation is generally taken to be that claims for or against collective decisions need to be justified to those subject to these decisions in terms that, given the chance to reflect, these individuals can accept. But in real-world deliberations, all or even very many of those affected do not appear to participate, thus rendering deliberative democracy vulnerable to demolition of its legitimacy claims. In the context of the supposedly exemplary case of health care rationing in Oregon,[3] Ian Shapiro asks, "Why should we attach legitimacy at all to a deliberative process that involved very few of those whose health care priorities were actually being discussed?"[4]

There are ways to fudge the issue; for example, Cohen specifies only that "outcomes are democratically legitimate if and only if they could be the object of a free and reasoned agreement among equals"[5]—*could* be, rather than actually being. Casting matters in terms of the universal right, capacity, or opportunity to deliberate, rather than actual exercise of that right, capacity, or opportunity, makes deliberative democracy more plausible. So for

Bernard Manin, "As political decisions are characteristically imposed on *all*, it seems reasonable to seek, as an essential condition for legitimacy, the deliberation of *all* or, more precisely, the right of all to participate in deliberation."[6] However, this sort of qualification places a major question mark by legitimacy. For surely the theory hangs by a slender thread if its viability depends crucially on the vast majority always choosing not to exercise the rights and capacities that are so fundamental to the theory—and whose exercise is taken by most proponents of deliberative democracy to be what makes for good citizens to begin with. Relying on mass apathy to make the theory work would return us to the dark days of the Schumpeterian, elitist models of democracy that deliberative democrats are otherwise so keen to reject.[7]

The key constraint here is one of economy. Robert Dahl and many others have pointed out that meaningful participation in collective decision by anything more than a tiny minority is inconceivable in contemporary nation-states (and, indeed, in most of their component units).[8] The time demands on participants are simply impossible in anything beyond a very small-scale political unit. As Michael Walzer puts it, "Deliberation is not an activity for the demos ... 100 million of them, or even 1 million or 100,000, can't plausibly 'reason together'."[9]

Here I will briefly survey and criticize the available solutions to this problem and propose a way to think about securing legitimacy while respecting the basic constraint of deliberative economy.[10] This proposal will require close attention to, and perhaps some rethinking about, what we actually mean by core concepts of deliberation, public opinion, and legitimacy—and so by democracy. It will specify the public sphere as the most important location for deliberation and conceptualize deliberation itself as a multifaceted interchange or contestation across discourses within the public sphere. Discursive legitimacy is then secured to the degree that collective outcomes are responsive to the balance of competing discourses in the public sphere, to the extent that this balance is itself subject to dispersed and competent control.

## Deliberative Legitimacy and Large Scale

The extant solutions to the problem presented by large scale are as follows. These solutions are not mutually exclusive and can indeed be combined.

First, deliberative democracy can be restricted to a small number of occasions when popular deliberation can occur. John Rawls believes that extended deliberation is appropriate only to matters concerning the constitution and legislation inasmuch as "basic justice" (equality of opportunity and material distribution) is at issue.[11] Yet the problem of scale remains even on such special occasions. Take, for example, the recent (1999) referendum in Australia on whether to ditch the British monarch in favor of a (particular model of) a republic. The failure of the republican proposal in the referendum compared with the overwhelming success of the model in a setting provided by a deliberative opinion poll (of which more shortly) suggests that this occasion, at least, was a deliberative failure at the national level—even in a population of (only) 19 million. The sheer impossibility of involving more than a handful of members of the population in deliberation remains overwhelming. As we shall see shortly, Rawls himself sees no problem in restricting deliberation to a well-qualified handful.

The number of occasions for society-wide deliberation is restricted still further by Bruce Ackerman, who argues that the political history of the United States has seen just three such occasions: the constitutional founding, the Civil War amendments to the Constitution, and the New Deal.[12] But even on these rare great crises of the state, it certainly was not a matter of *all* the people deliberating, however much deliberative circles may have been widened. And even if these three occasions were the only three rightful candidates, it would seem odd to rest an account of democratic legitimacy on events that most citizens may well go through their lives without ever seeing.

The second solution, perhaps more straightforward than the first, is somehow to restrict the number of people involved in deliberation, making sure that the individuals who do participate be in some way representative of those who do not. There are two main ways of securing representativeness: by popular election and by random selection. The former is of course acceptable to those theorists who see deliberation as an aspect of, rather than substitute for, conventional sorts of representative democracy.[13] But such an easy assimilation to representative democracy cannot straightforwardly deliver on the legitimacy requirements of deliberative democrats such as Cohen, Benhabib, and Manin. For to do so, election campaigns themselves would have potentially to involve the deliberation *of all*. So the problem of scale reappears, only this time in a slightly different location, and a legitimacy claim cannot be established at one remove simply by appeal to the electoral process.

Deliberative democracy's legitimation problems are compounded here to the degree elections themselves are not exactly deliberative affairs, even for those who do participate in them—deliberation often has to be subordinated to strategy in the interests of winning. One way to avoid this anti-deliberative aspect of election campaigns is to select deliberators by lot instead of election—as is done for James Fishkin's deliberative opinion polls, for citizen juries, for Dahl's proposed "minipopulus," and for John Burnheim's proposed "demarchy."[14] Such forums are usually constituted on an issue-specific basis and their role but advisory—though there is no reason why they could not be decisive or indeed act as general-purpose legislatures.

Random sampling of the relevant population followed by deliberation gives a simulation of what the population as a whole would decide if everyone were allowed to deliberate. This simulation may not hold if the deliberation so organized fails to capture the differentiated character of political interchange—that is, the fact that in reality people encounter each other largely within or across groups, as opposed to an undifferentiated forum.

(Sanders suggests that this means deliberative polls misrepresent group processes.[15]) However, even if we grant the simulation claim, it does not entirely solve the legitimation problem because decisions still have to be justified to those who did not participate. Still, such justification ought to be easier than for elections—provided that enough of the population could come to understand the logic of random sampling. The problem is that it is not easy to see how the outcome of a deliberative poll could be justified without somehow involving the population at large in deliberation. Simply televising and publicizing the poll is insufficient—as perhaps the Australian example indicates, where the majority of those voting in the referendum chose the opposite of the deliberators' recommendation. Another problem that may arise is that deliberative polls and citizen juries normally require that well-defined boundaries can be drawn around issues. Sometimes they can (for example, when it comes to a constitutional question such as the Australian transition from monarchy to presidency), but for some issues, there will be a variety of important interactions across issues (for example, concerning issues of free trade and capital mobility, which have major ramifications for environmental affairs and social justice).

Nondemocratic ways of restricting the number of participants in deliberation also merit attention. Consider in this light how Rawls specifies deliberative practice in terms of the exercise of public reason, a standard for the substantive content of arguments, which have to be framed in terms that can be accepted by all, thus excluding self-interest and partial perspectives.[16] Public reason for Rawls is singular and universal: its terms are identical for all, and all individuals who exercise it will reach the same conclusions. Public reason is defined by a body of principles that people must accept before they enter a political setting, not what they will be prompted to discover after they have entered the public arena.[17] Thus, any reflective individual can reach the correct conclusions, and so all that is really needed is one individual to deliberate about its content—an obvious solution to the problem presented by large scale. If some people are better able to reflect than others, perhaps political philosophers and legal theorists, then they should be the ones to whom society entrusts public reason. This perhaps helps to explain Rawls's own enthusiasm for the U.S. Supreme Court.[18]

Restriction of numbers of deliberators along Rawlsian lines means that public reason does not have to be tested in political interaction, and there is in fact no reason why it should be so tested. Political venues for deliberation, be they courts or legislatures (Rawls's favorite places), function so as to provide opportunity for expression; in this light, there is nothing interactive about them that induces proper public reason. Rawls is a deliberative theorist, but not a deliberative democrat, his own self-description notwithstanding.[19] The Supreme Court is a deliberative institution, but not really an interactive one, and most certainly not a democratic one. The problem of legitimation arises still more acutely for such nondemocratic deliberation than for deliberation on the part of the representatives. Institutions such as the Supreme Court can only contribute to legitimacy to the extent that the public accepts that public reason is indeed singular and that professional experts in the exercise of public reason do indeed know best.

A third solution to the challenge of deliberative economy is advanced by Robert Goodin, who wants those who do participate in proceedings to call to mind the interests of those who do not participate.[20] Thus, those who cannot or choose not to participate still have their interests entered into deliberation—but it is "internal-individual" deliberation as cogitation, within the minds of those who do participate. This sort of deliberation resembles Rawlsian public reason, at least inasmuch as deliberation is seen mainly as a matter of personal cogitation in light of public concerns, not as a social or interactive process.

This kind of partial substitution of internal-individual deliberation for real interaction is advocated in a somewhat different context by Robyn Eckersley, whose concern is with extending deliberation to a "community of the affected" that encompasses future generations and the nonhuman world.[21] Given that there is no conceivable way that future persons or nonhumans can give literal voice to their concerns, they can only be made virtually present in deliberations.[22] One could also imagine this sort of presence being used in connection with the extension of deliberative democracy across national boundaries as proposed by Thompson, who wants participants in decision making in state structures to be induced to internalize the interests of those residing in other states. (Thompson himself does not advocate internal-individual deliberation but rather representative devices such as a "tribune for non-citizens."[23])

Goodin's solution in fact presupposes that we have already restricted the number of deliberators. Given the criticisms he levels at selection by lot, in contrast with the free passage he grants more conventional representation, he appears to have the latter in mind. But in specifying a key role for "deliberation within," Goodin intensifies the legitimation problem for elected representatives. For he is asking members of the broader public to take it on trust that the deliberators really are calling to mind and internalizing broader sets of interests. At least in the case of the Supreme Court, a public record (or at least rationalization) of internal-individual deliberation is supplied, against which members of the public could, if so inclined, check the justices' version of public reason against their own. Goodin hints at no such check.

Having surveyed three available solutions to the problem of deliberative economy, my own view is that it is deliberation on the part of representatives selected by lot that presents the fewest problems for democratic legitimacy. But even here, substantial legitimation problems remain when it comes to persuading those who did not participate that their reflective opinions would in fact be the same as those who did deliberate, despite likely surface evidence to the contrary. Reacting to the results of the recent Australian deliberative poll on monarchy versus republic, one of the leaders of the "real republic" faction urging a "no" vote to the model of the republic on offer dismissed the deliberative poll as an exercise in "push-polling."²⁴ There are also issues of practicality, if we try to assemble such bodies on more than a few issues.

A fourth solution can be discerned in Jürgen Habermas's "two-track" account of deliberation in the public sphere and in the legislature, designed with contemporary complex and plural societies in mind²⁵ (unlike his earlier exemplar, the more direct and personal communication that defined the far simpler early bourgeois public sphere).²⁶ Legitimacy is secured by public acceptance of the procedures through which lawmaking achieves responsiveness to public opinion as formed in a broader public sphere. Public opinion is converted into communicative power as a result of the electoral process, then into administrative power via lawmaking. The problem of deliberative economy is solved because only a small number of legislators need to deliberate about the content of law.

In terms of the need to secure legitimacy while respecting the constraint of economy, the two-track model is inadequate for a number of reasons. First, it is a bit ambiguous about extra-constitutional agents of influence. There are times when Habermas remembers the myriad ways public opinion can affect state action without necessary reference to election,²⁷ other times when elections are central.²⁸ But he ignores the fact that public opinion can affect state action without reference to the legislature. For administration itself is political, sometimes even deliberative and responsive to public opinion, not necessarily the mechanical servant of the legislature. Later, I will argue that such extra-constitutional influences can be drawn into the service of legitimacy. Second, Habermas's stress on elections plays into the hands of social choice theorists such as William Riker and his followers who argue that the popular will has no content independent of the voting system used to measure it.²⁹ But the most serious flaw in the model is its unremitting proceduralism: Habermas gives no way to determine what the content of public opinion actually is on an issue. As I have noted, legitimacy for Habermas is secured by public acceptance of *procedural* responsiveness, not by the actual responsiveness of pieces of legislation to the substance of public opinion on an issue. Thus, it remains unclear what exactly it is that particular deliberations in the legislature are supposed to be responsive to (especially once we recognize that elections cannot easily answer this question). If the answer to this question is opaque to observers, it will be equally opaque to legislators and to actors within the public sphere. I will attempt to remedy these deficiencies.³⁰

## Deliberation as the Contestation of Discourses

Rather than wrestle further with the issue of legitimation in the context of these ultimately ineffective responses to the challenge of deliberative economy, let me suggest that the best way forward here involves detaching the idea of legitimacy from a head count of (real or imaginary) reflectively consenting individuals. Such a move might on the face of it seem to involve rejection of both the very idea of legitimation and of deliberative democracy itself. But on closer inspection, all it will prove to require is thinking in a slightly different direction about the entities that populate the political world—not all of which need to be reduced to individuals. My approach builds on a conception of discursive democracy that emphasizes the contestation of discourses in the public sphere.[31]

Deliberative democrats influenced by Habermas have long emphasized the public sphere as perhaps the most important location for deliberative politics.[32] Habermas himself now speaks of dispersed "subjectless communication" that generates public opinion.[33] Similarly, Benhabib speaks of an "anonymous public conversation" in "interlocking and overlapping networks and associations of deliberation, contestation, and argumentation."[34]

To give more substance to the idea of diffuse deliberation in the public sphere than the rather imprecise and intangible formulations of Habermas and Benhabib, I suggest we recognize that the public sphere is at any time home to constellations of discourses. A discourse may be defined in un-Habermasian terms as a shared way of comprehending the world embedded in language. In this sense, a discourse will always feature particular assumptions, judgments, contentions, dispositions, and capabilities. These common terms mean that adherents of a given discourse will be able to recognize and process sensory inputs into coherent stories or accounts, which in turn can be shared in intersubjectively meaningful fashion. Accordingly, any discourse will have at its center a story line, which may involve opinions about both facts and values.

Consider, for example, the area of criminal justice, which is currently home to at least three competing discourses. One treats crime as a matter of rational calculation on the part of potential lawbreakers; the story line is one of fully competent individuals weighing in their minds the expected subjective benefit of the crime against the probability of being caught and the severity of the punishment. A second emphasizes instead the circumstances of poverty and deprivation that cause individuals in desperation to commit criminal acts. A third emphasizes the psychopathology of criminals. Each discourse has at its heart a different model of the (criminal) human being, his or her capacity for autonomous agency, and likely motivations. Each is also entwined with values about what constitutes normal, criminal, and deviant behavior and about what kind of punishment or treatment is desirable. Each can be backed or undermined by empirical studies that are unlikely to convince adherents of different discourses. Each is entwined with ideological positions taken by politicians. The content of public policy at any time and place depends crucially on the relative weight of these discourses. Other contemporary examples of particularly powerful discourses would include market liberalism (arguably the dominant policy discourse of our time); sustainable development, which since the mid-1980s has dominated global environmental affairs; and various feminisms.

Now, followers of Michel Foucault often treat discourses as power/knowledge formations that condition—to the extent of imprisoning—human subjects. If so, then, it is hard to be a Foucauldian *and* a deliberative democrat because deliberation across discourses is hard to imagine. Still, I think it is useful to begin with a very loosely Foucauldian conception of discourses while recognizing that reflective choice across discourses is indeed possible (and this is where deliberation can come in). Foucault leaned closer to acceptance of this possibility toward the end of his life. Pierre Bourdieu speaks of a "discursive field" that actors, who may be in opposition to one another, can occupy.[35] The contours of this field limit the positions that actors can take, but the structure of the field is itself a result of their actions, interactions, and contestations. And though they do not use the "discourse" terminology, the notion of a reflexive modernity as advanced by Ulrich Beck and Anthony Giddens suggests that choices across discourses become increasingly possible and likely with the "de-traditionalization" of society.[36] The traditions that can be called into question include those that once took economic growth and technological change as inevitable and benign, as well as older traditions of deference and religious authority. Indeed, for Beck, the possibility of such choices becomes the defining feature of modernity proper (as opposed to the semi-modernity of industrial society). Which ought to augur well for the prospects for deliberative democracy.

Elsewhere I argue for a conception of discursive democracy in terms of the contestation of discourses in the public sphere on the grounds that it constitutes the only effective reply to two sets of critics of deliberation.[37] The first set is composed of social choice theorists inspired by Riker, who argue that the very conditions of structurelessness favored by deliberative democrats are exactly the conditions most conducive to arbitrariness, instability, and manipulation in collective choice.[38] This critique has force so long as deliberation is a prelude to aggregation of opinion, usually by voting. However, if we reconceptualize public opinion in terms of the provisional outcome of the contestation of discourses as transmitted to the state, the Riker-inspired critique dissolves. Such transmission from the public sphere can come about through a number of means. These include the deployment of rhetoric, through alteration of the terms of political discourse in ways that come to change the understandings of state actors (as Habermas puts it, "Communicative power is exercised in the manner of a siege. It influences the premises of judgment and decision making in the political system without intending to conquer the system itself."),[39] through creating worries about political instability, and sometimes even through arguments being heard by public officials. In short, there are many nonelectoral and nonvoting avenues of influence that bypass the social choice critique (in this light, it is hard to see why Habermas becomes so insistent in stressing elections as the main channel of influence from the public sphere to the state).[40]

Now, this respecification of discursive democracy and public opinion is not the only way to reply to the social choice critique (for example, David

Miller argues that social choice theory highlights some problems that deliberation can solve by disaggregating the dimensions of collective choice).[41] However, it has the benefit of also responding to a set of critics who arrive from precisely the opposite direction: difference democrats who charge deliberative democrats with perpetuating an exclusive gentlemen's club.[42] Where social choice theorists fear unmanageable diversity, difference democrats see stifling uniformity, under which deliberation is dominated by well-educated white males well versed in the niceties of rational argument. In this light, seemingly neutral deliberative procedures are systematically biased precisely because they traffic in unitary notions of public reason.

Taking difference seriously means attending to different identities and the different kinds of communication that accompany them, refusing to erase them in the name of a unitary public reason. This does not mean that "any thing goes" in terms of the kinds of communication that deliberative democrats ought to welcome, as well as argument. Many forms of communication can be welcomed (including gossip, jokes, performances) provided they are (1) capable of inducing reflection, (2) noncoercive, and (3) capable of connecting the particular experience of an individual, group, or category with some more general principle.[43]

Identity differences should not be allowed to warrant a relativism in which deliberation is impossible and identities are only asserted dogmatically (as feared, for example, by William Connolly).[44] Rather, we should remember that any identity is tightly bound up with a discourse. The possibility for deliberation is retained to the extent that reflective interchange is possible across the boundaries of different discourses—which, I would argue once again, is the defining feature of a reflexive modernity.

Deliberation as the contestation of discourses in the public sphere remains faithful to the core idea of deliberative democracy, which, as I noted at the outset, is that claims on behalf of or opposing collective decisions require justification to those subject to these decisions in terms that, on reflection, these individuals can accept. At the same time, conceiving of deliberation as the contestation of discourses enables effective response to the criticisms leveled by social choice theorists and difference democrats. Let me now try to make the connection to legitimation in a way that respects the constraint of deliberative economy.

## Discursive Legitimacy

Let me define *discursive legitimacy* as being achieved when a collective decision is consistent with the constellation of discourses present in the public sphere, in the degree to which this constellation is subject to the reflective control of competent actors. This conception accompanies a definition of *public opinion* as the provisional outcome of the contestation of discourses in the public sphere as transmitted to the state (or transnational authority).

Clearly, it is impossible for any decision fully to meet the claims of all competing discourses. That would only be possible if one could envisage consensus in collective choice, defined as agreement on both a course of action and the reasons for it. In a world of competing discourses, one can imagine such consensus only if the discourses were themselves either merged or dissolved—a prospect that is both unlikely and undesirable, inasmuch as it would erase the differences that make deliberation both possible and necessary. The ideal of consensus has long been rejected by most deliberative democrats, even those sympathetic to the Habermasian tradition where consensus once played a central role in the counterfactual standard of the ideal speech situation,[45] though their opponents have not always noticed. Workable agreements (or what Cass Sunstein calls "incompletely theorized agreements") in which assent can be secured for courses of action for different reasons are far more plausible.[46] Such agreements will vary in their degree of resonance with the prevailing constellation of discourses. More resonance means more discursive legitimacy.

How can this degree of resonance be ascertained? This issue can be unpacked into three questions. First, what discourses exist? Second, what is their relative weight? Third, are collective decisions consistent with this relative weight? The first question can be answered using empirical discourse analysis; qualitative and quantitative methods are available.[47] The second question is trickier. One might, for example, administer a sample survey with items informed by the results of discourse analysis,[48] but that would indicate only the percentage of the citizenry evidencing support for a discourse, not the depth or political significance of that support. The third question is easy once the first two have been answered, requiring only an examination of the content of public policy and other collective outcomes for consistency with the relative weight of discourses. So, for example, Maarten Hajer shows that environmental policy in the Netherlands features a disjuncture between a "Chamber of Concern" dominated by apocalyptic discourse accepting environmental crisis and a "Chamber of Regulation" where economic feasibility determines the content of policy.[49]

The availability of such procedures shows that tangible and measurable phenomena are at issue. The problem is that as presented, they substitute social science for democratic process, though in this respect they are no worse than ordinary opinion surveys and can be seen as just external checks on the operation of democracy. There is no reason why political actors cannot make corresponding tacit judgments. Gross violations of consistency at least may be easy to detect (for example, the imposition of a poll tax by Margaret Thatcher's government in the United Kingdom in 1990 that met with massive public protest). But one might say the same about elections as highlighted in more conventional models of democracy. Elections can register the massive and obvious in public opinion but cannot otherwise represent the popular will (again, as social choice theorists make clear).

Any possibilities for reasoned agreement resonating with the prevailing constellation of discourses notwithstanding, there will inevitably be times when particular discourses lose in the contest for influence. Those attuned to an individualistic ontology would probably ask why partisans of losing discourses should accept outcomes.[50] For surely, these individualists would say, we still have to ask this question because discourses as supra-individual entities are not in a position to confer or withdraw legitimacy, because they lack agency. The resonance of discourses with collective outcomes is something that can be discerned by an observer but not felt by discourses—because discourses cannot feel.

It is important here to resist reducing discourses to an individualistic ontology in such fashion because though discourses do not possess agency, they do possess the capacity to underwrite or destabilize collective outcomes—which, from the point of view of legitimacy, is the most important aspect of agency to begin with.[51] This resistance to reductionism does not mean that reflecting individuals need to be purged from the account. It is simply to imply that these individuals are not required to pass competent judgement on every collective outcome to which they are subject (this would of course run headlong into the economy constraint). They can, however, still engage the contestation of discourses as they see fit.

Indeed, it is important that such engagement be possible. For particular discourses might of course be slaves to tradition or religion or subject to manipulation by spin doctors, advertisers, and propagandists. Such is the very antithesis of deliberative democracy. Crucially, then, the constellation of discourses must itself be open to dispersed and communicatively competent popular control—which returns us to the idea of a reflexive modernity. (I will return to ways such control can be exercised shortly).

Having established what discursive legitimacy means, all that now remains to be shown is how it meets the constraint of deliberative economy. To restate the challenge: deliberative democracy requires that for a collective decision to be legitimate, it must be subject to the reflective acceptance of those subject to it, who should be able to participate in deliberation concerning the production of the decision. But reflective acceptance must be attained in a way that does not impose impossible burdens on the deliberative capacities of individuals or polity. As I have noted, the most plausible existing approaches respond to the challenge by somehow restricting the number of participants.

The approach I propose here solves the problem because the number of participants in deliberation is indeterminate. That is, it does not *require* any exclusions—not even exclusions based on not being selected at random for a citizen's jury, or not being elected to parliament, or on apathy, or on a choice not to exercise deliberative citizenship rights. At any given time, the contestation of discourses can be engaged by the many or the few, or indeed by none. Typically, that number will fluctuate widely over time for any given issue area; think, for example, of the upsurges in environmental concern in most developed countries around 1970 and again around 1990. Such upsurges might lead to dramatic shifts in the prevailing balance of discourses—which might then remain settled for a while and receive less public attention. Who can engage such contestation? Pretty much everybody; for the contestation of discourses overlaps with cultural change. Think, for example, of the life and times of feminism over the past three decades in its contest with patriarchy or environmentalism's rise in a (continuing) contest with industrialism. These discursive advances cannot just be measured in terms of legislation or policy decisions but also in everyday practice, in challenges made and resisted in households, in workplaces, in classrooms, and elsewhere (relatedly, Jane Mansbridge speaks of the role of "everyday talk" in the "deliberative system").[52]

This indeterminacy in numbers of participants in the contestation of discourses solves the seemingly incompatible demands of deliberative economy and the need for collective decisions to secure actual popular reflective acceptance. A Schumpeterian might argue here that all that has been done is to substitute packages in the form of discourses for individuals—paralleling the way Schumpeterians substitute the platforms of competing party elites for the will of the people. But there is a crucial difference, because Schumpeterians require that ordinary people do no more than vote and then sleep between elections. In contrast, discursive contestation can accept, even welcome, the participation of the many at any time. Moreover, party platforms are crafted by elites, whereas discourses can be made and remade by anybody.

My argument does not imply that the deliberative democrat can sit back and accept society's prevailing constellation of discourses, their changes over time, and the many ways in which these discourses can pervade policy making. There are still insistently critical roles to be played. First, deliberative democrats can expose occasions where state imperatives (related, for example, to the need to maintain the confidence of financial markets) override the constellation of discourses in determining the content of public policy.[53] Second, they can expose the degree to which popular discourses themselves are ideological (in the pejorative sense of specifying false necessities, perhaps even the necessity of always having to please financial markets; discourses are inescapably ideological in a more neutral sense of "ideology"). Third, they can criticize the degree to which the contestation of discourses is manipulated by strategy and power and not subject to reflexive control.

Democratic theorists can also think about ways in which that contestation can be subjected to more in the way of dispersed and competent democratic control. Let me illustrate with just one such way.

The role that networks can play in the public sphere has recently been investigated by David Schlosberg in a study of the U.S. environmental justice movement.[54] A network begins from the bottom up and is especially interesting from the point of view of the contestation of discourses when it brings together actors with quite different backgrounds. Such is certainly the case for the U.S. environmental justice movement. This began in 1978 in Love Canal, where working-class whites were upset at the toxic chemicals found buried beneath their homes—one of whom, Lois Gibbs, became a key figure in the development of the network. The movement grew to encompass groups from very different racial, ethnic, and class backgrounds and very different kinds of experiences—though of course they share the experience of exposure and resistance to environmental hazards. Networks of this sort can also extend across national boundaries—as is the case for international networks concerned with, for example, biopiracy, pollution from oil refineries, or landmines. With the possible exception of an informational clearing house (the most famous of which is perhaps the Citizen's Clearinghouse for Hazardous Waste, which in 1997 changed its name to the Center for Health, Environment and Justice), a network does not have any central organization, still less an organizational hierarchy.

From the point of view of the democratic contestation of discourses in the public sphere, networks are especially interesting because, to the degree they engage truly diverse participants, networks just have to work according to principles of equality, openness, respect, and reciprocity—the standard deliberative virtues. These principles do not just happen to describe particular networks; they are necessary for the network form. There is no centralized hierarchy or leadership promulgating goals, norms, and strategies to bring diverse participants into line. The norms that a network develops can, however, sometimes be formalized as constitutive principles.[55]

Networks do engage in discursive contests, but the positions they take grow out of the experiences of network participants. For example, the very concept of environmental justice emerges from what began as a collection of local anti-toxics struggles. The idea that environmental risks are systematically maldistributed across lines of race, ethnicity, and class came later, the product of a variety of local but eventually interconnected experiences. The discourse of environmental justice could then contest, engage, and change other kinds of environmentalism—as well as join them in a larger contest against the discourse of industrialism.

To return to the issue of legitimacy, environmental justice joins other discourses in pressing claims on collective decisions. It would be an oversimplification to say that a collective decision in environmental affairs is legitimate only to the degree of its consistency with the discourse of environmental justice. As I said earlier, no decision can ever fully meet the claims of all competing discourses, for consensus is in reality neither possible nor desirable. Workable agreements that can secure assent for different reasons are more plausible. Discursive legitimacy is achieved to the extent of the resonance of such an agreement with the prevailing constellation of discourses in the degree to which this constellation is subject to dispersed and competent control—to which networks in the public sphere can contribute.

What conditions are conducive to this sort of popular control? The difficulty here is that a public sphere is not a formal institution and so cannot be designed. In Habermas's terms, it is "a 'wild' complex that resists organization as a whole."[56] Networks, in particular, can only arise from the bottom up if they are to have the discursive qualities I have described. Yet public spheres take shape in relation to other authority structures that can be designed or at least reconstituted at the margins. Foremost among these is the state. The discursive vitality of the public sphere is facilitated by a state that is passively exclusive in the form of interest representation it allows.[57] The Federal Republic of Germany from the 1950s to the 1980s exemplifies this sort of state, featuring as it did tripartite corporatism (government, business, and labor) and a legalistic, unitary conception of the public interest in administration and law. Social movements flourished precisely because they were excluded from but not undermined by the state. Actively exclusive states (such as Thatcher's Britain in the 1980s) undermine the conditions of association in public spheres. Actively inclusive states (for example, Norway) have no public sphere with any distance from the state. And passively inclusive states (for example, the United States) convert public spheres into interest groups (though, as the environmental justice example suggests, such conversion can be resisted, at least temporarily).

## Conclusion

Democracy does not have to be a matter of counting heads—even deliberating heads. Nor does it have to be confined to the formal institutions of state or the constitutional surface of political life. Accepting such confinement means accepting a needlessly thin conception of democracy and a needlessly tenuous account of deliberative legitimacy. I have argued here that legitimacy can be sought instead in the resonance of collective decisions with public opinion, defined in terms of the provisional outcome of the contestation of discourses in the public sphere as transmitted to the state or other authorities (such as transnational ones). Moreover, legitimacy can be achieved in a way that meets the basic constraint of deliberative economy. But we should speak of *discursive* legitimacy only to the extent that contestation can be engaged by a broad variety of competent actors. Unlike other approaches to deliberative legitimacy, in the end it does not matter whether at any one time the number of such actors is large or small.

## Notes

1 Joshua Cohen, "Deliberation and Democratic Legitimacy," in *The Good Polity: Normative Analysis of the State,* ed. Alan Hamlin and Philip Pettit (Oxford, UK: Basil Blackwell, 1989), 17-34. See also Bernard Manin, "On Legitimacy and Political Deliberation," *Political Theory* 15 (1987): 338-68.
2 Seyla Benhabib, "Toward a Deliberative Model of Democratic Legitimacy," in *Democracy and Difference: Contesting the Boundaries of the Political,* ed. Seyla Benhabib (Princeton, NJ: Princeton University Press, 1996), 67-94 at 68.
3 See, for example, Amy Gutmann and Dennis Thompson, *Democracy and Disagreement* (Cambridge, MA: Harvard University Press, 1996), 144.
4 Ian Shapiro, "Enough of Deliberation: Politics Is About Interest and Power," in *Deliberative Politics: Essays on Democracy and Disagreement,* ed. Stephen Macedo (New York: Oxford University Press, 1999), 28-38 at 33.

5   Cohen, "Deliberation and Democratic Legitimacy," 22.
6   Manin, "On Legitimacy and Political Deliberation," 352.
7   Defenders of the approach to deliberative legitimacy taken by authors such as Benhabib, Cohen, and Manin might say they are simply presenting a counterfactual ideal through reference to which various practical proposals can be evaluated. But the ideal is so far from any plausible real-world proposals that it has little ability to sort them.
8   Robert A. Dahl, *After the Revolution?* (New Haven, CT: Yale University Press, 1970).
9   Michael Walzer, "Deliberation, and What Else?" in *Deliberative Politics: Essays on Democracy and Disagreement*, ed. Stephen Macedo (New York: Oxford University Press, 1999), 58-69 at 68.
10  Not to be confused with Gutmann and Thompson's proposed "economy of moral disagreement," which refers to the idea that deliberators who disagree on fundamental matters should nevertheless seek to identify points where they can agree. See Gutmann and Thompson, *Democracy and Disagreement*.
11  John Rawls, *Political Liberalism* (New York: Columbia University Press, 1993).
12  Bruce Ackerman, *We the People I: Foundations* (Cambridge, MA: Harvard University Press, 1991).
13  For example, Joseph M. Bessette, *The Mild Voice of Reason: Deliberative Democracy and American National Government* (Chicago: University of Chicago Press, 1994); Cass Sustein, "Deliberation, Democracy, Disagreement," in *Justice and Democracy: Cross-Cultural Perspectives*, ed. Ron Bontekoe and Marieta Stepaniants (Honolulu: University of Hawai'i Press, 1997), 93-117 at 94.
14  James Fishkin, *Democracy and Deliberation: New Directions for Democratic Reform* (New Haven, CT: Yale University Press, 1991); James Fishkin, *The Voice of the People: Public Opinion and Democracy* (New Haven, CT: Yale University Press, 1995); Robert A. Dahl, *Controlling Nuclear Weapons* (Syracuse, NY: Syracuse University Press, 1985); John Burnheim, *Is Democracy Possible?* (Cambridge, UK: Polity, 1985).
15  Lynn Sanders, "Poll Envy: An Assessment of Deliberative Polling," *The Good Society* 9, no. 1 (1999): 9-14.
16  Rawls, *Political Liberalism*; John Rawls, "The Idea of Public Reason Revisited," *University of Chicago Law Review* 94 (1997): 765-807.
17  See Benhabib, "Toward a Deliberative Model," 75.
18  Rawls, *Political Liberalism*, 231.
19  Rawls, "The Idea of Public Reason," 771-2.
20  Robert E. Goodin, "Democratic Deliberation Within," *Philosophy and Public Affairs* 29 (2000): 81-109.
21  Robyn Eckersley, "Deliberative Democracy, Ecological Risk, and 'Communities-of-Fate,'" in *Democratic Innovation: Deliberation, Association, and Representation*, ed. Michael Saward (London: Routledge, 2000).
22  For an argument that communications from nonhuman entities can be received by deliberators, see John S. Dryzek, "Political and Ecological Communication," *Environmental Politics* 4 (1995): 13-30.
23  Dennis Thompson, "Democratic Theory and Global Society," *Journal of Political Philosophy* 7 (1999): 111-25 at 122.
24  Phil Cleary, quoted in *The Age* (Melbourne), October 25, 1999, 1. Push-polling is a marketing tactic where interviewees are asked leading questions and given biased information to induce them to buy a product—or support a position or candidate.

25  Jürgen Habermas, *Between Facts and Norms: Contributions to a Discourse Theory of Law and Democracy* (Cambridge, MA: MIT Press, 1996).
26  Jürgen Habermas, *Structural Transformation of the Public Sphere: An Inquiry into a Category of Bourgeois Society* (Cambridge, MA: MIT Press, 1989).
27  For example, Habermas, *Between Facts and Norms*, 185, 308.
28  See especially Jürgen Habermas, "Three Normative Models of Democracy," in *Democracy and Difference: Contesting the Boundaries of the Political*, ed. Seyla Benhabib (Princeton, NJ: Princeton University Press, 1996), 21-30 at 28. See also Habermas, *Between Facts and Norms*, 368, 381.
29  William H. Riker, *Liberalism against Populism: A Confrontation between the Theory of Democracy and the Theory of Social Choice* (San Francisco: Freeman, 1982).
30  Other problems arise in applying the model to the real world that is supposedly its justification. Habermas recognizes but does not develop an adequate response to some serious constraints on lawmaking and policy making that do not emanate from and can override public opinion. These anti-democratic constraints include the pervasive political influence of money and corporate power and the policy imperatives dictated by the need to please financial markets and avoid disinvestment or capital flight. At a potentially high cost to his theory, at one point he suggests that the public sphere is more vulnerable to such distortions than is the legislature; see *Between Facts and Norms*, 307-8.
31  John S. Dryzek, *Deliberative Democracy and Beyond: Liberals, Critics, Contestations* (Oxford, UK: Oxford University Press, 2000). The terms *deliberative democracy* and *discursive democracy* are now used interchangeably and *deliberative democracy* more often. However, I believe it useful to recover the idea of discursive as a critical subcategory of deliberative democracy. When it comes to contestation, Fraser too speaks of contestation in the public sphere, though engaged by publics rather than discourses. Specifically, contestation for Fraser characterizes the orientation of "subaltern counterpublics" to dominant power structures. She treats contestation as an alternative to deliberation, rather than a category of deliberation. See Nancy Fraser, "Rethinking the Public Sphere: A Contribution to the Critique of Actually Existing Democracy," in *Habermas and the Public Sphere*, ed. Craig Calhoun (Cambridge, MA: MIT Press, 1992), 109-42.
32  For example, Benhabib, "Toward a Model of Democratic Legitimacy," James Bohman, *Public Deliberation: Pluralism, Complexity, and Democracy* (Cambridge, MA: MIT Press, 1996); John S. Dryzek, *Discursive Democracy: Politics, Policy, and Political Science* (New York: Cambridge University Press, 1990).
33  Habermas, *Between Facts and Norms*, 486.
34  Benhabib, "Toward a Model of Democratic Legitimacy," 74.
35  Pierre Bourdieu, *The Field of Cultural Production* (Cambridge, UK: Polity, 1993).
36  See, for example, Ulrich Beck, Anthony Giddens, and Scott Lash, *Reflexive Modernization: Politics, Tradition and Aesthetics in the Modern Social Order* (Cambridge, UK: Polity, 1994).
37  Dryzek, *Deliberative Democracy and Beyond*.
38  For example, David van Mill, "The Possibility of Rational Outcomes from Democratic Discourse and Procedures," *Journal of Politics* 58 (1996): 734-52.
39  Habermas, *Between Facts and Norms*, 486.
40  Habermas, *Between Facts and Norms*; Habermas, "Three Normative Models."
41  David Miller, "Deliberative Democracy and Social Choice," *Political Studies* 40 (special issue): 54-67.
42  For example, Iris Marion Young, "Communication and the Other: Beyond Deliberative Democracy," in *Democracy and Difference: Contesting the Boundaries*

*of the Political*, ed. Seyla Behabib (Princeton, NJ: Princeton University Press, 1996), 120-35; Iris Marion Young, "Inclusive Political Communication: Greeting, Rhetoric and Storytelling in the Context of Political Argument" (paper presented at the annual meeting of the American Political Science Association, Boston, September 1998); Lynn Sanders, "Against Deliberation," *Political Theory* 25 (1997): 347-76. Similar concerns were raised by Jane Mansbridge, "Feminism and Democracy," *American Prospect* 1 (1990).

43 Dryzek, *Deliberative Democracy and Beyond*, 68. On applying the third of these tests to testimony, see also David Miller, "Is Deliberative Democracy Unfair to Disadvantaged Minorities?" (unpublished paper, Nuffield College, Oxford, 1999).

44 William E. Connolly, *Identity/Difference: Democratic Negotiations of Political Paradox* (Ithaca, NY: Cornell University Press, 1991).

45 See, for example, Seyla Benhabib, "Communicative Ethics and Contemporary Controversies in Practical Philosophy," in *The Communicative Ethics Controversy*, ed. Seyla Benhabib and Fred Dallmayr (Cambridge, MA: MIT Press, 1990); James Bohman, "Public Reason and Cultural Pluralism: Political Liberalism and the Problem of Moral Conflict," *Political Theory* 23 (1995): 253-79; Dryzek, *Discursive Democracy*, 16-17; Carol Gould, *Rethinking Democracy* (Cambridge, UK: Cambridge University Press, 1988), 18, 126-7; Gerry Mackie, "Models of Democratic Deliberation" (paper presented at the annual meeting of the American Political Science Association, Chicago, September 1995).

46 Sunstein, "Deliberation, Democracy, Disagreement."

47 For a qualitative approach, see Maarten Hajer, *The Politics of Environmental Discourse: Ecological Modernization and the Policy Process* (Oxford, UK: Oxford University Press, 1995). For a quantitative method, see John S. Dryzek and Jeffrey Berejikian, "Reconstructive Democratic Theory," *American Political Science Review* 87 (1993): 48-60.

48 Elizabeth Theiss-Morse, Amy Fried, John L. Sullivan, and Mary Dietz, "Mixing Methods; A Multi-Stage Strategy for Studying Patriotism and Citizen Participation," *Political Analysis* 3 (1992): 89-122.

49 Hajer, *The Politics of Environmental Discourse*, 269.

50 In standard individualistic accounts of democracy, legitimacy is granted to collective outcomes by people who disagree with them either as a result of instrumental calculation that they have a good chance of winning at some future point under the prevailing system of rules or through recognition that procedures were transparent and fair. The latter principles can be applied in a deliberative context. As Cohen puts it, "Because the members of a democratic association regard deliberative procedures as the source of *legitimacy*, it is important to them that the terms of their association not merely *be* the results of their deliberation, but that it be *manifest* to them as such" (Cohen, "Deliberation and Democratic Legitimacy," 21).

51 An additional reason why an individualistic ontology is inappropriate is that discourses are not like parties or clubs or groups, for they do not have members and so are not reducible to a well-defined set of members. It is quite possible for any individual to have simultaneous leanings toward multiple, perhaps incompatible, discourses. Or, to put it another way, subjectivity can be multidimensional. See Jon Elster, ed., *The Multiple Self* (Cambridge, UK: Cambridge University Press, 1986). For example, part of me may subscribe to a radical green critique of industrial society; another part of me may evaluate government according to how well it is promoting economic growth and a positive investment climate. Different (discursive) situations may invoke these different

aspects of subjectivity, which can be latent or manifest at any given time or indeed not exist until the situation is such as to invoke the aspect in question.

52 Jane Mansbridge, "Everyday Talk in the Deliberative System," in *Deliberative Politics: Essays on Democracy and Disagreement*, ed. Stephen Macedo (New York: Oxford University Press, 1999), 211-38.
53 See, for example, John S. Dryzek, *Democracy in Capitalist Times: Ideals, Limits, and Struggle* (New York: Oxford University Press, 1996).
54 David Schlosberg, *Environmental Justice and the New Pluralism: The Challenge of Difference for Environmentalism* (Oxford, UK: Oxford University Press, 1999). See also Douglas Torgerson, *The Promise of Green Politics: Environmentalism and the Public Sphere* (Durham, NC: Duke University Press, 1999), 148-54.
55 For an example from the Southwest Network for Environmental and Economic Justice in the USA, see Schlosberg, *Environmental Justice*, 128.
56 Habermas, *Between Facts and Norms*, 307.
57 Dryzek, *Democracy in Capitalist Times*, 64-70.

# Part Seven: Multiculturalism

# Introduction

In recent years 'multiculturalism' has emerged as a distinct and yet varied political theory. While there is no consensus among multiculturalists concerning the principles, goals and policies they believe best promote multiculturalism, what unites these theorists is their concern that we should resist the wider society's homogenising or assimilationist thrust and its tendency to assume that there is only one correct, true or normal way to understand and structure the relevant areas of life (Parekh, 2000: 1). This assimilationist thrust is evident in the conception of citizenship implicit in the justice theories of egalitarian-liberals and libertarians. Despite the differences between the liberalisms of the distributive paradigm, what they share is the belief that justice requires *equal rights* for all citizens. Rawls, Nozick, Gauthier and Dworkin, for example, may disagree on what the foundation of the rights they defend are (for example, intuitions about impartiality and fairness, self-interest, etc.), but they agree that whatever rights justice does require these rights should apply equally to all citizens, regardless of their gender, religion or ethnicity. It is unjust, for example, to exclude women or Catholics or African Americans from exercising the rights other citizens enjoy, like freedom of expression and the right to vote. As Kymlicka notes, the logical conclusion of liberal principles of justice 'seems to be a "colour-blind" constitution – the removal of all legislation differentiating people in terms of their race or ethnicity (except for temporary measures, like affirmative action, which are believed necessary to reach a colour-blind society)' (Kymlicka, 1989: 141). But multiculturalists view the aspiration for a colour-blind society as ill-founded for it is not possible to separate, for example, the state and ethnicity and when the liberal state attempts to do this it unfairly privileges certain ways of life over others.

The charge that liberalism privileges certain ways of life over others might sound misplaced given the emphasis liberals like Rawls place on the fact of 'reasonable pluralism'. It is precisely *because* liberals take pluralism seriously, they might retort, that they endorse a neutral public philosophy that entails equal rights for all citizens. But multiculturalists do not believe that liberals take diversity seriously enough. Bhiku Parekh argues that Rawls, like many liberals, 'is sensitive to moral but not cultural plurality, and thus takes little account of the cultural aspirations of such communities as the indigenous peoples, national minorities, subnational groups, and the immigrants (Parekh, 2000: 89). Kymlicka argues that liberals like Rawls and Dworkin have falsely assumed that members of a *political community* are members of the same *cultural community*. Kymlicka describes these two kinds of community:

> On the one hand, there is the political community, within which individuals exercise the rights and responsibilities entailed by the framework of liberal justice. People who reside within the same political community are fellow citizens. On the other hand, there is the cultural community, within which individuals form and revise their aims and ambitions. People within the same cultural community share a culture, a language and history which defines their cultural membership. (Kymlicka, 1989: 135).

Many modern democratic societies are multinational and/or polyethnic and thus the liberal assumption that members of a political community are members of the same cultural community is unfounded. Multinational societies are states that have incorporated previously self-governing cultures such as aboriginal peoples whilst polyethnic societies are states where cultural diversity arises from immigration. Canada is an example of a country that is both multinational and polyethnic. It has national minorities (for example, Aboriginals and the Quebecois) as well as a significant immigrant population. The politics of equal citizenship and economic redistribution are not fully equipped, argue multiculturalists, to deal with the diverse concerns which are raised in multinational and polyethnic states. Multiculturalists thus endorse the politics of recognition (Taylor, 1994) which inspires a public philosophy premised on the concepts of identify and difference, instead of the principle of equal citizenship. The politics of recognition does, like the politics of equal citizenship, have a universal basis but that basis is not that everyone should be treated the same. On the contrary, the politics of recognition requires that '*everyone* should be recognized for his or her unique identity… The universal demand powers an acknowledgement of specificity' (Taylor, 1994: 38–9). In the first excerpt in this part Charles Taylor offers 'an historically informed, philosophical perspective on what is at stake in the demand made by many people for recognition of their particular identities by public institutions' (Gutmann, 1994: 6).

'Multiculturalism is not about difference and identity *per se*', claims Parekh, 'but about those that are embedded in and sustained by culture; that is, a body of beliefs and practices in terms of which a group of people understand themselves and the world and organize their individual and collective lives' (Parekh, 2000: 2–3). It is useful to see the current debates about multiculturalism as an extension of the liberal/communitarian debate because multiculturalists echo the communitarian's concern that we recognise that we are social beings who are embedded in particular cultures and value different cultural practices. Parekh argues that multiculturalism occupies a middle position between two dominant strands of political theory – naturalism (or monism) and culturalism (or pluralism). The former is espoused by a diverse array of philosophers ranging from Greek and Christian philosophers to Hobbes, Locke and Mill, all of whom 'assumed that human nature was unchanging, unaffected in its essentials by culture and society, and capable of indicating what way of life was the best' (Parekh, 2000: 10). Culturalists, on the other hand, like Vico, Montesquieu, Herder, and the German Romantics, argued for the opposite view. They believed that 'human beings were culturally constituted, varied from culture to culture, and share in common only the minimal species-derived properties from which nothing of moral and political significance could be derived' (Parekh, 2000: 10). But both of these positions, argues Parekh, are deeply problematic.

> Neither naturalism nor culturalism gives a coherent account of human life and helps us theorise multicultural societies. One stresses the undeniable fact of shared humanity, but ignores the equally obvious fact that human nature is culturally mediated and reconstituted and cannot by itself provide a transcendental basis for a cross-culturally valid vision of the good life; the other makes the opposite mistake. Neither grasps the two in their relationship and appreciates that human beings are at once both natural and cultural, both like and unlike, and like in unlike ways.
> (Parekh, 2000: 11)

# Introduction

Multiculturalists share the conviction that *cultural plurality* must figure prominently in our theorising about how we ought, collectively as a society, to live together. This has led them to defend a diverse range of policies ranging from granting national minorities rights of self-government to legal protection of certain cultural practices and special representation rights.[1]

In the second excerpt in this part Parekh argues that recognition of cultural differences requires that society sometimes permit members of certain groups to do things others are prohibited from doing. For example, granting turban-wearing Sikhs exemptions from the legal requirement that drivers and passengers on motorcycles wear a helmet. These exemptions do not mean that people have unequal rights; rather, such measures show respect for the importance religious practices have for the cultural groups involved. In the United Kingdom wearing a helmet became a legal requirement for drivers and passengers on motorcycles in the early 1970s. Critics campaigned against this law claiming that it was unfair to turban-wearing Sikhs. These individuals had to make a choice that members of other religious groups did not have to make – that between adhering to their religion or travelling by motorcycle.

According to the vision of citizenship espoused by liberalism there is no inequality in this case. The helmet law is not discriminatory as it does not explicitly declare that 'Sikhs shall not ride motorcycles'. Sikhs, like all other citizens, are at risk of injury from motorcycle accidents and thus they must take the same preventive steps required of all other citizens who wish to travel by motorcycle. If anything 'prevents' a Sikh from riding a motorcycle it is his religion and not the law, the liberal might argue.[2]

The helmet law was amended in 1976 and Sikhs were exempted from wearing helmets. Multiculturalists believe this change to the law was the right thing to do. The turban met the appropriate safety standards and thus it was deemed an adequate substitute for the helmet. Since the justification for requiring motorcyclists to wear a helmet was concern for their safety, and wearing a turban also satisfied that aim, then there was no reason not to permit turban-wearing Sikhs to be exempted from the law. Such a measure is a way of accommodating cultural diversity, it locates individuals against their cultural background and shows respect for the different beliefs and practices citizens of a pluralistic society have.

Similar concerns arise in the case of humane slaughter regulations. Many countries have passed legislation requiring the humane slaughter of animals for consumption (for example, stunning the animals prior to killing them). Most western countries have exemptions from humane slaughter regulations so that Jews and Muslims can slaughter animals in accordance with traditional methods that violate the procedures for humane slaughter. Are such exemptions justified? Multiculturalists argue that such exemptions are necessary as they show respect for the importance of the religious practices of Orthodox Jews and observant Muslims. This issue is more complex than the case of exemptions from motorcycle helmets as granting an exemption in the case of the latter was seen as consistent with the aim of the legislation (i.e. safety). But in the case of humane slaughter regulations the aim is to minimise the suffering of animals and permitting ritual slaughters[3] is not consistent with that aim. Unlike the helmet law example, where the aim of public safety could be achieved by having an exemption to the rule, in the case of humane slaughter regulation we have competing aims – minimise the suffering of animals or tolerate religious practices of butchery.

Multiculturalists argue that such exemptions are a reasonable compromise between these two aims. Such a measure shows respect for the value some people place on religion. But the difficulty with this position is deciding where to draw the line. If respect for custom can override the aim of protecting animal welfare when it comes to slaughtering them then why not permit something like cockfighting? Furthermore, customs change and if one truly believes that humane slaughter regulations promote an important interest then one will not view exemptions from these regulations as a *reasonable* compromise. As Brian Barry argues, 'it is hard to see why some cows and sheep should have to suffer in ways that are unacceptable generally in order to enable people with certain religious beliefs to eat their carcasses' (Barry, 2001: 43).

Exemptions from humane slaughter regulations is a difficult issue because proponents on both sides of the debate will find it difficult, indeed maybe impossible, to 'sympathetically enter into the world of thought' (Parekh, 2000: 240) of the other. Those who are passionate about animal welfare will not comprehend why some religious groups simply cannot change their customs whilst some religious groups might find the idea of altering valued traditions for the sake of animal welfare bewildering. When value systems differ in this way it is not easy to determine what constitutes a fair compromise.

Another issue which highlights the issues at stake in the debates about multiculturalism is the *l'affaire du foulard* which occurred in France. Parekh succinctly summarises the details of this affair:

> Three Muslim girls from North Africa, two of them sisters, wore *hijab* (head scarf) to their ethnically mixed school in Creil, some 60 kms north of Paris. In the previous year 20 Jewish students had refused to attend classes on Saturday mornings and autumn Friday afternoons when the Sabbath arrived before the close of the school, and the headmaster, a black Frenchman from the Caribbean, had to give in after initially resisting them. Worried about the trend of events, he objected to the Muslim girls wearing the *hijab* in the classroom on the grounds that it went against the laicité[4] of French state schools. Since the girls refused to comply, he barred them from attending the school. As a gesture of solidarity many Muslim girls throughout France began to wear *hijabs* to school and the matter acquired national importance. (Parekh, 2000: 249)

Eventually it was ruled that pupils could wear 'discreet' religious symbols (such as the cross) but not 'ostentatious symbols which in themselves constitute elements of proselytism or discrimination' (cited in Parekh, 2000: 250) and the *hijab* was deemed to fall into this latter category and thus was banned. The Headscarves affair deeply divided the French as different positions were taken with respect to the importance of symbolic significance. As Parekh notes, the main opposition to permitting the wearing of the *hijab* was that it went against the principle of secularism which was part of the French identity. To become French one must integrate, and the school is a central mechanism by which people are assimilated into French culture. But Parekh criticises the French decision, claiming that the decision to permit the cross and other Christian symbols but not the *hijab* amounted to treating Muslim girls unequally (Parekh, 2000: 253). Furthermore, the belief that the *hijab* symbolises and reinforces female

# Introduction

subordination, which Parekh argues was popular among most secular Frenchmen and feminists, fails to 'appreciate the complex processes of social change and intercultural negotiation [the *hijab*] symbolized and triggered' (Parekh, 2000: 254). Parekh argues:

> Muslim immigrants in France, Britain and elsewhere are deeply fearful of their girls entering the public world including the school. By wearing the *hijab* their daughters seek to reassure them that they can be culturally trusted and will not be 'corrupted' by the norms and values of the school. At the same time they also reshape the semi-public world of the school and protect themselves against its pressures and temptations by subtly getting white and Muslim boys to see them differently to the way they eye white girls. The *hijab* put the girls 'out of bounds' and enables them to dictate how they wish to be treated. Traditional at one level, the *hijab* is transgressive at another, and enables Muslim girls to transform both their parental and public cultures. (Parekh, 2000: 252)

Critics of multiculturalism might seize on the Headscarves example and use it to argue against polyethnic rights on the grounds that immigrants (and even national minorities) should assimilate into the culture of the society they live in. A strong sense of unity and common belonging, they might argue, is needed to ensure peace and stability and exemptions and similar measures for religious or ethnic groups threaten that sense of unity. But multiculturalists can agree that *some* degree of integration is necessary (and desirable), the difficult questions are how much assimilation is necessary and what is the just way of achieving that assimilation.

In the second excerpt in this part Parekh defends granting special exemptions from laws like the helmet law on the grounds that such measures are necessary if society is to recognise cultural differences. In the final excerpt Chandran Kukathas argues that multiculturalism does not pose a difficult problem for liberalism because liberalism is in fact the most plausible response to the fact of moral, religious and cultural diversity. The liberal response to pluralism is not, as multiculturalist critics argue, to assimilate all citizens into a uniform and common culture, but instead to accommodate diversity and tolerate differences. Pursuing the latter means allowing people to be free to live by different cultural standards. The counsel of liberalism, argues Kukathas, is to actually resist the demand for recognition. Liberalism is not united by any kind of common culture and thus 'it is indifferent to the goals pursued by the individuals and groups in society – unless they impinge upon the peace of society – and is not concerned to promote any particular form of the common good' (Kukathas, 1998: 696).

## Notes

1   See, for example, Kymlicka (1995).
2   This argument was made by Lord Wingley. See Poulter (1998: 293)
3   Which involve bleeding animals to death while conscious instead of stunning them prior to killing them (Barry, 2001: 41).
4   Which means secularism.

## References

Barry, Brian. *Culture and Equality*. (Cambridge, Mass.: Harvard University Press, 2001).

Gutmann, Amy. 'Introduction'. In A. Gutmann (ed.), *Multiculturalism* (Princeton: Princeton University Press, 1994).

Kukathas, Chandran. 'Liberalism and Multiculturalism: The Politics of Indifference', *Political Theory*, Vol. 26(5), 1998: 686-99.

Kymlicka, Wice. *Liberalism, Community and Culture*. (Oxford: Oxford University Press, 1989).

——— *Multicultural Citizenship: A Liberal Theory of Minority Rights*. Oxford: Oxford University Press, 1995).

Parekh, Bhikhu. *Rethinking Multiculturalism: Cultural Diversity and Political Theory*. (Basingstoke: Palgrave, 2000).

Poulter, Sebastian. *Ethnicity, Law and Human Rights: the English Experience*. (Oxford: Oxford University Press, 1998).

Taylor, Charles. 'The Politics of Recognition'. In A. Gutmann (ed.), *Multiculturalism* (Princeton: Princeton University Press, 1994).

# 23 The Politics of Recognition

## Charles Taylor

A number of strands in contemporary politics turn on the need, sometimes the demand, for *recognition*. The need, it can be argued, is one of the driving forces behind nationalist movements in politics. And the demand comes to the fore in a number of ways in today's politics, on behalf of minority or "subaltern" groups, in some forms of feminism and in what is today called the politics of "multiculturalism."

The demand for recognition in these latter cases is given urgency by the supposed links between recognition and identity, where this latter term designates something like a person's understanding of who they are, of their fundamental defining characteristics as a human being. The thesis is that our identity is partly shaped by recognition or its absence, often by the *mis*-recognition of others, and so a person or group of people can suffer real damage, real distortion, if the people or society around them mirror back to them a confining or demeaning or contemptible picture of themselves. Nonrecognition or misrecognition can inflict harm, can be a form of oppression, imprisoning someone in a false, distorted, and reduced mode of being.

Thus some feminists have argued that women in patriarchal societies have been induced to adopt a depreciatory image of themselves. They have internalized a picture of their own inferiority, so that even when some of the objective obstacles to their advancement fall away, they may be incapable of taking advantage of the new opportunities. And beyond this, they are condemned to suffer the pain of low self-esteem. An analogous point has been made in relation to blacks: that white society has for generations projected a demeaning image of them, which some of them have been unable to resist adopting. Their own self-depreciation, on this view, becomes one of the most potent instruments of their own oppression. Their first task ought to be to purge themselves of this imposed and destructive identity. Recently, a similar point has been made in relation to indigenous and colonized people in general. It is held that since 1492 Europeans have projected an image of such people as somehow inferior, "uncivilized," and through the force of conquest have often been able to impose this image on the conquered. The figure of Caliban has been held to epitomize this crushing portrait of contempt of New World aboriginals.

Within these perspectives, misrecognition shows not just a lack of due respect. It can inflict a grievous wound, saddling its victims with a crippling self-hatred. Due recognition is not just a courtesy we owe people. It is a vital human need.

In order to examine some of the issues that have arisen here, I'd like to take a step back, achieve a little distance, and look first at how this discourse of recognition and identity came to seem familiar, or at least readily understandable, to us. For it was not always so, and our ancestors of more than a couple of centuries ago would have stared at us uncomprehendingly if we had used these terms in their current sense. How did we get started on this?

Hegel comes to mind right off, with his famous dialectic of the master and the slave. This is an important stage, but we need to go a little farther back to see how this passage came to have the sense it did. What changed to make this kind of talk have sense for us?

We can distinguish two changes that together have made the modern preoccupation with identity and recognition inevitable. The first is the collapse of social hierarchies, which used to be the basis for honor. I am using *honor* in the ancien régime sense in which it is intrinsically linked to inequalities. For some to have honor in this sense, it is essential that not everyone have it. This is the sense in which Montesquieu uses it in his description of monarchy. Honor is intrinsically a matter of "préférences."[1] It is also the sense in which we use the term when we speak of honoring someone by giving her some public award, for example, the Order of Canada. Clearly, this award would be without worth if tomorrow we decided to give it to every adult Canadian.

As against this notion of honor, we have the modern notion of dignity, now used in a universalist and egalitarian sense, where we talk of the inherent "dignity of human beings," or of citizen dignity. The underlying premise here is that everyone shares in it.[2] It is obvious that this concept of dignity is the only one compatible with a democratic society, and that it was inevitable that the old concept of honor was superseded. But this has also meant that the forms of equal recognition have been essential to democratic culture. For instance, that everyone be called "Mr.," "Mrs.," or "Miss," rather than some people being called "Lord" or "Lady" and others simply by their surnames—or, even more demeaning, by their first names—has been thought essential in some democratic societies, such as the United States. More recently, for similar reasons, "Mrs." and "Miss" have been collapsed into "Ms." Democracy has ushered in a politics of equal recognition, which has taken various forms over the years, and has now returned in the form of demands for the equal status of cultures and of genders

But the importance of recognition has been modified and intensified by the new understanding of individual identity that emerges at the end of the eighteenth century. We might speak of an *individualized* identity, one that is particular to me, and that I discover in myself. This notion arises along with an ideal, that of being true to myself and my own particular way of being. Following Lionel Trilling's usage in his brilliant study, I will speak of this as the ideal of "authenticity."[3] It will help to describe in what it consists and how it came about.

One way of describing its development is to see its starting point in the eighteenth-century notion that human beings are endowed with a moral sense, an intuitive feeling for what is right and wrong. The original point of this doctrine was to combat a rival view, that knowing right and wrong was a matter of calculating consequences, in particular, those concerned with divine reward and punishment. The idea was that understanding right and wrong was not a matter of dry calculation, but was anchored in our feelings.[4] Morality has, in a sense, a voice within.

The notion of authenticity develops out of a displacement of the moral accent in this idea. On the original view, the inner voice was important because it tells us what the right thing to do is. Being in touch with our moral feelings matters here, as a means to the end of acting rightly. What I'm calling the displacement of the moral accent comes about when being in touch with our feelings takes on independent and crucial moral significance. It comes to be something we have to attain if we are to be true and full human beings.

To see what is new here, we have to see the analogy to earlier moral views, where being in touch with some source—for example, God, or the Idea of the Good—was considered essential to full being. But now the source we have to connect with is deep within us. This fact is part of the massive subjective turn of modern culture, a new form of inwardness, in which we come to think of ourselves as beings with inner depths. At first, this idea that the source is within doesn't exclude our being related to God or the Ideas; it can be considered our proper way of relating to them. In a sense, it can be seen as just a continuation and intensification of the development inaugurated by Saint Augustine, who saw the road to God as passing through our self-awareness. The first variants of this new view were theistic, or at least pantheistic.

The most important philosophical writer who helped to bring about this change was Jean-Jacques Rousseau. I think Rousseau is important not because he inaugurated the change; rather, I would argue that his great popularity comes in part from his articulating something that was in a sense already occurring in the culture. Rousseau frequently presents the issue of morality as that of our following a voice of nature within us. This voice is often drowned out by the passions that are induced by our dependence on others, the main one being *amour propre,* or pride. Our moral salvation comes from recovering authentic moral contact with our selves. Rousseau even gives a name to the intimate contact with oneself, more fundamental than any moral view, that is a source of such joy and contentment: "le sentiment de l'existence."[5]

The ideal of authenticity becomes crucial owing to a development that occurs after Rousseau, which I associate with the name of Herder—once again, as its major early articulator, rather than its originator. Herder put forward the idea that each of us has an original way of being human: each person has his or her own "measure."[6] This idea has burrowed very deep into modern consciousness. It is a new idea. Before the late eighteenth century, no one thought that the differences between human beings had this kind of moral significance. There is a certain way of being human that is *my* way. I am called upon to live my life in this way, and not in imitation of anyone else's life. But this notion gives a new importance to being true to myself. If I am not, I miss the point of my life; I miss what being human is for *me*.

This is the powerful moral ideal that has come down to us. It accords moral importance to a kind of contact with myself, with my own inner nature, which it sees as in danger of being lost, partly through the pressures toward outward conformity, but also because in taking an instrumental stance toward myself, I may have lost the capacity to listen to this inner voice. It greatly increases the importance of this self-contact by introducing the principle of originality: each of our voices has something unique to say. Not only should I not mold my life to the demands of external conformity; I can't even find the model by which to live outside myself. I can only find it within.[7]

Being true to myself means being true to my own originality, which is something only I can articulate and discover. In articulating it, I am also defining myself. I am realizing a potentiality that is properly my own. This is the background understanding to the modern ideal of authenticity, and to the goals of self-fulfillment and self-realization in which the ideal is usually couched. I should note here that Herder applied his conception of originality at two levels, not only to the individual person among other persons, but also to the culture-bearing people among other peoples. Just like individuals, a *Volk* should be true to itself, that is, its own culture. Germans shouldn't try to be derivative and (inevitably) second-rate Frenchmen, as Frederick the Great's patronage seemed to be encouraging them to do. The Slavic peoples had to find their own path. And European colonialism ought to be rolled back to give the peoples of what we now call the Third World their chance to be themselves unimpeded. We can recognize here the seminal idea of modern nationalism, in both benign and malignant forms.

This new ideal of authenticity was, like the idea of dignity, also in part an offshoot of the decline of hierarchical society. In those earlier societies, what we would now call identity was largely fixed by one's social position. That is, the background that explained what people recognized as important to themselves was to a great extent determined by their place in society, and whatever roles or activities attached to this position. The birth of a democratic society doesn't by itself do away with this phenomenon, because people can still define themselves by their social roles. What does decisively undermine this socially derived identification, however, is the ideal of authenticity itself. As this emerges, for instance, with Herder, it calls on me to discover my own original way of being. By definition, this way of being cannot be socially derived, but must be inwardly generated.

But in the nature of the case, there is no such thing as inward generation, monologically understood. In order to understand the close connection between identity and recognition, we have to take into account a crucial feature of the human condition that has been rendered almost invisible by the overwhelmingly monological bent of mainstream modern philosophy.

This crucial feature of human life is its fundamentally *dialogical* character. We become full human agents, capable of understanding ourselves, and hence of defining our identity, through our acquisition of rich human languages of expression. For my purposes here, I want to take *language* in a broad sense, covering not only the words we speak, but also other modes of expression whereby we define ourselves, including the "languages" of art, of gesture, of love, and the like. But we learn these modes of expression through exchanges with others. People do not acquire the languages needed for self-definition on their own. Rather, we are introduced to them through interaction with others who matter to us—what George Herbert Mead called "significant others."[8] The genesis of the human mind is in this sense not monological, not something each person accomplishes on his or her own, but dialogical.

Moreover, this is not just a fact about *genesis*, which can be ignored later on. We don't just learn the languages in dialogue and then go on to use them for our own purposes. We are of course expected to develop our own opinions, outlook, stances toward things, and to a considerable degree through solitary reflection. But this is not how things work with important issues, like the definition of our identity. We define our identity always in dialogue with, sometimes in struggle against, the things our significant others want to see in us. Even after we outgrow some of these others—our parents, for instance—and they disappear from our lives, the conversation with them continues within us as long as we live.[9]

Thus, the contribution of significant others, even when it is provided at the beginning of our lives, continues indefinitely. Some people may still want to hold on to some form of the monological ideal. It is true that we can never liberate ourselves completely from those whose love and care shaped us early in life, but we should strive to define ourselves on our own to the fullest extent possible, coming as best we can to understand and thus get some control over the influence of our parents, and avoiding falling into any more such dependent relationships. We need relationships to fulfill, but not to define, ourselves.

The monological ideal seriously underestimates the place of the dialogical in human life. It wants to confine it as much as possible to the genesis. It forgets how our understanding of the good things in life can be transformed by our enjoying them in common with people we love; how some goods become accessible to us only through such common enjoyment. Because of this, it would take a great deal of effort, and probably many wrenching break-ups, to *prevent* our identity's being formed by the people we love. Consider what we mean by *identity*. It is who we are, "where we're coming from." As such it is the background against which our tastes and desires and opinions and aspirations make sense. If some of the things I value most are accessible to me only in relation to the person I love, then she becomes part of my identity.

To some people this might seem a limitation, from which one might aspire to free oneself. This is one way of understanding the impulse behind the life of the hermit or, to take a case more familiar to our culture, the solitary artist. But from another perspective, we might see even these lives as aspiring to a certain kind of dialogicality. In the case of the hermit, the interlocutor is God. In the case of the solitary artist, the work itself is addressed to a future audience, perhaps still to be created by the work. The very form of a work of art shows its character as *addressed*.[10] But however one feels about it, the making and sustaining of our identity, in the absence of a heroic effort to break out of ordinary existence, remains dialogical throughout our lives.

Thus my discovering my own identity doesn't mean that I work it out in isolation, but that I negotiate it through dialogue, partly overt, partly internal, with others. That is why the development of an ideal of inwardly generated identity gives a new importance to recognition. My own identity crucially depends on my dialogical relations with others.

Of course, the point is not that this dependence on others arose with the age of authenticity. A form of dependence was always there. The socially derived identity was by its very nature dependent on society. But in the earlier age recognition never arose as a problem. General recognition was built into the socially derived identity by virtue of the very fact that it was based on social categories that everyone took for granted. Yet inwardly derived, personal, original identity doesn't enjoy this recognition *a priori*. It has to win it through exchange, and the attempt can fail. What has come about with the modern age is not the need for recognition but the conditions in which the attempt to be recognized can fail. That is why the need is now acknowledged for the first time. In premodern times, people didn't speak of "identity" and "recognition"—not because people didn't have (what we call) identities, or because these didn't depend on recognition, but rather because these were then too unproblematic to be thematized as such.

It's not surprising that we can find some of the seminal ideas about citizen dignity and universal recognition, even if not in these specific terms, in Rousseau, whom I have wanted to identify as one of the points of origin of the modern discourse of authenticity. Rousseau is a sharp critic of hierarchical honor, of "préférences." In a significant passage of the *Discourse on Inequality*, he pinpoints a fateful moment when society takes a turn toward corruption and injustice, when people begin to desire preferential esteem.[11] By contrast, in republican society, where all can share equally in the light of public attention, he sees the source of health.[12] But the topic of recognition is given its most influential early treatment in Hegel.[13]

The importance of recognition is now universally acknowledged in one form or another; on an intimate plane, we are all aware of how identity can be formed or malformed through the course of our contact with significant others. On the social plane, we have a continuing politics of equal recognition. Both planes have been shaped by the growing ideal of authenticity, and recognition plays an essential role in the culture that has arisen around this ideal.

On the intimate level, we can see how much an original identity needs and is vulnerable to the recognition given or withheld by significant others. It is not surprising that in the culture of authenticity, relationships are seen as the key loci of self-discovery and self-affirmation. Love relationships are not just important because of the general emphasis in modern culture on the fulfillments of ordinary needs. They are also crucial because they are the crucibles of inwardly generated identity.

On the social plane, the understanding that identities are formed in open dialogue, unshaped by a predefined social script, has made the politics of equal recognition more central and stressful. It has, in fact, considerably raised the stakes. Equal recognition is not just the appropriate mode for a healthy democratic society. Its refusal can inflict damage on those who are denied it, according to a widespread modern view, as I indicated at the outset. The projection of an inferior or demeaning image on another can actually distort and oppress, to the extent that the image is internalized. Not only contemporary feminism but also race relations and discussions of multiculturalism are undergirded by the premise that the withholding of recognition can be a form of oppression. We may debate whether this factor has been exaggerated, but it is clear that the understanding of identity and authenticity has introduced a new dimension into the politics of equal recognition, which now operates with something like its own notion of authenticity, at least so far as the denunciation of other-induced distortions is concerned.

And so the discourse of recognition has become familiar to us, on two levels: First, in the intimate sphere, where we understand the formation of identity and the self as taking place in a continuing dialogue and struggle with significant others. And then in the public sphere, where a politics of equal recognition has come to play a bigger and bigger role. Certain feminist theories have tried to show the links between the two spheres.[14]

I want to concentrate here on the public sphere, and try to work out what a politics of equal recognition has meant and could mean.

In fact, it has come to mean two rather different things, connected, respectively, with the two major changes I have been describing. With the move from honor to dignity has come a politics of universalism, emphasizing the equal dignity of all citizens, and the content of this politics has been the equalization of rights and entitlements. What is to be avoided at all costs is the existence of "first-class" and "second-class" citizens. Naturally, the actual detailed measures justified by this principle have varied greatly, and have often been controversial. For some, equalization has affected only civil rights and voting rights; for others, it has extended into the socioeconomic sphere. People who are systematically handicapped by poverty from making the most of their citizenship rights are deemed on this view to have been relegated to second-class status, necessitating remedial action through equalization. But through all the differences of interpretation, the principle of equal citizenship has come to be universally accepted. Every position, no matter how reactionary, is now defended under the colors of this principle. Its greatest, most recent victory was won by the civil rights movement of the

1960s in the United States. It is worth nothing that even the adversaries of extending voting rights to blacks in the southern states found some pretext consistent with universalism, such as "tests" to be administered to would-be voters at the time of registration.

By contrast, the second change, the development of the modern notion of identity, has given rise to a politics of difference. There is, of course, a universalist basis to this as well, making for the overlap and confusion between the two. *Everyone* should be recognized for his or her unique identity. But recognition here means something else. With the politics of equal dignity, what is established is meant to be universally the same, an identical basket of rights and immunities; with the politics of difference, what we are asked to recognize is the unique identity of this individual or group, their distinctness from everyone else. The idea is that it is precisely this distinctness that has been ignored, glossed over, assimilated to a dominant or majority identity. And this assimilation is the cardinal sin against the ideal of authenticity.[15]

Now underlying the demand is a principle of universal equality. The politics of difference is full of denunciations of discrimination and refusals of second-class citizenship. This gives the principle of universal equality a point of entry within the politics of dignity. But once inside, as it were, its demands are hard to assimilate to that politics. For it asks that we give acknowledgment and status to something that is not universally shared. Or, otherwise put, we give due acknowledgment only to what is universally present—everyone has an identity—through recognizing what is peculiar to each. The universal demand powers an acknowledgment of specificity.

The politics of difference grows organically out of the politics of universal dignity through one of those shifts with which we are long familiar, where a new understanding of the human social condition imparts a radically new meaning to an old principle. Just as a view of human beings as conditioned by their socioeconomic plight changed the understanding of second-class citizenship, so that this category came to include, for example, people in inherited poverty traps, so here the understanding of identity as formed in interchange, and as possibly so malformed, introduces a new form of second-class status into our purview. As in the present case, the socioeconomic redefinition justified social programs that were highly controversial. For those who had not gone along with this changed definition of equal status, the various redistributive programs and special opportunities offered to certain populations seemed a form of undue favoritism.

Similar conflicts arise today around the politics of difference. Where the politics of universal dignity fought for forms of nondiscrimination that were quite "blind" to the ways in which citizens differ, the politics of difference often redefines nondiscrimination as requiring that we make these distinctions the basis of differential treatment. So members of aboriginal bands will get certain rights and powers not enjoyed by other Canadians, if the demands for native self-government are finally agreed on, and certain minorities will get the right to exclude others in order to preserve their cultural integrity, and so on.

To proponents of the original politics of dignity, this can seem like a reversal, a betrayal, a simple negation of their cherished principle. Attempts are therefore made to mediate, to show how some of these measures meant to accommodate minorities can after all be justified on the original basis of dignity. These arguments can be successful up to a point. For instance, some of the (apparently) most flagrant departures from "difference-blindness" are reverse discrimination measures, affording people from previously unfavored groups a competitive advantage for jobs or places in universities. This practice has been justified on the grounds that historical discrimination has created a pattern within which the unfavored struggle at a disadvantage. Reverse discrimination is defended as a temporary measure that will eventually level the playing field and allow the old "blind" rules to come back into force in a way that doesn't disadvantage anyone. This argument seems cogent enough—wherever its factual basis is sound. But it won't justify some of the measures now urged on the grounds of difference, the goal of which is not to bring us back to an eventual "difference-blind" social space but, on the contrary, to maintain and cherish distinctness, not just now but forever. After all, if we're concerned with identity, then what is more legitimate than one's aspiration that it never be lost?[16]

So even though one politics springs from the other, by one of those shifts in the definition of key terms with which we're familiar, the two diverge quite seriously from each other. One basis for the divergence comes out even more clearly when we go beyond what each requires that we acknowledge—certain universal rights in one case, a particular identity in the other—and look at the underlying intuitions of value.

The politics of equal dignity is based on the idea that all humans are equally worthy of respect. It is underpinned by a notion of what in human beings commands respect, however we may try to shy away from this "metaphysical" background. For Kant, whose use of the term *dignity* was one of the earliest influential evocations of this idea, what commanded respect in us was our status as rational agents, capable of directing our lives through principles.[17] Something like this has been the basis for our intuitions of equal dignity ever since, though the detailed definition of it may have changed.

Thus, what is picked out as of worth here is a *universal human potential*, a capacity that all humans share. This potential, rather than anything a person may have made of it, is what ensures that each person deserves respect. Indeed, our sense of the importance of potentiality reaches so far that we extend this protection even to people who through some circumstance that has befallen them are incapable of realizing their potential in the normal way—handicapped people, or those in a coma, for instance.

In the case of the politics of difference, we might also say that a universal potential is at its basis, namely, the potential for forming and defining one's own identity, as an individual, and also as a culture. This potentiality must be respected equally in everyone. But at least in the intercultural context, a stronger demand has recently arisen: that one accord equal respect to actually evolved cultures. Critiques of European or white domination, to the effect that they have not only suppressed but failed to appreciate other cultures, consider these depreciatory judgments not only factually mistaken but somehow morally wrong. When Saul Bellow is famously quoted as saying something like, "When the Zulus produce a Tolstoy we will read him,"[18] this is taken as a quintessential statement of European arrogance, not just because Bellow is allegedly being *de facto* insensitive to the value of Zulu culture, but frequently also because it is seen to reflect a denial in principle of human equality. The possibility that the Zulus, while having the same potential for culture formation as anyone else, might nevertheless have come up with a culture that is less valuable than others is ruled out from the start. Even to entertain this possibility is to deny human equality. Bellow's error here, then, would not be a (possibly insensitive) particular mistake in evaluation, but a denial of a fundamental principle.

To the extent that this stronger reproach is in play, the demand for equal recognition extends beyond an acknowledgment of the equal value of all humans potentially, and comes to include the equal value of what they have made of this potential in fact. This creates a serious problem, as we shall see below.

These two modes of politics, then, both based on the notion of equal respect, come into conflict. For one, the principle of equal respect requires that we treat people in a difference-blind fashion. The fundamental intuition that humans command this respect focuses on what is the same in all. For the other, we have to recognize and even foster particularity. The reproach the first makes to the second is just that it violates the principle of nondiscrimination. The reproach the second makes to the first is that it negates identity by forcing people into a homogeneous mold that is untrue to them. This would be bad enough if the mold were itself neutral—nobody's mold in particular. But the complaint generally goes further. The claim is that the supposedly neutral set of difference-blind principles of the politics of equal dignity is in fact a reflection of one hegemonic culture. As it turns out, then, only the minority or suppressed cultures are being forced to take alien form. Consequently, the supposedly fair and difference-blind society is not only inhuman (because suppressing identities) but also, in a subtle and unconscious way, itself highly discriminatory.[19]

This last attack is the cruelest and most upsetting of all. The liberalism of equal dignity seems to have to assume that there are some universal, difference-blind principles. Even though we may not have defined them yet, the project of defining them remains alive and essential. Different theories may be put forward and contested—and a number have been proposed in our day[20]—but the shared assumption of the different theories is that one such theory is right.

The charge leveled by the most radical forms of the politics of difference is that "blind" liberalisms are themselves the reflection of particular cultures. And the worrying thought is that this bias might not just be a contingent weakness of all hitherto proposed theories, that the very idea of such a liberalism may be a kind of pragmatic contradiction, a particularism masquerading as the universal.

## Notes

1  "La nature de l'honneur est de demander des préférences et des distinctions...." Montesquieu, *De l'esprit des lois*, Bk. 3, chap. 7.
2  The significance of this move from "honor" to "dignity" is interestingly discussed by Peter Berger in his "On the Obsolescence of the Concept of Honour," in *Revisions: Changing Perspectives in Moral Philosophy*, ed. Stanley Hauerwas and Alasdair MacIntyre (Notre Dame, Ind.: University of Notre Dame Press, 1983), pp. 172–81.
3  Lionel Trilling, *Sincerity and Authenticity* (New York: Norton, 1969).
4  I have discussed the development of this doctrine at greater length, at first in the work of Francis Hutcheson, drawing on the writings of the Earl of Shaftesbury, and its adversarial relation to Locke's theory in *Sources of the Self* (Cambridge, Mass.: Harvard University Press, 1989), chap. 15.
5  "Le sentiment de l'existence dépouillé de toute autre affection est par lui-même un sentiment précieux de contentement et de paix qui suffiroit seul pour rendre cette existence chère et douce à qui sauroit écarter de soi toutes les impressions sensuelles et terrestres qui viennent sans cesse nous en distraire et en troubler ici bas la douceur. Mais la pluspart des hommes agités de passions continuelles connoissent peu cet état et ne l'ayant gouté qu'imparfaitement durant peu d'instans n'en conservent qu'une idée obscure et confuse qui ne leur en fait pas sentir le charme." Jean-Jacques Rousseau, *Les Rêveries du promeneur solitaire*, "Cinquième Promenade," in *Oeuvres complètes* (Paris: Gallimard, 1959), 1: 1047.
6  "Jeder Mensch hat ein eigenes Mass, gleichsam eine eigne Stimmung aller seiner sinnlichen Gefühle zu einander." Johann Gottlob Herder, *Ideen,* chap. 7, sec. 1, in *Herders Sämtliche Werke*, ed. Bernard Suphan (Berlin: Weidmann, 1877–1913), 13:291.
7  John Stuart Mill was influenced by this Romantic current of thought when he made something like the ideal of authenticity the basis for one of his most powerful arguments in *On Liberty*. See especially chapter 3, where he argues that we need something more than a capacity for "apelike imitation": "A person whose desires and impulses are his own—are the expression of his own nature, as it has been developed and modified by his own culture—is said to have a character." "If a person possesses any tolerable amount of common sense and experience, his own mode of laying out his existence is the best, not because it is the best in itself, but because it is his own mode." John Stuart Mill, *Three Essays* (Oxford: Oxford University Press, 1975), pp. 73, 74, 83.
8  George Herbert Mead, *Mind, Self, and Society* (Chicago: University of Chicago Press, 1934).
9  This inner dialogicality has been explored by M. M. Bakhtin and those who have drawn on his work. See, of Bakhtin, especially *Problems of Dostoyevsky's Poetics*, trans. Caryl Emerson (Minneapolis: University of Minnesota Press, 1984). See also Michael Holquist and Katerina Clark, *Mikhail Bakhtin* (Cambridge, Mass.: Harvard University Press, 1984); and James Wertsch, *Voices of the Mind* (Cambridge, Mass.: Harvard University Press, 1991).
10  See Bakhitn, "The Problem of the Text in Linguistics, Philology and the Human Sciences," in *Speech Genres and Other Late Essays*, ed. Caryl Emerson and Michael

Holquist (Austin: University of Texas Press, 1986), p. 126, for this notion of a "super-addressee," beyond our existing interlocutors.

11  Rousseau is describing the first assemblies: "Chacun commença à regarder les autres et à vouloir être regardé soi-même, et l'estime publique eut un prix. Celui qui chantait ou dansait le mieux; le plus beau, le plus fort, le plus adroit ou le plus éloquent devint le plus considéré, et ce fut là le premier pas vers l'inégalité, et vers le vice en même temps." *Discours sur l'origine et les fondements de l'inégalité parmi les hommes* (Paris: Granier-Flammarion, 1971), p. 210.

12  See, for example, the passage in the *Considérations sur le governement de Pologne* where he describes the ancient public festival, in which all the people took part, in *Du contrat social* (Paris: Garnier, 1962), p. 345; and also the parallel passage in *Lettre à D'Alembert sur les spectacles*, in *Du contrat social*, pp. 224–25. The crucial principle was that there should be no division between performers and spectators, but that all should be seen by all. "Mais quels seront enfin les objets de ces spectacles? Qu'y montrera-t-on? Rien, si l'on veut. ... Donnez les spectateurs en spectacles; rendez-les acteurs eux-mêmes; faites que chacun se voie et s'aime dans les autres, que tous en soient mieux unis."

13  See Hegel, *The Phenomenology of Spirit*, trans. A. V. Miller (Oxford: Oxford University Press, 1977), chap. 4

14  There are a number of strands that have linked these two levels, but perhaps special prominence in recent years has been given to a psycho-analytically oriented feminism, which roots social inequalities in the early upbringing of men and women. See, for instance, Nancy Chodorow, *Feminism and Psychoanalytic Theory* (New Haven: Yale University Press, 1989); and Jessica Benjamin, *Bonds of Love: Psychoanalysis, Feminism and the Problem of Domination* (New York: Pantheon, 1988)

15  A prime example of this charge from a feminist perspective is Carol Gilligan's critique of Lawrence Kohlberg's theory of moral development, for presenting a view of human development that privileges only one facet of moral reasoning, precisely the one that tends to predominate in boys rather than girls. See Gilligan, *In a Different Voice* (Cambridge, Mass.: Harvard University Press, 1982).

16  Will Kymlicka, in his very interesting and tightly argued book *Liberalism, Community and Culture* (Oxford: Clarendon Press, 1989), tries to argue for a kind of politics of difference, notably in relation to aboriginal rights in Canada, but from a basis that is firmly within a theory of liberal neutrality. He wants to argue on the basis of certain cultural needs—minimally, the need for an integral and undamaged cultural language with which one can define and pursue his or her own conception of the good life. In certain circumstances, with disadvantaged populations, the integrity of the culture may require that we accord them more resources or rights than others. The argument is quite parallel to that made in relation to socio-economic inequalities that I mentioned above.

But where Kymlicka's interesting argument fails to recapture the actual demands made by the groups concerned—say Indian bands in Canada, or French-speaking Canadians—is with respect to their goal of survival. Kymlicka's reasoning is valid (perhaps) for *existing* people who find themselves trapped within a culture under pressure, and can flourish within it or not at all. But it doesn't justify measures designed to ensure survival through indefinite future generations. For the populations concerned, however, that is what is at stake. We need only think of the historical resonance of "la survivance" among French Canadians.

17  See Kant, *Grundlegung der Metaphysik der Sitten* (Berlin: Gruyter, 1968; reprint of the Berlin Academy edition), p. 434.

18 I have no idea whether this statement was actually made in this form by Saul Bellow, or by anyone else. I report it only because it captures a widespread attitude, which is, of course, why the story had currency in the first place.

19 One hears both kinds of reproach today. In the context of some modes of feminism and multiculturalism, the claim is the strong one, that the hegemonic culture discriminates. In the Soviet Union, however, alongside a similar reproach leveled at the hegemonic Great Russian culture, one also hears the complaint that Marxist-Leninist communism has been an alien imposition on all equally, even on Russia itself. The communist mold, on this view, has been truly nobody's. Solzhenitsyn has made this claim, but it is voiced by Russians of a great many different persuasions today, and has something to do with the extraordinary phenomenon of an empire that has broken apart through the quasi-secession of its metropolitan society.

20 See John Rawls, *A Theory of Justice* (Cambridge, Mass.: Harvard University Press, 1971); Ronald Dworkin, *Taking Rights Seriously* (London: Duckworth, 1977) and *A Matter of Principle* (Cambridge, Mass.: Harvard University Press, 1985); and Jürgen Habermas, *Theorie des kommunikativen Handelns* (Frankfurt: Suhrkamp, 1981).

# 24 Equality of Difference

## Bhikhu Parekh

In multicultural societies dress often becomes a site of the most heated and intransigent struggles. As a condensed and visible symbol of cultural identity it matters much to the individuals involved, but also for that very reason it arouses all manner of conscious and unconscious fears and resentments within wider society. It would not be too rash to suggest that acceptance of the diversity of dress in a multicultural society is a good indicator of whether or not the latter is at ease with itself.

In 1972, British Parliament passed a law empowering the Minister of Transport to require motor-cyclists to wear crash-helmets. When the Minister did so, Sikhs campaigned against it. One of them kept breaking the law and was fined twenty times between 1973 and 1976 for refusing to wear a crash-helmet. Sikh spokesmen argued that the turban was just as safe, and that if they could fight for the British in two world wars without anyone considering their turbans unsafe, they could surely ride motor-cycles. The law was amended in 1976 and exempted them from wearing crash-helmets. Although this was not universally welcomed, Parliament was right to amend the law. Its primary concern was to ensure that people did not die or suffer serious injuries riding dangerous vehicles, and it hit upon the helmet meeting certain standards as the best safety measure. Since the Sikh turban met these standards, it was accepted as an adequate substitute for the helmet.[1]

This became evident in the subsequent development of the law as it related to Sikhs. Although the Construction (Head Protection) Regulation 1989 requires all those working on construction sites to wear safety helmets, the Employment Act 1989 exempts turban-wearing Sikhs. The latter does so because it is persuaded by its own scientific tests that the turban offers adequate though not exactly the same protection as the helmet, and is thus an acceptable substitute for it. One important implication of this argument is that if a turbaned Sikh were to be injured on a construction site as a result of another person's negligence, he would be entitled to claim damages for only such injuries as he would have suffered if he had been wearing a safety helmet. The law does not allow anyone to work on a construction site without an acceptable headgear. However, it is willing to compromise on the helmet if two conditions are satisfied. First, the alternative headgear should offer an equivalent or at least acceptable level of protection. And second, those opting for it should themselves bear the responsibility for such *additional* injury as it may cause. The law lays down a minimally required level of protection and uses it to regulate the permissible range of cultural diversity. So far as the minimum requirement is concerned, it places the burden of injury on those causing it. The burden of additional injury is borne by those who for cultural reasons choose to meet the minimum requirement in their own different ways. Such an arrangement respects differences without violating the principle of equality, and accommodates individual choice without imposing unfair financial and other burdens on the rest of their fellow-citizens.

In Britain, Sikhs in the police and armed forces are entitled to wear turbans. In Canada it has led to a heated debate. Although most major police forces across the country allowed Sikhs to wear turbans, the Royal Canadian Mounted Police did not. When it finally decided to allow them, a group of retired officers organized a campaign involving 9000 letters and a petition signed by 210 000 people. They argued that the RCMP should be, and seen to be, free from political and religious bias and that the Sikh's turban, being a religious symbol, 'undermined the non-religious nature of the force' and violated other Canadians' 'constitutional right to a secular state free of religious symbols'. They also contended that since the Sikhs insisted on wearing the turban, they gave the impression of valuing their religion more than their police duties and would not be able to inspire public trust in their impartiality and loyalty to the state. In the eyes of the critics, Canada had taken its multiculturalism too far and should insist on the traditional Stetson. The matter went to the Trial Division of the Federal Court of Canada, which ruled that the objection to the turban was 'quite speculative and vague', and that the turban did not compromise the non-religious character of the RCMP. Three retired officers of the RCMP appealed to the Supreme Court, which dismissed the appeal and upheld the right of Sikhs to wear the turban.

Although the objection against the turban smacks of cultural intolerance and treats Sikhs unequally, it is not devoid of merit. The RCMP is a powerful and much-cherished national institution and, since Canada has few national symbols, there is something to be said for retaining the Stetson. However, one could argue that precisely because the RCMP is a national institution, it should permit the turban and become a representative symbol of the country's officially endorsed multicultural identity. Furthermore, several provincial forces as well as the Canadian Courts and House of Commons allow Sikhs to wear turbans with no suggestion that this compromises the discharge of their official duties, diminishes their loyalty to the state, or detracts from the country's secular character. There is no reason why the RCMP should be different. Besides, wearing a turban does not signify that the wearer values his religion more than his professional integrity, nor does his replacing it with a Stetson indicate the opposite. Pushed to its logical conclusion, the criticism of the turban would imply that those wearing the traditional Stetson are likely to be partial to whites and hostile to others. One would therefore have to replace the Stetson with a culturally neutral headgear, which would have the double disadvantage of satisfying neither Sikhs nor whites and leaving the basic problem unsolved. Again, it is not at all true that Canada is committed to a narrow and bland form of secularism. If it were, it would have to change its coat-of-arms, disallow prayer in the Federal Parliament, expunge reference to God in the swearing-in ceremony of Cabinet ministers, and so on. Since opponents of the turban are unsympathetic to these changes, their objection is specious and discriminatory.

The diversity of head-dress has raised problems in other societies as well, especially in relation to the armed forces and the police, the official symbols and guardians of national identity. Samcha Goldman, an orthodox Jew serving in the secular capacity of a clinical psychologist in the United States Air Force, was asked to resign when he insisted on wearing his yarmulke, which the Air Force thought was against its standard dress requirement. When the matter reached the Supreme Court, it upheld the decision of the Air Force by a majority of one, arguing that the 'essence of the military service is the subordination of the desire and interests of the individual to the needs of the service'. It is striking that the Court saw the yarmulke as a matter of personal desire or preference rather than a religious requirement which Goldman was not at liberty to disregard (Sandel, 1996, pp. 69f)[2]. Justifying the Court's decision, the Secretary of State argued that the uniforms of the armed forces were the 'cherished symbols of service, pride, history and traditions', and that allowing variations in them was bound to 'operate to the detriment of order and discipline', foster 'resentment and divisiveness', 'degrade unit cohesion', and reduce combat effectiveness. The Supreme Court decision rightly outraged many members of Congress, which by a sizeable majority passed a law permitting religious apparel provided that it did not interfere with military duties and was 'neat and conservative'.

There is much to be said for uniforms in the armed forces. Since they are closely identified with the state and symbolize its unity, their uniforms reinforce the consciousness of their national role and create an appropriate corporate ethos. And it goes without saying that they should be suitable for combat. However, this has to be balanced against other equally important considerations. If the yarmulke, turban and other religious apparels were to be disallowed, Jews, Sikhs and others would be denied both an avenue of employment and an opportunity to serve their country. Furthermore, the United States is a culturally diverse society made up of people of different religious faiths. There is no obvious reason why its national symbols including military uniforms should not reflect that fact. Besides, if differences of mere headdress are likely to detract from collective solidarity and unit cohesion, the differences of colour, accent and facial features are likely to do so even more, and we would have to exclude blacks, Asians and others from joining the armed forces. In short, while the uniform should not be discarded, it should be open to appropriate modification to accommodate genuine religious, cultural and other requirements, provided of course that they do not compromise military effectiveness.

The controversy concerning uniforms occurs in civilian areas of life as well, where it raises issues that are at once both similar and different. Since no question of national unity of symbolism is involved, the controversy has no political significance. However, it involves far more people, usually women, and has a great economic significance.

Many Asian women's refusal to wear uniforms in hospitals, stores and schools had led to much litigation and contradictory judgments in Britain. A Sikh woman who, on qualifying as a nurse, intended to wear her traditional dress of a long shirt (*quemiz*) over baggy trousers (*shalwar*) rather than the required uniform, was refused admission on a nursing course by her Health Authority. The Industrial Tribunal upheld her complaint on the ground that since her traditional dress was a cultural requirement and did not impede the discharge of her duties, asking her to replace it with a uniform was unjustified. The Tribunal was overruled by the Employment Appeal Tribunal, which took the opposite and much criticized view. Since rules about nurses' uniforms are laid down by the General Nursing Council, the latter promptly intervened under government pressure and made more flexible rules. This enabled the Health Authority to offer the Sikh woman a place on the course on the understanding that as a qualified nurse her trousers should be grey and the shirt white.

This was one of many cases in which lower courts took one view and the higher courts another, or the same court took different views in similar cases. The discrepancy arose because courts used two different criteria in deciding such cases. Sometimes they asked if the job requirements were *plausible* or understandable; that is, if 'good reasons' could be given for them. On other occasions they thought that such a criterion justified almost every demand, and insisted that job requirements should be *objectively necessary*; that is, indispensable for discharging the duties of the jobs concerned. It sounds plausible to say that since loose hairs could cause infection or pose a risk to public health, surgeons or those working in chocolate factories should not be allowed to sport beards. However, the requirement turns out to be objectively unnecessary, for beards do not mean loose hair and, if necessary, they can always be covered by a suitable clothing. After all, we do not ask people in these jobs to shave hair off their heads and arms.

Although the test of objective necessity is reasonable, it runs the risk of taking a purely instrumental view of job requirements and stripping the organizations concerned of their cultural identity. Take the case of nurses' uniforms. One could argue that since these are not objectively necessary for carrying out the required medical tasks, anyone may wear anything. This is to miss the crucial point that they symbolize and reinforce the collective spirit of the nursing profession and structure the expectations and behaviour of their patients. The instrumental view of rationality implicit in the test of objective necessity is also likely to provoke resentment against minorities whose cultural demands might be seen to undermine a much-cherished tradition. It is also unjust because, while it respects the cultural identity of the minority, it ignores that of the wider society. The concept of objective necessity should therefore be defined in a culturally sensitive manner and do justice to both the minority and majority ways of life. This means that uniforms should be kept in hospitals, schools and wherever else they are part of the tradition and perform valuable symbolic, inspirational, aesthetic and other functions, but be open to appropriate modifications when necessary. Such an arrangement neither deculturalizes the organizations concerned and renders them bland, nor eclectically multiculturalizes them and renders them comical, but preserves and adapts the tradition to changing circumstances and facilitates minority integration into the suitably opened-up mainstream society.

## Equal treatment

In the cases discussed so far, it has been relatively easy to identify what aspects were relevant and what equal treatment consisted in. Situations sometimes arise when such judgements are not at all easy.

In most societies the law declares that a marriage is void if contracted under duress, a concept not easy to define in a culturally neutral manner. A British Asian girl, who had married her parentally-chosen husband because of the threat of ostracism by her family, asked the court to annul her marriage on grounds of duress. The court declined, arguing that duress only occurred when there was a 'threat of imminent danger to life and liberty'. This culturally insensitive interpretation of duress was rightly criticized. Not surprisingly the court did a complete *volte face* a few years later and declared void the marriage of another Asian girl under similar circumstances. It took the view that although acute social pressure did not amount to duress for a white British girl, it did so for her Asian counterpart.

The Asian girl is clearly treated differently, raising the question whether the difference amounts to privileging her. *Prima facie* it would seem that she is offered an *additional* ground for dissolution of marriage, and is thus being privileged. However, this is not the case. The law lays down that absence of duress is the basis of a valid marriage. Since ostracism by the family virtually amounts to social death and hence to duress in Asian society but not in white British society, the differential treatment of the Asian and white girls does not offend against the principle of equality. It does not give the Asian girl an additional ground for divorce, only interprets the existing one in a culturally sensitive manner.

The recognition of cultural differences might sometimes entitle a person to do things others cannot do without necessarily implying unequal rights. Many countries allow Sikhs to carry a suitably covered *kirpan* (a small dagger) in public places on the ground that it is a mandatory symbol of their religion. If other citizens asked to do that, their request would be turned down. This raises the question whether non-Sikhs can legitimately complain of discrimination or unequal treatment. There is no discrimination because their religious requirements are just as respected as those of the Sikhs. As for the complaint of inequality, there is a *prima facie* inequality of rights in the sense that the Sikhs can do things others cannot. However, the inequality arises out of the different demands of the same basic right to religion and does not confer a new right on the Sikhs. Some religions might require more of their adherents that do others, and then the same right would encompass a wider range of activities. Their adherents have the same right as the rest and its scope too is the same, only its content is wider.

## Note

1. For a most thorough discussion of some of these cases, see Sebastian Poulter (1998) *Ethnicity, Law and Human Rights* (Oxford: Clarendon).
2. Michael Sandel, *Democracy's Discontent* (Cambridge, MA: Harvard University Press, 1996).

# 25 Liberalism and Multiculturalism

## Chandran Kukathas

My business in this state
Made me a looker-on here in Vienna,
Where I have seen corruption boil and bubble
Till it o'errun the stew: laws for all faults,
But faults so countenanc'd that the strong statutes
Stand like the forfeits in a barber's shop,
As much in mock as in mark.

—*Shakespeare*[1]

The greatest liberty of subjects, dependeth on the silence of the law.

—*Hobbes*[2]

In modern societies, particularly the societies of the liberal democratic West, cultural diversity poses a challenge not only to the makers of government policy, but also to the philosopher looking to understand how it might be possible—in principle—for people of different ways to live together. The challenge is posed because society's institutions have been challenged, as the members of different groups have demanded "recognition". They have demanded not simply recognition of their claims to a (just) share of the social pie but, more important, recognition of their distinct identities as members of particular cultural communities within society. The persistence and, in some cases, the ferocity of demands for recognition have led many to concede that recognize them we must. The problem that arises for a liberal society, however, is that there quickly emerges a conflict between two demands: on one hand, that the dignity of the individual be recognized (by respecting certain fundamental rights); on the other hand, that the claims of the groups or cultural communities to which individuals belong be recognized. Philosophers such as Charles Taylor, who have viewed the problem in this way, also see that no simple solution to this conflict is available. A more complex, and nuanced, answer must therefore be given to the problem posed by the politics of recognition; and that answer must acknowledge the need for institutions that facilitate public deliberation and for attitudes of openness and tolerance.

The argument I wish to present here, however, is that the problem is not a complex one. Or, at least, it is not a complex problem in philosophical terms.

Multiculturalism does not pose a difficult problem for liberalism—or for liberal "political ethics." This is not to say that it poses no problems for politics; but politics is not philosophy, and my concern here is with philosophy.

The reason multiculturalism does not pose a philosophical problem for liberalism is that liberalism's counsel is to resist the demand for recognition. Politicians have always found this advice difficult to follow, for the demands of constituents are nothing if not compelling (especially at election time). But philosophers (including many avowedly liberal ones) have also found this advice hard to take, perhaps because it seems to suggest that there is not much they can contribute to making the world a better place. Nevertheless, I wish to argue here, this is what liberalism recommends. In a sense, it recommends doing nothing. But, of course, doing nothing is a very difficult thing to do. The rest of this essay is devoted to explaining what it means to do nothing, and why nothing should be done; although it cannot really say very much—for reasons that will, I hope, become clear—about how nothing is to be done.

The reason why liberalism does not have a problem with multiculturalism is that liberalism is itself, fundamentally, a theory of multiculturalism. This is because liberalism is essentially a theory about pluralism; and multiculturalism, is, in the end, a species of pluralism. Liberalism is one of the modern world's responses—indeed, its most plausible response—to the fact of moral, religious, and cultural diversity. Its response has been to say that diversity should be accommodated, and differences tolerated; that a more complete social unity, marked by a uniform and common culture that integrates and harmonizes the interests of individual and community, is unattainable and undesirable; that division, conflict, and competition would always be present in human society, and the task of political institutions is to palliate a condition they cannot cure. Political institutions would be liberal institutions if they left people free to pursue their own ends, whether separately or in concert with others, under the rule of law. By implication, many liberals have argued, this requires leaving people free to worship as they see fit; but it also requires leaving them free to live by different cultural standards—provided their doing so does not threaten the legal and political order that allows for peaceful coexistence.

But the point is not simply that liberalism does not have any difficulty with accepting some form of multiculturalism. While liberalism is a term that is properly used to identify a particular movement of European thought, it also denotes a philosophical outlook whose primary concern is to articulate the terms under which different ways may coexist. There is a historical liberalism; but there is also a philosophical liberalism. The fact that philosophical liberalism is the invention of particular historical circumstances (or of particular culturally identifiable figures) has no bearing on the coherence or plausibility of liberalism as a philosophical idea.

What is it, then, that liberalism has to say about multiculturalism? In the end, what it offers is not a thesis about individual dignity, or about how that dignity should be recognized. To be sure, thinkers like Kant (drawing inspiration from Rousseau) thought this important; so did von Humboldt and J. S. Mill, among others. But while human dignity may have been an important consideration for such thinkers, it is not central to liberalism. For this reason, liberalism is not troubled by the question of whether respecting human dignity requires recognizing individual identities or recognizing the identities of groups. Liberalism is not concerned with granting recognition to either. It does not offer recognition at all.

In this regard, liberalism is indifferent to the groups of which individuals may be members. Individuals in a liberal society are free to form groups or associations, or to continue their association with groups that they have joined or into which they may have been born. Liberalism takes no interest in these interests or attachments—cultural, religious, ethnic, linguistic, or otherwise—that people might have. It takes no interest in the character or identity of individuals; nor is it concerned directly to promote human flourishing: it has no collective projects, it expresses no group preferences, and it promotes no particular individuals or individual interests. Its only concern is with upholding the framework of law within which individuals and groups can function peacefully. To be sure, upholding the rule of law may require intervention in the affairs of individuals and groups (and this may, unavoidably, have a bearing on individual and group identity); but liberal politics is not concerned with these affairs in themselves. Indeed, it is indifferent to particular human affairs or to the particular pursuits of individuals and groups. Liberalism might well be described as the politics of indifference.

To assert this, however, is not only to offer a particular view of what liberalism amounts to; it is also to present a view with which thinkers like Taylor take issue. For them, a politics of indifference is neither feasible nor desirable in the face of persistent demands from various groups for recognition. The question, then, is: Can these demands indeed be resisted—if they should be resisted at all?

In one way, thinkers like Taylor are clearly right to suggest that it is difficult for the liberal state—or any state, for that matter—to resist the demands of particular individuals and groups for recognition. Tamil and Basque separatists in Sri Lanka and Spain cannot easily be ignored. And when a *fatwa* is issued against a writer like Salman Rushdie, the conflict between religious traditions seems to require more than indifference. Yet, to describe liberalism as the politics of indifference is not to say that in a liberal state there are no issues of public policy that cannot be ignored. It is, rather, to make a point about the goal of public policy in a liberal state. That goal is not to shape the culture of the polity, or to uphold the dignity of the individual, or to rescue minority groups from their marginalized status in society. Liberalism is indifferent to these matters. Its only concern is to preserve the order within which such groups and individuals exist. From a liberal point of view, it does not matter what happens to the identities of particular groups or to the identities of individuals. Whether some cultural groups fragment into a number of smaller associations or are assimilated into the dominant culture of the wider society, or disappear altogether, does not matter from the liberal standpoint. Of course, it may matter enormously to the groups and individuals in question; but while liberalism does not counsel obstructing those who wish to preserve or enhance their identities, it takes no interest in supporting such endeavors either.

Is this standpoint untenable, as Taylor and others suggest? I wish to suggest that it is not; although it will often be difficult to hold to—for the reason that, in politics, the demands of powerful interests will always be difficult to resist. And the higher the stakes, the more vigorously will the demand for recognition be pressed. Yet, there are two points that should be made. The first is that, while resistance to demands for recognition may be difficult, it does not mean that it is impossible. The second is that the feasibility of adopting the standpoint of indifference should be judged against the feasibility of the alternative, which is to accede to such demands. Attempting to grant recognition to those who demand it, however, is almost always dangerous. This is because demands for recognition are often in conflict with other similar demands, or other interests. For example, when in 1993 immigrants from parts of the former Yugoslavia claimed recognition as Macedonians who formed a distinct ethic community in Australia, it immediately brought about a challenge from others who regarded themselves as people of Macedonian descent—a challenge that escalated to acts of violence between ethnic communities when the Australian government saw fit to rule on which identification would be officially recognized.

The problem is that, when transformed into the politics of recognition, multicultural politics quickly descends into the politics of interest group conflict.[3] Groups are themselves not in any way natural or fixed entities but mutable social formations that change shape, size, and character as society and circumstances vary. To some extent, they vary according to economic and political circumstances. Groups do not always demand recognition because they exist; sometimes they exist (at least in their particular sizes and characters) because they have been granted recognition. In the United States, policies of affirmative action for selected minorities supply incentives for people to identify themselves as members of those particular groups.[4] Preferential policies have acted similarly as incentives (or disincentives) in other countries, where the benefits of membership work to increase the size, and strength, of particular groups.[5]

Yet, even when groups are relatively stable, recognition is troubling because it signals an elevation of the conflict between groups over material gains into conflict over the character or the identity of the society. At worst, the danger in this development lies in the fact that it induces a conflict over which compromise is difficult—if not impossible. If the identity of the society becomes an issue—one that cannot be regarded as trivial and, so, a matter of indifference—conflict over it can only become more bitter, particularly since some will be regarded as winners and others as losers.

In this light, I argue that the idea of a liberal polity, understood as one that is, as much as possible, indifferent to such matters as identity (including national identity) and group recognition, has much to commend it. It does not offer a philosophical attempt to reconcile the competing claims of different groups and different identities, all demanding recognition. It assumes, instead, that no resolution is possible in philosophical terms; and it would be better not to try. Its recommendation, therefore, is that political institutions try to resist attempts to put the issue of recognition at the center of political debate.

Yet, there are further objections to the liberal move that need to be considered. The most important argument that Taylor might make here is that this does not get around the problem for the simple reason that the attempt to evade the politics of recognition will have its own, undesirable, implications. For it will, without doubt, favor some people over others. More precisely, it will simply allow the standards of the majority culture to dominate. In such circumstances, the claims of liberalism to be offering no more than a framework of law within which different ways may coexist will ring hollow.

To some extent, this objection is well founded; no political arrangements are neutral in their outcome. The large majority culture will tend to assimilate the small minority culture—although the contributions of the minority will also (to some degree) reshape the dominant culture. While liberalism asserts that the minority is under no obligation not to resist assimilation (by trying to keep to its own ways), it does not impose upon the majority any obligation to help the smaller cultural community succeed: if people are assimilated, that is the way of the world.

Now, Taylor's objection to this standpoint would be that it does not meet the demand—or satisfy the yearning—of those such as the Quebecois, whose concern is not just to be free to pursue their own way of life, but, more important, to ensure the survival of their particular culture: now and far into the future. Here, however, liberalism can only take a stand that is surely not unreasonable: a stand that says that cultural survival cannot be guaranteed and cannot be claimed as a right. And while this is not to say that members of different cultural communities may not take some measures that increase the chances of that group's enduring, the state should not be in the business of trying to determine which cultures will prevail, which will die, and which will be transformed.

The state, in the liberal view, should not be concerned about anything except order or peace. It cannot accomplish any more—it cannot determine which cultures will survive. The danger in its attempting to do more is, in part, that it may fall down in its primary role. This is, to some extent, what is happening in societies such as the United States, as well as in other divided societies. The state, in trying to shape society (under the influence of its modern monks and clergymen—intellectuals—who in the past tried to influence the state's religious character) has tended to exacerbate conflicts. For the sake of order, it may be preferable that the state stick to its primary function of maintaining the peace.

This does not mean that political institutions should not be sensitive to conflicts over power between different groups. If the goal is peace, political institutions may, for example, have to develop explicit power-sharing arrangements between ethnic or religious groups. In Malaysia, for example, many political parties are racially based, but the government consists of a ruling coalition of such parties (the *Barisan Nasional* or National Front). In many democratic countries, electoral systems are adopted to ensure that minorities are assured of a place in the political structure.[6] Peace may require, among other things, different ways of devolving political power. But for liberalism, the polity would still have to be there, in principle, not to promote any particular collective. Liberalism does not care who has power; nor does it care how power is acquired. All that matters is that the members of society are free to pursue their various ends, and that the polity is able to accommodate all peacefully.

Now, Taylor has objected that this kind of view holds out a promise that turns out to be illusory: the promise that liberalism will turn out to be the meeting ground of all cultures. This is illusory because liberalism is itself simply the political expression of one range of cultures; thus, it cannot accommodate Islam, which refuses to separate religion and the state. There is something to be said for Taylor's view, since liberalism clearly cannot accommodate all views. But we should be clear, nonetheless, about what liberalism cannot accommodate: it cannot accommodate views that insist a state be dedicated to the pursuit of some substantive goal that is to be embodied in the structure of that political society. This does not, however, mean that it is not capacious enough to accommodate a very wide range of cultures—including some, like certain Islamic traditions. This is very clearly the case in countries with an Islamic minority, such as Britian and the United States. But even in countries with a clear (or even large) Muslim majority—such as Malaysia and Indonesia—it is quite possible for liberal institutions to prevail. In Malaysia, for example, Hindus, Buddhists, and Christians—indeed, all religious minorities—are guaranteed freedom of worship under the constitution of what is, essentially, a secular state. This is in spite of the fact that the king of this constitutional monarchy is always a Muslim, as are a preponderance of members of Parliament. Indonesia is populated by an even larger Muslim majority; yet, it also offers freedom of worship. Indeed, it upholds an effective separation of church (or mosque) and state, as well as a formal or principled one. (In the United Kingdom, on the other hand, there is an effective separation of religion and politics, but still an established church.)

To the extent that it is able to accommodate a variety of ways, and does not pursue collective ends of its own, that polity may be described as a liberal one. It is not so because it has members a majority of whom share a particular European heritage. It is so if it may be described as a society, not of majority and minority cultures but of a plurality of cultures coexisting in a condition of mutual toleration. There is much to be said for Joseph Raz's view that "[w]e should learn to think of our society as consisting not of a majority and minorities, but of a plurality of cultural groups."[7] But doing this is best accomplished by refusing, in the first place, to recognize such distinctions between cultural groups as having any relevance to the fundamental purpose of the state.

One problem that will, of course, be raised is that this is easier said than done. Groups will not cease demanding recognition, and rulers will always be tempted to satisfy their demands—whether for material gain, or in an attempt to hold on to political power, or because they regard the claims of the group as just. Thus, there is always the prospect of the liberal state being distracted from its business and induced to pursue particular collective goals. In particular, rulers are always likely to be tempted to reshape society to promote (even if not exclusively) some particular religion, or culture, or (not unusually) some favored conception of the nation. Yet, while we should recognize that this will always be so, there is no need to make a virtue out of what is unnecessary. And in the liberal view, it is unnecessary; for liberalism's counsel is that the state do nothing. It does nothing not by refusing to engage in any activity at all—it still has a task to perform in securing peace within political society. It does nothing by refusing to engage in activities that have no bearing on that task.

Social harmony, I would maintain, is more likely the less vigorously social unity is pursued. In a multicultural society, this, I suggest, is what liberalism offers. It offers the opportunity, under a state indifferent to the ways or the goals of the different peoples living under the law, for people to coexist and for their different arts and letters and sciences to flourish (or die out) with them. It offers this opportunity, however, not because the laws grant them recognition, but because the laws are silent.

## Notes

1 *Measure for Measure*, act 5, scene 1, lines 314-20.
2 Thomas Hobbes, *Leviathan*, ed. Richard Tuck (Cambridge: Cambridge University Press, 1991), ch. 21: "Of the Liberty of Subjects," 152.
3 Michael Walzer, "Comment," in *Multiculturalism. Examining the Politics of Recognition*, 99.
4 I have discussed this in *The Fraternal Conceit. Individualist versus Collectivist Ideas of Community* (Sydney: Centre for Independent Studies, 1991).
5 Recently, in California, the category of Portuguese American was added to the list of officially recognized minority categories, this presenting a substantial incentive for those with any Portuguese ancestry to identify with this group (and secure the substantial funding benefits offered to minority students at California universities).
6 On this topic, see Donald Horowitz, "Democracy in Divided Societies," in *Nationalism, Ethnic Conflict and Democracy*, ed. Larry Diamond and Marc F. Plattner (Baltimore, MD: Johns Hopkins University Press, 1994), 35-55.
7 Joseph Raz, "Multiculturalism: A Liberal Perspective," in *Ethics in the Public Domain. Essays in the Morality of Law and Politics*, ed. Joseph Raz (Oxford: Clarendon Press, 1994), 155-76.

# Index

aboriginals, 264, 269, 276
abortion, 109–10, 186–7
absolute property rights, 53–4
accountability, 171–4, 175, 176, 229–30, 239
Ackerman, Bruce, 244
acquisition, 53
  justice in, 55–6, 62–3, 65–7, 81–2, 85, 86
  Locke's theory, 63, 65–7
adaptive preferences, 37, 38, 42
added value, 66
Adorno, T., 195
affinity groups, 210–11, 215, 216
affirmative action, 45, 291
African Americans, 184, 211, 213, 216, 263
Afrocentrism, 218
agreement, morals by, 57, 95–6, 99–102
alienation, 197, 198
Allen, Anita, 187
ambition, 9, 10, 37
American Indians, 183
American Revolution, 153–4, 155
*Anarchy, State and Utopia* (Nozick), 53–7, 69–80, 81
Anderson, Elizabeth, 7
animal slaughter regulations, 265–6
antipower, 147–9, 151–6
antipoverty policies, 45, 48
appropriation, 66–7
approximate validity (theory), 28
Arab-Americans, 211
Archimedean point, 94–5
Aristotle, 40
armed forces, 283, 284
Arneson, Richard, 5–6, 31–5, 41–2
Asian-Americans, 211
Asian culture/society, 265, 282–7
assets, 119–20
  natural, 40, 81, 83, 84
assimilation, 263, 267, 276, 292
auctions, 9–10, 37
Augustine, Saint, 271
Australia, 291
  referendum (1999), 243–4, 245, 246
authenticity, 198–9, 224, 271–2, 274–6
authority, 153, 191
  constitutional, 151, 152
  political, 149, 169–78, 233
autonomous will, 115, 116
autonomy, 3, 41, 110, 140–2, 239

average life span, 95
average utility level, 29
avoidability, voluntary, 31–5

*Barisan Nasional*, 293
bargaining theory, 18, 93, 94–5
Barry, Brian, 266
barter economy, 134
basic justice, 243
basic liberty, 3, 4, 15, 20, 118–19, 232, 236–8
basic needs, 64
basic rights, 101
basic structure, 3, 7, 16–20, 33, 34, 73–7, 207
Basque separatists, 290
Bay, Christian, 196
Bayesian theory, 23, 24, 28, 91
Beck, Ulrich, 249
Beer, Samuel, 122
Bellow, Saul, 278
Benhabib, Seyla, 242, 244, 248
benign dictator model, 155
Bentham, Jeremy, 4, 5, 22, 151, 154
Berlin, Isaiah, 151, 169
best-off individual, 28, 46–7
beta interferon, 236, 239
biological difference, 181
Black-son/White-son (case example), 82
Blacks, 130, 183, 215
Bohman, James, 149–50, 169–78
Bourdieu, Pierre, 211, 249
bribery, 139
Britain, 154, 293
  Asian culture, 265, 282–3, 285, 286
  health care 225, 234, 235–6, 239
  monarchy, 243–4, 245, 246
  Thatcher government, 251, 255
'brute luck', 37, 38, 41
Buchanan, Allen, 57–9, 99–106
Buddhists, 293
Bull, Hedley, 174
bureaucracy, 198
Burnheim, John, 244

Callinicos, Alex, 7, 36–44
Canada, 264, 270, 276, 283–4, 292
capabilities, 38–41, 96, 207, 209
capacities, 99, 242, 243
  mental/physical, 57, 95
capital, 141

capitalism, 42, 75, 140–1, 195, 198, 199, 200
Carter administration, 122
Catholics, 263
Center for Health, Environment and Justice, 254
'Chamber of Concern', 251
'Chamber of Regulation', 251
Chamberlain, Wilt (case example), 54–5, 63, 72–3
child abuse, 188
children, 17, 188, 190–1
Chodorow, Nancy, 190–1
choice, 5, 38, 40
   collective, 294, 250, 251
   rational, 57, 90–2, 94, 95
   social, 247, 249–50, 251
   voluntary avoidability, 31–5
   see also impartiality; preferences
choice/chance distinction, 7
Christians, 139, 293
Cicero, Marcus Tullius, 147
citizen-principals, 175
citizens, 13, 15–20, 127, 159–60
citizenship, 118, 147, 264
   cosmopolitan, 169, 174–6
   duties, 149, 160–3, 164, 166
   rights, 252, 263, 275
   'thick', 149, 169
   world, 149, 169, 171–4
city-states, 170
city life, 200–3
civic virtue, 147, 149, 159–60, 161, 162, 166
civil liberties, 126–7, 156
civil rights, 173, 275–6
civil society, 147, 175, 232
Civil War (USA), 244
class habitus, 211, 215
coercion, 57, 95–6, 130, 151–2, 154, 163, 165–6, 198
Cohen, G.A. 34, 36–9, 40, 41, 54
Cohen, Joshua, 175, 224, 242, 244
collective choice, 249, 250, 251
collectivities, 210–12
Commission on Social Justice, 42
commodification, 198
Commodities and Capabilities (Sen), 207, 209
common good, 121, 160, 164, 166
communitarianism, 109–12
   complex equality, 109, 111, 134–43
   liberal individualism/neutrality, 110–11, 126–33
   procedural republic and unencumbered self, 109–10, 113–25
community
   ideal of, 182–3, 195–204
   justice and, 117–21

compensation, 47–50, 56, 62, 82, 85–6
complex equality, 109, 111, 134–43
compliance, 93, 94
Connolly, William, 250
consensus, 251, 254
consequentialism, 126–7, 151
constitutional authority, 151, 152
constitutional balance of power, 163–4
constrained maximisation, 57, 93–4, 95
contract, social, 3, 18, 19, 22, 57
contractarian liberalism, 161–6
contractarian morality, 92–3, 95–6
contractarian theory, 22, 92, 93, 95
   Gauthier, 56, 57, 58–9
   Rawls, 4, 56, 58
contributors, 57–8, 100, 101, 103
convertibility (social goods), 142
cooperation, 5, 92–4, 96, 99, 102
   social, 13–20, 31, 33, 102–3
cooperative schemes, 101, 102
cooperative surplus, 99, 100, 101
corruption, 159, 160, 161, 165
cosmopolitan citizenship, 169, 174–6
cosmopolitan republicanism, 149, 169–78
crash-helmets (UK law), 265, 282
criminal justice, 248
Croly, Herbert, 122
cultural background, 81, 84, 265
cultural community, 263–4
cultural difference, 205–6, 208–12, 214–15, 218, 267, 286
   see also multiculturalism
cultural disadvantage, 129–31
cultural domination, 205
cultural freedom, 128–9
cultural identity, 285
cultural imperialism, 183, 207, 213–15, 217
cultural nationalism, 218
cultural plurality, 264, 265
cultural revolution, 208, 213, 214
cultural tradition, 111

Dahl, Robert, 172–3, 243, 244
Dallmayr, Fred, 203
Davis, Lawrence, 54, 56
decentralized communities, 200
decision-making, 224, 228, 234–6, 239
decision rule, 23, 24, 25, 28
decision theory, 23, 24, 28, 91
defective conception of law, 149, 163–4
deliberative democracy, 223–6
   beyond process, 225, 232–41
   deliberative model, 224, 227–31
   legitimacy and economy, 225, 242–59
*Deliberative Democracy and Beyond* (Dryzek), 223

# Index

democracy, 122–3, 171–7, 191, 196, 270
  aggregative model, 223–4
  *see also* deliberative democracy
*Democracy and Disagreement* (Guttman and Thompson), 232, 237, 239
*Democracy's Discontent* (Sandel), 109, 110, 169, 284
democratic control, 171
democratic self-government, 159
democratic socialism, 195, 197
democratic society, 3–5, 13–21
deontological theory, 4
Derrida, Jacques, 195
deserving poor, 6, 8
difference
  denial of, 196–200
  differentiated politics of, 217–18
  equality of, 264–7
  politics of, 182–4, 195–204, 210–18, 276
  recognition of, 183–4, 205–19
difference principle, 3–6, 8, 15, 25–7, 38, 53–4, 56, 118–20, 183
  voluntary avoidability and, 31–5
dignity, 270, 272, 276–8, 289–90
Diogenes, 170
disabled people, 183, 211
*Discourse on Inequality* (Rousseau), 274
discourses, 247–50
discursive legitimacy, 243, 250–5
distribution, 8, 15, 86, 119
  of holdings, 69–71, 72, 74, 77
  income, 74–5, 76, 77–8
  material, 182, 243
distributive justice, 3, 5, 20, 42, 58, 76–8, 99, 101, 205
  complex equality, 109, 111, 134–43
  entitlement theory, 53–6, 61–8, 81, 83–6
  pattern theories, 63–5, 71, 74
  primary goods standard of, 31–5
  theory of goods, 136–40
distributive paradigm, 182–3, 206–7, 223, 263
  *see also* deliberative democracy
division of labour, 134, 211
  gender, 182, 185–6, 191–2, 216
  oppression and, 209, 210, 212–15
divorce, 189, 190, 286
domestic sphere/life, 181–2, 185–94
dominance, 147
  monopoly and, 140–1, 142
domination, 111, 170, 197, 198
  non-, 147–9, 151–8, 176
  of women, 182, 183
Dryzek, John S., 175
  *Deliberative Democracy and Beyond*, 223
  'Legitimacy/Economy in Deliberative Democracy', 225, 242–59

duties, 166
  moral, 57, 89–90, 115
  political participation, 160–2, 164
  priority of rights, 120, 121, 149, 162–3
Dworkin, Ronald, 7–10, 37–8, 40, 162, 163, 223, 263

Eckersley, Robyn, 246
economic inequalities, 3–4, 15, 20, 118–19
economic theory, 90–1
egalitarian-liberalism, 3–10
  equality of what?, 6–10, 36–44
  justice as fairness, 3–5, 13–21
  maximin principle, 5, 22–30
  primary goods reconsidered, 5–6, 31–5
  question for egalitarians, 10, 45–50
egalitarian belief, 10, 45–50
egalitarian metric, 6, 10
ego, 203
elections, 244, 245, 247, 249, 251
employees, 154–5, 183–4, 216
employment, 154–5
  laws/regulations, 282–3, 285–6
  of women, 186, 191
Employment Appeal Tribunal, 285
end-state theory, 55, 61, 63–5, 69–80, 183, 207
endowment-sensitive distribution, 9–10
Enlightenment, 118
entitlement theory, 53–6, 61–8, 81, 83–5, 86
environment, 84
environmental justice movement, 253–4
environmentalism, 149, 253–4
envy test, 9
Epicurus's thesis, 99
equal basic liberties principle, 3, 4, 15, 118, 119
equal importance, 7–8, 9, 10
equal respect, 278
equal rights, 263
equal treatment, 286–7
equality
  access to advantage, 38, 41
  capabilities, 39–41
  complex, 109, 111, 134–43
  of difference, 264–7, 282–7
  distributional, 8, 15
  focal variables, 36, 37, 39
  freedom and (incompatibility), 53–4
  of income, 38, 41
  of opportunity, 3, 4, 15, 17, 20, 53, 232, 243
  of resources, 7, 8–10, 37–9, 127, 183
  of welfare, 8, 36–7, 39, 41–2, 127
  of what? debate, 6, 36–44, 233
  *see also* egalitarian-liberalism
*Equality* (Callinicos), 7
'Equality of What?' (Sen), 6, 36–44
equi-probability assumption, 28

ethical individualism, 7–10
ethics, 4–5, 91, 113–14, 115
ethnic minorities, 182, 291, 292–3
ethnicity, 211, 212, 216, 263
  see also race/racism
eudaimonia, 40
Europe, 278
expectations, 74, 78
expected-utility maximization
  principle, 23, 24, 28
expensive tastes, 36, 37, 38–9, 127
exploitation, 205, 212–13, 214
'eye lottery', 54

face-to-face relations, 195–202
fair equality of opportunity, 3, 4, 15, 17,
  20, 53, 232, 243
fair reprocity, 100–2
fairness, 22, 93, 232
  justice as, 3–5, 13–21, 23–5, 119
'Fairness to Goodness' (Rawls), 32, 34
false consciousness, 205
family, 84
  divorce, 189, 190, 286
  law, 17, 148
  public/private dichotomy, 181–2, 185–94
  violence, 188–91
Federal Appeals Court (Minnesota), 186
Federal Court of Canada, 283
Federalists, 122
feminism, 149, 181–4, 253, 269, 275
  ideal of community and politics of
    difference, 182–3, 195–204
  public-private dichotomy, 181–2, 185–94
  recognition or redistribution, 183–4, 205–19
Filmer, Sir Robert, 153
Fishkin, James, 244
focal variables (equality), 36, 37, 39
forced labour, 64
Foucault, Michel, 249
foundationalism, 56–7
France, 266–7
Fraser, Nancy, 183–4, 205–19
Frederick the Great, 272
free-riders, 57–8, 160
free state/society, 159–61, 164, 169, 170
freedom, 36, 40, 41, 115, 116
  as anti-power, 147–9, 151–6
  of association, 126
  cosmopolitan republicanism, 149, 169–78
  equality and (incompatibility), 53–4
  loss of, 5, 53
  as non-interference, 3, 62, 147, 148,
    151–6, 169
  of speech, 126, 183, 228
  value of (primacy), 53, 61–8
functionings (beings/doings), 39–41

game theory, 91, 93
Gauthier, David, 56, 58–9, 89–98, 223, 263
  Morals by Agreement, 57, 99–102
gay men, 184, 211, 213, 215, 216
gender, 181, 218, 263
  division of labour, 182, 185–6, 191–2, 216
  see also men; women
General Nursing Council, 285
general welfare, 164
genes/gene pool, 84
George, Henry, 66
German Romantics, 264
Germany, 211, 255
Gibbs, Lois, 253
Giddens, Anthony, 249
Gilligan, Carol, 218
Glaucon, 96
global political authority, 149, 169–78
God, 17, 137, 141, 271, 274, 284
Goldman, Samcha, 284
good, 14, 17, 40, 118, 129, 271
  common, 121, 160, 164, 166
  right and, 4, 113–14, 116, 117
good society, 199–200
Goodin, Robert, 246
goods
  theory of, 136–40
  see also primary goods; social goods
government, 3
  action (liberal neutrality), 109,
    110–11, 126–33
  see also state
Great Society, 45, 121
group-differentiated society, 183
group defamation, 110
groups, social, 210–12, 213
Guttman, Amy, 170, 225, 232–41, 264
gynocentrism, 218

Habermas, Jürgen, 129, 224–5, 247, 248,
  249, 254
Hajer, Maarten, 251
Hampshire, Stuart, 235
handicaps (physical/mental), 57, 58
happiness, 4, 8, 64
Harrington, James, 153, 155
Harsanyi, John, 5, 22–30, 91
Hawking, Stephen, 58
headgear, 266–7, 282–4
health care, 10, 47, 57, 225, 234–7, 239, 242
Health Maintenance Organization, 237
Hegel, G.W.F., 128, 270, 274
Herder, J.G., 264, 271–2
*hijab*, 266–7
Hindus/Hinduism, 293
Hispanics, 130
Hobbes, Thomas, 56, 151, 153, 264, 288

# Index

holdings, 84
  distribution, 69–71, 72, 74, 77
  transfer, 55, 56, 62–3, 81–2, 85
  see also acquisition
honour, 270, 274
'How Liberty Upsets Patterns' (Nozick), 55, 63–5, 69–80
human welfare, 4
humanism, 218
Hume, David, 4, 22, 89–90, 99, 101
Hurley, Susan, 172

Idea of the Good, 271
ideal of community, 182–3, 195–204
ideal speech situation, 251
identity, 273–5, 276
  cultural, 285
  difference, 250
  logic of, 195
  national, 284, 291
  politics, 205
immediacy/immediate presence, 197–8
immigrants/immigration, 129, 235, 264, 266–7
impartiality, 4, 93, 94, 95
inauthentic society, 198, 199
inclusion, 224, 228, 230–1
income
  distribution, 74–5, 76, 77–8
  equality of, 38, 41
  regimes, 74–5, 76, 77–8
incompetents, 102–3
independence, 117
Indianapolis (1984 ordinance), 110
individual freedom, 53
individual liberty, 164
individual people (inviolability), 61–2
individual rights, 53, 109, 119, 121–2, 123–4
individualism
  ethical, 7–10
  liberal, 109, 110–11, 126–33
individualistic ontology, 252
Industrial Tribunal, 285
industrialism, 253, 254
inequality
  material, 205
  in primary goods, 33–4
  social, 3–4, 15, 20
  unjustified, 10, 45–50
inheritance patterns, 85
injustice, 70–1, 72–3
  see also rectification
innocuous actions, 75–6
institutional structure, 3, 7, 16–20, 33, 34, 73–7, 207
institutionalization (of justice), 69, 71, 74, 75
instrumental reasons, 40

instrumental republicanism, 149, 159–64, 166
insurance, 9, 10, 38
interference, freedom from, 3, 62, 147, 148, 151–6, 169
intergenerational rectification, 82, 83, 84–6, 87
internal–individual deliberation, 246
interventionism, 74
intragenerational rectification, 82–3, 85, 86
inviolability, 61–2
'invisible hand' doctrine, 149, 161–2, 166
Islamic traditions, 293

James, William, 138
Jefferson, Thomas, 122, 147
Jews/Jewish community, 110, 211, 213, 265, 284
job requirements, 285–6
Johnson, Sonya, 218
just entitlements probability distribution, 86
just initial acquisition, 55
just society, 3–5, 13–21
  egalitarian belief, 10, 45–50
just transfer, 55
justice, 22
  in acquisition, see acquisition
  community and, 118–21
  entitlement theory, 53–6, 61–8, 81, 83–5, 86
  as fairness, 3–5, 13–21, 23–5, 119
  - initiating application, 55, 69
  as mutual advantage, 56, 57–8, 89–98
  as reciprocity, 57–9, 99–106
  two principles of, 3–4, 15–16
  see also distributive justice
'Justice as Fairness' (Rawls), 3–5, 13–21, 23–5, 119
*Justice and the Politics of Difference* (Young), 182–4, 205–19
justificatory neutrality, 126, 127–8

Kant, Immanuel, 3, 22, 26–7, 61, 114–16, 117, 118, 277, 289–90
'Kantian Constructivism in Moral Theory' (Rawls), 32
Kantian principle, 26–7, 53
Kekes, John, 10, 45–50
Kentucky study, 188
Kukathas, Chandran, 267, 288–94
Kymlicka, Will, 263
  'Liberal Individualism and Liberal Neutrality', 109, 110–11, 126–33

labour, 64–6
  see also employees; employment; division of labour
*laissez-faire* economy, 9
land, 141
languages (of expression), 273

Latinos, 183, 213
law
    defective conception of, 149, 163–4
    moral, 114, 115–16
    natural, 17, 18
    rule of, 152–3, 159, 289–90
least-advantaged, 3, 6–7, 34, 53
legitimacy, 224
    deliberative, 243–7
    discursive, 243, 250–5
    of state action, 83
'Legitimacy and Economy in
    Deliberative Democracy' (Dryzek),
    225, 242–59
legitimate expectations, 74, 78
legitimation, 139, 225
leisure, 34, 47, 64, 127
lesbian women, 183, 184, 211, 213, 216
Leviathan (Hobbes), 56, 151, 153, 288
lexical difference principle, 47
liberal/communitarian debate, 109
liberal democratic politics, 227
liberal individualism, 109, 110–11, 126–33
'Liberal Individualism and Liberal
    Neutrality' (Kymlicka), 109, 110–11, 126–33
liberal neutrality, 109, 110–11, 126–33
liberalism, 111, 120, 147
    commitment to invisible hand, 149, 161–2
    commitment to priority of rights
        over duties, 149, 162–3
    defective conception of law, 149, 163–4
    hostility to utilitarianism, 149, 164
    republic critique, 149, 159–68
    see also egalitarian–liberalism Liberalism
        and the Limits of Justice (Sandel), 109
libertarianism, 53–9, 119
    critique of justice as reciprocity,
        57–9, 99–106
    entitlement theory, 53–5, 61–8
    how liberty upsets patterns, 55, 63–5, 69–80
    justice as mutual advantage, 56–7, 89–98
    on rectification in Nozick's minimal
        state, 56, 81–8
liberty
    equality and (incompatibility), 53–4
    how liberty upsets patterns, 55, 63–5, 69–80
    negative, 3, 147, 149, 160, 163, 165–6
    as noninterference, 151–2
    see also egalitarian-liberalism
life choices, 6, 33, 34
life expectancy, 10, 45–8, 49, 50
life goals, 32
life span, average, 95
lifetime income, 74–5, 76, 77–8
limited government, 3
limited rectification, 81–4
Lincoln, Abraham, 122

Lind, John, 154
Litan, Robert, 56, 81–8
Locke, John, 3, 19, 22, 57, 95–6, 264
    acquisition theory, 63, 65–7
logic of identity, 195
Love Canal (USA), 253–4
Lucca, 153
luck, 7, 37–8, 41
lynching, 215

Macedonians (in Australia), 291
Machiavelli, Niccoló, 147
Mack, Eric, 55, 69–80
MacKinnon, Catharine, 110, 218
majority rule, 164, 223, 239
Malaysia, 292–3
Manicas, Peter, 196
Manin, Bernard, 243, 244
Mansbridge, Jane, 253
marginalization, 213, 214, 217
market, 92, 96, 119
marriage, 148, 185, 186, 188–90, 286
Marx, Karl, 40, 42, 141, 215–16
Marxism, 42–3, 207, 210, 211, 212–13
material distribution, 182, 243
material inequality, 205
material prosperity, 4
maximin principle, 5, 22–30, 93
maximin relative benefit, 93
Mead, George Herbert, 273
means of production, 53, 67, 141
mediation, 197, 198
medical care, see health care
medical insurance, 47–8
men, 17
    gays, 184, 211, 213, 215, 216
    life expectancy, 10, 45–8, 49, 50
    patriarchal society, 188, 189, 195, 199,
        200, 269
    see also divorce; family; marriage
mental capacities, 57, 95
mental powers, 37–8
metaphysics of presence, 195
'midfare', 41
Mill, John Stuart, 4, 22, 115, 119, 138, 264, 290
Miller, David, 249–50
Miller, Richard, 169
minimal state, 53, 54
    rectification in, 56, 81–8
minimax relative concession, 57, 93, 95, 223
minority groups, 45, 48–50, 130–1, 235
money, 111, 134, 139
monopoly, dominance and, 140–1, 142
Montesquieu, Baron de, 264, 270
moral duties, 57, 89–90, 115
moral intuitions, 4, 6, 17, 57, 58
moral law, 114, 115–18

moral order of values, 17, 18
moral principles, 57, 89, 90
moral rights, 58, 101–2
moral side-constraints, 53, 54, 56
moral value judgements 23, 28–9
morality, 14, 29, 99–101, 233, 271
　contractarian, 92, 93, 95, 96
　rational, 22, 23, 90–2, 94, 95
morally free zone, 92, 95
morals by agreement, 57, 95, 96, 99–102
*Morals by Agreement* (Gauthier), 57, 99, 100, 101–2
motorcycle helmets, 265, 282
multiculturalism, 149, 183, 263–8
　equality of difference, 264–7, 282–7
　liberalism and, 267, 288–94
　politics of recognition, 264, 269–81
Muslims, 265, 266–7, 293
mutual advantage, 56, 57–8, 89–98
mutual friendship, 199
mutuality, 14

Nagel, Thomas, 31, 45
Nash, Ogden, 89
nation state, 121–2, 149, 170–1, 173–4, 243
National Front (Malaysia), 292–3
National Health Service, 225, 234, 235–6, 239
national identity, 284, 291
National Institute for Clinical Excellence (NICE), 225, 234–6, 239
nationalism, 170, 269, 272
Native Americans, 211, 213, 216, 218
natural assets, 40, 81, 83, 84
natural duties, 120
natural law, 17, 18
naturalism, 264
Nazism, 110, 211, 217
negative liberty, 3, 147, 149, 160, 163, 165–6
negative rights, 58, 101–2
neo-feudalism, 174
neo-Nazism, 110, 217
nepotism, 139
Netherlands, 251
networks, 253–4
neutrality
　liberal, 109, 110–11, 126–33
　state, 110, 111, 128, 129–31
New Deal, 121, 122, 244
new social movements, 208, 255
*New York Times*, 186
Nicholson, Linda, 187
non-domination, 147–9, 151–8, 176
non-governmental organisations (NGOs), 175, 177
non-interference, 3, 62, 85, 147, 148, 151–6, 169
non-moral premises, 57, 58, 92

non-waste condition, 66, 67
noncontributors, 57–8, 101–2
nonprofessional workers, 183–4, 216
normative ideals, 224, 228–30
normative theory, 90–1, 102–3, 181
North, Lord, 154
Norway, 255
Nozick, Robert, 36, 40, 109, 223, 263
　*Anarchy, State and Utopia*, 53–7, 69–80, 81
　entitlement theory, 53–5, 61–8, 81, 83–5, 86
　'How Liberty Upsets Patterns', 55, 63–5, 69–80
　minimal state, 56, 81–8
nurses (uniforms), 285
Nussbaum, Martha, 40–1

object-relations theory, 190
O'Brien, Mary, 187
offensive tastes, 36
Okin, Susan M., 181–2, 185–94
old people, 183, 211
Osen, Frances, 190
ontology, 252
opinion polls, 244–5
opportunity, 41–2
　equality of, 3, 4, 15, 17, 20, 53, 232, 243
oppression, 207, 218
　defining, 208–10
　five forms, 183, 206, 212–15
　real-world applications, 183–4, 215–17
'option luck', 37
Oregon health care, 242
original position, 4, 160, 162, 164, 223
　basic structure and, 17–20
　maximin principle, 5, 22–30, 93
　unencumbered self, 116–19, 121
Other/otherness, 203, 215
ownership, 65–6
　self-, 36, 54, 55, 69–80, 109, 223
　*see also* acquisition; holdings

Paley, William, 155
Parekh, Bhikhu, 263, 264–7, 282–7
participation in politics, 224
　ad duty, 160–1, 162, 164
Pateman, Carol, 187
patriarchal society, 188, 189, 195, 199, 200, 269
Patten, Alan, 149, 159–68
pattern theory, 55, 63–5, 69–80
peace, 292–3, 294
perfectionism, 40, 41, 42, 129–31
personal grievances, 82–3
personal as political, 181–2, 185–92
personal preferences, 29
personal rights, 94
Pettit, Philip, 147–9, 151–8, 169
physical capacities, 57, 95

physical powers, 37–8
plaintiffs (rectification scheme), 82–3, 86
Plato, 135
pleasure, 48, 64–5
pluralism, 18, 134–6, 137, 156, 263, 289
political
   authority, 149, 169–78, 233
   community, 7, 263–4
   economy, 206, 208, 209, 211–15
   equality, 224, 228
   ethics, 289
   justice, 3–5, 13–21, 23–5, 119
   liberalism, 7
   personal as, 181–2, 185–92
*Political Liberalism* (Rawls), 7
politics
   American, 109–10, 113–25
   of difference, 182–4, 195–204, 210–18, 276
   of recognition, 208, 264, 269–81, 288–9, 291–2
pornography, 110
positive freedom, 147
potential, 277–8
poverty, 6, 8, 45, 48–50, 183, 275–6
power, 147, 152
   *see also* antipower; authority; autonomy
powerlessness, 213, 214, 215–16
preferences, 29, 41, 43, 64, 96, 127, 270, 274
   adaptive, 37, 38, 42
   for equality, 70
   voluntary choice of, 31–5
prescription drugs, 235
Price, Richard, 153–4
Priestley, Joseph, 153–4, 156
primary goods, 36, 39–41, 111, 127, 138
   reconsidered, 5–6, 31–5
   unjustified inequalities, 10, 45–9
priority, 26, 27
   of rights over duties, 120, 121, 149, 162–3
'Priority of Right and Ideas of the Good, The' (Rawls), 34–5
private/public dichotomy, 181–2, 185–94
private property, *see* property
probability, 23–4, 62, 86
procedural principles, 224–5, 232–40
procedural republic, 109–10, 113–25
procedural responsiveness, 247
Progressives, 122
proof, rectification and, 82, 84
property
   private, 17, 67
   rights, 17, 27, 53–4, 65, 66, 83–4, 94, 189
   unowned, 66, 67, 86
   *see also* entitlement theory
prostitution, 139
proviso (bargaining position), 94, 95

Przeworski, Adam, 171
public/private dichotomy, 181–2, 185–94
public opinion, 244–51, 255
public philosophy (American politics), 109–10, 113–25
public service, 149, 161, 164–6
public spaces (in cities), 201–2
publicity, 224, 229–30
punishment, 139
pure practical reason, 116, 118
push-polling, 247

Quebecois, 264, 292
'Question for Egalitarians, A' (Kekes), 10, 45–50

race/racism, 110, 129–30, 183, 184, 195, 237
radical feminism, 185
rational advantage, 14
rational bargaining, 93, 100
rational choice, 57, 90–2, 94, 95
rational self-interest, 100–2
Rawls, John, 7, 45, 109, 116–17, 126, 166, 223, 263
   contractarianism, 4, 56, 58
   deliberative legitimacy, 243–4, 245
   difference principle, *see* difference principle
   equal basic liberties principle, 3, 4, 15, 118, 119
   equality debate, 36–8, 40, 42
   'Fairness to Goodness', 32, 34
   'Justice as Fairness', 3–5, 13–21, 23–5, 119
   'Kantian Constructivism in Moral Theory', 32
   maximin strategy, 5, 22–30, 95
   *Political Liberalism*, 7
   'Primary Goods Reconsidered', 5–6, 31–5
   'The Priority of Right and Ideas of the Good', 34–5
   *A Theory of Justice*, 3–6, 13–20, 22–3, 31–4, 36–7, 83, 91–2, 114, 152, 162, 164
Raz, Joseph, 126, 293
Reagan administration, 122
reasonableness, 14, 15, 224, 229
reciprocal advantage, 17
reciprocity, 14
   justice as, 57–9, 99–106
   requires substantive principles, 225, 234–40
   thesis, 57–8, 100
recognition
   critical theory of, 217–18
   of difference, 183–4, 205–19
   politics of, 208, 264, 269–81, 288–9, 291–2
   predominance of, 206–8
   redistribution or, 183–4, 205–19
rectification
   alternative rules, 84–6

# Index

rectification *cont.*
  of injustice, 55–6, 62, 64
  intergenerational, 82, 83, 84–6, 87
  intragenerational, 82–3, 85, 86
  limited (case for), 81–4
  in minimal state, 56, 81–8
  principle of, 55–6, 62, 64
redistribution, 41, 42, 64
  or recognition, 183–4, 205–19
  unjustified inequalities, 10, 45–50
redistributive justice, 78
redistributive policies, 33–4, 36, 54
referendum, 227, 243–4, 245, 246
reflective equilibrium, 58
reflexive modernity, 249, 250, 252
relative autonomy, 140
Relenza (anti-flu drug), 236
religion, 110, 263
  apparel, 265–7, 282–4, 286–7, 292–3
  beliefs, 138, 148, 265–6
  symbols, 138, 266, 283, 286
representation democracy, 244
republic, procedural, 109–10, 113–25
republicanism
  cosmopolitan, 149–50, 169–78
  critique of liberalism, 149, 159–68
  freedom as anti-power, 147–9, 151–8
  instrumental, 149, 159–64, 166
*Republicanism* (Pettit), 147
resources, 71, 72
  assigned, 69–70
  equality of, 7, 8–10, 37–9, 127, 183
reverse discrimination, 277
right, 4, 113–117, 119
rights, 252, 263, 275
  individual, 53, 109, 119, 121–4
  moral, 58, 101–2
  to natural assets, 81, 83
  negative, 58, 101–2
  priority of, 120, 121, 149, 16203
Riker, William, 247, 249
Ripstein, Arthur, 56
risk, 67, 91
*Roe v. Wade* (1973), 109–10
Roemer, John, 38, 39, 42
Rousseau, Jean-Jacques, 3, 22, 271, 274, 290
Royal Canadian Mounted Police, 283
rule of law, 152, 153, 159, 289–90
ruling class, 141
Rushdie, Salman, 290

Sabel, Charles, 175
Sally/Harry (case example), 76
Sandel, Michael J.
  *Democracy's Discontent*, 109, 110, 169, 284
  *Liberalism and the Limits of Justice*, 109

Sandel, Michael J. *cont.*
  'The Procedural Republic and the Unencumbered Self', 109–10, 113–25
Sanders, Lynn, 245
Scanlon, T.M., 32, 172
Schlosberg, David, 253
Schwartz, Adina, 31
seat belt laws, 148–9
self-determination, 183
self-government, 159, 169–70, 265
self-interest, 57, 90, 99–102, 160–1, 245
self-ownership, 36, 54–5, 69–80, 109, 223
'Self-Ownership, Marxism and Egalitarianism' (Mack), 55, 69–80
self, unencumbered, 109–10, 113–25
Sen, Amartya, 172, 207, 209, 223
  'Equality of What?', 6, 36–44
sense of justice, 162, 166
servants, 155
sexual difference, 181
Shapiro, Ian, 223, 242
Shaw, G.B., 38
Shaw, William, 4
side-constraints, 53, 54, 56, 61, 64
Sidgwick, Henry, 5, 22
Sikhs, 265, 282–4, 285, 286–7
simony, 139
Skinner, Quentin, 149, 169
  instrumental republicanism, 159–61
  objections to contractarian liberalism, 161–6
Skokie controversy (1977–78), 110
slavery, 147, 153
slaughter regulations, 265–6
Smith, Adam, 4, 22
Smith-Jones-Johnson-Black case (life choices), 6, 33, 34
social background, 84
social choice theory, 247, 249–50, 251
social contract, 3, 18, 19, 22, 57
social cooperation, 13–14, 15–20, 31, 33, 102–3
social duty, 162–3
social engineering, 72
social goods, 111, 135–42, 223
  cost of, 61
  primary, *see* primary goods
social groups, 210–12, 213
social inequalities, 3–4, 15, 20
social justice, 17, 42, 182, 223
social meanings, 139–40
social movements, 208, 255
social ontology, 195
social security, 47–8
'Social Unity and Primary Goods' (Rawls), 34
socialisation of women, 182, 186, 190, 216
socialism, 41, 149, 155, 218
  democratic, 195, 197

socialist feminism, 182
society
  basic structure, 3, 7, 16–20, 33, 34, 73–7, 207
  as fair system, 3–5, 13–21
  well-ordered, 13, 16
Socrates, 96
*Sovereign Virtue* (Dworkin), 7–10
sovereignty, 170–4, 176–7, 233
Soviet Communism, 205
space/spatial distancing, 195–201
special responsibility, 7–8, 9, 10
*Spheres of Justice* (Walzer), 111
'starting-gate' theory, 9
state, 135, 190
  minimal, 53, 54, 56, 81–8
  neutrality, 110–11, 128, 129–31
Statistical Abstract of the United States, 45–6
Steiner, Hillel, 71–2, 76
Stetsons, 283–4
stringent requirement (appropriation), 66, 67
subcultures, 130
subject-centered conceptions, 101
subjugation, 151, 152, 155
subordinate groups, 131
subordination, 170
subsidy policies, 74
substantive principles, 224–5, 232–40
Sunstein, Cass, 251
Supreme Court, 109, 131, 245, 246, 284
symbols/symbolism, 138, 266, 283, 285, 286

Tamils (Sri Lanka), 290
taste, 36, 37, 38–9, 127
Tawney, R.H., 40
taxation, 10, 45, 64, 74, 75
Taylor, Charles, 264, 269–81, 288, 290, 291–3
Taylor, Michael, 196
technocracy, 140–1
teleological theory, 4, 114, 117
Texas, 109–10
Thatcher government, 251, 255
*Theory of Justice*, A (Rawls), 3–6, 13–20, 22–3, 31–4, 36–7, 83, 91–2, 114, 152, 162, 166
Third Way, 41
Third World countries, 40, 272
Thompson, Dennis, 225, 232–41, 246
time/temporal distancing, 195, 196–201
Tobin, James, 173
toleration, 3
Toulmin, Stephen, 170
transcendental subject, 116, 117–18
transfer, 55, 56, 62–3, 81–2, 85
Trilling, Lionel, 270–1
turbans, 265, 282–4
two-track model, 247
tyranny, 141–2, 173, 235, 237, 240

unanticipated ways/gains, 75, 77
uncertainty, 23, 91, 171
undeserving poor, 6, 8
*Uneasy Access* (Allen), 187
unencumbered self, 109–10, 113–25
Unger, Roberto, 196
uniforms, 283, 284–6
unilateral transformations, 69–70, 75
United National Development Programme, 40
United States, 82, 95, 255
  African Americans, 184, 211, 213, 216, 263
  American Revolution, 153–4, 155
  city life, 199, 200–1
  civil rights movement, 275–6
  environmental justice movement, 253–4
  excluded groups, 129–30
  life expectancy, 10, 45–8
  New Deal, 121, 122, 244
  political philosophy, 109–10, 111, 113–25
  social groups, 211–12, 213, 291–3
  Supreme Court, 109, 131, 245–6, 284
  women in, 186–7, 188
United States Air Force, 284
universalism, 275, 276
unjustified inequalities, 10, 45–50
unowned objects, 66, 67, 86
utilitarianism, 8, 36, 53, 118–19
  liberalism's hostility, 149, 164
  maximin principle, 5, 22–30
  Rawl's alternative, 4–5
utility, 4–5, 38, 41, 53, 100

value-added, 66
veil of ignorance, 4, 18, 22, 92, 94, 121
Vico, Giambattista, 264
violence, 183, 188–9, 191, 213–15
voluntary avoidability, 31–5
voluntary exchange, 69, 70, 72
voting, 164, 223, 227, 237, 243–7, 275

Walzer, Michael, 109, 111, 134–43, 170, 173, 191, 243
weaker requirement (appropriation), 66–7
wealth, 7, 41, 48–9, 75, 84, 141, 159
Weitzman, Lenore, 189
welfare, 47, 118
  equality, 8, 36–7, 39, 41–2, 127
welfare state, 15, 45, 121, 123
welfarism, 36, 39, 41–2
well-being, 40–1, 96, 156
well-ordered society, 13, 16
Western Europe, 95
Whigs, 122
wife abuse, 188, 190, 191
Williams, Bernard, 139
Wolff, Jonathan, 53, 54

# Index

women, 17, 130, 148, 154–5, 269
   employment of, 186, 191
   lesbians, 183, 184, 211, 213, 216
   life expectancy, 10, 45–9, 50
   oppression of, 181–3, 185, 186
   public/private dichotomy, 181–2, 185–94
   wife abuse, 188, 190, 191
   *see also* divorce; family; marriage
working class, 183–4, 211
world citizenship, 149, 169, 171–4
worst-off individual, 25–6, 28, 32–3, 37, 46–7, 49–50, 54, 86
worst possibility, 23–4
WTO meeting (Seattle 1999), 174

yarmulke, 284
Young, Iris Marion, 195–204
   deliberative model, 224, 227–31
   *Justice and the Politics of Difference*, 182–4, 205–19
Yugoslavia, 291

Zulu culture, 278
Zurn, Christopher, 224

Lightning Source UK Ltd.
Milton Keynes UK
20 December 2010

164678UK00001B/6/P

9 780761 941842